**This book is to be returned on or before
the last date stamped below.**

17. JAN. 1994

17. MAR. 1994

-8. JUN. 1994

-6. NOV. 1995

24. OCT 1996

LUTON SIXTH FORM COLLEGE

LIBREX

THE
COMPLETE
POTTERY
COURSE

THE
COMPLETE
POTTERY
COURSE

SUSAN PETERSON

EBURY PRESS LONDON

First published in 1992 by Ebury Press
an imprint of
The Random Century Group Ltd
Random Century House
20 Vauxhall Bridge Road
London SW1V 2SA

Published in 1992 in North and South America and Canada by
Prentice Hall, Inc. under the title *The Craft and Art of Clay*

A catalogue record for this book
is available from the British Library

ISBN 0–09–177003–3

This book was designed and produced by
JOHN CALMANN & KING LTD
71 Great Russell Street, London WC1B 3BN

Designed by Peter and Vanessa Luff
Typeset by Fakenham Photosetting Ltd, Norfolk
Printed and bound in Hong Kong by Mandarin Offset

Half-title Adding a pedestal to make a goblet

Frontispiece Jane Ford Aebersold: "Winter Suite 1985, Number 6";
stoneware, lusters, multiple firing; Boston Museum of Fine Arts.
"I aim to infuse the surface with a sense of depth and light
to establish a richness of color that is indivisible from the form.
I don't regard the glazes as coloring the surface, but as being
absorbed in the form, wedded to it inseparably in a visual sense."

CONTENTS

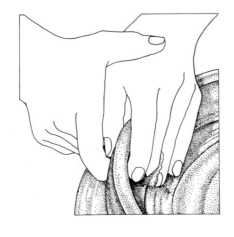

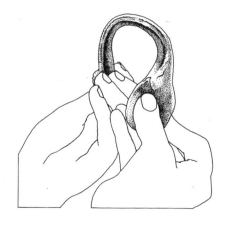

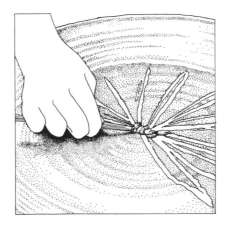

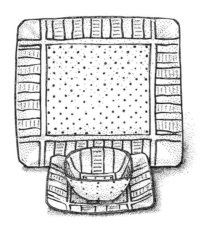

PREFACE

I have wanted a book like this since I began teaching. At Chouinard Art Institute, Los Angeles, in 1952, I developed a system of written and photographic visuals mounted on huge "multiplex" frames. In the 1960s at the University of Southern California I split up topics and made films for the four-minute single concept continuous roll cassettes that Technicolor Corporation developed to be used with the projectors they made for sealed cassettes, and I played the films continuously on my classroom walls. In the early 1970s I did a series of 54 half-hour television programs on all facets of ceramics, called "Wheels, Kilns, and Clay." The programs were broadcast live on major network television. I still keep tapes of them in my Hunter College classroom for student use on a chained-down video machine.

This book is the realization of everything I have felt a clayworker needs to do claywork: how to, what to, what others are doing, and self helps. The book will supplant my visuals. *The Complete Pottery Course* should be used like a dictionary, picked up and put down, but always at hand.

I have been aided by many of my students, and by clayworkers the world over. Without everyone who contributed photographs and other assistance, such a complicated book could not have been realized, and I am grateful to them.

I must individually thank Vanessa Adams, who did all the process photography of me in my studio, and much in other parts of the book; Ada Cruz, who culled the several thousand fabrication negatives; Françoise Gilot, for sharing photographs of her large Chinese ceramic drawings; Laurie Burruss Myers, who made the 34 fusion button and low-fire commercial color tests and wheel drawings; Jeanne Otis and the Arizona State University ceramics class, who mixed and fired the cone 5 50/50 blends of 34 basic glaze raw material tests; Bill O'Bryan, who ran the cone 10 series of those tests in my kiln; the laboratory at Westwood Ceramic Supply in California, for doing the clay, feldspar, and some of the glaze tests; Mildred Wolkow, for compiling the clay data chart; Jude Golden, for some of the color tests; Betsy West, administrator of the Portfolio; Rebecca Medel, who researched the museum compilation and helped in many ways for several years; computer assistants Aram Quaratessi and John Hirx; Joseph Masny, my "above and beyond" all-round assistant; Arthur Pogran and Jennifer Martin, who proofread; Mary Pat Fisher in Connecticut, who helped immensely with the text; and Bud Therien at Prentice Hall and Hilary Arnold at Random Century, who adopted the manuscript for publication. I must express my delight and appreciation for the verve and commitment of Laurence King at John Calmann & King, London, and his staff who produced *The Complete Pottery Course*, and give special thanks to Rosemary Bradley, who worked on the early stages of the book, the excellent designer, Peter Luff, and Ursula Sadie, who edited with amazing skill and uncommon diligence.

I owe my family everlasting thanks — my parents for their understanding guidance and for my education, my three children for their continuous help, and Robert Schwarz for his constancy. Charles Harder, Daniel Rhodes, Marion Fosdick, and Loyal Frazier — my primary professors at Alfred Ceramic College — gave me a love and respect for ceramic materials and a bouncing start. From the many exceptional teachers in my life, I must single out Clarence Merritt, who was my glaze "wizard". As well as my teachers, my mentors have included some particularly good students (who know who they were), my lifelong friends, and my colleagues. I am deeply grateful for my fortuitous associations with Shoji Hamada, Bernard Leach, Maria Martinez, Lucy Lewis and all their families, and the numerous encounters everywhere in the world that broadened my vision.

All of you, please keep in touch and accept my thanks.

Susan Harnly Peterson
New York City, 1991

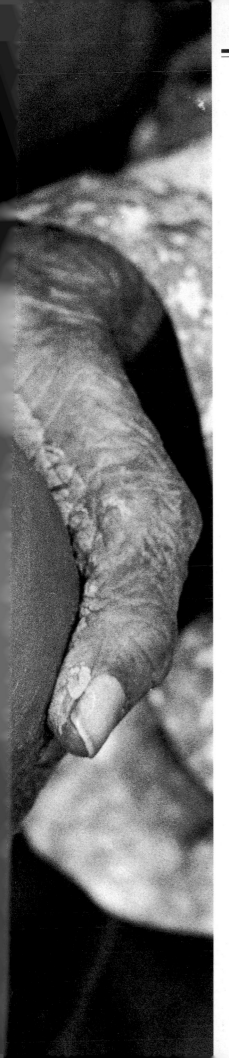

1

THE CRAFT AND ART OF CLAY

The late Maria Martinez, nearly 100 years old, pinches a small vessel

THE CRAFT AND ART OF CLAY

Ancient pit kiln; drawings at excavation site, Bang Po, Thailand

Hans Coper's beautifully made pot is a synthesis of old and new, reminding us of the past but evoking the future

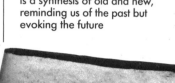

Claywork is full of paradoxes. It is one of the most technically challenging of art media, and yet it is used by children. It is one of the most ancient media, made of the stuff of the earth itself, and yet it is also at the forefront of modern materials science. Those of us who work in clay follow an ancient tradition in which a great deal is still new, still to be done.

The term *ceramics* refers to all non-metallic, inorganic materials that lend themselves to permanent hardening by high temperatures. Ceramics are more resistant to heat than any other materials on the face of the earth. From the beginning of human history into as much as we can see of the future, we have been and will be dependent upon ceramics.

I am fond of saying that you will be going to the moon in a glazed pot. That's not literally true, of course, but to withstand the extreme heat, everything on the outside of a spaceship is probably made of or coated with ceramics. Metals cannot withstand the temperatures of space or the corrosion of ocean depths. Human beings are conquering space, as well as building ceramic submarines and exploring the great waters, with the basic materials we are discussing.

Ceramics thus range from an increasing array of industrial products — such as computer chips, jet engine components, the nose cones of rockets, electrical insulators, blast furnace linings, bathroom fixtures, diamond-hard grinding and drilling units — to more ancient uses of clay. In addition to vessels and ritual objects, the use of clay brick for structures has been described through time in age-old records. Egyptian tomb paintings depict dredging clay from a river, bringing it to the bank, tamping it in wooden molds, drying the bricks in the sun, and eventually building a "firing mound" through which flames from twigs and brush must have raged for a few hours, burning the brick to a degree of hardness; it is still the same today.

Historically, clay has been used to create some of the world's best art: the tiles of the Persian mosques, the sculpture of the early dynasties of China, Pre-Columbian figures in Mesoamerica, the jars of Mycenae from 2000 B.C., and much more. *Porcelains*, glass-like translucent wares, from the Sung dynasty of China were brilliant achievements of technique in fabrication and firing. Anyone who understands the ceramic process will be in awe of the claywork of past ages.

How then can we account for the soulful expressions of pure form, appealing to today's minimalistic esthetic, that have appeared in isolated cultures, such as the water jars of the Jivaro Indians in the South American jungle? Surely it must have to do with profound aspects of clay itself. And much of art develops through the energies bouncing among people where cultures are juxtaposed.

Shoji Hamada, the potter who was declared a Living National Treasure of Japan, said that to work with clay is to be in touch with the taproot of life. Confrontation with clay can bring us into contact with the self — earthy,

CHINA REVISITED

Françoise Gilot showed me these drawings when she brought them from the museum in Valluries, France, to New York City at the end of the 1970s. She made them in very sharp graphite pencil, similar to intaglio, on large grey oil-painted panels 13 ft (4 m) tall by 6 ft 6 in (2 m) wide. They were painted and drawn while Françoise lived with Pablo Picasso.

Françoise explains: "In 1949 or 1950 we were spending a good part of the year in the South as Pablo was doing so much ceramic work in Valluries. In an antique shop by the harbor we found a small 18th-century book which had eight actual etchings in it. Pablo and I were very amused by the book.

"As I looked at these tiny etchings I thought it would be nice to make panels of my own interpretation of them, so I extended the scale. Large scale allowed me to keep the spirit but make changes — to take the 18th century to the 20th century, but really to show that ceramics is a very ancient thing which can be rejuvenated, and which is both a craft and an artistry. It took me about a month to make the eight-panel series. I made small drawings first, and then drew direct on the oil panels.

"Even now in Valluries, potters beat the clay with the same instrument as in China. After refining the clay they fold it and fold it — folding rearranges the molecules and makes clay more elastic. Pablo was enchanted; he always liked technical things. I use my palette knife to do the same folding with oil paint.

"See the sense of humor in the faces! We were intrigued that the carrying of pots was just as in Valluries, and so was working at the wheel or coiling, by the master with assistants. See the barrel of rainwater being carried in — the rain goes direct from the roof to the barrel and is carried to mix with clay or glazes. In Valluries distilled water is used for glaze. Engobe or glaze dipping and pouring into different shapes is the same over the centuries."

Bringing clay from the mountains and screening it

Turning the wheel manually for the potter

Glazing and painting porcelain

intense, passionate. The material is soft and sensuous, as well as a strong, hefty substance, at once resistant and pliable. It is so plastic that it can take any shape.

Yet claywork is not easy. It is not immediate; it requires a series of processes that are hard to control. Only at the end, after the firing, can one see the finished work. This limitation decreases as skill increases and experience makes pre-visualization possible. Ideas tend to be superseded by the sheer physical problems of working with clay. Moreover, some finished pieces are fragile, despite the hardness of the material. Let me briefly introduce the processes of claywork as an overview for the step-by-step chapters that follow, and then comment on the art of clay.

THE CRAFT OF CLAY

Claywork begins with prospecting or buying clay, the natural material. Clay is basically a hydrated (water-containing) silicate of alumina. People with materially simple lifestyles have used clays just as they come from the ground. We struggle to improve the characteristics of natural clay, such as its plasticity, texture, color, absorption capability, density, and firing temperature; clayworkers blend materials to create *clay bodies*. Today, clay bodies may be mixed by a supplier or blended by the artist. Clay should be kneaded in a process called *wedging* to remove air and prepare it for working.

I photographed this updraft wood-fired test kiln near a large climbing kiln in Japan. Even indigenous societies, reproducing claywork constantly, frequently test new materials and glazes

Grace Knowlton in her studio with large handbuilt forms, applying engobe; small pinched forms in the background

The clay piece is fabricated, or shaped, by handbuilding, pulling up on a potter's wheel, casting, or pressing (chapter 2). Although sizes and shapes have traditionally been limited by physical constraints, new technologies are increasing the possibilities. The complexity of design of such things as ceramic turbine blades has compelled the introduction of new processes. Eventually these new processes will make their way into the studio. Factories, such as the one in Shigaraki, Japan, can create shapes or sizes that were previously impossible to produce and fire ceramically. Hydraulic machinery is too expensive for a studio, but artists can buy or be granted time at plants with all kinds of machinery, such as Kohler (the sanitary-ware ceramic

factory in Sheboygan, Wisconsin), for experimental, creative ceramic work. In addition, composite clay pieces of any size can be developed by joining smaller pieces with cement or glue, or nuts and bolts, or caging them in metal.

Once the piece is made, it can be *bisqued* in an initial firing at a relatively low temperature (perhaps 1600°F [870°C]) to harden. If it is still intact after this firing, it can be *glazed* — coated with a liquid that turns powdery dry, that will fuse onto the clay during a final firing to form a glassy surface. Glaze makes functional ware easy to clean and serves a decorative purpose, providing color, sheen, and texture. The clay may have been textured with patterns incised into the surface while it was damp or *leather-hard*

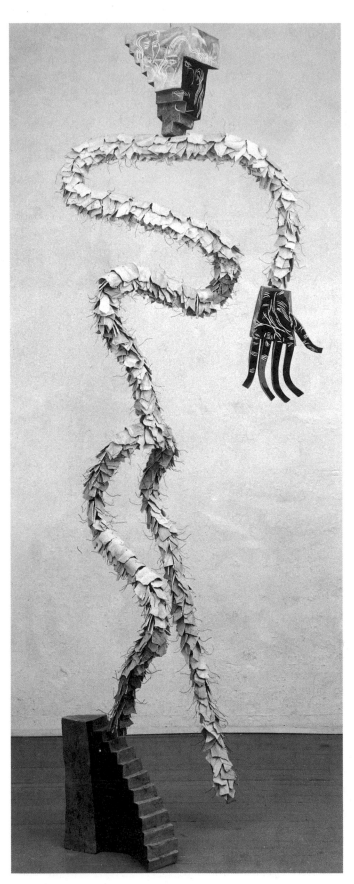

(stiff enough to hold its shape), or color or inert material-bits may have been added in the initial mixture. Chapter 3 of this book covers a great range of decorative techniques with clay and glaze, while chapter 4 looks further at the properties of these materials.

Finally, the piece can be *fired* in anything from an open-air fire of dung or wood to a space-age kiln. Chapter 5 covers the technicalities of kilns and firing. The temperature used for the firing affects the end product, as does the *atmosphere* — the mixture of air and carbon surrounding the work; control of these factors will be discussed.

THE ART OF CLAY

The unique difficulty for the clay artist is that with this material more than with any other, it is impossible to see the end at the beginning. In other media, you can see the paint or ink as it is laid down, you can look at the metal as you weld or the marble as you carve, and watch the work develop; it doesn't change and you always have an awareness of its look. Clay looks very different in every state: fat and soft and wet in the plastic state, waxy and cheese-like when leather-hard, lighter in color and chalky in the bone-dry state. Bisqued clay changes again, in color, look, and feel, to something totally different, hard and harsh but porous. Liquid glaze that is applied to the bisque before firing a second time dries in minutes to a chalky skin of another color and quality, and when the piece is fired, behold, it has still another look! None of the beginning stages has looked or felt anything like the finished piece. The clayworker searches for the pre-visualization and waits until the end of the fire.

Clay processes take a great deal of technical expertise before control is assured. Often, whatever you have made — and spent a lot of time on — ends up in a shambles in the kiln. Air bubbles in the clay are likely to cause explosions in the fire. If construction is incorrect, the work may break or fall over. Even in industrial ceramics, there is a high failure rate, especially with porcelain. At Lennox China, the "recovery rate" is about 50 percent; only half of what goes into the kiln can be sold as first quality.

Much claywork is a "happening," but even happenings can be — must be — controlled. Natural materials and natural fires are the hardest to control. There are more impurities in hand-dug materials than in filtered, refined ingredients from the supplier. Natural clays and fires such as those still used by some indigenous peoples only succeed when the clayworker has a great deal of experience. We in the studio are continually learning about the kiln and experimenting. The folk artist uses the same few simple materials and the same simple fire over and over again, and develops an ability to predict exactly what will happen.

Michael Lucero: "Untitled (Nude Descending the Staircase)," 1982, and amalgamation of ceramic skill and imagination

George Geyer's "Tidal Erosion," 1978, is a good example of clay handled conceptually

Sometimes, something else may happen; another ingredient slips into the clay, another phenomenon takes place in the fire, and the results might change a whole direction.

Working with standardized materials and temperature-controlled firings demands that you learn to document each process. Keep a journal and a sketchbook. Write down what you see or effects that occur and analyze why things happened as they did. Intellectual endeavor is utterly necessary.

On the other hand, the technical aspects of the process can become so important that they negate the art of working with clay. Ideally, you must become so familiar with the process and ways of controlling it at each stage, that the information is part of your bones. Expertise sinks into your subconscious and allows you to work more spontaneously. We artists try hard not to be too technical, not to concern ourselves too much with process. When process gets in the way, ideas can't come through. Learn, then try to forget, so that the work comes instinctively rather than didactically.

Since this freedom to make art comes from years of experience, how then can we teach and learn the art of clay from the beginning? I have spent years trying to

rationalize whether it might be best to give people a chunk of clay and tell them to go to the top of a building and throw it down to the ground, or to stand far away and throw it against a wall, just to get some form out of the clay without the effort of the building process. Skills of fabrication alone are major problems — to make the clay stand up, to bring it in or out, to gain facility with this wet, inert material. Should we throw away all the aspects of skill and work from intuition only? (Yes, but only when you know how.) Or should we start with the beginner techniques and hope that something more than personal satisfaction takes place? Yes.

Over all this time, I seem to have come to a middle ground, which is that "happening" is important, but decision-making is, too. It is important to be able to look at something and say, "That's great!" But it is also important to be able to say that it is bad and throw it away. To do that, you must develop a set of standards for yourself.

Academic institutions, museums, and galleries question

whether clay as such is art, whether a piece of wood furniture, beautifully crafted, is art, or whether a piece of glass in the form of a bowl is art. We tend to think that something that is nonfunctional, like sculpture, is art, and something that holds a pear is not art. However, the definition of sculpture offered by Michelangelo and others is that sculpture bisects, or in some way changes, space. A hollow object that can serve as a bowl can do that as well as a nonfunctional work.

What is art? All we can probably agree on is that art is difficult to explain and that it can occur in a five-year-old's painting, or in the work of an untrained folk artist, or in a tribal setting where someone who has never gone to an art academy makes a wonderful piece. If a work has the unusual quality that causes it to evoke emotion of some kind in the observer as well as in the artist, it probably is art. It could be constructed of clay or any other material.

The boundaries of what is considered art have been stretched considerably in this century, and they encompass conceptual art which exists largely as an idea, and largely in the moment. Clay can be handled conceptually. It does not have to be shaped, glazed, or fired in the traditional ceramic vocabulary, though these processes are also as valid as they have been for millennia.

Exhibitions devoted solely to unfired clay art have occurred. Conceptual artists have worked with the ephemeral dust or dissolved the wet mud. Clay can be presented as art in its dry state, in chunk or powder form, as an additive to paint, or as a base for paint or lacquer or sequins or cut paper. Clay houses, clay furniture, earthworks, are all potential visual, environmental, or installation experiences. Is the art experience in the doing or the documentation or the watching?

Art produced in clay today is strong and valid, and is crossing the boundaries of other art forms and media. As definitions of art expand, claywork is earning growing recognition. The science of ceramics is difficult, but approached with patience or with nonchalance and verve, it is intensely expressive. There are galleries that show clay along with other forms of sculpture; and clay — not just ancient clay — is shown in museums. Nevertheless, an unfortunate distinction is still being made between functional and nonfunctional work, with the latter commanding much higher prices.

The goal of this book is to present the whole spectrum of the craft and the art of clay, with beginnings at many levels, to be explored either in depth or merely tasted, or to extend previous experiences with clay. There are step-by-step approaches for the beginner, detailing suggested methods of progression, along with technical and chemical data and safety instructions. There are ways of conducting original research into materials, documenting new tests and results — including an exciting method for visual compounding of glazes for any texture and temperature desired.

Contemporary, traditional, and historical examples of claywork are woven throughout the text, with a timeline in chapter 6 and a portfolio displaying the visual energy of many contemporary clay artists in chapter 7. And in chapter 8 there is an unprecedented survey of museum ceramic collections around the world. The information and the experiences developed in this book are applicable to the full range of approaches to clay, from working as a functional potter to dealing totally with ideas.

Ray Meeker is fabricating experimental clay dwellings in villages around Pondicherry, South India, using tons of local mud. The ingenious brick construction forms the kiln, which is wood-fired, rendering the house indestructible (left)

Arnold Zimmerman's arch for a private residence in Arizona (right)

FABRICATION METHODS

Susan Peterson closing a donut form

INTRODUCTION

Clay can be shaped in many ways, but for our purposes there are three general ways: built up by hand, pulled up or "thrown" on a rotating potter's wheel, or cast or pressed in plaster molds. Knowing which method to choose for fabricating a specific piece depends on your experience with the materials, personal preference, size, form, or the requirements of a particular process.

The wheel is very sensuous, rhythmic, and hypnotic, and many clayworkers are fond of these qualities. But artists who build with tiny 1/4 in (.6 cm) coils or enormous chunks of clay find hand methods equally appealing.

Once the wheel is learned, it is the fastest method of fabricating a form, but mastering the skill completely takes years. It is faster to make a 12 ft (3.6 m) totem from a number of wheel-thrown forms and fit them together than to build the same piece by hand. Coiling and pinching techniques are inevitably slow, but they can create remarkable textures. Slab building in large sections is possible if a material such as nylon screen or nylon fiber is added to give the clay more stability. Methods can also be combined.

Certain methods are naturally more conducive to specific forms. Coil fabrication easily produces a round form; slab fabrication produces flat-sided, angular forms, but either method can make any shape. Wheel-throwing makes round forms, but they can be made off-round by beating or cutting.

Beginners practice all the methods of clayworking. Artists choose according to intuitive feel or what is best for the project. In addition to the methods described in detail in the following pages, other general considerations must be kept in mind when shaping clay, such as drying, shrinkage, air pockets, and the need to put clay into a homogeneous condition before working it.

DRYING

It is essential to remember that as soon as clay is exposed to air, it begins to dry. There is chemical water in the very composition of clay, and physical water is added as well, to bring it to a workable, plastic state. Evaporation of this water must be even throughout the piece, for clay shrinks as it dries. If clay dries on the outside and not in the middle or if it dries on thin edges, some areas will shrink at different rates, part company, and crack. Even if the piece dries evenly, improper construction or some impediment to the drying claywork, something that does not allow it to shift as it dries, may cause warping or distortion of the shape.

During construction, it is best to keep the clay moist enough to manipulate, or to let it set up slowly in order to support new additions. You will learn to sense how the clay needs to look and feel in its various stages. It can be kept continually wrapped in plastic and remoistened with a gentle spray of water. Traditionally, potters have kept small storage rooms damp by pouring water on the floor or by

standing buckets of water nearby, and some still do. Thin plastic bags or plastic drop cloths from the hardware store can be a great help in keeping clay damp, but plastic will not keep it moist forever. Learn to sense when clay needs more moisture or when it needs to be allowed to stiffen.

You can tell whether a piece is drying by watching and feeling it. Clay gets lighter as it dries from the initial moist working state to the stiff, waxy, *leather-hard* state to the chalky, *bone-dry* state. In all these unfired states, the clay is known as *greenware*. Clay also gets warmer to the touch as it dries. If clay isn't dry, it will feel cool. Once the piece passes the leather-hard state, wet clay cannot be added because shrinkage has taken place. However, clays differ. The local clays prospected by some Pueblo Indian families in the American Southwest are full of volcanic ash; about half of their *clay bodies* consist of non-clay, non-shrink materials, and wet coils can be added to bone-dry work. Once you have finished a piece, let it dry before firing it in a kiln.

MOISTURE AND SHRINKAGE

Clay does not dry completely at room temperature. Additional evaporation and shrinkage take place during firing. Clay construction methods are typically hollow, with relatively thin walls, because if the remaining physical and chemical water in the clay is constricted in thick cross-sections, it can accumulate and cause blow-ups from steam in the initial stages of firing. This fact makes clay building different from sculpture techniques in all other materials. Clay, handled more or less wet, must be engineered structurally to support weight and height and must be built well enough to move as it shrinks and hardens during firing.

Clay bodies can be chemically brewed to have little or no shrinkage, as discussed in chapter 4, by compounding clay bodies with a small percentage of clay and a large percentage of materials having little or no shrinkage. However, in so doing, plasticity is lost, and the clay body cannot be handled with the flexibility that is its seductive quality. New non-plastic methods of working non-shrink clay bodies are often invented by artists who use them.

One solution to the problem of drying and shrinkage is to build thin walls. The thinner the wall, the more easily moisture is lost and the gentler the shrinkage movement. A cross-section measurement from 3/16 to 1 in (1 to 2 cm) is optimum, though not realistic for some sculpture projects. As clay gets thicker or larger in scale, drying and firing become more difficult, but not impossible, to control, and the time needed for drying and firing increases. A thick piece must be fired very slowly, sometimes for days, with the temperature raised very gradually and cooling slowed more than usual. Unfired clay art avoids this problem!

Inert materials may be added to clay to lessen shrinkage, ease strains from drying, and perhaps aid construction. At the same time, these materials can also add color or

Susan Peterson in her California studio, where the photographs for handbuilding and wheel-throwing were taken.

texture, decrease plasticity, and change density. Materials such as dried pet food — and other combustible food products such as coffee grounds — burn out, leaving holes; sand adds color and texture; strands of nylon or fiberglass add support during construction; dirt, pieces of ground-up fired clay shards, mica, cement, crushed rock, and impure metallic ores add interest and diminish shrinkage; and lightweight insulating materials such as vermiculite or perlite lighten the weight of the fired clay.

AIR POCKETS

Air trapped in the wall of a clay piece is a decided hazard if clay is fired. Air bubbles can be created either by construction method or thickness. Trapped air causes pockets in which moisture can change to steam during firing with such power that the clay will explode. Air may be caught whenever two pieces are joined, when a structure is built up of clay wads, when a profile line is folded over or layered, or when solid clay is carved out. Be careful!

While clay can be built up solid and then hollowed out before drying, it is better to construct pieces hollow from bottom to top or to add sections to each other before drying, so that the thickness of the cross-section is under control at all times. If large thicknesses are necessary, pinholes can be hidden in the structure for ease of drying and safety in firing. Closed hollow forms must have a tiny hole to release moisture and air.

THE IMPORTANCE OF CLAY PREPARATION

Before clay fabrication, the character of the clay to be worked is a major consideration. Fine-grained clay bodies are plastic and throw easily; coarse-grained clay bodies have good *tooth* (texture and workable strength), and they pinch or pound easily. Getting to know and understand clay takes time and may be frustrating, but the importance of a good clay body cannot be overemphasized. All clays must be carefully prepared before they are worked.

Clay can be prospected, refined, and mixed, or a clay body can be compounded from individual raw materials as described in chapter 4. Ready-mixed clay bodies of many colors and for different temperatures can be bought. Prepared clay usually comes as a 25 lb (11 kg) rectangle wrapped in a plastic bag and sometimes shipped in a cardboard box. This size and shape can be psychologically limiting. A big mound of clay on the floor or in a container is more conducive to creativity.

Whether you begin by compounding the clay body from basic materials or buy it pre-mixed, each time you work the clay, it must be returned to an even condition with any trapped air removed. Although there is little tactile training in Western cultures, all clayworkers must learn to sense when the clay is ready to work.

This awareness requires intellectual concentration as well as a sense of touch. It can even be useful to talk to yourself, asking important questions about the clay. Does it feel soft? Lumpy? Full of air? As if it has stones in it? The clay mix should not have hard or soft lumps; it should have an even wetness or dryness. For wheel-throwing, clay should be relatively soft; a stiffer clay is needed for handbuilding. You learn from experience what condition is best and how to achieve it.

Clay has many personalities and must be read with empathy. No matter how well formulated the clay body or how skilled the artist, clay does not always respond. Sluggish, it may sit down rather than stand up, or refuse to pull out, push in, or lift up. Wedging or kneading the clay just before working it should be a period of communication between the clay and the clayworker, a "discussion" about the workability of the artist's wishes and the clay's capabilities. Clay knows what it wants to do.

Commercially produced plastic clay comes ready to work, sometimes even de-aired in a vacuum chamber. However, wedging or kneading the clay after it has been hand or mechanically mixed and before it is used is important to its workability. It is also an important form of communication, potter to clay, clay to potter.

There are many hand techniques to prepare clay for working, such as kneading it like bread, or slapping, cutting, or beating it. However, these methods can actually force air into the clay. *Spiral wedging* is the most effective way of getting air out of clay and can be used to condition amounts of clay that would be too heavy to wedge in a bread-kneading manner. In spiral wedging, the clay is only pivoted, never lifted. Large amounts of clay can be wedged on the floor. Otherwise, stand with full shoulder over the clay, leaning your weight into it.

The longer clay is aged after mixing and the more it is handled, the more workable it will be. Traditional Japanese folk potters dig clay, *slake* it (let it homogenize in a watery slurry), and screen it back and forth from one pit to another for weeks. They then eliminate some of the moisture in drying *bats*, store the plastic clay for another six months in a large mound before it is used (so the molecules keep each other company), foot-wedge it before storing it again, and finally hand-wedge 100 lb (45 kg) batches for several hours, breaking each batch into workable amounts and wedging each lump again before use. Clay prepared with this prolonged slaking, storing, and wedging process has an abundance of *plasticity* and *elasticity* with which most of us are simply not familiar.

By contrast, clay mines dig, filter out the metallic impurities (which many artists wish were kept in the clay), bag, and ship — nothing else. If possible, clayworkers should buy their materials in quantity, mix them into a wet state, and store them for a long time. Even commercially prepared clay bought in 25 lb (11 kg) rectangles can be sliced with a cutting wire and stored in large quantity in moisture-proof, airtight containers such as zinc-lined wooden boxes, galvanized metal cans, or plastic tubs. Storing plastic clay in good condition in large quantity promotes plasticity. There is no telling what improvements there might be if more people really cared about the preparation and processing of clay.

Almost all of the demonstration photographs of handbuilding and wheel-throwing were made of me, working in my California studio. I believe that these methods, developed over years of teaching, are easiest for beginners to master, as background from which to develop their own ways. Advanced clayworkers may find some new pointers. Each of us finds an individual way from a beginning way.

HANDBUILDING

Because ancient peoples made their pots and clay figures by hand processes thousands of years before the potter's wheel was developed, it is easy to assume that handbuilding techniques are simple. This is not necessarily so. Learning to control handbuilt shapes and to support them by profile line, weight, and cross-section can be more difficult than learning to throw on the wheel. Understanding clay and its movement in the wet to dry stage, together with its physical and chemical changes in the kiln fire, is a prerequisite to building large or small forms in clay by hand.

TECHNIQUES

The basic handbuilding techniques are pinch, coil, and slab. *Pinching* is usually monolithic, working clay with the fingers from a single ball or from pinches of clay. *Coiling* involves building up walls with a series of long clay ropes. If the piece has to hold water, the coils must be carefully *luted*, or joined together by *scoring* (crosshatching or scratching) both surfaces, moistening, scoring, moistening again, and then pressing the coils together. Coil technique is one of the oldest and most universal of ceramics techniques and demands precision, skill, and time.

Coils can be carefully smoothed or left visible for textural pattern. The lines of coil construction may even be emphasized decoratively by pressing with fingers or tools.

Slabs are rolled or thrown flat and then luted together or used large, formed in one piece. In all handbuilding, luting is critical. Unless you really dig into the two clay surfaces to mate them, they will shrink apart as they dry. Brushing the surfaces with water or slurry is not enough.

For reproduction or similar copies of the same piece, or for esthetic reasons, plastic clay can be formed mechanically by processes such as *extrusion* — forcing clay through a die — or *jiggering* — pressing a clay slab between a metal template which is attached to an arm on an electric wheel and a plaster mold rotated on the wheel. Machines can be helpful in other ways: slab rollers for large flat shapes, hand-operated or electric extruders for solid and hollow shapes, augers (channels through which clay can be pushed) and vacuum extruders for shaping large forms, mechanical cutting devices, hydraulic presses, and forklifts for carrying big pieces around. Machines also make it unnecessary to think of clay pieces as monoliths. All saws will cut greenware; most saws cut *bisque* ware, and diamond blades will cut vitreous ware. Breaking, nut-and-bolt construction, wire caging, and epoxy glues allow the potter to handle large or small works as components after the initial fabrication.

Tom McMillin in the process of building a rammed earth and clay sculpture which will be fired in place with a coat of charcoal

CONTROLLING STRESSES

In handbuilding, learn to think in terms of the contours and cross-sections of walls. Support for the line of the exterior profile is important; projections must be engineered so that they are supported from below. It is also important to control cross-section thickness. Clay can be thick if it is thick everywhere, but the thicker it is, the longer it takes to dry and fire. If cross-sections vary too much from thick to thin in too many places across the entire piece, drying and shrinking will be uneven. This variation is almost always the reason that pots warp, slump, or crack in drying or firing.

Pots may not crack from these strains in low-temperature firing, but all strains become more dangerous as the temperature increases. Clay achieves greater density at high temperatures, and hazards cause more damage. Finishing claywork at low earthenware temperatures causes less strain, but the ware is porous. The color palette and look of clay change as temperature goes up, and the clay becomes more dense. These facts are basic to the artist's choice of material, temperature, and method of working.

Rudy Autio in his studio with huge handbuilt, engobed forms: 1978, Missoula, Montana

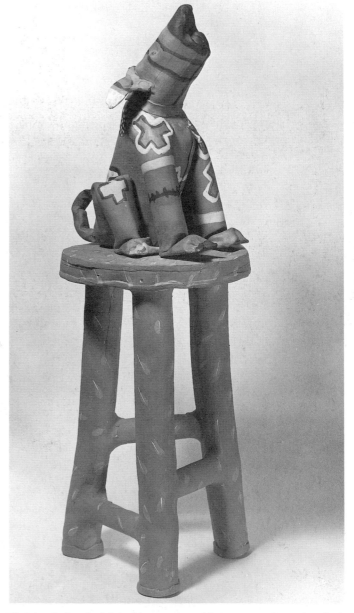

Christine Federighi slab builds animals and figures around loosely rolled paper bundles

John Mason with handbuilt sculpture, 1963

Strains of which the beginning potter may be unaware develop as the piece is built. Clay's plasticity — its ability to assume shape and then remember it — is its unique property. If you attack clay in one way and then hit it from another direction in the same place, you will be creating opposing strains that cannot be seen, but that may cause cracks in firing. Slow, careful firing is not always available until you learn to handle your own kiln; it is better to learn to avoid creating unnecessary strains in the piece.

Cores can be used to support handbuilt pieces (see the Federighi illustration, p. 28). Again, it is necessary to understand one of the principal properties of clay: because clay shrinks as it dries, it will crack against any core that has no give. A core may be made of combustible material that burns up in firing. If noncombustible forms are used under the clay, they must be porous materials like *plaster* or bisque that clay can dry on and release from, or the cores must be covered with paper or cloth to provide a movable surface on which the clay can dry and shrink without strain. Wood or metal armatures cannot be used unless they are loosely wrapped or continuously turned to prevent the clay

from sticking. When possible, remove cores or armatures before firing, or fire them in the piece if there is leeway for shrinkage.

Clay is alive from the time it is mixed with water until the final firing. Throughout this period, it is moving and reacting, so it must be built on something that also moves. You might use an entire issue of your local newspaper or a pile of towels beneath a large clay work.

Children like to make solid clay figures, but holes should be poked through thick parts to facilitate even drying and firing. As soon as possible, encourage children to make hollow things that look solid. Close them like a balloon, using a pinhole for air. Children can create a whole story by putting groups of small figures together on a flat slab of clay.

Some of the most beautiful clay objects and some of the best architectural ceramic sculptures have been made by hand techniques without the use of a wheel or template. Learn to respect handbuilding techniques and use them properly. There is no limit, large or small, to the forms that are possible.

Clayton James' handbuilt forms in his studio, Seattle, Washington

CLAYWORKING TOOLS

Many tools can be used by the clayworker, but knowing what to look for beyond the basics comes from experience. Most potters make a habit of collecting things that can be used as clay tools from hardware stores, secondhand and antique stores, yard sales, and ceramic suppliers. Be inventive!

Wood has a natural affinity for clay, withstands moisture, and can be kept edged by sanding. **Metal tools** rust, corrode, wear down, and need frequent sharpening.

Brushes give strokes of various widths, depths, and shapes. Find different whisk brooms, shaving brushes, scrubbing brushes, house-painting brushes, artist's brushes, and calligraphy tools, or make your own from animal hairs and plants.

Many **kitchen utensils** such as sieves, spatulas, wooden spoons, paddles, and knives are useful to the potter. Metal hardware such as nuts, bolts, screws, screens, trowels, wires, nails, bearings, and cogs should be investigated for clay texturing and for what may happen during firing when they are embedded in or wrapped around a clay piece.

Certain **objects** make characteristic marks when pressed or rolled into clay: crisp edges from blocks of wood, extruded sprigs from metal sieves, fine lines from a serrated blade, stamps or roll-ons from carved wooden casters, rope, spools, and rollers. Use a syringe or Rapidograph pen with engobes or stains to draw on clay.

1 Basic set: calipers, wood knife, cutting wire, small natural sponge, needle, flat-wire end tool, loop corer, rib

2 Decorating brushes

3 Wooden paddles for forming

4 Shaping tools

5 Wooden blocks for decorating and texturing

6 Metal cutting, shaping, carving tools

7 Objects for pressed textures

8 Scoring and combing tools

9 Syringes, extruder, cutting, rolling and stamping tools

10 Banding wheels for sculpting or for decorating around a piece

11 Ball bearing and rigid rolling pins

12 Water sprayer

SPIRAL WEDGING

1 Starting position of clay and hands

2 Left hand pushes down with wrist and palm, then lifts off quickly

A clay body made by adding water to a dry mixture and blended in a dough mixer, in a pug mill, or by hand, must be kneaded in a process called "wedging" to remove air pockets and make it homogeneous. Wedging is not as necessary if commercially pre-mixed and de-aired clay is bought, but to be used more than once, clay must be conditioned every time by wedging against plaster, wood, cloth, or any semi-porous surface.

Clay must be the right consistency for handbuilding or throwing. It takes a while to learn what "good consistency" is. If you are in doubt, ask. If clay is too stiff, make fingertip holes, add water, and wedge it to the proper condition; if it is too soft, stiffen it by wedging it against a surface that absorbs moisture.

Decorative effects can be obtained by wedging powdered metallic coloring oxides, commercial ceramic stains, or liquid colored clays called *engobes*, into plastic clay. With clay of two or more colors, brief wedging produces marbled effects, longer wedging produces one color.

Techniques of wedging vary from bread-kneading methods (which put air into the clay and are unsatisfactory), to cutting clay on a wire and slapping the pieces together (which traps air and is unsatisfactory), to some variation on oriental "chrysanthemum" spiral wedging (which is most satisfactory for expelling air from the clay and insuring an even consistency). Learn to judge the condition of clay as you wedge.

3 Right hand pivots the clay one quarter turn to left

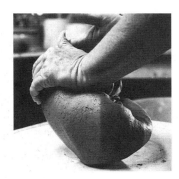

4 Left hand down

5 Right hand pivot

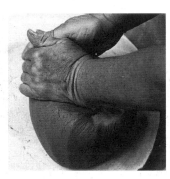

6 Left hand down

STEPS IN CHRYSANTHEMUM WEDGING

1 Pat a ball of clay that your two hands fit around into an oval shape.

2 Stand the oval on end, angled toward the right. Place fingers and palm of left hand horizontally in the middle of the left side of clay oval. Fingertips and palm of right hand are on top of clay, ready to pivot counterclockwise.

3 Left hand begins the wedging motion from the back and middle of the clay by pushing down into the clay, then lifts off quickly.

4 Right palm on top of the clay pivots immediately — does not pick up the clay, does not grasp the clay — just gently turns the clay on its end a quarter of a circle, counterclockwise to the left. Left hand holds its position against the middle left side of the clay as the right hand pivots.

5 Heel of left palm pushes down into the clay again, left fingers stay toward back of the clay. Right palm pivots clay toward you with counterclockwise quarter turn again.

6 Repeat process, push down, pivot, push down, pivot, over and over, keeping a steady rhythm until you feel that the clay is in good working condition, free of lumps and air.

Note: the steps outlined above apply more to right-handed people who need to strengthen the left hand for clay ambidexterity. If you are left-handed and need to strengthen your right hand, reverse the process.

7 Right hand pivot, etc.

8 Finished spiral

PINCHING A VESSEL

Pinching is a useful method of building forms in clay on any scale, and it is frequently used in the studio or classroom as a first experience in clay. Objects both hollow and solid — if the cross-section is less than 2 in (5 cm) thick — can be made by pinching.

Most people are right-handed, but potters must learn to use both hands. In this exercise of pinching a footed bowl, strengthen the weaker hand by making it the pinching hand.

Hold a ball of clay in the hand you use for writing. Use the thumb of the other hand to indent the ball to within ¾ in (2 cm) of the base.

Pinch all around once, squeezing the clay between thumb and fingers with a firm, even stroke. Pinch around once more to make the wall thinner.

Lift the form with thumb and fingers. Begin at the base and pinch straight up to the top in four strokes. Turn the clay slightly. Again pinch up from base to top in four strokes; continue all around to raise the wall evenly. Pinching straight up keeps the bowl tall and narrow; pinching and pushing out from the inside rounds the shape.

To make the foot, turn the pot upside-down on your fist. Pinch up a hollow foot with thumb and finger, turning as you pinch; squeeze fingers to narrow the pedestal foot.

1 Left thumb pushes down, right hand holds

2 Turn and pinch all around

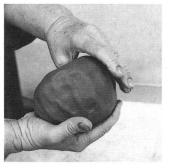

3 To raise, pinch four strokes up bottom to top

4 Turn, repeat bottom to top pinching to make shape taller

5 Place bowl upside-down on right fist; left hand pinches up a foot

6 Fingers inside and out shape hollow foot

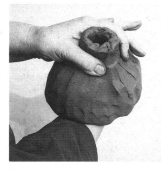

7 Squeeze in a circle to narrow the foot

8 Paddling can be used for shaping

9 Fingers refine the edge

10 Smooth inside and out, or leave finger pinching marks

11 Other textures can be added with tools

12 Straighten form right side up

COIL BUILDING: SMOOTH SURFACE

1 Begin to roll a patted oval form, fingers flat

2 Stretch coil between rolls, pick up, stretch, and drop it

Building with clay coils is a technique that demands precision, skill, and time, yet it is one of the most ancient and universal of ceramic techniques. Coil-built pots and figures can be studied in museums, especially pre-Columbian ritual vessels and effigy figures of North and South America, the life-sized Etruscan sarcophagus figures, and the huge temple and tomb sculptures of early China.

Today the coil method is still used by many indigenous handbuilders, including Southwest American Indian potters, the Mexican Tree of Life makers, and the builders of the big clay horses in South India, as well as by contemporary ceramic artists.

Coils can be made by rolling clay on a flat surface or between the palms or by extrusion with a machine.

Construction principles are the same everywhere: place one coil above another for a cylindrical shape, outward from the last coil for a flared form, inward from the last coil for curving in.

To lute, or join, two clay surfaces, apply crisscross indentations and water on a narrow space where each clay area joins another, then press to mate. To smooth between the joints, move a tool, paddle, or your fingers against the pot, up and down first, then in an "X" motion, to eliminate the high spots, fill in the low spots, and refine the form and surface. The "X" motion over any clay surface is the best way to make it smooth.

3 Move fingers from center out, quickly, each time

4 Fix uneven spots

5 Crosshatch and moisten to lute between coil and base

6 Place coils outward of each other to expand shape

7 Move clay up and down to join coils outside

8 Move clay up and down to join coils inside

9 Fingers make "X" motion to smooth outside surface

10 Fingers make "X" motion to smooth inside surface

11 A serrated-edged tool refines more, in "X" motion

12 Paddling can be used to smooth and finish shaping

COIL BUILDING: TEXTURED SURFACE

If the joints are not smoothed, the lines of coil construction can be used as decoration, or more textural decoration can be created by making patterns, with fingers or a tool, during the joining process. When the direction or shape of the coils becomes the decorative element, the coils can be left in their original rounded form or flattened with a paddle.

Historically, the technique of using tools to stamp patterns where coils join together was employed in the Anasazi vessels of the American Southwest and by the prehistoric Jomon of Japan, as well as other early cultures.

Tools for pressing into the coils vary. Sticks, rocks, decorative stamps carved from stone or clay, or other objects from nature can be, and were, used. Potters of the Jomon and other civilizations used ropes and corded string rolled over the clay to create various textured patterns. Some early pots were probably pressed in woven baskets and retained that texture after bonfiring; examples of the idea of texturing were repeated and modified from generation to generation.

Leaving the coils exposed requires careful crosshatching, moistening, and joining of each coil only at the point of contact. Where one coil touches another also requires care if the form is a vessel that should hold water. If the design permits, smooth the interior as an added precaution for sealing when coils are not smoothed on the outside.

Splits occur easily in building with coils — or wherever there are many joinings — whether the surface is smooth or left with exposed construction. Make sure you crosshatch each joining surface deeply, moisten the crisscrossed area, crisscross and moisten again, and repeat until a real glue is made on each spot where surfaces will touch. After pressing and paddling the connection, test each joint by wiggling it to see if it can be separated; re-do it if the joint is not strong.

Long, slow drying of the final form is desirable if the coiled piece is large. Quick drying can create stresses that later cause cracks and warping, which often do not appear until the piece is fired to bisque or glaze temperature. Keep the piece wrapped airtight in plastic when it is not being worked on so that minimal drying takes place until all is finished. You can let the work stiffen gradually by poking small holes in the plastic periodically.

Process is an important part of claywork, but it doesn't have to show. Some artists prefer to obliterate signs of construction or for that matter of the material. Determining what you believe is integral to becoming an artist.

1 Fingers flat, roll coil from center out each time

2 After scoring, moisten seams with water again

3 Coils can be wound evenly or unevenly

4 Test fit of areas to be crosshatched, then moisten for joining

5 Additional texture can be added

6 Leave inside coil texture or smooth it

7 Place coils inward on each other to curve shape in

8 Finish the lip, refine textures

COIL AND PINCH SCULPTURE

1 Robert Brady works figures upside-down, luting coils and pinching up to extend height

2 Body parts demarcated by coil separations, then coiled and pinched up

Many artists use the coil-pinch method for small or big work.

Robert Brady, rolling and pinching up coils, constructs figurative sculptures up to 9 ft (3 m) tall. He uses a low-fire clay body with colored clay patinas and fires in electric, gas, or raku kilns for different effects. Octagon ring-type electric kilns can be stacked up indefinitely to accommodate height.

Elsbeth Woody builds sculptural columns any height by coiling and pinching in tall sections.

David DonTigny demonstrates that the coil and pinch method is as fast as, or faster than, any other method as he constructs a forest of sculptural vessels.

3 Brady usually works figures in series

4 Two coils separated begin legs

5 Figures stand upright for gas kiln firing

6 Finished pieces in the studio

7 Elsbeth Woody pinches tall buttressed sections

8 Newspaper dividers keep sections from sticking during construction

9 Each section is begun over the previous one

10 Finished installation of columns

11 David DonTigny textures his coil sculptures with emphatic pinching

SLAB BUILDING

Slabs can be made with a rolling pin, by wire-cutting through a block of clay, or on a slab-rolling machine. To put the least amount of strain on the clay, though, "throw" out a slab by hand. Fling the clay out or down to your side so that it spreads flat. Repeat for thinness and size. Make large slabs by overlapping and joining several slabs.

To make a form, lute pieces, compress edges, and paddle.

For tall shapes, let slabs partially air-dry or stiffen them with a propane torch between additions. Leather-hard slabs stay moist for months wrapped well in plastic. Use water spray to keep pieces moist but not wet during construction.

1 Pound clay several times on both sides to condition and flatten

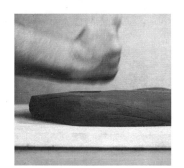

2 Pick up on one edge

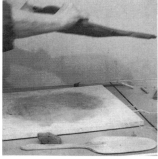

3 Throw clay outward and ...

4 ... fling it down toward you, repeat

5 Cut shapes from slab

6 Begin form, moisten crosshatched surfaces to be joined

7 Firmly press seam inside and outside

8 Cut and lute a base

9 Paddle form to shape it

10 Add clay slabs for accent

11 Should you make a lid?

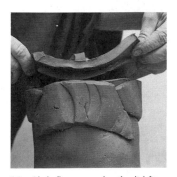

12 Slab flange under the lid fits the pot

13 Add a knob

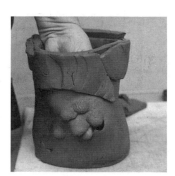

14 Play with the clay — maybe it's a lantern

LARGE SLAB CONSTRUCTIONS I

1 David Middlebrook throws slab out

2 Pull to stretch slab

3 Make a big slab from several slabs; heavy paper underneath makes handling easier

4 Sand-filled cotton core placed on slab

5 Slab and paper backing rolled over core; sand removed when dry

6 Assembled sculpture, dried and sanded, ready for burnished engobe patina

7 Dry sculpture sawed into pieces before firing

8 Shapes reassembled, sawmarks creating line decoration

9 Another technique: Middlebrook crosshatches and moistens interior buttresses

10 … to mate with and support massive top slab

11 Ron Fondow casts or presses clay in a removable plaster slab mold

12 With top slab on, removal of plaster forms creates negative shapes

Artists who build large pieces develop their own techniques. Slab building seems natural for monumental forms; coil building takes more time, but it can give more control.

Slab works should be handled little and carefully at all stages, to prevent strains that develop later into warps or cracks. All clay works, but especially wide or large ones, should be constructed on beds of whole newspapers, burlap, or terry toweling, to allow the clay to move and shrink easily during drying. Try to construct large works in one place, and move them only once, into the kiln. Place them on a layer of grog, sand, or powdered clay that will shift as the piece shrinks more in firing. Alternatives: build on ¾ in (2 cm) thick plywood and let it burn out in the kiln, or build a loose-brick kiln over a piece and dismantle it after firing.

David Middlebrook throws out large slabs and rolls them together into even larger units. He sometimes supports huge forms on cloth structures filled with sand or foam which he empties when the clay hardens. He cuts dried, unfired pieces with a saw and leaves the cuts as patterns. Some constructions are buttressed inside with slab supports.

Ron Fondow makes small sculptures and large site pieces by pressing or pouring a core grid of clay slabs in plaster molds with removable pieces of plaster that create negative spaces.

LARGE SLAB CONSTRUCTIONS II

Adding fibers to clay. Marilyn Levine was one of the first artists to add nylon denier fibers to clay for extra workability and strength. Additives that allow clay more elasticity, causing less stress in the forming stage, include nylon fibers, fiberglass cloth soaked in clay slurry, embedded nylon screen, and ground nut shells or animal fodder mixed into clay. Other possibilities must exist — experiment!

For her *trompe l'oeil* leather-like sculptures, Levine rolls clay on a slab machine, rolls the slabs thinner by hand, and stores them until needed. The plastic-covered slabs are cut with scissors, joined at the seams, formed into sculpture, and covered tightly again for slow drying.

Levine finishes with metallic oxides rubbed on the clay, scratching and bending the shapes to achieve the look of leather. Copper and gold lusters are fired on for the hardware; finally the fired piece is paste-waxed.

Armature construction. Jerry Rothman works large sculptures over wood scaffolding wrapped with paper to allow for clay shrinkage and removal of the wood.

Rothman also developed a non-shrink cement-clay body, in which stainless steel wire can be embedded and fired at 2000°F (1100°C). He supports the structure externally with wood during building.

1 Marilyn Levine's buttressed slab-built suitcase encased in plastic, ready for top

2 Finished suitcase in kiln for first firing

3 Levine applies oxide patina

4 Detail of "leather" finish, "stitching," and "metal" hardware

5 Jerry Rothman laying clay on a wooden scaffold support

6 Triptych fountain units ready for carving

7 Non-shrink clay body will be laid over this stainless steel armature that will fire in the piece

8 Clay on the steel armature, supported by wood while it dries

HANDBUILDING WITH PORCELAIN

Porcelain is the most difficult type of clay body to work. It has the least plasticity of any clay body, cracks easily, and doesn't support well. Thin pieces are fragile both before and after firing. Porcelain has a wonderfully hard, dense, stony appearance when it is built thick and fired to high temperature maturity, but it is the look of the thin translucency that we generally associate with the "material of kings."

Porcelain can be handled thin enough to fire translucent with plastic clay slabs. Jan Peterson throws out a clay slab in the usual manner, then rolls it to less than ⅛ in (.5 cm). She cuts shapes from the fragile clay slab with a sharp metal knife. Joints are patiently luted with a drop of vinegar poised to drip down the joining seam and then squeezed to insure the fit. She uses detailed edges, cuts, and overlaps to alter the form. If cracks develop during drying, they can be patched with dry powdered clay body and vinegar or Epsom salts; she patches cracks in bisque pieces with a paste of Epsom salts, water, and powdered bisque.

Peterson also constructs 25 in (65 cm) diameter platters by hand in porcelain that is glazed with bright, low-temperature colors. Thin porcelain slabs have less strain if they are made from liquid casting slip poured against plaster and tipped to spread, then stiffened evenly with infrared lamps. Shapes cut from the leather-hard slabs are luted together against a plaster form, paddled, and rolled to secure joints. A second layer of porcelain strips reinforces and accents the piece. The platter is supported underneath by cloths or rolled paper while drying right side up.

1 Jan Peterson flattens and throws out a slab of plastic porcelain clay body

2 Roll to ⅛ in (.5 cm) or less

3 Cut and lute base to cylindrical form

4 Squeeze gently to fuse joints; make decorative alterations with delicate pressure

6 Peterson makes slab by pouring casting slip onto plaster, tipping to spread evenly

7 Cut shapes with sharp metal knife

5 Finished tumblers will be translucent when fired to density

8 Reinforce with more slabs

9 Paddle joints to insure fit

10 Dry finished platter right side up

HANDBUILDING IN OR OVER FORMS

Large forms are often constructed in or over something that gives support as well as shape. Armatures such as wood or wire, on which clay might be buttressed, cannot be left in because the clay shrinks as it dries and would crack over the framework; wrap armatures with paper and remove them before the clay dries. Clay can be supported in or on a shallow rigid form of metal, wood, rock, plastic, ceramic, or glass that is covered with enough paper or cloth to let the clay shrink and still be supported as it dries. Remember that clay has to survive without crutches in the kiln. Clay still warps or cracks if a form is dangerously cantilevered.

Cloth hammocks draped between table legs or over a scaffold will support and even create handbuilt forms; adjust the cloth for shape and tack it securely; attach clay appendages or decorative appliqués to the base form and dry in the hammock. Several leather-hard hammock shapes can be joined together, or fired separately and attached later with glue or by other means.

Balloons and balls can support similar shapes, but balloons can be popped and do not have to be removed. **Plaster**, a common material for forming against, absorbs moisture and allows clay to dry easily. **Armatures with some flexibility**, such as soft plastics, linoleum, and tar paper, should be removed before firing because of unpleasant fumes, but cardboard supports can burn out in the kiln.

1 Hammock of cloth draped and nailed

2 Drop clay into hammock, change shape by adjusting cloth, dry in hammock

3 Lay clay over porous form (here, a seashell)

4 Remove leather-hard vessel from form

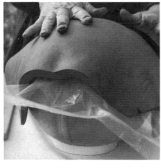

5 Drape slab over beachball covered with plastic

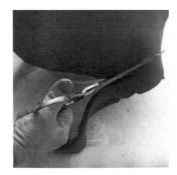

6 Clay can be cut with scissors or knife

7 Textured clay scraps luted on and slab pedestal foot added

8 Finished vessel, quickly and easily fabricated

9 Concave or convex plaster forms

10 Wads of clay pressed into concave plaster show texture when removed

11 Wads of clay pressed over a hump (reverse of previous mold) and paddled together

12 ... give an inside texture when removed

MECHANICAL METHODS OF FORMING

Mechanical processes are particularly suited to production in quantity or numbered repetitive editions. To maintain involvement with the clay, try to use mechanical processes creatively.

Extruding lengths of clay with a plunger and die is at least as old as the Egyptian faience necklaces of Cleopatra's time. Extruders from ceramic suppliers, a cookie press, hand-operated extruders like the one pictured here, or a pug mill (normally a clay-conditioning machine) fitted with dies, are among the mechanical means that can be used to push clay into long hollow or solid shapes.

1 Hand-operated extruder with solid coil die

2 Sculpture made from extruded coils

3 John Glick uses dies for extruded forms

4 Wood die forms built-in lid flange

5 Wood pieces form concave curves in extruded box side

6 Wood and foam shapes used to stamp liquid engobe decoration

7 Darryl Clark readies silicone to mix with liquid clay

8 Liquid silicone clay extruded thread

9 Weaving silicone clay threads

10 2 ft (60 cm) tall porcelain silicone clay sculpture

11 Metal jigger tool cuts back of 24 in (60 cm) clay plate on a plaster mold

John Glick extrudes clay strips to make boxes; one die has a built-in lid flange. He uses formed pieces of wood to keep components the same and decorates quickly, using foam and wood stamps with colored clay engobes that will be visible later under a high-fire reduction glaze.

Darryl Clark discovered the use of silicone rubber lubricant as an additive to clay "to make things happen that ordinarily wouldn't, like paper-thin sheets or extruding thread-thin strings of clay for weaving." With silicone added, liquid clay will assume any shape without breaking. Clark constructs porcelain pieces more than 2 ft (60 cm) tall by this method.

A potter's wheel can be used like an industrial jigger wheel. An arm is attached to hold the metal template that carves one side of a form, while plaster shapes the opposite side.

MAKING WALLS I

Ceramic artists all over the world are making clay walls and murals using a variety of techniques, for residential, commercial, subway, ecclesiastical, and site-specific installations. These are a few examples:

Bruce Howdle was commissioned by the Iowa Beef Processors, Dakota City, Nebraska, for a ceramic mural. He completed the modeling and carving in eleven days with 12,000 lb (5,450 kg) of clay. Cutting the wall into hundreds of pieces, coding them, disassembling, salt-firing, and installation took six months. The wall is 27 ft (8.2 m) at the top, 25 ft (7.6 m) at the bottom, 9½ ft (2.9 m) tall and varies in thickness from 1½ in (3.8 cm) to 1½ ft (.5 m).

Tom McMillin cast and installed a wall in white hydrocal (a special hard plaster) for a bank lobby. In a vacant lot, he dug the form of the whole wall in dirt, divided and shimmed the individual shapes with metal and wood, and cast the hydrocal into them. The units with their earth textures came apart for installation.

Ruth Duckworth's wall, 12 ft (3.65 m) long, is made of hundreds of protruding pinched clay slabs.

Gunnar Larsen modeled sand molds for casting stoneware and concrete sections of a 17 ft (5.2 m) wall in Sweden.

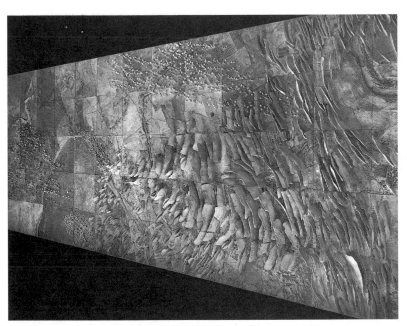

Ruth Duckworth

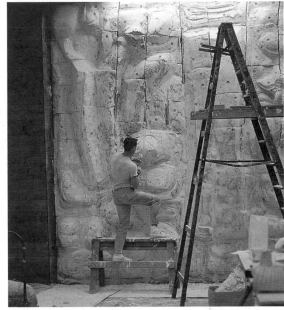

Tom McMillin

Bruce Howdle

MAKING WALLS II

Gunnar Larsen

WALLS

John Stephenson: raku and steel

Nancy Selvin: unglazed earthenware

Frank Matrenga: stoneware fireplace

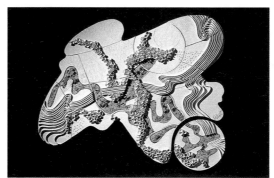

Dave and Pat Dabbert: porcelain and red clay, unglazed

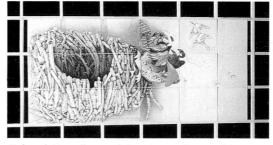

Deborah Horrell: porcelain, prisma color, graphite

JOHN MASON'S HANDBUILT SCULPTURE

John Mason in his Los Angeles studio, a wall in progress, and clay strip sculptures, 1960. All Mason's work is in high-fired stoneware

John Mason working on "Blue Wall," 1959

John Mason, in the 1950s in California, was one of the first to work clay on an enormous scale using handbuilt techniques and high temperature firing. At about the same time, Peter Voulkos was constructing large sculptures from wheel-thrown forms (p. 86). Innovations with scale became possible partly because of the heavy-duty wheels and large kilns that I developed in 1952 at Chouinard Art Institute, Los Angeles.

Mason's 1966 exhibition of monumental clay sculptures at the Los Angeles County Museum of Art was one of the first major solo exhibitions of contemporary clay in a museum. It was followed several years later by a solo exhibition on a similar scale by Ken Price, in the same museum.

In the catalog of Mason's next solo exhibition in 1974, at the Pasadena Art Museum, the art critic Barbara Haskell wrote, "These pieces have a monumentality and physical size that have no precedent in contemporary ceramics."

The flamboyant spontaneous style and exuberant execution of 1950s clay came to be called "Abstract Expressionism," after the term art critic Harold Rosenberg had coined for mid-century painting. We clay artists involved in the vortex at the time did not give names to what was being done, or think of it as a "movement." Many clay artists have since found their own methods for handling clay on an extremely large scale.

JOHN MASON'S HANDBUILT FORMS

"Plate," 1982

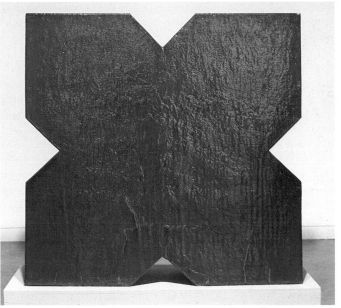

"Red-X," geometric series, 1960

"Wall-Cross," 1963

"Desert Cross," 1963

Doors for Sterling Holloway house, 1962

WHEEL-THROWING

Throwing is another method of clay fabrication. The *potter's wheel* is designed for making round forms of varying thickness from plastic clay, but throwing can produce other forms.

Use of the potter's wheel dates from about 5000 B.C., beginning in Egypt, the Middle East, and Asia. Some cultures — particularly in the Western hemisphere, such as the Indians of North and South America, Eskimos, and South Sea Islanders — have never used the wheel for making clay vessels, although they used the wheel for carts. Their vessels were handbuilt, usually by pinch or coil. Sometimes the vessels were built in saucers that were rotated as coils were added or on rocks that were turned on other rocks; sometimes the artist moved around the pot while making it. These methods might be similar to wheel work, but none of them was centrically perfect.

EVOLUTION OF THE WHEEL

In cultures that did develop the potter's wheel, ancient wheels had large diameters. Usually made of wood, bamboo, or stone, they were mounted on a stick in the ground or on a shaft anchored in stone. The potter bent over from a standing or squatting position and turned the wheel with a rod placed in a hole on top. Another option was to have an assistant to turn the wheel with a rope or lie on the ground and kick the wheel.

Eventually, wheel designs evolved to a more controllable size. The potter could then sit at or above the disk, kicking another wheel placed below to turn it, or rotating it by hand with a short stick in a hole on the top edge.

After thousands of years, electricity was added, although many potters continue to use kick, treadle, or hand-turned wheels. Variable-speed motorized wheels were developed on the kickwheel principle using a flywheel. In 1950, Jack L. Peterson and I built what I think was the first high-horsepower gear-reduction motorized potter's wheel. This new development unleashed large-scale construction in clay on a potter's wheel. The potter could now work with 300 to 400 lb (140 to 180 kg) of clay on the wheel, and could accelerate or decelerate the speed of the wheel with a foot pedal similar to the accelerator pedal in a car. Further refinements have included cone drives and rheostats.

On most kickwheels, the body's kicking motion is separate from its throwing motion; one must kick and then throw. Throwing therefore takes place as the rotation is decelerating, further slowing the motion of the wheel against the pressure of hands on the clay. With a flexible-speed electrically driven wheel, the motion of the wheel can increase during throwing, irrespective of the weight of the clay or the hand pressure on it.

However, some potters still prefer kickwheels to electrically driven ones, for reasons of sensitivity and empathy. The late Bernard Leach, the famous British potter who is thought of as the founder of studio ceramics in our time, used a traditional European-style treadle wheel that limited the size of the piece that could be thrown. The late Shoji Hamada used a Chinese-style hand wheel, rotated by a stick, which made only a few revolutions before the stick was needed to rotate the wheel again after pressure on the clay. That very act made its particular mark on the look of the work. After about fifty years of potting, Hamada refused an American offer of a gear-reduction motor-driven wheel, saying that he was too old to learn to use it. This statement probably implied several things, the most important of which were that tradition was a major virtue in his value system and that the limits of his wheel were a visual characteristic of his work.

Some wheels have a flat metal wheelhead; others have a concave wheelhead into which a *bat* made of wood or plaster must be placed. Plaster, wood, or presswood are the best materials for the bat because they are porous, allowing the piece to dry and release easily in place. With

Berndt Friberg's porcelain bottles in his studio at Gustavsbergs Fabriker in Gustavsberg, Sweden, 1966

a cupped wheelhead, the bat and drying piece can be removed together, and the wheel can be used with another bat or returned for working or decorating at will. If the wheelhead is metal, the piece must be cut off and transferred somewhere to dry. Cutting pieces off a bat is a learned skill, more difficult for large shapes than small.

THE THROWING PROCESS

Throwing shapes on a potter's wheel makes you think about the *profile line*, the outside edge or the contour edge of the form. But you are confronted with two profile lines, one inside and one outside. To get the inside to be like the outside, it is easiest to fix your mind on the outside except when the shape is low and open. The fingers pull up the "line" as the wheel rotates.

It is important to have only one pressure point on one place on the clay at one time. If there are more pressures — more fingers or too much hand against the clay — the pot will accept all those pressures and will be taken off center.

Centering, the first part of the process of throwing, is needed to persuade the clay ball to take shape symmetrically. It does not matter which direction the wheel rotates; the potter adapts to the motion and works on the left or right side of the clay according to which is the best spot for "catching" clay as it comes around, and for pushing on it in the proper place, "on center." In the United States and some European countries, the potter's wheel turns counterclockwise, and the potter centers on the left and pulls up on the right. In Asian countries, the wheel is turned clockwise. (The diagrams and demonstration photographs in this book use a wheel rotating counterclockwise.) No matter what the shape of the wheelhead or bat, the potter must learn to feel the centrifugal motion of the wheel and the clay as it responds to that motion with pressure of the hand.

After initial centering, throwing basically consists of opening the ball of clay, pulling the cylinder up, and shaping. At first, this whole process should be practiced over and over, so the potter learns to feel the rhythm of the whole motion. After some weeks of practicing the whole, the beginner should divide the process into parts, studying the initial sequences on the following pages and working with each segment separately to improve each part of the process. That done, the parts can be reunited into the whole process. Repeat and practice until throwing is second nature. Think the line, think the shape, see the volume. Fingers will do as you think.

THE IDEA OF FORM

Gaining control of the potter's wheel takes several years. Once hands know where the pressure really is and can feel the clay's response, advanced potters evolve their own ways of throwing. For beginners, my recommendation is to

Nepalese potter

Traditional wheel, stick turned

Standing up and sitting to work the clay

Shoji Hamada sitting, lotus position, at his chestnut Chinese hand wheel rotated with a stick

work on **five forms** in succession, thinking of them as "forms" rather than utilitarian objects. The idea of "bowl" is psychologically limiting; thinking "half-sphere" conjures an unlimited concept of roundness. Repeat the forms until making them is subconscious; then consider variations of line.

Take a ball of clay the size that your two hands almost, but not quite, go around. Begin this series of forms by making a straight-sided **cylinder** of even thickness, but slightly heavier in the cross-section at the base of the wall. Pull the form as tall and narrow as possible.

Next try a **half-sphere**, as in half a grapefruit. This is not an easy form, but it is the second necessary step in learning to perfect the technical control of a profile line and to understand the engineering of support.

Next throw a **whole sphere**, where the line is brought all the way around in profile and nearly closed, leaving a small opening. Try to make a true circle. This form is full of throwing pitfalls; walls will collapse if the curve is not properly drawn and supported from underneath.

A whole sphere and cylinder combined (sometimes called a "bottle"; see p. 48) requires pulling the clay form out, in, and up, keeping the shape symmetrical and the cross-section relatively even all the while. This is one of the most difficult forms to throw.

The **low open form**, last and quite different in technique, is pulled from a low-centered mound perhaps 12 in (30 cm) in diameter. Avoid thinking of words like plate or platter. Think only of the profile line, interior and exterior, and the shape it makes in space.

When the five forms are mastered on one scale, double the size of the ball of clay and go through the series again. Repeat it, doubling or at least increasing the clay until a limit is reached. Like any skill, throwing will grow with practice, although once the basic technique is mastered, it will never vanish.

Traditional throwing techniques used for functional ware can also be adapted to innovative sculptural projects. The pages that follow illustrate the basic centering, opening, and pulling process, with possible mistakes, and then proceed to throwing specific functional forms. The last sequences illustrate special techniques such as throwing hollow "donuts" to cut into other forms, throwing several small pieces off a single hump of clay, throwing large vessels, building large pieces in sections, altering the symmetry of thrown forms, and cutting thrown pieces into slab-like pieces for sculptural constructions.

Tom Coleman adds one thrown leather-hard porcelain section to another to make a composite piece

Peter Voulkos assembling thrown and altered volumes into monolithic volumes, and brushing on pigments, in his studio in 1958. The works shown are "Black Butte Divide," left, "Rondera," center, and "Black Bulerias," right

THROWING ON THE WHEEL

Throwing on the potter's wheel takes practice. Anyone can learn this quickest method of clay fabrication, but not everyone chooses this technique as the major way to work clay.

Principles of pressure in throwing are the same no matter what method is used. When the wheel turns counterclockwise, as it does in all my demonstration photographs, centering pressure is on the left side of the clay. To center, lean in to the clay at 8 o'clock; that is, lean in against the movement. After the mound is opened, pull up on the right side of the clay at 4 o'clock position to lift the wall. Lift up with the inside and out-side fingers together, in an absolutely straight line from bottom to top.

The smallest pressure point against the clay gives greatest control; too much hand-touching drags. Feel the motion of the wheel and the response of the clay. The clay must revolve at least once each time before you move up — wheel speed dictates your speed. Practice the five basic shapes of the throwing process (p. 50), then increase size. Not everyone throws alike; find your own way. My way, easiest for beginners, is documented in this section.

1 Place mound of clay on wheel going counterclockwise; palms squeeze into clay, lift up evenly

2 Base of each palm presses into clay, lifts up, several revolutions between lifts

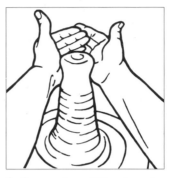

3 Squeeze in and lift up to make a tall cone

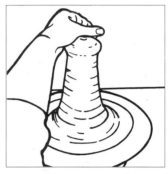

4 Press down on top with base of left thumb and heel of left palm in 8 o'clock position

5 Left palm pushes down and leans in toward center at the same time

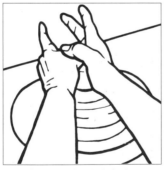

6 Add base of right little finger and palm on top, parallel to left thumb; push down

7 Left hand is the primary pressure centering hand

8 Right hand gives a secondary helping pressure

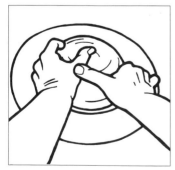

9 First fingertip of right hand trues base of clay from right side in 4 o'clock position

10 Left middle fingertip opens centered ball, right middle finger on top supports left

11 Right fingertip at 4 o'clock trues base of open form

12 Centered open mound ready to be lifted into hollow form

THROWING FAULTS AND REMEDIES

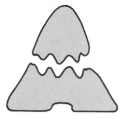

1   Clay breaks in two because you squeezed too hard in one place lifting up.
Remedy: keep pressure steady on the way up; don't press in too hard.

2   Uneven pressure on the cone, with one hand pressing more than the other.
Remedy: steady yourself, with back of neck, shoulders, upper arms, forearms, wrists, and palms rigid; both hands must move up with equal pressure.

3   Spiral, because hands moved faster than the wheel was going.
Remedy: allow more rotations of the wheel each time before moving both hands upward.

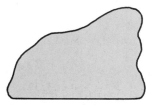

4   Off-center mound.
Remedy: left palm must lean into clay with steady pressure at exactly 8 o'clock position.

5   Opening hole is uneven and off-center.
Remedy: left middle fingertip or tip of left thumb, supported by right fingers, must push straight down in the center.

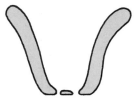

6   No bottom, because fingers pushed too fast or too hard.
Remedy: stop wheel, fill hole with pancake of clay, re-throw smooth.

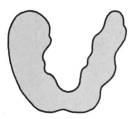

7   Lumpy off-center wall.
Remedy: exert even pressure on inside and outside fingertips at 4 o'clock position and move up evenly.

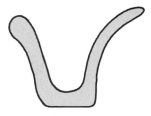

8   Top lip is higher, with wall thicker on one side than the other because hands moved up on the diagonal or one hand was in front of the other.
Remedy: inside and outside fingertips must move up in a straight line, together.

9   Air bubble in wall.
Remedy: stop wheel, poke bubble with needle, fill void with wad of clay, re-throw the wall.

10   Top lip is cut off unevenly.
Remedy: to cut it evenly, hold wall in 4 o'clock position at the lip with left fingers. Push needle through clay wall evenly to inside finger for several revolutions; lift off ring of clay.

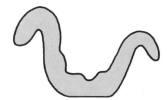

11   Wall collapses.
Remedy: use as little water as possible during throwing. Always move hands up, bottom to top; never press down.

12   "S" crack in base, usually discovered after drying or bisque firing.
Remedy: compress clay better when throwing. Drop clay ball down harder on bat to start; press fingers down harder to open ball.

CENTERING

Many methods exist for getting clay centered with the centrifugal motion of the wheel. My way centers clay by leaning into it from one position. This method is always successful and there is no limit on the size of mound that can be centered.

Raise a cone to begin centering. Drop or place a wedged cone of clay onto the moving or stopped wheel — and learn now to use minimal water in all throwing processes. Start the wheel, place the base of both palms parallel to the wheelhead, squeeze into the clay about 1 in (2.5 cm) horizontally, lift straight up. Body is rigid, arms taut; if you move, the clay moves. Hold hands steady for several revolutions, then lift. Moving too fast creates spirals; too hard chops off clay.

Push the cone down. With end of the left wrist against the top of the clay at 8 o'clock, press down and lean in toward center. Practice squeezing up, then pushing down until you understand the power of the left hand. Right hand position is added when you understand the left: place the flat of the right hand parallel to the left thumb, and push downward.

Centering. When downward pressure forms a mushroom, lean heel of left palm 90 degrees to its wrist into clay at 8 o'clock position. Clay is centered when it revolves evenly without lumps or bumps, absolutely smooth. To begin, push down, then lean into the mushroom, in two motions. Eventually you will be able to do the down-lean as one motion.

Squeeze up, push down, lean in to center several times. True up the base, moving tip of first finger of right hand down toward the bat at 4 o'clock position.

Lifting the cone up and pressing it down several times is a form of wedging. Clay can be centered as soon as it is put onto the wheel, but you develop empathy with the clay while lifting it up and pushing it down; production potters may cut out this step to save time.

1 Moisten hands

2 Start with cone-shaped mound

3 Squeeze both hands in toward center and lift clay to make a tall cone

4 Squeeze only with the base of each palm; lift both hands evenly

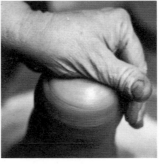

5 Wrist end of left palm pushes down and leans into clay at 8 o'clock

6 Thumb and heel of palm push down and in toward center; other fingers exert no pressure

7 Further down, use only the bones at left wrist to center

8 To add right hand, place base of right palm and little finger parallel to left palm

9 Push down from top with heel of left palm leaning in at 8 o'clock; press down with right hand

10 True base with tip of first finger of right hand at 4 o'clock

OPENING THE BALL

Sit or stand at the potter's wheel with weight in lower body. Back, shoulders, neck, upper arms, forearms, and wrists rigid, move as one unit. Clay should be at lap level. Sit or stand high enough over the clay for your back and shoulders to give stability; don't let wrists and forearms do all the work. You stay still; the clay moves. Catch the clay in one place as it turns.

To center, body thrust is from the left. To open the ball, equal pressure is applied with both hands from mid-body. Arms lie close to ribs, hands drop from wrists, fingertips rest on top in the middle of the mound.

Opening the ball. There are basically two methods for opening the centered mound. Each is useful at some point, so learn both. Open a low, wide mound for low, wide forms, and a taller mound for taller forms.

Method A. Push middle fingertip of left hand straight down into clay, supported with right middle fingertip on top. Let other fingers ride. Allow at least one wheel revolution each time before pushing down more, to about ¾ in (2 cm) from the wheelhead. To widen the hole, pull fingertips toward you, keeping a U-shaped interior.

Method B. Push tip of left thumb straight down, supported on knuckle with two right fingertips; bottom remains about ½ in (1 cm) thick. To widen, move left thumb at center bottom toward the left, supported with right fingertips, wrists steady. Press slowly; widen cautiously.

Recenter. If mound goes off center, your pressure is wrong or in the wrong place. To recenter at any time, even when mound is open, lean in with left palm in 8 o'clock position and right fingers inside, opposite the left palm; press both hands steadily against each other until clay recenters. Feel the clay establish itself. Steady pressure is paramount. One spot on the hand does the pressing, everything else rides or supports. When clay is on center, release pressure and remove your hands slowly, without causing any movement; the clay must not know you are going.

Practice locking muscles, especially of the left arm and its centering palm. Stiffen the left palm and wrist, then release the rigidity without moving. This ability to stiffen and relax muscles at will is the basis of skill in throwing. Throwing is only a skill; art is something else.

1 Method A. Right middle fingertip supports left middle fingertip in center mound

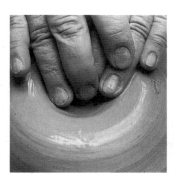

2 Left middle fingertip pushes straight down, right supports

3 Keep wrists low and rigid, body steady

4 When base is ¾ in (2 cm) thick, pull fingertip from center out to widen cylinder

5 Method B. Tip of left thumb is supported by right fingertip

6 Thumbtip pushes straight down; move toward palm to widen, wrists steady

7 Steady the wall after opening; hold with left thumb and fingers, press down with right

8 Shape and straighten lip before lifting wall

PULLING UP

All wheelthrown forms start as a cylinder – tall for tall forms, short and fat for wide forms. The secret of lifting is to indent ½ in (1 cm) into the clay wall at the base, and lift that roll of clay from bottom to top evenly. Clay must slither through hands without dragging, but throw with minimal water. Strains put in clay now become cracks or warps later.

Begin the lift with left fingertip inside and right fingertip outside, on the right-hand side of the clay wall in 4 o'clock position. Outside fingertip makes the indentation to lift the roll of clay; inside fingertip exactly opposite rides up, exerting no pressure. Both hands lift in a diagonal line toward your left shoulder. Fingertips must be exactly opposite, or clay goes off center.

Indent from the base, and lift to the top several times. If the roll isn't visible, you aren't lifting. Measure with ruler to see what you have lifted.

Squeeze palms to narrow cylinder between pulls. Hold steady, only moving your hands; don't breathe. Stop partway up if necessary, relax, begin again at that place, go to the top. The smallest pressure point on each fingertip against the clay gives the most control; reduce that contact to a pinpoint. Make the cylinder needed for the shape you want, and cut off excess clay.

1 First fingertip makes outside indentation; inside finger does the same

2 Push in with outside first fingertip backed by second finger to lift the roll

3 Pressure is on the outside; inside hand rides

4 Each pull continues to the top, pushing in toward center while lifting up

5 Squeeze with base of palms to narrow cylinder and thicken wall for next lift

6 Fingers at back pull slightly toward you, palms lift and squeeze

7 Repeat wall roll lift from bottom to top, with inside fingertip opposite outside fingertip

8 Squeeze palms to narrow cylinder between each lift

9 Palms and fingertips make three-point collar to narrow top

10 Cut top evenly, with needle through clay to inside finger

11 Lift off severed ring of clay after several wheel revolutions

12 Smooth and shape lip with fingertips

THROWING A BOWL

1 Left thumb and right palm press down from center out to left to flatten a low mound

2 Or fingers of both hands press down from center out to right for low, flat mound

The bowl, one of the most basic ceramic forms made by all pottery-producing cultures, can be functional, decorative, sculptural, or non-functional.

In ceramics, we need to learn to pre-visualize form and finished concept. Draw on paper or in your mind the profile of the shape you wish to throw. Keeping that shape in mind will enable you to throw it.

Rule: the top of a thrown bowl can safely exceed the bottom radius by 2 in (5 cm), or 4 in (10 cm) on the diameter. Using that rule, draw a curved shape that can be made between a given foot and a lip diameter.

Throwing: center clay as wide at the base as the form will be. Open the mound; pull up a short cylinder. Shape the lip now, before thinning the wall. Begin the curve by pushing out and up with the inside fingertips; outside fingertips support. Avoid a reverse curve inside by pushing out once more than seems necessary.

Bowls are best made this way: pull the curve out to about halfway up, release pressure, and finish the inside curve to that point. Then pull the top diameter out in several moves, return to the base, and re-throw the entire curve.

Refine the lip, trim excess clay at base with wood knife. See p. 61 for directions to finish foot.

3 Right finger presses clay down to wheelhead

4 Open mound with left middle finger supported by right, pulling toward you to widen

5 Widen more by rolling edge over and pressing down

6 Lift curve, with fingers inside opposite fingers outside. Watch curve develop on left of interior

7 Press rib from center out to smooth and reinforce bottom curve

8 Lift, thin, shape again with wheel moving slowly

9 Left hand holds; right fingertip defines edge

10 Trim base. Hold wood knife parallel to wheelhead, perpendicular to clay; cut

11 Cut base profile. Hold wood knife parallel to clay and shape curve; remove excess clay

12 Sponge interior smooth

THROWING A PITCHER

Pitcher forms are indigenous to almost all cultures except in East Asia. Mesopotamian and Egyptian pouring vessels were tall, elegant shapes; medieval forms were broad based and strong. European peasant pitchers were often embellished with decoration, while Early American pitchers had simple shapes and were slightly patterned. The pitcher form, thrown or handbuilt, poses design questions: body fat or thin, pouring spout indented low or beginning high at the lip, handle low or high, body altered or round. The spout controls the flow of liquid and should not drip; exaggerate the extension of the pouring lip, and sharpen the edge at a right angle to the body of the pot.

Raise a cylinder to the desired height by lifting with the first fingertip backed by the second one outside, against the middle or first fingertip backed by the other inside. To make a cylinder, the inside hand moves up toward the left shoulder. Never push out to the right; pressure from the outside hand against the inside one does the lifting.

Shape the vessel. Bow the form out from the inside, with fingertips pushing out; inside and outside fingers together draw the profile, pushing out and lifting up simultaneously. The natural pitcher form contains liquid in a wide base and collars inward to limit the flow.

Collar by squeezing in with three-point pressure from thumbs and fingers held horizontally on the clay. Touching three places on the clay will keep it round; using only two pressure points creates an oval shape.

Stop the wheel to make the spout. Press left thumb and middle finger into the body and lift up to begin the pouring form. Inside right finger matches movement and pulls over the top edge to form spout. Bring inside edge of the wall to the outside edge at the lip, making one sharp horizontal edge exactly parallel to the wheelhead.

Refine base by trimming with wood knife. Cut under the pot with twisted wire and lift it to another board; finish foot when leather-hard.

1 Begin lifting cylinder, with outside finger lower than inside finger; press in and lift up

2 Inside pressure from fingertips pushes out the body curve; outside fingers ride

3 Inside and outside fingertips opposite each other; push out to expand or push in to narrow profile

4 Thumbs and fingers collar in and lift up

5 Three-point pressure on the clay keeps it round

6 Inside fingertip lifts up and out to flare lip; outside fingers support

7 Begin pouring lip. For pouring indentation, press outside opposite inside finger; move up

8 Inside finger follows upward and pulls clay edge over at top to make one sharp lip edge

9 Trim base profile with wood knife; lift off excess clay

10 Re-establish throwing marks; cut pitcher off and finish leather-hard

BOWL FORMS

James Makins: porcelain, colored clays

Robert Sperry: stoneware, low-fire glaze

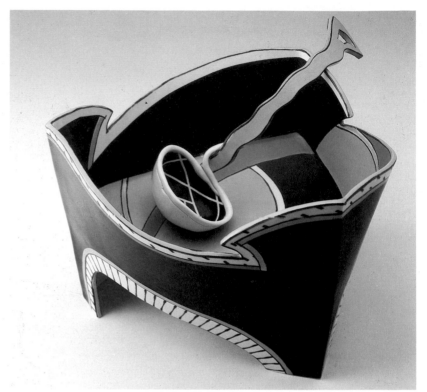

Dorothy Hafner: cast tureen, porcelain

Pat Kenny: cut earthenware

Nan McKinnell: ribbed porcelain

Robert Duca: translucent and bloated low-fire porcelain

PITCHER AND BOTTLE FORMS

Taäg Peterson: stoneware, salt-glazed

Cynthia Bringle: stoneware

Regis Brodie: glaze with stain washes

Bill Farrell: stoneware with crayon

Victoria Littlejohn: poured glazes, stoneware

Harrison McIntosh: stoneware, engobe

THROWING A BOTTLE

1 Inside hand pushes cylinder out to expand bottle

2 Fingertips of both hands draw the desired profile line

Bottle shapes are fun to make, but those with narrow bases, wide bellies, and narrow necks are the most challenging to throw on the wheel. Bottles can be altered to other shapes, split open for trays, turned sideways for teapots, clustered as candelabra, used abstractly, or shaped as parts of animal or people figures.

Center as tall a cone of clay as can be opened easily. If a cylinder is too wide, it is difficult to squeeze narrow, while too tall a cylinder is hard to get into for lifting and shaping.

Open a cylinder approximately the width at the base that the foot of the bottle will be. Lift, keeping a roll of clay at the top that will become the neck. When your hand no longer fits inside, use a long stick with a piece of sponge attached to the end, or the rounded end of a long wooden spoon handle, to work inside against your outside fingertip for lifting.

Draw the shape from inside with the fingertips of both hands, as if drawing the outline of a bottle on paper. Moisten your arm as it goes down into the long cylinder, or use the sponge on the stick inside to expand the form. Tall, thin bottle forms with long necks are the most difficult.

Bottle neck. Collar the extra roll of clay kept to make the neck with three pressure points; squeeze and lift. As the neck narrows, hold a pencil, dowel, or needle inside vertically. Lift the outside finger against the object inside. Rotate the wheel more slowly as neck narrows. Flare the lip gingerly; too much pressure throws clay off center. For a very tall neck, keep a very thick roll of clay at the top edge of the cylinder. Belly the bottle under that roll and form the neck with it.

Refine base with wood knife. Narrow shapes can be wire-cut and lifted with fingers or trowels off the wheelhead; wide shapes can remain on bats to dry.

3 Hold thumbs and fingertips in a triangle to narrow neck. Don't push directly in; lift up and squeeze

4 Squeeze and lift several times to narrow slowly

5 Raise wall with fingertips inside and outside to lift and shape neck between upward squeezes

6 Straighten neck and refine lip slowly

7 Narrow neck with three-point pressure

8 Finished bottle form with decorative finger marks is wire-cut off wheelhead

9 Instead, bottles can become lidded pots; needle-cut into bottle at an angle for lid

10 Be sure lid is cut through, then let it dry on the pot

ROLLING OR TRIMMING A FOOT

Pots can be footed in different ways: by rolling, wheel trimming, paddling, carving, or adding another foot form.

Rolling the base is fine for large pots, thin bottoms, production potting, or uneven top edges. Roll the base edge of a leather-hard piece against a flat surface for a short bevel; roll more of base to make a larger bevel. To aid drying and firing, indent rolled foot by pressing inward gently with fingers or palm.

Carving a foot. Bottles or uneven lips must be trimmed upside-down in another pot, a jar, or a thrown cylinder, called a chuck. Center chuck and secure it with a coil of clay. Place pot upside-down; make sure it is level. Hold pot down with middle finger of left hand, and carving tool with right (or vice versa if left-handed), but always carve on right side at 4 o'clock.

Trim the outer profile first with sharp tool, cutting with one small point of tool against clay. Trim indentation inside bottom of vessel last, moving tool from center out to the right. Size and shape of the foot enhance the vessel form. After cutting, smooth the footrim with fingers or rib; use a monogram stamp or sign your name, or paint it on after bisquing.

1   Rolling: roll base evenly on flat surface, around in a circle

2   Hold pot lightly with both hands

3   Angle pot more for larger bevel

4   Press in bottom; foot indentation aids drying and firing

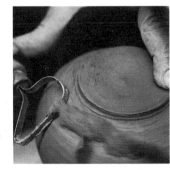

5   Trimming: invert pot in centered chuck to trim with tool

6   Level pot; secure chuck to wheelhead with clay coil

7   Small wire-end tool cuts small amount, left middle finger holds pot securely on chuck

8   Loop corer trims clay faster; move tool up or down to shape profile

9   Rib refines, smooths, shapes; concentric fingermarks can be reinstated

10   Begin foot indentation with tool moving from center out; stop for appropriate footrim width

11   Smooth finished tooled foot with fingers or rubber rib

12   A narrow foot profile accentuates curve

PULLED AND THROWN HANDLES

Handles for various kinds of vessels can be coil-rolled, pinched, or slabbed; but handles for thrown vessels should be pulled out of a lump of clay much as the thrown pot was, so the clay is strained in the same way. Usually the handle is made separately and attached in the leather-hard stage. It can be formed and attached when both pot and appendage are wet, but the look will be different.

Pulled handle. Start a pulled handle with an oval lump of wedged clay. Hold the clay in one hand and pull with the other, keeping the clay moist. Narrow the handle toward the bottom; if it breaks or weakens, start again. Place it in a curved

position to stiffen. Attach to trimmed leather-hard pot while handle is still movable — after about 20 minutes. Handles can also be pulled on a pot (p. 63).

Thrown handle. Throw a wide, curved, open ring. Cut it into one or more handles for one or a group of pots. The ring can be thrown the desired finished handle curvature, or a narrow thrown ring can be pulled into a larger arch.

Experiment with coils or slabs of clay in various curvatures on pots to decide about form and placement before shaping the real handle. Handle-making becomes a type of personal signature.

1 Pulled handle: draw clay from oval lump, with thumb and first finger holding round or flat shape

2 Turn wrist to and fro to keep handle even on all sides

3 Thumb makes indentation for grip, if desired

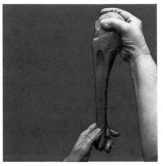

4 Pull until long and thin enough; pinch off excess clay

5 Long handles stiffen best in wide arch; extra clay will be wire-cut off for handle attachment

6 Short handles stiffen with short curve

7 Crosshatch and moisten both handle and pot when attaching

8 Handle should be placed low for weight, exactly opposite spout

9 Thrown handle: open a low, wide mound for thrown handle. Tool cuts clay away

10 Lift open ring, shape handle curvature

11 Cut handle sections from the large ring

12 Lute thrown handles to pots

ATTACHING A HANDLE

Some potters make lots of cups, all different; some just make sets; others use cups as beginnings for other abstractions. Non-functional cups have been metaphors for centuries and still are, in the work of many artists, today.

Try cup shapes — hold them, lift them, drink from them. Think of weight, balance, size, curve, lip flare. Experiment with lugs, knobs, handles, loops. Foot cups by rolling, carving, paddling, or wheel trimming, before adding handle.

Handle design. Roll practice coils to make trial tests of handle shapes and placement on cups before pulling and attaching the real handle. Some handles are better for some cups than other cups. Observe the enclosed space that occurs between the handle and the cup. This negative space is the most important element of the design, and it dictates the way in which the handle is held.

To pull a handle separately, do so without twisting. Attach the top and bottom of the handle in a straight vertical line on the cup. If handles are strained during forming or attaching, cracks or distortions will result in the firing.

To pull a handle directly on a cup, attach a clay lump to a leather-hard cup. Pull the lump slowly with thumb and fingers into an arch relating to the shape of the cup, adjusting the curve, and secure the end.

1 Center cup upside-down for trimming, with left palm holding position at 8 o'clock

2 Middle finger holds cup down, loop tool cuts profile first, then bottom indentation

3 If shape allows, rolled footing is fast

4 Indent base of rolled foot with heel of palm

5 To form an off-cup handle: pull a short handle from clay lump with thumb and fingers

6 Loop handle to stiffen before attaching

7 Crosshatch and moisten cup to attach handle

8 Crosshatch and moisten handle ends in water

9 Be certain handle is squarely vertical when attaching

10 To pull handle on a cup: lute clay lump to cup, pull out with moistened thumb and fingers

11 Arch handle and attach base to cup

12 Work handles and cups in series

THROWN AND CUT LUG HANDLES

1 Cut lugs: throw cylinder; cut wet to allow shaping

2 Attach handle, bringing ends over for fingerhold

3 … or flare a ledge for support

4 Throw taller cylinder to cut larger lugs

5 Spread the form wide against the pot

6 … or bring ends together

"Lug" is defined as a projection piece by which anything is held or supported. This style of handle has been used historically on peasant folkware and often appears as an extra handle on large functional vessels. Lug handles can be made by cutting portions from thrown cylindrical or spherical shapes or by throwing solid or hollow lengths to be attached to pots as lugs.

Handles cut from thrown shapes. Throw several forms from which to cut experimental lug shapes; try them on pots. Often more than one is used. These handles are particularly good for casserole dishes or serving dishes for hot food.

Thrown lug handles. This handle is usually shaped as a long reverse (concave) curve. It must have the right width and flare for handling and balancing the vessel. The lug can be open, nearly closed, or closed, with a pinhole for air escape. Usually just one such lug is used on a pot; the form must hold the necessary weight and provide leverage.

Throw long lug handles with the attachment side against the wheelhead or bat. Shape the length, width, and end open or closed, based on the shape of the vessel to which the handle will be attached. Attach wet or leather-hard. Attaching handles leather-hard is crisp; attaching wet is more spontaneous. Lute the joint carefully.

7 Thrown lugs: fingertips center clay mound of correct diameter

8 Open and lift wall of long reverse curve; flare lip of lug form

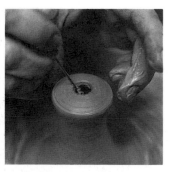

9 Attach handle wet or leather-hard

10 For closed-end lug, bring clay over nearly or all the way (make pinhole if closed)

11 Wire-cut handle off bat

12 Attach wet or leather-hard; experiment with forms; lug shapes change look of vessel

FLAT LIDS FOR FLANGED POTS

A flat lid, made right side up, suits most pots, is easy to measure with calipers for an accurate dimension, needs no trimming, and is the simplest lid for beginners to learn. A small, flat lid can be cut off and placed on its pot right away to dry. If the lid is large and wide, allow it to stiffen slowly on the bat where it was made before picking it up to place it on its pot for further drying.

Make a pot with an inside flange — a ledge to hold the lid — or with a flared rim just wide enough for the lid to sit on, or flare the edge of the pot wide enough to act as both a hand-hold for the vessel and a ledge for the lid, dramatizing the form. Decide exactly where the lid will sit on the flare or the inside flange, and measure diameter of the exact spot before constructing the lid.

Measure the dimensions for the lid when the pot is wet. Despite some excuses, the only reason for lids that do not fit properly is inaccurate measurement or incorrect fabrication.

Center the clay needed for throwing a lid on the wheelhead or bat; throw small lids off-the-hump (see p. 81). Lids often use less clay than anticipated; experience helps in gauging the amount.

A flat lid is made right side up, about the same thickness as the cross-section of the pot. Flatten the centered mound of clay to the diameter needed for the lid; clean the bat of excess clay. Don't open the mound. Instead, form a flat lid with a solid knob by squeezing the clay with fingers of both hands from the edge of the mound in toward the center and up.

Cut off excess clay with a needle at the knob and at the edge of the lid as you trim and shape. Refine the stem as you throw a solid knob or open a hollow knob. Measure width several times, shaping the lid with reference to the pot. Bevel the inside edge of lid with wood knife in the right direction to sit properly on the flange.

Flat lids can have a flange to fit pots with no flange. Construct the lid right side up, of appropriate diameter, but thick enough for a flange: press inward with finger or tool at 4 o'clock position to make a ledge under the top edge of the lid that will fit into the pot. It should not be necessary to hollow this flange.

Flat lids are shaped and made to exact measurement and finished after throwing. No further trimming is needed. Don't wire-cut under the lid unless you are using an impervious bat. Allow the flat lid to stiffen on the bat until it can be moved without strains, to continue drying on its pot.

1 Flared lip serves as flange ledge for a flat lid

2 Make pot first; measure diameter where lid will fit with calipers or ruler while wet

3 Center small lump of clay on bat or throw lid off-the-hump (p. 81)

4 Press down to widen; squeeze solid knob up

5 Spread clay for lid diameter; flatten and shape knob

6 Sharp edge is important for fit; angle it underneath

7 Open the solid knob to make it hollow if desired

8 Try lids with both solid and hollow knobs on pot

LIDDED POT FORMS

Rick Pope: stoneware, salt-glazed

James Makins: porcelain, colored clays

Bruce Van Valen: porcelain, engobe

Byron Temple: tie-box with string,
stoneware, saggar-fired

Andrea Leila Denecke:
stoneware

DOME LIDS FOR FLANGED POTS

1 **Upside-down lid:** indent under solid ball of clay before opening, to narrow for the stem

2 Open, lift, and shape the lip while wall is thick

3 Press under; lift again to raise dome from the stem

4 Small lids need fingertip pressure, not hard work

Dome lids to fit flanged pots are made upside-down or right side up. Carve a knob out of the supporting stem or add a handbuilt or thrown knob. Take measurements for the lid on the wet pot.

Upside-down dome lid. Center a ball of clay on the bat or throw small lids off-the-hump. Indent the base for a stem of extra clay to carve a knob later or throw the bowl flat to add a separate knob. The lip edge of the lid must be sharply pointed so it will sit level against the pot.

A dome lid made right side up is difficult to throw, but it has the advantage of needing no trimming. This method is best for large pots that need a lid with a tall curve to complete the vessel form. Open a centered ring of clay down to the bat, and tool away excess clay. Raise and shape the open wall into a dome, stem, and knob, squeezing the clay closed as tightly as possible where the stem begins. To prevent a spiral twist, stop short of closing the stem. Fill the hole with clay and continue throwing the knob.

Lids should dry on their pots. When possible, a glazed lid should fire with its unglazed edge supported on the unglazed edge of its pot; lids fired separately may warp.

5 Place fingertips exactly opposite each other to flare the dome lid

6 Measure lid and pot with calipers to check fit

7 **Right-side-up lid:** open centered mound down to bat, tool away clay inside

8 Raise dome; squeeze and lift hollow knob

9 Narrowing the stem for accent, close it almost shut

10 Put a ball of plastic clay in to close the hole

11 Throw the ball of clay to become part of the knob

12 Hollow dome-shaped lid fits its pot with no trimming; refine fitting edge when leather-hard

FLANGED LIDS: DOMED AND FLAT

1 Dome lid with flange: measure diameter of pot where lid will fit

2 Begin lid with centered ball of clay that has diameter of outside of pot

3 Open without expanding mound

4 Push fingertip into wall to construct flange; throw and shape dome from underneath flange

5 Caliper outside edge of lid to fit exactly, or extend out from vessel wall

6 Caliper flange of lid where it will fit into the vessel wall, allowing some leeway

7 Cut under lid with wood knife as far as possible to minimize trimming

8 Trim lid right side up; prepare for knob attachment if knob is necessary

9 Flat lid with flange: push into centered mound to begin flange for lid upside-down

10 Open; move the pre-set flange to measured dimension

11 Flatten edge of lid that rests on pot edge

12 Raise flange enough to stay securely inside pot

13 Check measurements a final time

14 Wire-cut lid off bat

A pot without a flange must have a lid with a flange that fits down inside the pot. Make this hollow-flanged lid upside-down to have more control over the height and width of the flange.

Dome lid with flange. Set the flange by pressing a ledge into the wall of an open cylinder. Lift the dome shape from under the pre-set flange. Measure flange to fit into pot with some leeway; measure outside edge of lid to fit exactly or extend over vessel edge. Try to visualize the upside-down lid right side up.

Flat lid with flange. Push into the mound to make a solid or hollow flange; add knob when leather-hard.

CASSEROLE DISH WITH INSIDE FLANGE

Clay pots are excellent for baking or serving hot food, but fired clay cracks with thermal shock. Earthenware bodies take temperature changes best because heat passes through a porous clay body. Vitreous bodies — stoneware or porcelain — may crack with quick temperature change, but will withstand gradual changes in temperature. Any ceramic vessel can be used for baking if it is put at room temperature into a cold oven before the heat is turned on.

To make a wide, shallow casserole, center and open a mound to the diameter desired for the pot. Widen the cylinder with fingertips of both hands held flat, moving from center out. Lift a thick wall and flatten its top edge.

Form the flange in the thick wall now, before shaping the vessel. Press down into the wall from the top edge, making a ledge. Fingertips of both hands, underneath and on top of the ledge, squeeze lightly to thin the flange, drawing it toward the center.

Needle-cut the inside edge of the flange so that the ledge is about ¾ in (2 cm) wide, big enough to support the lid that has yet to be made. Round the flange edge with fingers or moistened chamois (a sponge would drag off the fine-grained wet clay, leaving a coarse edge).

Lift and shape the casserole wall, bottom to top, stopping under the already-constructed flange each time. True the flange and top edge of the pot after each lift if necessary.

While the pot is wet, measure for the lid, exactly where it will sit. Keep the measurement until the casserole has been fired. Lids without flanges, on baking dishes with flanges, seem most functional for cooking food. If the flange is on the lid, it sits in the food. Lids without flanges can be turned upside-down as serving dishes, too.

Small pots with interior flanges are thrown the same way as flanged casseroles.

1 Both hands pull out center toward right

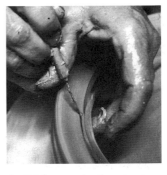

2 Lift wall and flatten wide lip to prepare for flange

3 Left finger under, right finger presses down to create flange; fingertips extend flange

4 Cut flange edge from top to finger underneath, working on right side of clay

5 With right fingers outside and left inside, lift and shape wall, stopping under flange

6 True lip and flange

7 Finish shaping wall

8 Cut off excess clay with wood knife held parallel first to bat, then to pot

9 Use two calipers: inside caliper measures where inside cross-section of lid will sit

10 Outside caliper measures where outside edge of lid will sit

CASSEROLE TRIMMING AND LID MAKING

1 Casserole and bowl trimming: invert leather-hard pot on wheelhead

2 Center pot with wrist end of dry left palm; lean in at 8 o'clock

Center pots for foot trimming upside-down on the wheel by leaning into the leather-hard pot at 8 o'clock position with end of the left palm. Beginners should attach the centered pot to the wheelhead with three coils of clay, but learn to do without the coils soon because they damage the lip. Hold pot down with middle finger of left hand while trimming.

Throw the lid to measurements already taken. Center, lower mound to lid dimension, open, and move from center out, perfecting the inside curve. Visualize height of this (upside-down) lid on its pot; cut if it is too tall. Then pull lid out to exact dimension, point the edge to sit level on casserole flange, and trim leather-hard.

3 Beginners who haven't learned to center can make a line; needle hits high spot

4 With fingers on far ends of line and thumbs bisecting line, push opposite; repeat until centered

5 Middle finger holds pot down; loop corer at 4 o'clock trims outside profile

6 Begin indentation, moving from center out toward footrim

7 Smooth footrim with fingers or rubber rib; feet smoothed this way will never mar a table

8 Lid throwing: open low centered mound as wide as measurements for pot indicate

9 Finish interior curve; pull lip to exact dimension. Triangular edge sits square on pot flange

10 Caliper shows lid too wide; cut with needle to fit

11 Trim underneath as far as possible with wood knife to remove excess clay

12 Lid trimming: center leather-hard lid right side up with wrist end of left palm

13 Middle finger holds lid down on bat, while writing hand tools at 4 o'clock

14 Smooth tool marks with rubber rib, or leave carving lines as decoration

CASSEROLE KNOB

Handles and knobs for lidded pots can be pulled, made by slab or coil, carved, or thrown, but the knob should complete or develop the form.

Lute a fat coil of clay with a small central hole and a solid bottom to the lid — the same method works well for thrown feet or pedestals. Use minimal water and press lightly, as the lid is leather-hard and can be dented.

Center the thick coil with fingers; open and center the hole for a hollow knob. Shape knob to suit pot and lid. When finished, lay edge of lid against the pot flange touching as little as possible, and set it evenly in place. Lid and pot will shrink together.

1 Roll fat coil, square it, angle-cut each end

2 Crosshatch and moisten each edge; pull coil into a circle and lute seam

3 Smooth a solid bottom to the coil

4 Draw a circle on the centered leather-hard lid where knob will attach; crosshatch and moisten

5 Crosshatch and moisten bottom of knob into glue

6 Moisten knob in water one more time

7 Lute knob to lid, with fingers pulling downward to join

8 Begin throwing knob on lid: fingertips center knob, first finger begins hole

9 Fingertips raise wall of hollow knob

10 Needle-cut to even edge of knob

11 Press from outside to accent stem; smooth lip

12 Smooth lid, or re-throw fingermarks on lid

13 Pull lid off bat toward you, lifting with one hand supporting from underneath

14 Place leather-hard lid on leather-hard pot immediately after trimming

PLATTER THROWING

Large platters need larger bats for throwing; make or buy plywood or presswood circles 15 to 30 in (40 to 80 cm) or more in diameter to attach with a pancake of clay to a plaster or metal wheelhead. Nine-tenths of throwing a platter is in laying out the low flat mound and opening it with a shallow curve from the center out to the wall; one-tenth is pulling out the rim into a platter at the very end. Set the lip early. Thickness at the base should be about the same as the wall. Allow just enough extra for footing; if a platter is too thick, drying strains will warp or crack it.

1 Left palm and end of right wrist lean in, centering 10 lb (5 kg) or more clay at 8 o'clock position

2 Right first finger presses clay down from top to bat, trues edge at 4 o'clock position

3 Left thumb and base of right hand press down and out to flatten more

4 Base of right hand flattens clay down to bat; right first finger will true up base

5 To lower and widen mound more, push down in center to get more clay, pulling toward you

6 Stop wheel; to check thickness, push needle through the bottom

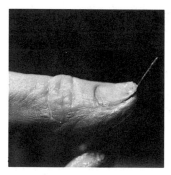

7 1 in (2 cm) is about the right thickness through center foot of a large-diameter platter

8 Continue pulling more clay from center out to widen diameter

9 Flatten; refine interior curve with fingertips or rib

10 Shape and finish lip of platter before final pulls up and out

11 Fingertips inside and outside lift and shape wall of wide, shallow cylinder

12 Cut underneath with wood knife as far as possible to remove ring of excess clay

13 Inside and outside fingertips pull, lay platter out flat

14 Finished platter stiffens on bat until leather-hard

PLATTER AND PLATE TRIMMING

Platters and plates vary only in size. When thrown, their foot-rims are usually carved out of the base on the wheel; handbuilt plates and platters often have feet added.

Touch clay as little as possible. Cracks and warps are due to handling strains and uneven drying. Trimming is a strain to clay that has already been strained in the throwing process. Turning low flat forms over for footing is tricky. Anticipate the potential strains, and think ahead to avoid stress to the piece. Flip a platter over on someone's hand, or place a larger bat on top and then flip the platter and the bat. Clay reacts to every uneven strain.

Attach a large bat on to the wheelhead, wide enough to trim the upside-down platter, using a pinch of soft, sticky clay between wheelhead and bat. Wiggle the top bat to secure.

Recentering: leather-hard plates and platters turned upside-down for trimming are too low to recenter by leaning in with left palm at 8 o'clock. Instead, watch the plate as it goes around, tapping the piece toward center on the high spot as the plate revolves. Tapping the high spot takes practice. Until you have mastered it, hold a needle pointing at the plate. Move the needle toward the clay until it hits the high spot and makes a line. With fingers holding the ends of the line and thumbs bisecting the middle, push opposite you toward center. When the plate is centered, the needle line will go all around.

Placement of the foot is important to the support of the piece. The spot inside where the curve begins to form is where the foot will support best. Mark that spot on the bottom of the plate, and trim the footrim there. Make two concentric lines about ¼ in (.5 cm) apart on the bottom of the plate to be sure that an even foot can be trimmed.

Dry low, flat shapes like platters right side up on many layers of newspaper or cloth for air circulation; cover the lip edge with plastic. Slow drying is essential.

1 Put crosshatched wet pancake of clay on wheelhead to adhere to bat

2 Slap large-diameter bat down to secure for platter trimming

3 Place platter upside-down gently on bat; center as directed

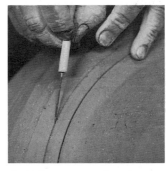

4 Make concentric lines for an even footrim, corresponding to beginning of inside curve

5 Hold plate down on bat with one hand; trim with other hand at 8 o'clock position

6 Carve outside profile first

7 Decide to keep trimming lines or rub them off

8 Indent foot: move sharp tool from center out to right, cutting without pressure

9 Place a straight edge across foot diameter to make sure center is indented below footrim

10 Remove plate with both hands and turn it right side up; dry slowly

PLATTER FORMS

James Lawton: raku

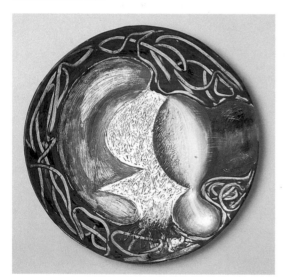

Patrick Loughran: earthenware, engobes

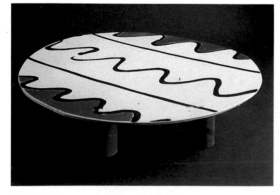

Judith Salomon: earthenware, engobes

Norman Schulman: porcelain, engobes and salt

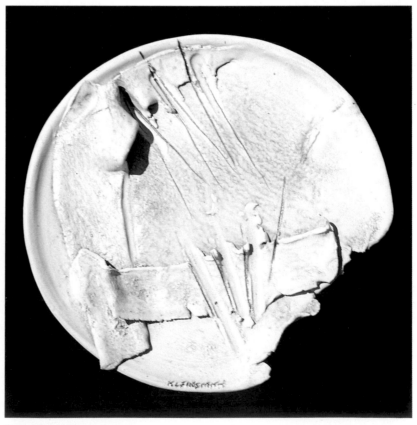

Gene Kleinsmith: stoneware

TEAPOT FORMS

Barbara Tipton: porcelain, engobe trailed

James McKinnell: porcelain

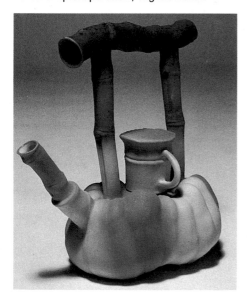

Lynn Turner: earthenware, stains

Joe Soldate: earthenware

Peter Shire: earthenware, low-fire glazes

TEAPOT THROWING AND TRIMMING

1 Pull a cylinder

2 Inside fingertips opposite outside fingertips belly out round teapot body

Tea and herbal brews have been used in most societies for centuries. Tealeaves need to steep in hot water for a few minutes, either directly in the water to be strained at pouring, or in special containers in the pot. In this demonstration, the teapot is made with holes which strain tealeaves at the spout.

Certain cultures consider porous earthenware better for brewing tea than vitreous stoneware or porcelain. Some connoisseurs claim to taste a difference in tea made in a red clay pot.

The teapot form offers functional and abstract potters a design challenge. Where the handle is placed on a teapot, what the handle is made from — clay, wood, metal, bamboo — as well as handle size and proportional relationships, placement of spout, type and shape of lid, and decoration and glaze, provide never-ending opportunities for invention and change.

A coffeepot traditionally has a long spout and a tall body, a teapot a short spout and a squat body. Long thin spouts are harder to throw. Coffee and tea can both be made and served in pitcher-style vessels with lids with deep flanges so they stay in during pouring.

Throw a round teapot body with a rather narrow opening, to keep the liquid hot and the lid on during pouring. Belly out the form with inside fingertips supported by outside fingertips. Keep the shoulder of the curve rising at all times as you lift the shape. Take lid measurement while the pot is wet, and trim foot on the leather-hard pot upside-down in a chuck before making and adding appendages.

Glazing the teapot. It is not necessary to glaze the inside of a stoneware or porcelain teapot. If you do, wipe glaze from the strainer and from the edge of the pouring lip. If the lid is glazed inside, wipe the edge and the pot lip clean, so they can glazefire together without sticking.

3 Press with outside fingertips to narrow opening

4 Narrow more by squeezing three points with thumbs and fingertips

5 Fingertips carefully raise a short neck; be sure to keep it centered or lid won't fit

6 Hold wood knife first perpendicular, then parallel to the pot to cut excess clay

7 Measure for lid while wet

8 Turn leather-hard pot upside-down, level in centered chuck

9 Finger holds pot; carve outside profile with sharp tool, then indent foot from center out

10 Soften footrim with fingertips or rubber rib

TEAPOT LID AND SPOUT

Lids and spouts can be thrown off-the-hump (p. 81), especially if you are making several at a time, or make them singly on a bat. It is a good idea to make several spouts and lids and choose one of each to suit the pot.

Lids: a solid flanged flat lid made right side up, as shown here, measured accurately to fit the teapot, needs no trimming. Domed or flat lids made upside-down with hollow flanges must be turned over and trimmed, and some sort of knob can be added. The rule of thumb for the depth of a teapot lid flange, to keep it on the pot while pouring, is to make the flange slightly longer than half the diameter of the opening.

Spouts are thrown taller than necessary to have extra length for cutting and fitting on to the body of the pot. The spout needs to be wide enough at the pouring edge not to gurgle, have a sharp lip to prevent dripping, and be attached so that the open end of the spout is higher than the highest liquid level in the pot.

If the spout is twisted during throwing, it will twist more in the fire. Pay attention to the speed of the wheel; work with its centrifugal motion to make narrow spouts with small openings without spiral strains. Or pay no attention to circular perfection — be unconventional with the whole pot, slap it around, alter the whole shape, go against tradition.

Before throwing lids and spouts, it is useful to try on different shapes at different angles. Keep the extra spouts and lids you make for this purpose. Observe spout, lid, the kind of handle, and its place of attachment; compare relationships of spacing and proportion as you try on various appendages. Handles fill in and complete forms; the spout protrudes, but must complement the whole arrangement. Longer spouts pour better than short ones; a taper and flare at the end give direction to the flow.

1 **Lid:** fingers indent base for flange that fits inside teapot opening

2 Caliper flange frequently as you make lid

3 Lift flange tall, indent lid, raise and shape solid or hollow knob

4 Caliper inside of pot opening, check lid fit once more

5 **Spout:** raise tall narrow cylinder

6 Belly out base of spout with thin wooden dowel when fingers aren't long enough

7 Collar in gently and gradually, with three pressure points on clay

8 Straighten spout; shape narrow pouring flare; sharpen pouring edge to stop drip

9 Final narrowing and shaping of spout

10 Cut spout off; lift it to another bat to stiffen before attaching

ATTACHING TEAPOT SPOUT AND HANDLE

1 Smooth bottom of lid, leaving flange deep and solid for stability during pouring; place on pot

2 Needle-cut spout in "V" shape to fit pot, try it on, determine angle, cut again until correct

3 Carve and shape cross-section of spout until angle and fit are perfect

4 Fit spout exactly, draw line on pot to mark position

Before attaching a spout to the teapot, pull a handle from a lump of clay or cut it from a thrown donut (p. 80), make a lug handle, or pull short loops to be added to the teapot to hold a bamboo, wood, or metal handle. The handle stiffens while the spout is being attached. Put lid on pot.

Try spout position at various angles and heights; make sure the top of the spout will be higher than the liquid line. Try experimental handles also, to get the whole picture.

Draw a line on the body where the spout will attach. Punch holes with a drill bit, pencil, or end of needle tool, to make openings for straining leaves. Dust excess clay and scraps out; when glazing, wax this strainer to resist glaze. Crosshatch edges, and lute spout well.

Attach handle as soon as possible, luting both body and handle edges particularly well and adding coils to reinforce joints. If clay loops are used to hold handles of another material, they must be tall enough and strong. Soaked vines become supple and can be wound into handles; split or round bamboo or bamboo root can be steamed and bent; silver or brass handles can be forged. The design made by the negative space — that space between the body of the pot and its handle — is all-important.

5 Holding top of pot steady, make holes with tool and crosshatch body for spout attachment

6 Carve spout edge thin so it will glide into pot on attaching

7 Crosshatch thinned edge of spout, moisten; crosshatch spout and pot several times

8 Press spout on gently but firmly; replace throwing marks, if desired

9 Try pulled handle on, fix length and arch, bevel ends, crosshatch pot and handle, and lute well

10 Handle on top balances easily for pouring

11 Handle can go on side. Knob shown on lid is solid

12 Attached clay loops now hold Oriental-style bamboo handle. This knob on lid is hollow

SUSAN PETERSON'S WHEEL-THROWN FORMS

Stoneware, incised wax over magnesium matt glaze, inlaid with iron oxide, reduction

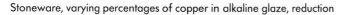

Stoneware, varying percentages of copper in alkaline glaze, reduction

Stoneware, sgrafittoed colemanite white glaze over iron oxide, reduction

Stoneware, wax resist, black stain over cream matt, oxidation

Stoneware with chrome, rutile, and manganese engobes, reduction

DONUT THROWING AND TRIMMING

1 Throwing: lower centered mound with left palm and flat end of right palm to donut diameter

2 Open away from center with left middle finger. Pull to widen

A hollow ring — a donut — is a form often used by European, Middle Eastern, and Asian potters for wine jugs, braziers, and other containers. Attachments to the donut such as feet, handles, bottle necks, pouring spouts, and lids have made the form applicable to many functions. A horizontal donut quite naturally becomes a candelabra or an ivy pot when holes or holders are added, and many artists use the form for thrown sculpture segments. Cutting up the donut is a good beginning for thinking about cutting up other thrown forms.

Make the donut by opening the centered mound away from center, not in the center. A large or small hole for a fat or narrow ring is determined by where you make the indentation. Open the chosen spot, pull out slightly, lift a short wall. Now open the center, pull out depending on the width of the hole, and raise a wall. Refine curves, and draw the two walls together into a donut. Remove clay from center hole with tool, and cut underneath the outside profile.

The technique is the same for double-walled vessels, except that a base is left in the pot. Chinese potters make such vessels in porcelain, left double for insulation or with one wall pierced and carved for decoration.

3 Overhead view: left middle fingertip, supported by right, opens in center, pulls to widen

4 Cut away excess clay inside ring to bat; cut underneath to round the ring

5 Raise and curve both inside and outside walls, with left fingertip against right fingertip

6 With wood knife, cut under as far as possible outside to round ring; remove excess clay

7 Bevel edges of both walls toward each other; pull closed, holding fingers steady

8 Seal joint well with finger pressure, then with rib pressure

9 Trimming: center leather-hard donut with left hand at 8 o'clock

10 ... or hold needle to make line at high spot; thumbs bisect line, push opposite you

11 Round donut ring inside and out at base with loop tool

12 Hollow ring ready to be cut or adapted in another form

OFF-THE-HUMP THROWING

Making many small vessels from one solid lump of clay on a wheel is called throwing *off-the-hump*, a method often used by production throwers for a number of pieces all alike. This method is quick, but precarious.

Off-the-hump throwing. A large cone of clay is placed on the wheel and not necessarily centered. Fingers squeeze a lump on the top, setting the size needed for the object; center that lump with palm or fingertips. Open the ball and raise the wall, making a decided finger line indicating where the base of the pot is. Cut the shape off the large mound of clay at the finger line. Continue throwing objects from the lump until the clay is used up.

Off-the-hump throwing works for *goblet* bowls and stems, for lids and other small pots, but cutting the pot off evenly takes some practice; throwing each shape flat on a bat may be best.

The goblet form is made by setting a small bowl on a tall or short stem. Goblets have had a celebratory and joyful history through the ages, and they are among the nicest forms for potters to make. Stems can be thrown solid right side up or hollow upside-down (upside-down is easier). Solid stems are best for fragile forms. Level the leather-hard goblet stem so it stands true before attaching the cup.

1 Throwing off-the-hump: center enough clay on top of solid mound to make desired object

2 Make finger indentation for base of pot; raise the wall

3 Emphasize finger indentation under the bowl after each lift

4 Cut pot off at the base indentation; move pot to another bat

5 Making goblet stem: open for a stem thrown off-the-hump upside-down

6 Raise and narrow stem, using stick inside if needed. Shape stem, and flare footrim upside-down

7 Finish footrim smooth and level; cut shape straight off hump with string or twisted wire

8 Lift stem off; leave to stiffen upside-down before attaching

9 Attaching stem: trim cup by hand or on the wheel; crosshatch and moisten base

10 Crosshatch and moisten leather-hard stem

11 Join bowl and stem by hand or by throwing

12 Set goblet upright, level if necessary. Dry right side up

PEDESTAL VESSELS

Chalices, bird baths, samovars, and other forms with pedestals must be planned for possible firing problems at construction time. Porcelain or dense stoneware requires different support patterns from those of porous earthenware bodies; shapes cantilevered out wide from narrow pedestals may work in earthenware but will warp, deform, or crack in porcelain due to physical and chemical shrinkage as the clay becomes glass-like.

For the best support, attach the pedestal at the spot where the inside curve of the bowl begins. Wide vessels need pedestals wide at the base; tall narrow bowls need bases wide enough not to fall over. Thicken the wall where support is needed — at the footrim and the joint. Sharpening the footrim to a triangular beveled point helps a pedestal pot stand level in the kiln and on the table, while a flat rim might drag as the pot shrinks in firing, causing warp. Keep the weight of the pot toward the center of gravity.

Greco-Roman chalices and other ancient pedestal forms have profiles breaking all rules for support, but they are eggshell-thin and were always low-fired. In high-temperature stoneware and porcelain firings, extreme shapes — wide diameters with narrow feet — are almost impossible if symmetry is important. If you make several, you might get one that is round out of the fire.

1 Tall pedestal: cut out base of thrown pedestal for attachment to trimmed bowl

2 Carve the wall thin; crosshatch and moisten well before attaching

3 Mark a line on the upside-down bowl where foot will attach. Crosshatch and moisten

4 Attach pedestal to bowl and throw the joint; if pieces are wet enough, shape can be changed

5 Short pedestal: center leather-hard; carve joining wall thin, crosshatch, and moisten

6 Crosshatch bowl well for luting to foot

7 Dunk crosshatched bowl in water; join it to pedestal right side up

8 Fingertips throw the joint, reinforcing it

9 Pedestal thrown on pot: crosshatch and moisten fat coil; lute it to leather-hard bowl

10 Center and raise the coil; shape pedestal foot

11 Move pot to edge of bat; with hand underneath and hand at foot, flip pot

12 All pots should dry right side up on layers of cloth or paper for even shrinkage

THROWING LARGE VESSELS

Vessels too large to be thrown in one piece are made by the ancient method of *throw-and-coil*. Coils added to a thrown base are thrown on each other as they stiffen, or thrown sections are luted together, or cut or altered forms are attached randomly to others. Each method can be repeated to indefinite height, as tall as your kiln, or fired in sections or in a loose-brick kiln built around the pot, or with electric kiln rings piled over it.

Todd Piker, a production potter making large jars, planters, and dinnerware, uses the throw-and-coil method for oversized vessels, as shown. He fires 4,000 lb (2,000 kg) of wet clay (600 to 1,000 pots) ten times a year in a six-day fire in a wood-burning Korean-style climbing kiln, in Cornwall Bridge, Connecticut.

Taäg Peterson joins leather-hard thrown forms into a monolithic piece, throwing the joints together with added coils of clay. Each joint becomes a decorative line change and gives rise to texture or pattern, with no attempt at a smooth profile.

1 Todd Piker adds coil to large wheel-thrown jar on kick wheel

2 After luting a coil, he throws it on wheel and pulls up wall

3 Shape grows and changes

4 Finished large jars drying

5 Smaller jars drying in yard

6 Piker's Korean-style climbing kiln wood-fires 4,000 lb (2,000 kg) of pots in six days

Taäg Peterson throwing already-thrown sections together

THROWN AND HAND CONSTRUCTION

1 Don Reitz levels the wheelhead, important for throwing several sections for a large piece

2 Reitz lifts and shapes wall upside-down, forming a narrow foot

3 Slab is attached to make the bottom; rim is wrapped in plastic to keep moist for joining

4 Second section, calipered to fit first section, is thrown right side up with flange for a lid

5 Crossed calipers measure inside diameter where lid will sit

6 Lid is thrown upside-down; handbuilt knob will be added later

7 Recentered first and second sections are luted; joining edge is re-thrown with base supported by extra clay

8 Reitz rolls slabs for decoration; dowel supports, turned hourly to prevent sticking to clay, are removed before firing

9 Finished piece with lid to be salt-fired. "I make a statement about a bowl, or whatever; I don't just make a bowl."

THROWN SLAB CONSTRUCTIONS

Linda Rosenus demonstrates her method of constructing slabs from thrown spheres and bowl shapes: she drops wet thrown pots on to newspaper-covered plywood boards and cuts the clay into modules. The thrown slabs are worked together compositionally with tools.

Ends for the wedge-shaped totem sculptures will be made from tall thrown cylinders which are cut open and flattened into ribbons.

Leather-hard, the slab squares are scored and assembled into hollow wedge-shaped triangles that will stack 6 to 12 ft (1.8 to 3.6 m) high. The plywood backing comes off when each clay piece can stand. Newspaper placed between sections keeps the leather-hard edges from sticking to each other during construction. 1 in (2.4 cm) holes are punched in the sections to allow for final installation on a metal pipe set in a concrete base.

1 Linda Rosenus drops spheres on to newspaper-covered plywood then rearranges the forms

2 Shapes are altered

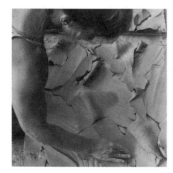

3 Surface texture is created with fingers and tools

4 Cut slabs are assembled into a standing totem; plywood will be removed when clay is stiff

5 After a low temperature soda-firing for coloration and patina, the finished sculpture is installed

PETER VOULKOS' ALTERED WHEEL FORMS

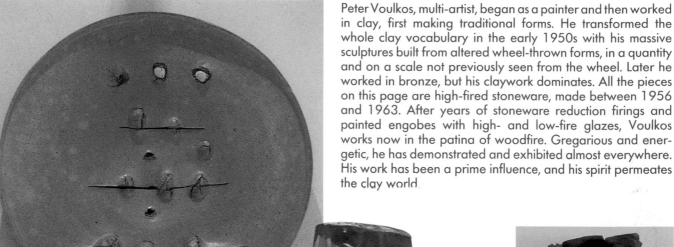

Peter Voulkos, multi-artist, began as a painter and then worked in clay, first making traditional forms. He transformed the whole clay vocabulary in the early 1950s with his massive sculptures built from altered wheel-thrown forms, in a quantity and on a scale not previously seen from the wheel. Later he worked in bronze, but his claywork dominates. All the pieces on this page are high-fired stoneware, made between 1956 and 1963. After years of stoneware reduction firings and painted engobes with high- and low-fire glazes, Voulkos works now in the patina of woodfire. Gregarious and energetic, he has demonstrated and exhibited almost everywhere. His work has been a prime influence, and his spirit permeates the clay world.

PLASTERWORK

Plaster — a mineral called gypsum with the chemical composition of calcium sulfate — has many uses during the processing and fabricating of clay because of its dense but porous surface. Plaster can be an art material for its own sake, but it is fragile and impermanent. Work in clay does not mean you have to work in plaster, but knowledge of its problems and possibilities is useful.

Plasterwork is complicated. I give an overview of plaster techniques and ways of using plaster here. Please refer to my bibliography for more specific information, particularly to Don Frith's book, *Plaster Molds for Ceramics*.

Cheap, readily available, easy to mix with water, fast to harden yet porous, plaster is a practical material for surfaces to dry wet clay and wedge plastic clay, for slip casting and press molding, and for wheelheads and bats. Plaster in a *slurry* (semi-paste) condition can be used for experimental mockups modeled in the wet state and refined when hard. Wet plaster can be laid over armatures of wire, metal, wood, or paper to explore forms that can

be used as models for molds. Plaster mixed 50/50 with clay yields a material pliable enough for direct carving.

Freshly made plaster forms should air-dry slowly for maximum strength and durability. If plaster is heated above 130°F (54°C), it becomes soft and powdery and loses its strength. Plaster that is too wet will not absorb moisture from clay; it is better to wipe plaster with a damp sponge than wash plaster surfaces and bats, and molds should be cast only a few times a day. Plasterwork areas must be kept separate from clayworking areas, as chunks of plaster contaminants leave holes in clay after firing. All plaster surfaces that are used with clay in any form will wear out in time and need to be replaced when scuffed and chipped, before they cause imperfections.

The plaster. Major companies, particularly U.S. Gypsum and Blue Diamond in America and British Gypsum in the U.K., manufacture a number of different plasters with various brand names for different uses in the building and manufacturing trades, in dentistry, and in industrial ce-

Harriet Brisson: "Schwarz Surface," a sculpture made by assembling a number of porcelain pieces slip-cast from the same mold

ramics. Read the literature. Some mixtures set harder than others and have greater durability with varying densities and absorption; choose for the job to be done. For molds American potters usually use U.S. Gypsum Pottery Number 1 or Blue Diamond Green Tag, both of which set hard in about twenty minutes when mixed with water. The former company, with headquarters in Chicago, Illinois, and the latter with headquarters in Los Angeles, California, will send literature about various brand names and respond to questions. In Britain a popular type is fine casting plaster.

Buy plaster in 100 lb (45 kg) bags, store in a warm dry place off the floor, and discard if moist or lumpy. Stack bags only a few high and try to use old plaster first. Both powdered and wet plaster can create a mess. Small amounts of wet plaster can be cleaned up easily with cold water, but hard plaster sticks to surfaces and clogs drains. Pour excess wet plaster onto newspaper and discard it in the wastebasket. Wash mixing utensils immediately with lots of cold water and continue running cold water into the drain for some minutes.

Mixing plaster. Sculptors in materials other than clay frequently use plaster as a sketch element or for "waste molds" that will be scrapped after a model is cast in some other compound. Because durability is not essential, these artists often mix plaster in hit-or-miss style by adding the powder to water until it mounds up above the waterline, then stirring it to a creamy consistency. Clay artists, who need plaster to be strong and to have a specific, duplicatable absorption quality, mix plaster and water in a prescribed fashion.

Each brand of plaster has a recommended weight of plaster per quart or liter of water (plaster–water ratio). The volume to fill with plaster can be measured (details p. 89). Use a hard-rubber or plastic bucket, rather than metal, large enough to contain the appropriate quantity. Dry plaster should be a fine powder; if not, sift it or use another bag. Add the weighed amount of plaster by shaking it into the measured water quickly but evenly and allow it to slake without stirring for one minute.

Most plasters set hard 20 minutes after immersion in water. Stirring the plaster–water mixture speeds up setting; mixing with an electric propeller and hot water instead of cold further hasten the setting time. Electric mixing of the plaster batch is fastest, but probably too fast except for professionals in production mold shops. Vinegar or boric or acetic acid added to plaster retards the setting time and can keep the mix pliable for several hours.

Stir plaster and water by hand with a wide arm motion in circles around the container. Periodically turn the palm upward on the bottom of the bucket, wiggling the fingers and moving the palm up and down slightly to bring air to the surface; remove the foam with paper towels. Pour when a finger line drawn on the surface will almost hold.

Parting compounds (sometimes called soaping or sizing coatings). All surfaces of wood, metal, plaster, linoleum, glass, and other impervious materials, and objects that liquid plaster will be cast against, must be coated with soap, grease, or oil. White Vaseline is fine for flat surfaces with no carving. Liquid English Crown Soap or Green Soap are the universally preferred sizing for forms with fine detail. Leather-hard clay or plasticine forms do not need to be coated.

How to soap. Apply soap foam liberally to a plaster model with a soft natural sponge. Sponge off excess foam with a less foamy sponge and dry for a few minutes between each coat. Continue applications until a high shine remains on the plaster when the soap is dry; soap it once more before pouring wet plaster against it. The process of *soaping* or *sizing* may also be called "*dressing.*"

Removing the model after casting. Plaster becomes hot to the touch while it sets and expands slightly; try to remove plaster surfaces from each other at this point. Models rarely drop out easily from a newly made mold. Clay models can be dug out, but will be destroyed. Rigid models can be extricated by running hot water or a jet of compressed air into the seam between two pieces, or by tapping the mold with a wooden mallet.

Defects in plaster casts. Patch blemishes or airholes with "dead plaster" made by dropping dry plaster down the side of a shallow bowl half-filled with water until the plaster powder forms a mound over the waterline. When the powder above the water has moistened, use only that plaster to patch holes, leaving the part below the water in the bowl undisturbed.

"Hard spots" in plaster, adversely affecting carving and casting, result from use of old or hydrated plaster, improper stirring, pouring the plaster–water mixture unevenly or in layers, or mixing and pouring the required volume in sections rather than all at once.

Making casting slip. Plastic clay can be pressed into or over plaster shapes, but *deflocculated clay slip* is necessary for liquid casting in molds. A maximum of 40% water is added to 100 parts of dry clay body along with .002 to .005% deflocculant such as soda ash, sodium silicate, "Darvon Number 7," or other catalyst to make the clay and water mixture liquid with a minimum of water (details in chapter 4). If more than 40% water is used, the water evaporation will leave the clay shell weak or subject to cracking on drying.

Molds for slip casting. "*Hollow cast*" refers to a hollow mold into which deflocculated slip is poured. A firm clay shell sets up against the plaster mold surface, and excess slip is then poured out of the mold. The thickness of the finished piece is even and the inside and outside profiles are alike. "*Solid cast*" (sometimes called "core cast") molds have a plaster surface on both sides of the void that will be filled with clay. All slip poured in is used to make the shape, no excess is poured out, and the wall thickness varies according to design.

The photographs on the following pages were made in the plaster shop of Geoffrey Meek, Hudson Valley Clayworks, Middletown, New York.

PREPARING PLASTER

1 Clamp linoleum coddle; calculate cubic volume for plaster mix

2 Secure base of coddle with clay

3 Stir measured plaster and water; pour when creamy

4 Coddle removed; set plaster is ready to work

To insure consistent absorption and durability, potters make plaster models, molds, wheelheads, bats, and wedging tables with measured plaster and water amounts recommended by the manufacturer.

A general 3 to 2 plaster–water ratio is used by many professional mold-makers regardless of the brand of plaster, that is, 3 lb plaster to 2 pints (lb) of water. Another common formula is 20 oz of plaster to one U.S. pint, which is equivalent to 24 oz of plaster to one U.K. pint, or 120 grams of plaster to 100 cc of water. "A pint is a pound the world around" is an axiom that can be used to equate liquid and dry materials. Some plaster companies recommend their own plaster–water amounts; U.S. Gypsum advises 2¾ lb plaster per quart (2 pints) of water for its Pottery Number 1 plaster brand.

Plaster forms and molds are made by pouring liquid plaster into a contained space or by mocking up plaster slurry. Use the following formulas to relate the volume to be filled with the amounts of water and plaster.

Measure the volume to be filled with plaster. (a) For a cube, compute height × width × width ÷ 81 (there are 81 cubic inches in a quart of water) = quarts of water for this volume. To determine the amount of plaster needed, multiply this volume of water by the recommended weight of plaster per liquid volume of water recommended for your plaster.

(b) For a cylinder, compute height × width × width ÷ 81 × .8 (the equivalent of *pi* for reducing a cube to a cylinder) × the number of pounds of plaster per quart of water for your plaster brand.

Example for a cylinder: 8 in × 8 in × 3 in = 192 ÷ 81 × .8 = 1.9 or almost 2 quarts of water (4 pints) and 6 lb plaster on the 2 to 3 generalized ratio, and 5½ lb plaster for U.S. Gypsum Number 1's recommended amount.

Cast into a coddle. Build a clay, linoleum, wood, or metal wall, called a *coddle*, to contain the plaster; size surfaces with vaseline or soap to prevent sticking. Measure and mix the plaster and water required to fill the volume. Pour plaster mixture into the coddle when a vague line can be drawn across the surface. Pour excess plaster, if any, onto newspaper and discard.

Plaster tools are not the same as clay tools. A basic set of plasterworking tools includes a square, large sponge, sanding sponge, mold knife, metal scraper, dusting brush, sureform file, single-edged razor blades, and wood modeling tool. You may also need wood files and rasps, plaster rasps, flat-wire loop tools, hard steel knives, wood and rubber mallets, brace and bit, putty knife, tree-pruning saw with no-pitch teeth, shavehooks, plaster turning tools, water sandpaper, wooden mold frames or linoleum coddles, and C-clamps. Plaster tools should be kept clean, and metal tools can be oiled to prevent rust.

1 Basic plasterworking tools

2 Files, rasps, knives, loops

3 Mallets, saw, brace and bit

4 Wooden mold frames, C-clamps

MAKING A ONE-PIECE MOLD

1 Plaster carving tools, rasps, sureforms, scrapers; keep tools sharp

2 For solid model of cup, cast a block of plaster on wheel; carve with tool held against stick

A plaster mold can be made over any model — handcarved or wheel-turned clay, plaster, oil-based modeling clay (plasticine), wood, natural things or found objects. Commercial molds are usually made over plaster forms.

The number of pieces in a *mold* is determined by the number of undercuts or line changes in the model. For a one-piece mold, the model must have a simple outside profile, narrowest at the point opposite the mold opening; the mold lifts off the solid model easily because there are no undercuts.

A *trim shelf*, a ½ in (1 cm) thick slab that is 1 in (2.5 cm) wider in diameter than the top of the cup, can be built on or carved with the model. The trim shelf permits the pouring of extra clay slip above the actual mold edge, allowing an even edge to be finished on the piece.

Make the mold. Place the widest part of the model (usually upside-down) against a flat surface; construct a coddle wall 1 to 2 in (2.5 to 5 cm) from the model all around. Apply soap, oil, or Vaseline to the model to prevent sticking. Measure the volume of the coddle, subtract the volume of the model; calculate and mix the water and plaster and pour the mold.

Remove the model when plaster is hot to the touch, using compressed air or running water at the seam between model and mold.

3 Plaster tool begins to shape cup from wet plaster; use one small point of tool

4 Hold tool in both hands and steady with "bellystick" anchored to wall

5 Use wet sanding sponge or water sandpaper to smooth model

6 Saw model off wheel

7 Soap-sized model on trim shelf slab ready to be molded

8 Size model, set coddle, pour plaster mold

9 Sized model releases easily from mold

10 Finished one-piece mold ready for slip casting

MAKING A TWO-PIECE MOLD

A mold of two or more pieces is necessary if one or more *undercuts* exist on the model.

Forms should be designed to need the fewest possible mold pieces. Multipiece molds chip easily and take more time to cast and finish than one-piece molds. Each piece causes a seam on the clay casting that must be scraped off and sponged but still may show. Design so that seams occur at places on the shape such as contour changes, where they will not be obvious.

A plaster model of a cup will need a two-piece mold if an indented shelf over the lip has been added to form the actual thickness of the lip in the cast.

Prepare the model for the two-piece mold. Mark the seam line for dividing the model into two pieces by finding the center on the bottom of the model. Then draw a line in indelible pencil from the center point up both sides of the cup. For clay models, push thin-gauge copper or brass shims into the seam line. (To find the seam line on an asymmetrical model, place it directly under a light; where the shadow falls can be marked for the seam.) For a more perfect mold seam, carve a smooth plaster template to serve as the divider.

Make a seam divider. Lay clay to the seam mark on the model, or underneath the metal shims, or make a thin clay slab seam-marker supported behind by wads of clay, or use a plaster template.

Build a coddle wall for the mold (here, wooden mold boards). In a cradle of clay, rest the model horizontally with the widest end directly against one of the mold boards, for the casting opening. (The model could stand vertically, upside-down, against the table for the pouring opening.) Leave 1 to 2 in (2.5 to 5 cm) around the other three sides for mold thickness; bring the clay seam flush with the mold boards. If possible, make a mold's outside shape conform to that of the model, for even absorption and therefore even slip casting. You will learn by casting molds whether the clay slip you use needs more plaster thickness, and can construct molds accordingly.

Cast the first half of the mold. Be certain the coddle and model are secure. Measure the mold volume, subtract that of the model, calculate plaster–water mix, stir, and pour down one corner of the coddle to minimize air bubbles. When the plaster is hot, remove the mold boards. Turn the mold over with the model still in it, make indentations to serve as fitting-locks for the second half, soap-size the plaster half just poured, replace the boards, and cast the second half (see next page).

1 Construct seam around model at chosen dividing line, leaving pouring hole against board

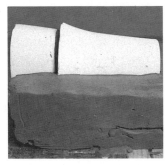

2 Level and smooth the clay seam

3 Clamped mold boards form wall for 1 to 2 in (2.5 to 5 cm) mold thickness; model rests in clay

4 Shake the weighed plaster into correct amount of water

5 Professionals can stir plaster with an electric mixer

6 Beginners should stir plaster by hand or with a wooden stick

7 Pour plaster down one side of coddle

8 Finished half; turn mold over and cast second half as explained on next page

TWO-PIECE MOLD WITH HANDLE

1 Remove coddle from first half of mold; scrape smooth

2 Remove clay seam

Handles for hollow-cast molds are made several ways. (1) A clay handle is cast in a separate mold from its vessel and attached later (p. 93, photographs 1–5). (2) Form and handle are cast together in a multipiece mold; the holes left in the interior when the slip drains out of the hollow handle are filled with clay wads. The model for a vessel handle can be carved in the mold, as shown, or attached to the model before making the mold. The process illustrated can yield a waste mold from which a plaster model can be perfected, or this mold can be slip cast.

Prepare for the second half of a two-piece mold of which the first half has been cast (see previous page). Drill or carve concave locks into the first half of the mold 1 in (2.5 cm) from each edge to insure fit of both mold pieces.

Draw a handle on the first half of the mold with an indelible pencil, inscribing a line that will make a matching handle mark on the second half. Soap-size the model and mold (p. 88).

Cast the second half; the handle imprint appears on both sides in the mold. Carve identical handle halves with a loop tool and smooth with water sandpaper.

If the foot of the vessel is indented, a three-piece mold must be made. Cast the foot section against the first two halves, remembering to carve locks for fit.

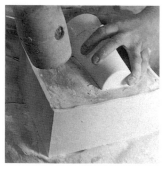

3 Remove model with sharp taps

4 Level surface with sureform file

5 Make locks for the second half with drill bit, tool, or spoon

6 Sand lock indentations smooth

7 Draw handle with indelible pencil

8 Soap first half

9 Replace model, clamp coddle, cast second half of mold on this half

10 Carve half-handles in each mold, using indelible guide

11 Two-piece mold; put it together and tie securely for slip casting

12 Three-piece mold for indented foot

SLIP CASTING AND PRESS MOLDING

A casting slip for any clay body or firing temperature can be mixed in the studio or purchased commercially. Different clays, different deflocculants, tapwater impurities, and the weather can cause casting problems and affect the setting-up time of slip in molds — usually 30 minutes for a 3/16 in (.5 cm) clay wall. Make the best molds, then experiment to develop the best slip (see chapter 4).

Most molds can be cast three times daily, about 100 times before a new mold is needed. If release is uneven, as it can be with complicated shapes or with porcelain slip, dust the mold with talc or silica. Hold multipiece molds together with cord or rubber bands, tightening with a piece of wood.

Store casting slip in an airtight container to prevent water evaporation. Clayworkers either develop a sense of slip consistency, or they control slip viscosity by measuring specific gravity. A casting slip that pours and drains well has a specific gravity (s.g.) of 1.7 (water has a s.g. of 1; 1.7 s.g. means that 100 cc slip weighs 170 g). If your slip weighs too much, carefully add a few drops of water to thin it.

Hollow cast. Pour the mold full of clay slip. The slip level in the mold recedes as the plaster mold absorbs moisture from the slip. Provide more slip with a trim shelf in the mold, with a funnel or tube on the pouring hole, or by continuous refilling of the mold.

The clay shell will begin to form in minutes. Check the wall for thickness until the desired cross-section is achieved. Then drain the mold directly upside-down to prevent an uneven accumulation of clay. Remove the piece as soon as it is stiff.

Press mold. As shown in Dorothy Hafner's hand-produced dinnerware studio, a slab of plastic clay is pressed into a plaster form and removed when leather-hard. Laying a slab of clay over a plaster form or pressing clay between two plaster molds is also possible.

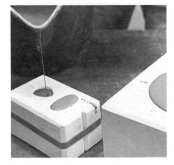
1 **Slip casting:** pour slip in one-piece cup mold and two-piece handle mold

2 Pour out excess clay slip and drain both molds on sticks until clay is semi-leather-hard

3 Cut and remove clay from the trim shelf, sponge cup edge

4 Cup is out of mold, handle still in two-piece mold

5 Attach handle to cup with slip

6 Another way: handle cast on cup in two-piece mold from p. 92

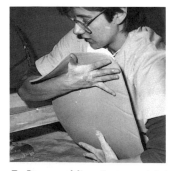
7 **Press molding:** laying a slab in a platter mold at Dorothy Hafner's dinnerware studio

8 Press clay down against plaster surface

9 Press rib tool to smooth clay and eliminate air

10 Turn leather-hard piece out as soon as possible

MULTIPIECE MOLDS

1

2

3

4

5

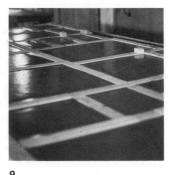

6

7

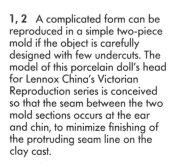

8

9

9 Studio techniques incorporated into an industrial situation were pioneered by Gustavsbergs Fabriker in Sweden, and Arabia Factory in Finland. Here, stoneware slip is cast into handcarved sand molds at Gustavsberg.

1, 2 A complicated form can be reproduced in a simple two-piece mold if the object is carefully designed with few undercuts. The model of this porcelain doll's head for Lennox China's Victorian Reproduction series is conceived so that the seam between the two mold sections occurs at the ear and chin, to minimize finishing of the protruding seam line on the clay cast.

3, 4, 5 Using more than two pieces for a slip-cast mold allows greater design flexibility and more precision. Richard Notkin's six-piece mold for the garbage can part of a large assembled composition shows pour and drain holes in the top and bottom sections. The center picture shows the cast clay can with one piece of mold removed. All components of the whole 5 ft (1.5 m) sculpture were cast in porcelain slip, fired to cone 10.

6, 7, 8 Casting can be as difficult as making molds. Notkin uses a hose casting system from which to pour slip into a number of molds at a time. Funnel on mold holds extra slip to allow for absorption. When Notkin casts a very large mold too heavy to move, he supports it on wooden planks so that a plug at the bottom can be removed to drain the excess slip from the hollow mold. Casting is sometimes used for large flat tiles instead of pressing — for very smooth surfaces or for detail. Notkin slip casts flat 2 × 3 × 2 ft (61 × 91 × 61 cm) wall panels using two pourholes simultaneously.

WHEELHEADS AND COMPLICATED MOLDS

A plaster wheelhead mold should be made for casting plaster wheelheads and bats for cup-shaped or flat metal wheelheads. Make a one-piece mold for a new wheelhead by casting plaster over an old one upside-down: after soaping, pour plaster in a coddle around the wheelhead, only to the top edge of the wheelhead, thus leaving the top and bottom of the mold open. Embed wire in the wet plaster to strengthen the mold. (Flat bats can be made in pie pans.)

Cast the plaster wheelhead by placing the widest diameter of the soap-sized mold against the table — this casts the top of the wheelhead against the smooth table surface. Seal the joint between the table and the mold with a coil of clay and pour the measured volume of plaster. Molds, wheelheads, and bats should cure for several days after they are made, before use.

Complex forms require complicated molds. *Solid cast molds* are always at least two-piece molds. The model is made exactly as the piece will look finished. Pour plaster against one side of the soap-sized model, clayed to the edge to make the divider. Cut locks in that half of the mold; soap and cast the second half around the rest of the model. Remove model, cut a pouring hole for casting at the seam or at the foot. Place a funnel there when casting slip into the void; no slip is poured out. Remove the clay piece as soon as possible before it cracks in the mold.

A *jigger mold* is similar to a solid cast — because the wall thickness can vary — except that plaster forms one side of the shape and a metal tool attached to an arm on a throwing wheel or a plaster wheel forms the opposite side from a slab of plastic clay (see p. 97). The hydraulic Ram Press ® presses plastic clay between two plaster molds (also allowing varying wall thickness) and hot air in tubes through the mold stiffens the clay. Use variations of these industrial processes in your studio.

A *gang mold* is a single mold of a number of small pieces that will be cast together.

Block-and-case is a mold of a mold. The block is the original mold; the case is the multipiece mold made of the block (original mold) for casting more molds.

1 Making a wheelhead: grease table, soap-size mold cast from old wheelhead

2 Coil of clay seals joint

3 Pour when mixed plaster is creamy

4 Pound mold to break air bubbles

5 Remove wheelhead with mallet

6 Mold and new wheelhead, ready to be trimmed and sanded smooth

7 Complicated molds: plaster model of a bowl; wall varies

8 Solid cast mold of bowl model

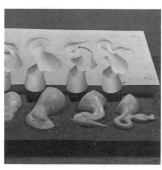

9 Gang mold for multiple casting

10 Block-and-case of the cup and handle mold

INVENTING WITH MOLDS

Here are some examples of the many possibilities that artists explore with repetitive methods. Fragments from one or more molds can be combined to make sculpture or vessels. Clay units can be luted together in the wet or leather-hard stage, or attached after firing with glue or nuts, bolts, wire, etc. Or molds can create more models for composite or single forms.

Jolyon Hofsted casts body parts from a nude model. Later, for a sculpture, he will press clay into these plaster molds and ultimately distort the form until its real source is hardly recognizable.

Patriciu Mateescu casts or presses a number of forms from several different molds and assembles them at varying angles into individual works of architectural scale.

Karen Koblitz makes plaster molds of real fruit and vegetables, casts them in low-fire clay, and combines the forms in *trompe l'oeil* sculpture.

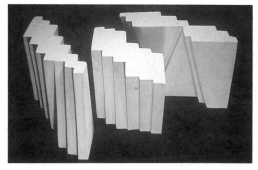

Charles Nalle designs and produces dinnerware with themes (here an accordion), first experimenting with geometric shapes.

Jim Stephenson uses talc to coat a two-piece mold into which he presses individual clay components for massive walls. Hinged wooden molds allow interchanging parts of the units but may not release clay as well as plaster molds do.

A CERAMIC INSTALLATION

Several years ago, sculptor Judy Chicago decided to execute a large environmental work in clay. She had no experience in clay, but felt that only clay and ceramic surface could respond to her needs, because of its plasticity, color, and potential for repetition. The project took five years to complete. Chicago and her assistants experimented with many different porcelain-body compositions and all methods of fabrication for making the 39 relief-modeled platters, each one a 14 in (35.6 cm) wide eulogy for an historically important woman. Each platter was 1 to 2 in (2.5 to 5 cm) thick. Cracks in drying or firing of the porcelain occurred constantly due to the intricate variations in thickness. Finally, jigger molds and handbuilding with the best clay body of the experiments netted one finished plate every ten tries.

Each place setting for the massive sculpture was completed with a slip-cast porcelain goblet and flatware. After the high temperature firing with clear glaze, a palette of china paints, mixed from many color experiments, was applied to each plate and fired again at low temperature. Names of 999 other historically important women were fired on in gold luster over the 5,000 tiles making up the floor of the sculpture. The installation opened at the San Francisco Museum of Art in 1981.

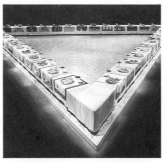

1 "The Dinner Party," a ceramic installation by Judy Chicago

2 Jigger arm on a potter's wheel; template cuts profile over plaster mold

3 Lace dipped in casting slip laid on Emily Dickinson plate

4 Chicago carves a plate

5 Slip-cast flatware

8 Glazed floor tiles coded and packed for the San Francisco installation

6 Hundreds of china paint tests were made

7 Painting the Elizabeth Blackwell plate with china paints

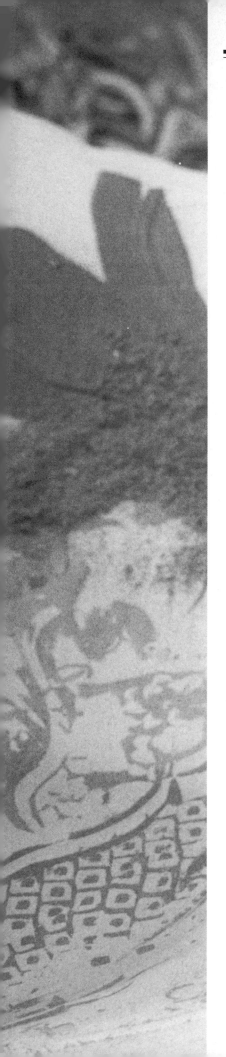

DESIGN, DECORATION, AND GLAZING

John Glick incising and inlaying decoration on a greenware plate

DESIGN: FROM IDEA TO ART

Having an idea in mind and being able to execute it in clay are two different things until you have gained a certain amount of expertise. As we have seen, there are many ceramic skills to master before anyone can be in control of this material. On the other hand, it is possible for beginners to mis-handle the techniques, unaware of problems, and find the resulting form to have tension and grace, thought by some to be qualities of "art."

Knowing what is or isn't art, or if art is craft or craft is art, may not occupy your thinking now, but these questions are always of some concern. Most clayworkers are down-to-earth people who function in their chosen material intuitively. Most clayworkers use clay because it does for them what no other material could do. And most clayworkers are able to articulate what they do. Criteria and values can be established for functional pots or for sculpture. The trick is to know when a piece is good, no matter what it is or how it was made.

The clay artist builds on and from experience. Beginners "begin" for a long time. The process of learning about clays and temperatures and colors takes so long that it might be discouraging, if clay were not such a fascinating medium.

Art is more than the sum of processes. Now and then, we encounter people who were seemingly born with a native ability that provokes art in everything they touch. More often, the way to art must be learned as arduously as the skills involved.

Whether we are making vessels or sculpture, there are age-old principles to apply to three-dimensional form, such as movement, repetition, contrast, variety, proportion. There are perceptions to communicate, such as soft, hard, light, heavy, fragile, strong. There are adjectives to attain, such as exciting, dramatic, powerful. These are all words that should be in your head as you work in clay. Creativity requires being able to see the whole image ahead of time, find the steps to reach it, and change as new possibilities occur. Learn to carry the broad picture in your mind, visualizing it from start to finish.

In wheel-shaped forms, we choose from many possibilities: to use or not to use the concentric fingermarks that develop in the process and that will react differently from a rubbed-smooth surface under a glaze; to alter or not to alter the round form or to cut it apart and reattach those parts to other parts; to place a vessel form on a short or tall pedestal to give it lift; to exaggerate a line for emphasis or to soften the line to make it flow; to choose just to make a cup or to make a piece that transcends cup.

In clay sculpture, initial choices include stabile or mobile, unfired or fired (if so, how), documented (photographed before disassembling) or permanent, monolithic or not, for indoors or out. Ideas are paramount. Keep a sketch book, draw, paint, write things down. Execute, evaluate, invite criticism, throw out, start again.

Today artists, and students, are encouraged to talk and write about their work and to interpret it intellectually and esthetically. As a result, an art vocabulary has developed that is general and is used with any material.

Read and look at everything possible in the literature of art of the ages — ceramics in particular (see the Annotated Bibliography) — and follow the monthly art magazines, the ceramic periodicals, and video documentaries of art and artists. Everyone lives near an art museum of some sort: go often. As you look, think about the works you see, ancient or contemporary, as if they were your own. Make judgments about appeal and lack of appeal; try to decide why. You must teach yourself what fits you, what is you, and then project it in your work.

SEEING AS AN ARTIST SEES

One has to learn how to see. To train one's eye to see line, form, light, and color in others' work as well as one's own is not only possible but necessary to any artist. A photographer trains for this concentration in the process of taking pictures; eventually, the picture takes itself. This happens after long experience in visualization. Keeping a dialogue going in your mind about what you see makes the imprints deeper and more spontaneous each time. Few are born with this ability; fortunately, it can be nourished and developed.

To practice seeing form, sit or stand in a room and simplify what can be seen. Sort out the dramatic lights and darks, horizontals and verticals, without seeing them as objects. See the large space divisions without reference to detail. Form squares or rectangles according to the spaces; watch the lines of the room, dividers, cabinets, windows; determine which lines are dynamic, which are subordinate; the dark areas and the light areas. This exercise is the beginning of space sensibility. Apply it anywhere — on the train, in the supermarket.

Lights and darks, and sometimes the middle values, make three-dimensional breaks in a given space, or they can create sculptural areas on a flat plane. Discriminate; think about which shapes or light and dark patterns appeal most and which least and try to decide why. Working through these analyses intellectually many times will make the ideas and visuals second nature.

It is important to make the decisions freshly and individually. Keep seeing the spaces, out of the window, along the street, and in the country — the masses that trees make and the solid forms of houses. Watch only the outlines so that spaces, receding or coming forward, assume singular importance.

In addition to space, learn to see line. Line can be a real line cutting space, or a shape perforated by another shape that acts like a line, moving, going somewhere, directing, leading and forcing. Find lines everywhere. Look them over, beginning to end. Eventually, when working in clay, you will see line directions and define shapes and planes on the form automatically. Fast lines, slow lines, big shapes or small, bright or dark accents, create tension one to another. Another aspect is color, which often supersedes line and even space. Try to find out about colors, what each one does by itself and in combination. Introducing a red spot or a yellow square causes a dramatic tension. See in your mind's eye what a pink spot would do, a white one.

Make these judgments alone so they are personal and meaningful to you. No one today makes adamant statements about what design is any more than what art is: no one can tell you that — you tell yourself.

Clay itself is best looked at leather-hard. Clay is the only art material that changes, that never stays the same until after the final firing, that evokes different emotions at different stages, that does not reveal itself until the final cooling. Every other art medium remains the way it was when it was worked and, even if it is changed, the visual is the same, visible. Looking at leather-hard forms, we see shadows, light and dark lines, and shapes revealed by a light source in the room. Some of these revelations can be translated to engobe patterns, *intaglio* drawings, or glaze directions. These revelations are just a matter of looking, of being aware all the time of how things look.

Ken Price's "Wedge," 1981, illustrates the translation of seeing line to actualizing it in form

AN EXERCISE IN HOW TO SEE

This is an exercise in developing line directions with form and space allocation. Try the idea yourself and carry on the dialogue while doing it. Add color or paint for emphasis as the piece develops and to train the eye to understand the dramatic effects color makes.

Knowing that I wanted to study line visually and then form, I began the work shown in the photographs with one horizontal and two vertical slabs of clay. An added upright, filling the middle space, had a hole in it that drew the eye to the center. A dramatic horizontal added at the left brought the direction around and back again; an arched element, also added on the left, spoke of symmetry and did not seem as interesting or dynamic as the previous grouping. A floppy rectangle pulled the piece off-center, away from symmetry, and another shape giving height diverted the eye up. Take away the dramatic pull-down, add a slab to the left, and you have a sturdy substantial feeling that still has a feeling of lift.

As you fabricate your own piece as an experiment in seeing, let your eye look at the shadows under the clay edges where darker lines form. Watch the line directions flowing with them. Line directs, mass stabilizes. Height compacts or extends. Seeing the same piece from a different angle forces the understanding that three-dimensional work cannot be stationary. One must keep moving and watching the form develop on all sides.

Breaking up mass, slicing into flat surfaces, poking holes, opening up, making forms recede or come forward, layering clay, drawing lines — these are the elements. Passion, solitude — such are the emotions to be felt in clay by the clayworker, to be extended toward the observer.

EXPERIMENTING WITH DESIGN

Design ideas for vessels or sculpture can come from the fabrication process itself, especially in the early stages of claywork. Watch for the relationships of form, texture, and space that happen to clay whenever it is touched. Make notes or sketches for other forms as ideas occur to you during your work.

Drawings help in previewing images, at least in profile, but there is no substitute for visualizing directly in clay. Working out solid clay forms that will later be constructed hollow so they can be fired is a fast, exciting way to arrive at design concepts. A *maquette* (model) is often used to prepare for making large vessels or sculptures. Line, proportion, space division, and weight distribution should be worked out in small dimensions before being translated into large volumes.

Experiment with forms to build with. For example, pound or drop clay and watch the forms that result; wire-cut some of them into other shapes. Pay attention to edges as they occur. Work with a single form or combine shapes. Look for tools or objects to work clay against.

Cut and add clay components one at a time, analyzing each composition. Be sensitive to why one placement seems better than another. Watch highlights and shadows as they define the form. Be aware of your own reactions as forms are moved, cut, changed, added to, or subtracted from.

1 Pressing a chunk of clay against a door frame

2 ... suggests sculpture

3 Press clay over patio stones

4 ... for another texture

5 Cut from large simple blocks

6 Add and subtract

7 Coil units luted together

8 ... can be used to construct airy structures

9 Wire-cut shapes suggest line drawings

10 ... or sculpture

11 Create an environment with cut components

12 ... or make composite forms

DESIGN IDEAS FROM NATURE

Forms in nature are said to be similar to pottery forms; for instance, there are seed pods that look like vessels. Lines and textures seen in plants and trees are reminiscent of those reproduced over the centuries in clay. The words artists use to describe basic principles of art are implicit in nature — line, form, mass, volume, color, light, half-tone, shadow, repetition, rhythm, positive and negative space, dynamics, tension. Study natural forms individually and in groups and note where and how those words apply. Make detail photographs and sketches from the world around you, perhaps not just plants, but buildings, junkyards, street scenes — compositions whose lights and darks and line directions can be transferred to three-dimensional work.

DECORATION

Decorating into and with clay does not require glaze. Techniques of stamping or pressing objects into clay, scratching or carving clay in the wet or dry state, and attaching clay patterns to clay pieces, appear very early in ceramic history. Next, potters explored coloring clay surfaces with various earth pigments from their surroundings — which were really impure clays or metallic oxides — and mixing them into the clay body as well. We know that the exteriors of ancient clay dwellings were often decorated with colored clays combined with rice paste or calcium, a process still found in some parts of the world.

Since ancient times, potters have collected **objects to press or roll into clay** that leave their impression when they are removed. Combustibles such as coffee grounds, rice kernels, dry dog food, pasta, etc., can be added to the clay itself, to burn out in the kiln and leave holes corresponding to their shapes. Small objects can be pressed or wedged into clay and left in during firing for texture or color, such as ground bits of previously fired clays (called *grog*), metal cuttings, gravel, sand, chunks of quartz, and anything else that will not melt or cause deformities in the ware during firing. If larger rocks are desired on the clay surface, press them in, take them out, fire, and replace them with glue (clay would crack around rocks if they were embedded).

Ceramic artists also make collections of **brushes**, bought or handmade, to use in applying colored clays to other clays. Whiskbrooms, shaving brushes, all manner of paintbrushes, textured cloths, and stalks of plants make their individual marks and contribute to the individuality of clay decorating techniques. Pueblo Indian potters in the southwestern United States still chew the ends of yucca fronds to make their brushes. Asian potters often use the hair clipped from the back of the neck of the Akita dog for handshaped brushes.

Engobe is the ceramic term that refers to a liquid clay, usually colored, used on claywares for decoration. Engobes can be colored clays prospected from nature, or mixed in the laboratory using any basic clay that might be a clay-body component — even iron-bearing red clays or white china clays. However, *ball clay* (the most plastic and white-burning of natural clays) is the best choice for an engobe base because of its plastic workability and therefore bonding quality, and its whiteness. Metallic oxides and glaze stains, the same colorants used in clay bodies and glazes, can be added to engobes as colorants in varying percentages (see p. 165).

Ancient engobes and those used today in indigenous cultures are natural clays colored with metallic earth oxides found in the ground close to the surface or by streams of water. These clays can be brushed on and *burnished*

(rubbed) with a cloth or smooth pebble to a high shine that will remain shiny in a bonfire or up to cone 04 in a kiln. If polished clay is fired higher, the molecular structure of the burnished surface reverts to smooth rather than shiny.

A clay or mixture of clays that will produce a good shine when burnished or pre-ground is called *terra sigillata* and was probably first used in ancient Greece on the famous red and black vases we see in museums. The Greeks probably didn't burnish those intricate drawings to get the shine, but found clays that had already been burnished by nature over centuries in rocky streambeds; when painted, they shone without polishing. We can find clays in or near mountain creeks that will function similarly. (See p. 145 for technical information on making sigillata.)

Historically, the term *slip* has been applied in the same way as engobe; English "slipware" is engobe-decorated. Also there are *slip glazes* made from common surface clays that become glassy at high temperatures. Albany slip clay from New York State (no longer mined there, but other natural clays with parallel compositions are available) is a classic example of a clay that makes a glaze when fired hot enough, as is the famous *kaki glaze* used by folk potters in Mashiko, Japan, which is ground from a local clay shale.

All liquids in ceramics, except water, can be called "slips"; for instance, engobes or clay slips, glaze slips, and casting slips for molds. I myself reserve the term "slip" to mean casting slip — the liquid clay mixture including a deflocculant (liquifying catalyst) and made with minimum water content for casting and for coating combustible objects or cloth that will burn out in firing (like the porcelain-dipped lace applied and fired on ballerina figurines, or the articles of clothing dipped in clay and fired for *trompe l'oeil* effects). I use the term "engobe" to differentiate the liquid clay mix that is used for decoration; however, many books still call engobes slips.

Engobe decoration, or any decoration in the wet or leather-hard clay, has a vitality that cannot be duplicated in any other clay process. Engobe mixtures can be made that will work on bone-dry clay or bisqueware, but the effect is not the same. For me, the essential quality of engobe is applying it thick for opacity or thin for translucency, building it up, sloshing around in it with fingers or tools, or carving through it — against wet or leather-hard clay. Working engobes in this manner is a powerful means of surface treatment. Engobe, clay mixture that it is, cannot move during firing and holds its shape exactly as applied, with or without a glaze coating.

The quality of the unglazed engobed surface will be different at different firing temperatures — sometimes more harsh or more quiet than glaze, but well worth exploring.

DECORATING WITH CLAY

1 Pine needles rolled into soft clay

2 Stains sprinkled on wet clay over stencil

3 ... then rolled to blend, make an "engobe" on the clay

4 Carved wet clay, with engobe brushed over it

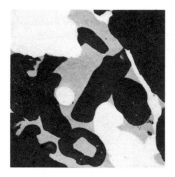

5 Colored clay shapes rolled onto a clay slab

6 Black engobe splashed over rust engobe

7 Engobes brushed on as wheel turns

8 Scratch through engobe to clay

9 Ladle-pour engobes

10 Comb one engobe into another

11 Press objects into clay through engobes

12 Wax design brushed on, scratched through, engobe brushed over

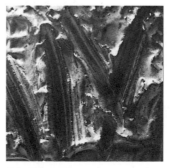

13 Textured wet clay painted with colored engobes

14 Clay appliqué, with engobes over it

PRE-PATTERNED DECORATION

1 Jane Arnold brushes engobe over cut-paper patterns, then removes paper before bisquing

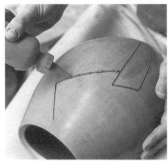

2 Engobe is inlaid in lines drawn through wax

Jane Arnold decorates with damp cut-paper patterns applied to a leather-hard bowl, brushes engobe over it, and removes the paper. Various types of sticky labels also work. Another technique Arnold uses involves line drawings through wax inlaid with a dark engobe. She fires both techniques with matt glaze coating or without any glaze.

Jay Kvapil mixes plastic clay with ceramic stains and oxides for a variety of colors and works by one of two methods: (a) rolling colored clays together flat, or (b) cutting the colored clay slabs into shapes and re-rolling them. These pre-patterned slabs are used to construct other forms.

Katie Kazan's *millefiore* slab plates are derivations of the Oriental or Italian technique of forming clay and glass by pre-patterning and slicing. She forms a large block from many pieces of colored clays, or just two clays, laid together geometrically or pictorially, at random or intentionally. Slices from the large block are used to make functional or sculptural forms.

Dorothy Hafner is a well-known studio artist who produces five dinnerware lines for international distribution and also designs for commercial ceramic manufacturers. The forms are cast or pressed and hand-decorated in a number of colors with stencil guides.

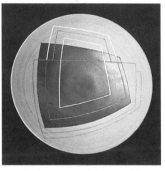

3 Brushed and inlaid engobes show through matt glaze

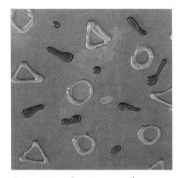

4 Jay Kvapil squirts engobe shapes onto an engobe background

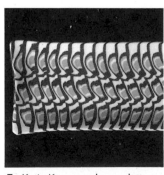

5 Colored clay shapes are rolled into another clay

6 Platter made from a pre-patterned engobed slab

7 Katie Kazan makes a platter from a composite slab produced by millefiore technique

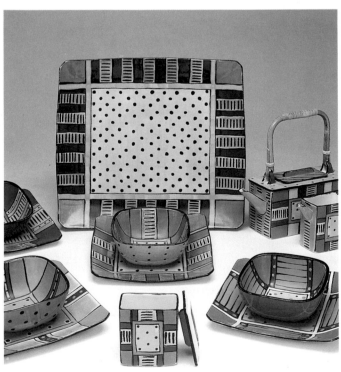

8 Removing paper design after engobe is applied in Dorothy Hafner's dinnerware studio

9 Finished engobe-decorated tablewares by Hafner

CREATING LINE IN CLAY

Mary Frank: line drawing in red clay, unglazed

Dora de Larios: stoneware and porcelain clay inlay with drawing

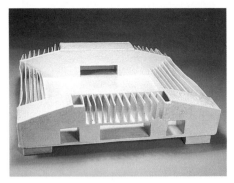

Marge Levy: unglazed white earthenware, line-building

Sandra Blaine: metal and object burnouts used for line direction

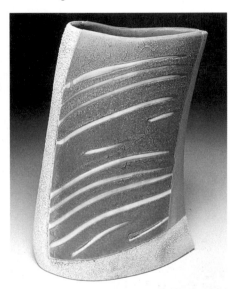

Kurt Weiser: sgraffito through engobe on porcelain

Tom Supensky: sculpted lines with clay extensions

TEXTURING CLAY

Everything pressed into moist clay makes a mark, and almost anything can be carved into dried clay. Ancient cultures, discovering this, used clay for various means of printing, for stamping seals, and for impressions on fabric; clay tablets and other ceramic artifacts of communication have been found in excavations.

Often we use this receptive quality of clay as a means of adding decoration. Leaving spontaneous marks of the fingers, the hand, or the tool in the clay results in ornamentation. More controlled embellishments are achieved by designing special implements or finding natural or readymade objects to press into the clay.

Patterns or textures can be made by (a) Impressing objects into clay and removing them, or leaving them in to melt or disintegrate in the fire. (b) Rolling clay over textured cloth or natural materials, such as leaves or twigs. (c) Paddling plain or carved wood against clay. (d) Pushing or wedging combustibles that will burn out into clay, such as coffee grounds, pasta, sawdust, dried pet food, etc. (e) Pushing or wedging non-combustibles into clay, such as iron filings, metallic tracings, cut-up metal kitchen scrub pads, colored and fired crushed clays, black sand, mortar sand, ground glass, pellets, and so forth; each material leaves its own mark in the clay depending on the firing temperature.

Above textures, left to right, from the top:
Row 1 gravel, matches, split peas, rice, macaroni
Row 2 pine needles, ferns, leaf, coffee, sawdust
Row 3 stamp, stencil, pulled wire, aluminum hot pad, wire screen
Row 4 nails, hot-metal type, printer's stencil, twine, heavy wire.
Each textural material was laid out on the table, and the clay tile pressed over it; the reverse is also possible.

PRINTS FROM CLAY

Many clay concepts are similar to printmaking techniques. Here two professional printmakers explore raw and bisqued clay "plates" to use in making paper prints on and off a press. Wet or leather-hard clay, inked and pressed against paper by hand, may be more or less off-register. Sharper prints occur with bisqued plates and a printing press. Whether the bisqued clay tiles are earthenware, stoneware, or porcelain seems to make a difference to the resulting print; lines from fired earthenware plates are softer, while those from porcelain are crisper.

Cornelia Von Mengershausen applied ceramic stains — although any kind of paint pigment could be used — to raw clay slabs. She printed from the wet-inked clay on wet 3-Arches paper, on rice paper, on newsprint, and on cloth, and found that the second or third print in all cases was usually best. After making paper prints from the slabs, she fired them as tiles.

Patricia Clark used traditional etching technique in carving her clay plate. After bisque firing to cone 04, she coated the plate with printing inks and used felt and foam mats to protect the clay plate as it rolled into the Dickerson etching press. It seemed important to soak the paper for one hour and to print extremely wet. Clark fired some of the tiles to stoneware temperature. Prints made from them had an effect similar to an aquatint, and this was easier to achieve with clay than with the usual metal plate, she said.

1 Cornelia Von Mengershausen lays found objects on clay slab, presses in with slab roller

2 Objects are removed and details carved

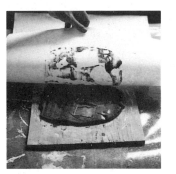

3 Roll acrylic or ink onto clay; press paper onto surface

4 Paper print from clay

5 Pat Clark's bisqued clay plate is inked before pressing

6 Clay plate is laid on etching press

7 Soaked paper, felt, and foam on top of clay plate

8 Roll press, pull proof

9 Finished etching from the fired clay plate

GLAZING

Clay decorated with engobes and textures can be fired without *glaze*. Glaze adds another dimension of color and yields a hard, dense, smooth surface that is easy to clean.

Unfired glazes are liquid mixtures of powdery ceramic minerals and water that when fired in the usual temperature range of 1300 to 2500°F (700 to 1350°C) will melt into a glassy coating and bond to a clay or metal form. Glazes are composed chemically and mathematically for specific results (see chapter 4) and can be mixed from raw materials or bought ready-made.

Fired glazes run the gamut from clear transparent, translucent, or opaque glossy surfaces to stony, dull-surfaced *matts*. Glazes made to the same formula usually work in the same way no matter what colorants have been added. Glossy glazes vacillate while they melt in the kiln, whereas matt glazes tend to stay in one place, but all glazes will run if the application is too thick or the fire too hot.

A glaze can be poured, dipped, brushed, sponged, sprayed, or applied in any other way to a clay piece. Each application technique leaves its own mark — brush marks, pour marks, sponge marks. Only very even applications finish even. Learning the look of each application method for each particular glaze, its proper wet glaze consistency, and the thickness of coating for various effects, is a long process.

THICKNESS OF GLAZE

The consistency of the liquid glaze is important; it should be adjusted according to the effect you want and the speed at which you work. Stir the glaze well by hand. Some skin should be visible through the glaze coating on your hand, and the glaze should run off your fingertips as a long drool, followed by a few drops. This is the normal consistency for glazing.

Generally, glaze is applied to porous bisqueware that absorbs the liquid quickly. A normal glaze application thickness for an average coating is 1/32 in (less than 1 mm). In industry, this is measured with a micrometer. In studio work we use a pin-tool to poke through the dry glaze after it is applied, to judge thickness. Raw glaze 1/32 in thick will feel like a cushion as the pin point goes through it. If the point hits bisqued clay immediately, the application is too thin. Artists with years of glaze experience still check application thickness when the results are crucial. You will gain an intuition about glaze thickness with practice, but only from pin-checking through the raw glaze and analyzing the fired results.

GLAZING EVENLY

An even coating of glaze is best achieved by pouring and dipping. If the form is hollow, pour glaze first into the interior, rotating the vessel quickly to cover, then pour glaze over the outside or dip the piece into the glaze. Brushing usually shows stroke marks, but glaze brushed in several alternating coats will blend more evenly. Spraying should result in an even coating, but will only if the glaze is sprayed on evenly.

All other methods leave the imprint of their process because of irregularities in the application tool or the technique. When the mark of an uneven method is desirable, use it with rhythm and verve, knowing the result will show. Try to utilize this characteristic of glaze to advantage.

Overlaps of the same or different glazes should be applied in thin, successive layers to add up to the total correct thickness. Glaze should not dry for a long time between coats; air bubbles can develop, leaving unglazed holes in the surface of the piece. A glossy glaze over a matt one will cause the matt to become shiny in the fire. A matt glaze applied over a gloss will retard the latter's shine. Clear glaze sprayed or poured over other glazes will cause diffusion of colors. Glazes, chemically calculated and fired in extreme heat, do not react like paints at room temperature and cannot be mixed together with the same color results that occur with paints. Most potters make tests continually for new color ranges and new base glazes.

VISIBILITY OF UNDERLAYERS

A thinly applied opaque glaze will be translucent enough after firing to show the underlying clay color, texture, or decoration. On the other hand, too thick a coat of opaque glaze will obliterate the clay quality or decoration underneath. Only transparent glossy glazes are really clear, and even they become cloudy if the application is heavy. Matt glazes are never totally transparent, because of their chemistry. Translucent glaze effects can be obtained by controlling the glaze composition or the application.

To reveal the contrast between clay and glaze surfaces, glaze can be wiped off in various places, or stencils or wax can be used against the clay or between glazes. Metal oxides and stains can be mixed with water and applied by any means under or over unfired glaze, resulting in *underglaze* and *overglaze* (*majolica*) decoration.

Engobes used on the raw clay and fired on in bisque-firing will be visible in some measure under almost all glazes, albeit differently according to the color and type of glaze. Liquid clays used on top of glazes before firing produce shrinkage patterns called crawling; other effects result from experimental textural additions to glaze such as copper or iron filings, coffee grounds, and sand.

ENAMELS AND LUSTERS

Glazes maturing in the lowest temperature range (around 1300 °F [700 °C]) and glazes that are applied on metals are called *enamels*. In ceramics, enamels and low temperature *lusters* and precious metals such as gold and platinum (for silver color), can be applied to glazed and unglazed porcelain, stoneware, or earthenware, but in a subsequent firing or firings. Pieces that have been previously glazed can always be fired again — carefully. Clay doesn't like going up to temperature and down again too many times, and glazes never melt the same way twice, but high-temperature glazes already fired on will be unaffected in subsequent lower firings. (Technical details of glaze formulations can be found in chapter 4.)

EFFECTS OF FIRING

Firing factors make a definite difference to glazes, sometimes quite dependent upon the way glaze is applied. If the fire is too fast at the end or not quite hot enough, thick glazes may be harsh or bubbled, or may not mature; and thin glazes may not show at all. The type of kiln and the kiln atmosphere, the speed of firing and cooling, and the placement of pieces inside the kiln also influence glaze results. Records of firing curves indicating time and temperature are important to the final analysis of glazes and glaze application and should be kept for every firing.

DRY FOOT

In stoneware and porcelain firings, the foot is left "dry," that is, wiped clean of glaze or coated with wax resist prior to glazing. The late Shoji Hamada, the famous Japanese folk potter, used to say that it took longer to brush wax on feet than it did to wipe glaze off (but he had several workers whose main job was to clean glaze off feet).

Glaze will not make a porous earthenware body impervious, but it will help to seal the surface. For low temperature firing, earthenware can be glazed all over. Support the glazed foot in the kiln on a pointed stilt to keep it from melting onto the shelf (see chapter 5). Stilts must not be used at high temperature because they will warp vitreous ware and may even melt into the piece.

Peter Voulkos' "Walking Man" shows the rhythm of a brushed on glaze application

WEIGHING AND MIXING A GLAZE

1 Balance gram scale at zero; balance empty scoop with tearbar; add weights

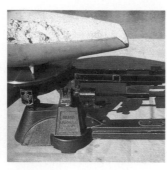

2 Add glaze material to scoop until scale balances perfectly

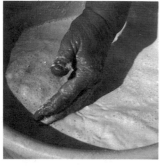

3 Add dry materials to water; stir glaze smooth and adjust water

4 Screen glaze

Dry materials for glazes can be (1) weighed on a gram scale, (2) measured in larger quantities on an ounce/pound scale, or (3) batched on a parts-by-volume basis using a consistent container.

Most gram scales weigh 500 g, 100 g, and 10 g on three beams, and most accompanying scoops hold only about that much fluffy dry material. If the gram scale has an extra tearbar, a larger container can be balanced and used with additional weights, up to 1,500 g at a time.

There are 454 g to a pound and approximately 3,000 g dry material make one gallon of liquid glaze.

Mixing. Dry materials should be added to water to slake evenly and mix without lumping. Use several inches of water, add dry materials, then add additional water to bring glaze to the correct consistency. Stir by hand or with a blender.

Screening. Most glaze mixes need to be screened through at least 20 mesh to 80 mesh window screen, according to application needs; screen again before using if necessary. Hand mixing without screening will leave glazes colored with metallic oxides or speckled stains, sometimes a desirable condition. If complete homogeneity is required in colored glazes, ball milling for 20 minutes can be preferable to screening.

Most wet glazes store well, except high alkaline and wood ash glazes, which tend to solidify and can be kept dry until needed. Suspension agents — one percent Epsom salts, CMC (metho cellulose), gum arabic, or magnesium carbonate — added to the batch help keep liquid glazes from settling.

It is best to store glazes in wooden containers, which do not react chemically with liquid glazes as plastic containers often do. If glazes must be stored in plastic tubs for several months, it is best to let the batch dry out each time and then add water again for the next glazing. For consistency or to get clear uncontaminated colors, some potters use distilled water to mix the glaze.

Different glazes require different amounts of water. Glaze consistency can vary, depending on the requirements of the application technique. Water amounts for each glaze can be measured and recorded, or a specific gravity of the correct viscosity can be obtained.

The rule of thumb for most glaze viscosities, especially for dipping and pouring, is: after stirring the liquid mix well, test it by lifting your hand. The glaze should coat the hand (skin of your hand should be partly visible through the glaze) and drain off in a long stream, then make three or four droplets. Adjust glazes when necessary by adding water little by little and testing the way they drain. If glazes get too thin, add more dry batch or leave time for evaporation.

Always stir glaze by hand, at least at the end.

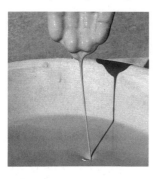

GLAZE APPLICATION

1 Adjust glaze consistency; add water if necessary

2 Pour glaze into vessel; turn it quickly

3 Pour out, being aware of the overlap pattern

4 Glaze dries instantly; sponge excess glaze off lip

5 Scrape glaze drips off exterior

6 Pour glaze evenly or in pattern over exterior

7 Scrape lip clean in preparation for final lip treatment

8 Brush air bubbles with fingertips to fill holes, preventing pinholes

9 Dip lip in same or different glaze

10 … or brush the lip and rub down uneven spots

11 Patch fingermarks with dots of glaze

12 Leave the dribbles to show after firing, or scrape now to even the application

13 Dipped patterns follow shape of pot

14 Glaze can be poured in patterns, with pot on sticks

15 Spray glaze for accent or to coat evenly

16 Signature can be carved or stamped in wet clay or written with oxide or stain during glazing

GLAZING A LARGE VESSEL

Large vessels need large troughs for draining glaze. Here, Chris Guston is using an old metal washtub to catch the excess while glazing a huge platter.

Glaze is usually poured inside a piece first and then outside, or applied outside by another method such as spraying.

ORGANIC OR PROSPECTED GLAZES

Almost anything on earth will melt in a kiln if it is fired hot enough. Wood ashes or ashes from plants, fruits, and grains can be burned, perhaps washed, and then dried for use alone as glaze *patinas* or in combination with other glaze materials (see p. 161). Keeping the ash glaze and water mixture in suspension is difficult, but it can be accomplished by adding 1 percent bentonite, CMC gum, Epsom salts, or magnesium carbonate. It is better to store ash dry and mix only enough to use.

Ash glazes need frequent stirring during the glazing process. Application of all organic-material glaze mixtures must be thicker than normal because of the ignition loss.

Volcanic ash presents the same problems as burned ash and will need one of the additions mentioned above for suspension of the liquid glaze. Volcanic ash varies in its metallic content and impurities — and therefore its firing range — according to where it is found. Kansas, a flat state with no volcanoes, nevertheless has volcanic ash that is quite different, for instance, from Mt. St. Helen's ash found around that mountain in Washington State.

The late Glen Lukens was one of the first potters to crush agate, amethyst, jade, and other semi-precious stones from the deserts of California. He ground the rocks with a *pestle and mortar*, then suspended the water solution with Epsom salts and recommended painting as the only method of application for these materials when they were used as glazes in low temperature firings.

GLAZING GREENWARE

Generally, clay is bisque-fired and then glazed for maximum control as well as to give an absorbent surface. However, glazing greenware (unfired clay) in a once-fire process is particularly useful for large or precarious wares when handling is a strain, for certain decorative techniques where digging through glaze into the clay is effective, and

almost always for special firings such as salt or wood.

Applying a glaze to greenware is as hazardous as putting a piece of dry clay under a water faucet. Spraying glaze wets the greenware body least. The dip-and-pour method can work on leather-hard wares, but bone-dry greenware should only be sprayed. Bonding chemicals (from DuPont) can help in the glaze slip, as does the water-soluble wax resist called Ceremul A mixed 50/50 with water to the glaze materials.

Glazes used on greenware are compounded differently, with a higher percentage of raw clay in the batch. Raw glazed pieces are once-fired to maturing temperature in a long cycle, approximating the time taken in separate bisque and glaze firings except for a few hours saved in cooling and restacking.

Commercial ceramic factories employ the method of glazing greenware because it saves labor and firing. Clay artists may use once-fire for the prospect of unusual results.

CLAY BODY INFLUENCE

Clay body color makes a decided difference to all glazes. Clear glaze looks white over a white clay, or rust-red over an iron-bearing clay body, when really it is a colorless glass. Opaque glossy or matt glazes show subtle variations over light and dark clays, depending on thick or thin applications. One glaze can look like many when it is applied in layers over a dark engobe or a highly colored clay. How to enhance the clay body with glaze is an intuitive sense to be mastered with experience.

UNFIRED FINISHES

Non-ceramic coatings are important alternatives to glaze. Called "room temperature glazes," the possibilities include paint of all types, varnishes and lacquers, paste wax, epoxies, polymers, shoe polish, wood stains, food coloring, felt-tip pens, crayons, pasted papers, and fabric. Particular application demands may result, depending on the basic surface — soft or dense bisqueware or an already-fired glaze — and the texture of that surface.

Room temperature pigments have a certain durability and longevity, but none has the quality and permanence of fired glaze. Alternative surfaces are fine for non-functional ceramics, they work well for children, and they can be used to enhance other glazes after firing.

DECORATING WITH GLAZE

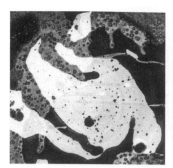

1 Ladle-pour glazes over other glazes

2 White glaze overlaps brown glaze

3 Fluid glazes pool together

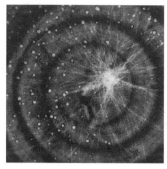

4 Stain over clear glaze, scratch with needle

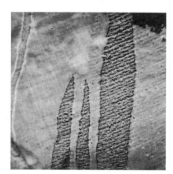

5 Glaze poured against unglazed clay

6 Scratch through unfired iron oxide sprayed over white glaze

7 Glaze, brush wax, engrave, and brush stain inlay before firing

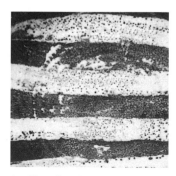

8 Glaze first; brush stripes with wax resist; brush stain over

Decorative glaze application. Dipping or pouring glaze in patterns is one of the easiest ways to achieve a decorative surface. Try overlapping colors; try matt and gloss glazes together; try unglazed next to glazed areas. Pour with different utensils or dip pieces into glaze at different angles.

One glaze can be sprayed over another using a spray gun. Colors blend or stay put, depending on the moisture content of the spray, thickness, the type of glaze, and the firing.

Stains with glaze: 1 Underglaze technique. Metallic oxides such as copper, cobalt, iron, manganese, rutile, nickel, etc. and the manufactured palette of stain colors made from these oxides, or any of the commercial so-called underglazes, can be mixed to watercolor consistency and applied to bisqueware, then covered immediately with a sprayed glaze. Stains adhere to the clay body without glaze if fired to cone 1 or above.

2 Overglaze or majolica technique. Oxides and stains mixed with water are painted, sprayed, or otherwise applied over an unfired glaze, then fired. Glaze moves during the melt, giving majolica decoration its characteristic fused or watery appearance.

Wax and other resists such as liquid latex or stencils can be used against bisque with glaze as background, between two glazes, or over glazes with stains. Hardened wax can be carved through and inlaid. Ceremul A or a similar wax can be bought, but it is water soluble. Paraffin melted with benzine resists perfectly, but can't be washed out of the brush; keep a separate brush for paraffin. Waxes burn out in the kiln at 300 °F (150 °C), and stencils made from paper or other combustibles will burn out in the fire. Latex resists must be removed before firing.

Glaze-on-glaze is usually mottled, with one glaze boiling up through another during the molten stage of firing. If the kiln cools fast after firing, the molten boiling effects are caught and the bubbles will be visible. If firing is slow at the top temperature and cooling is slow, the glazes mingle.

Texture in glaze can be achieved by adding sand, dirt, grog, granular metals, etc., to the glaze slip. Copper or other wires can be wrapped around a glazed piece and will blend into the fired glaze. These same wires, or organic materials such as plants or vegetables, can be laid or wrapped on unglazed clay. Fired on, especially at high temperature, they leave the vapor marks of their encounter with the clay.

Drawing through one layer to another (called *sgraffito*) is usually associated with engobe on raw clay. But the potter can tool through glaze to the bisque or from one layer of freshly applied glaze to another. If the glazes are not chemically fluid in the fire, the engraved lines will hold.

DECORATING OVER AND UNDER GLAZE

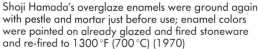

Shoji Hamada's overglaze enamels were ground again with pestle and mortar just before use; enamel colors were painted on already glazed and fired stoneware and re-fired to 1300 °F (700 °C) (1970)

Overglaze enamels, used for centuries in China and Japan on glazed porcelain and stoneware, are metallic oxides ground to an extraordinary fineness and mixed with water and a low-melting glaze, which is held in suspension with tea (tannic acid). Enamels are painted on already-fired ceramics and fired again, usually at low temperatures (such as 1100 to 1500 °F or 600 to 800 °C), depending on the desired melt. Fired enamels should look and feel raised above the surface of the glaze.

The late Shoji Hamada used traditional enamel colors — grass-green from copper, amber from iron, and a particular cinnabar red — on glazed stoneware. Hamada said, jokingly, that enamels should be ground for three years. His enamels were ground to his specifications in Kyoto; he ground them even more before use.

We make enamels by grinding metallic oxides with a commercial low-fire frit (glass) in a ball mill. China paints, bought ready-made from ceramic suppliers, are similar to glaze enamels but not the same. Lusters, such as mother-of-pearl and the precious metals gold and platinum (for silver color), can also be bought for use over already glazed ware, to be fired again low, according to directions on the bottle. (See pp. 168, 186–8.)

John Glick demonstrates his method of decorating under and over the glaze by inscribing raw clay, rubbing and dusting stain and glaze into the line, covering with a clear glaze, and working stains on top of the unfired glaze. Glick once-fires to porcelain temperature. The second photograph shows the glaze-fired plate.

THE JAPANESE WAY

Hamada and team glazing 3,000 pots for the five-chamber kiln, 1970

Mass glazing. The traditional Japanese way of making pottery, where thousands of pieces are made, decorated, glazed, and fired in huge climbing kilns, over and over again, year after year, is almost a thing of the past. But many clayworkers around the world strive to achieve the abandon that comes from this way of working daily with clay. Hamada said, "Making pottery should not be like climbing a mountain; it should be more like walking down a hill in a pleasant breeze."

Decorative patterns. Hamada used only a few decorative patterns, with engobes, underglaze and overglaze stains, and enamels, that he had developed in the 1920s. He explored these few patterns all his life, repeating them countless times with a brush, his fingers, a ladle, or a carving tool.

Discussing patterns, Hamada said that one evening when he was in his twenties, he sat on a porch in Okinawa watching sugarcane blow in the breeze. Several years later he began to paint one stalk of sugarcane repeatedly, with his handmade brush. This, he said, was how to develop patterns, and the doing of a thing over and over made the heart the hand.

Soetsu Yanagi, the authority on Buddhist esthetics, said that "Hamada's painting, the same painting year after year, becomes part of his hand." Hamada said, "It isn't the same, since each one is different. It is Hamada's variation on the same theme, the variety of sameness."

Hamada painting his bamboo and sugarcane patterns with manganese and iron, using one of the brushes he made by hand from the ruff of his Akita dog, 1970

Hamada's ash glazes, applied very thick because organic materials burn out in the firing, 1970

Hamada's sugarcane pattern: "It is my painting, and I never grow tired of it even though I repeat it."

PHOTO-EMULSION AND DECALS

Photographic techniques have a natural association with ceramics, in decorative duplication in mass production, as well as in one-of-a-kind work. Photographic silk-screen *decals* are made with ceramic pigments and fired to permanence in the kiln. With *photo-emulsion*, clay artists have another way to explore *trompe l'oeil* and surreal effects.

Photo-emulsion is a non-permanent photographic darkroom process. For the finished result shown here, Bill Davis exposes the surface of a glazed and fired piece with liquid emulsion in the darkroom and dries it. After that, a photographic negative or a group of objects — or literally anything — can be exposed on the emulsion covering the ceramic surface, developed with developer and a stop bath, and dried. The process is suitable only for sculpture and non-functional ceramics because it is not permanent.

Ceramic decalcomanias, also called transfer prints, date from an 18th-century European technique: paper was pressed on to copper etching plates to make transfer patterns and then inked with ceramic oxides for reproduction on glazed ware. These decals, properly fired on, are permanent.

Making a decal. Use a photographic screen or a stencil drawing on a silk screen. Mix ceramic colorants — glaze oxides or stains, glaze or overglaze enamels — with a commercial suspension agent, and screen onto flat or flexible decal paper. Apply a plastic coating over the design on the decal paper when the color is dry. Buy decal-making materials from ceramic suppliers.

Readymade ceramic decals can be bought in hobby shops or ordered in large quantity from decal manufacturers such as Commercial Decal, Inc. To transfer the image to a ceramic piece, the decal is moistened or placed in water until it floats free of its paper and is attached to the glazed or bisqued surface. Excess water is gently squeezed away, and the design should dry for 24 hours before firing. The late Howard Kotler was one of the first artists to use commercial ceramic decals, "the perfect readymades," as he saw them.

Direct transfer. After application to glazed ware, fire decals on at any temperature, but experiment with the temperature range to achieve different color effects. Most commercial decals are made of high-temperature stains and can be fired high, except for cadmium reds and yellows. Photographic or drawn images on silk screens can also be screened directly on to ceramic forms, particularly flat surfaces such as tiles, without making decals. When this technique is employed on round objects on a commercial scale, the screens are molded to the shape of the piece.

"Cloud One," photo-emulsion on porcelain by Bill Davis

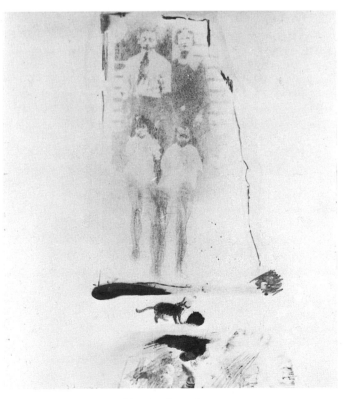

Detail of the drawing used for decal transfer

A collage of several decals fired on the glazed plate

Silk-screened overglaze enamels on decal paper, made from Davis' drawing

Commercial decals fired on commercial porcelain by Howard Kotler

DECORATIVE TECHNIQUES WITH GLAZES

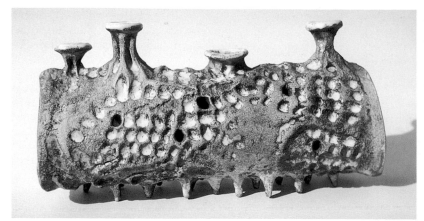

Paul Berube: glaze inlaid in the texture of a weed sculpture on stoneware

Robert Hudson: room-temperature glaze painted on porcelain

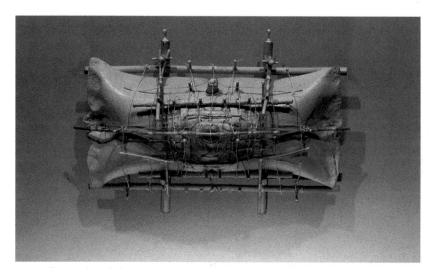

Don Miller: unglazed clay, lusters, and paints

Faith Banks Porter: ladle-pour pattern over double-dipped glaze on stoneware

Malcolm Wright: "Angle Vase," showing light breaks over sharp edges in a dark glaze on stoneware

SURFACE DETAILS

Raul Coronel: wax-resist collage of stencils between engobes

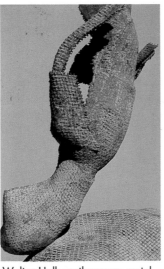

Walter Hall: earthenware, metal screen in clay, glazed so texture shows

Marilyn Dintenfass: porcelain pieces layered and glazed, detail from a large wall

Rina Peleg, stoneware, woven clay, stained with metallic oxides

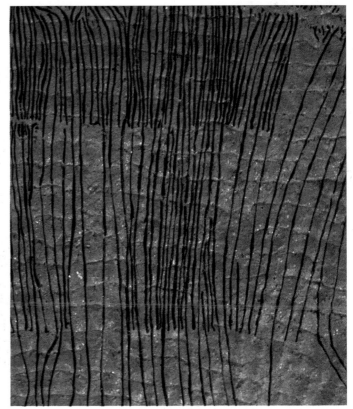

Bruno Lavadiere: stoneware, rapidograph drawing with oxide over glaze

4
CLAYS AND GLAZES

All outer-space exploration is dependent upon ceramic materials

During the 20th century, scientific research has had a marked effect on the previous thousands of years' ceramic materials and processes. The discovery of more high-temperature chemicals has widened the clayworker's scope, especially in this era of space travel.

Metals rust and corrode, wood disintegrates with water and fire, but ceramics processed by heat have longevity and permanence like no other materials. For this reason, we can study ancient cultures from the ceramic artifacts that remain from long-gone civilizations. Now, for use in outer space, however, some ceramic materials must be made impermanent so that they disintegrate when they are no longer wanted; others must be capable of being dissolved when they are used as cores.

Esoteric uses made of the new materials in high-temperature science include rocket and jet technology, spaceships, computer chips, and refractory insulators, as well as the construction of entire ceramic submarines and underwater housing for communities of "aquanauts" who are harnessing aquatic plant and animal life for human benefit. Scientists have not finished investigating all the properties of clay, the oldest and still by far the most widely used ceramic material.

Today, even the word "ceramics" has an enlarged connotation because of the extreme temperature ranges used by the space industry. Ceramic materials such as silicon carbide, uranium dioxide, and the like, have little in common with naturally occurring clays. Carbon is considered a ceramic because of its highly refractory nature, not because of any characteristic relating it to any other ceramic material. It is thus no longer possible to define ceramics only in terms of composition. Instead, ceramics must be defined as those materials that lend themselves to manufacture in a certain way, the essential part of which is the application of heat in one form or another at some point.

For the first time in history, ceramics as a science or an art has almost no limitation. At the same time, it functions in much the same way as it did 35,000 years ago. In this world of expanding possibilities, it becomes particularly important to pre-think and find answers before working in clay. Learn about the characteristics of materials and test them before proceeding; the variables are too numerous and the new substances too remarkable for a trial-and-error approach.

Start with three basic questions:

1 How is the piece to be used? Is it a decorative work to sit on a shelf or be shown in a museum? If so, strength is not a major objective. Is it a piece of dinnerware to go through a dishwasher hundreds of times? If so, it should be vitreous enough to shed food easily. Is it a piece of outdoor sculpture that children will climb on? If so, strength is a major consideration. Will the sculpture be installed in a place where temperatures range from 32°F (0°C) in the winter to 100°F (40°C) in the summer? If so, a dense clay body that won't absorb water is probably the best choice, but it should not be too dense, to avoid thermal shock.

2 How do you want the work to look? Should the materials appear coarse or fine; do you envisage the surface as shiny, chalky, crackled? There are ways to make all of these textures, even on the same piece. Will the form be vertical, rising straight up, in which case gravity works for you; or will it spread horizontally, in which case the clay body must be able to support the fabrication process?

3 What materials are available? Can you order anything you choose from a supplier? Must you work with materials already at hand? Are you limited to materials you can prospect from the local environment?

The pages that follow present both general principles and specific answers that can guide your thinking about what materials you need to meet your goals. They include many unique visual examples and charts of information from original tests I made for this book, which I show you how to repeat for yourself. You can use my photographs to shorten the process of coming up with your own answers. I want you to be able to understand the techniques and then develop them from your own vantage point.

CLAYS

There was no clay at the beginning of the earth, but clays have been continuously forming for millions of years as alteration products from original igneous rock such as granite. Physical and chemical actions of wind, rain, erosion, and gases cause the continuous decomposition of rock into clay. As long as the earth exists, clay is being formed. Chemically, it is a hydrous aluminum silicate with the formula $Al_2O_3 \cdot 2SiO_2 \cdot 2H_2O$. The differences among clays are caused by the original geological process and the position of the deposit.

Plasticity, the important physical property of clay that belongs to no other material on earth, allows clay that has been mixed with water to be coaxed into any form in any size. When it has dried, clay uniquely holds its shape; when fired, it will retain that shape and become hard, dense, and rock-like again, never to change. Claywork fired to red heat and above remains the same forever unless it breaks. The purest clays are the whitest burning,

the highest firing, the least plastic, and the most rare. Impurities add color and plasticity to clay. Clays can be graded on a scale from least plastic to most plastic, a property that depends on their geological formation and on the impurities resulting from the movement of clay from its original site to another one.

Natural clays, as they exist in the ground, differ in workability, texture, and raw and fired color. This has to do with their juxtaposition with other materials in nature, and depends on whether the movement from the site of original formation occurred by glacier, volcano, water, or other means. Clayworkers choose from the many commercially available clays or prospect clay from the ground, and they compound clay bodies according to the properties they need for their work. If fabrication is complicated, the most important choice of clay property may be the degree of plasticity needed; all other properties follow. Set priorities first, then test.

Fire clay rises to the surface when wet, and shrinks in the sun; Africa

GEOLOGICAL TYPES OF NATURAL CLAYS

All natural clays around the world are grouped into categories based on their geological formation. You need to understand these general types whether you are buying them from a supplier or prospecting them yourself. The clay bars on page 130 show what fired colors you might expect from some representative kinds of American clays sold commercially; they were photographed after being fired at different temperatures and atmospheres, and are displayed in alphabetical order.

On page 131, the same clays are grouped on a chart by geological types, with extremely valuable information derived from tests of each clay in terms of shrinkage, absorption, warpage, and water of plasticity (p. 135), as well as fired color, at three mean temperatures. These factors are very important in choosing clays for the particular function and look you want. For instance, if you want to build a 12 ft (3.6 m) tall sculpture, you probably won't want to choose a clay that will shrink 20 percent. The sections that follow describe these geological types of clays, from the purest to the most impure. Most types of clays exist in many parts of the world in small amounts that can be prospected, if not in amounts large enough to be mined.

KAOLIN OR CHINA CLAY

Primary kaolins (also called "residual kaolins") are found on the exact spot where they were formed; they have not been moved. The purest and rarest of all clays, they fire the whitest and are the least plastic. They are used for the finest porcelain. In the United States, primary kaolins exist in mineable amounts only in North Carolina. Most English china clay is primary kaolin, as are the china clays in Germany, China, Japan, Korea, and India.

Secondary kaolins (also called "sedimentary kaolins") have been moved from the spot where they were formed. They are almost as pure as primary kaolins, but are slightly yellower, more plastic, and a bit less refractory. Also rare, they are found in mineable amounts in the United States in the Southeast, especially Georgia, Florida, and South Carolina, and in the few countries of the world mentioned above where primary kaolins exist. Kaolins, used in the making of all whitewares, mature alone at 2700°F (1480°C) or above. Outcrops of china clays exist in other parts of the world in small amounts and have been used conspicuously in some ancient cultures — where otherwise most of the earth and the pots are red — notably by tribes in the western hemisphere and in early Greece.

BALL CLAY

Ball clays are always clays that have been moved by, under, or with water. They contain carbonaceous material that often colors them gray or brown in the raw state, but which burns out. Ball clays are fine-grained and highly plastic, but they have the highest shrinkage of all clays. They fire off-white, are rare, but less rare than china clays, and they mature at a slightly lower temperature, around 2400°F (1300°C). In the United States, ball clays are mined in Kentucky and Tennessee. Porcelain clay bodies and all whitewares fired at any temperature may contain only china clays, or china and ball clays together; but all clay bodies firing any color or temperature should use some ball clay if possible, to enhance plasticity.

STONEWARE CLAY

This is a term some geologists use for a natural clay that is classified between ball clay and fire clay in texture, plasticity, color, shrinkage, and firing range. *Stoneware clays* are very rare. It might be easier to find a stoneware clay to prospect yourself than to find one that is mined and sold.

FIRE CLAY

Fire clays have been moved generally by wind and erosion and redeposited, carrying with them metallic oxides and free silica which cause them to fire in a variety of colors and to be coarse-grained and tough. Abundant in the world, fire clays are found in mountains and deserts, often on top of the ground or in the upper strata of rock. In the United States, mined fire clays come from California, Ohio, Colorado, Missouri, New Jersey, and Pennsylvania. Almost every country in the world has and uses fire clays for "heavy clay" products like blast furnace and fireplace brick, water pipes, and flue lining, as well as other durable products such as beer mugs and containers. Alone, most fire clays become dense at 2200 to 2400°F (1200 to 1300°C) and range in fired color from light buffs and

Mining china clay commercially

grays to rust reds and darker browns.

A special kind of fire clay called "flint fire clay" contains an excess of silica or alumina in the natural state. It is particularly hard-packed geologically and serves to give tooth and texture to clay bodies, making large work easier to form. In the U.S.A., flint fire clays are mined in Missouri.

COMMON SURFACE CLAY

Surface clays are the ground of the earth, found everywhere, and familiar to all of us from the artifacts of primitive cultures of the world. These clays have moved geologically a great deal, been redeposited by natural forces, and moved again. Along the way, they pick up impurities that add color and aid plasticity, and also cause them to become dense at firing temperatures lower than all other clays. Common surface clays, often in the form of hard-packed shales or trap rock, have been used historically as "slip glazes" because some melt enough to form glazes at temperatures around 2100°F (1150°C). The famous kaki glaze of Mashiko, Japan, is a local clay rock crushed fine and *calcined* (disintegrated by heat) at low temperature to eliminate moisture before use.

Common surface clays can be collected everywhere — in the back yard, at the beach, on the desert, in rocky palisades — or they can be bought at a local brick or sewerpipe yard. Fine by themselves for earthenwares, or in combination with other clays as colorants or plasticizers, common surface clays can be extended to higher temperatures, or can help more refractory clays to mature at lower temperatures. They are among the easiest and most interesting materials to prospect and experiment with by yourself. Density occurs from 2000 to 2200°F (1100 to 1200°C), but these clays become hard and durable enough to use at much lower temperatures.

Slaking a mountain deposit of clays in Japan

Common surface clay area in Old Cairo, Egypt

Feldspathic clay area in California (this is a natural blend of feldspar and kaolin)

Common surface clay near water; Katmandu, Nepal

Common surface clay from road work

COMMERCIAL CLAYS AFTER FIRING

This is a small sampling of commercial clays available in the U.S.A. Test the materials you can get locally within each of the five classifications of kaolins (china clays), ball clays, stoneware clays, fire clays, and common surface clays, as I have done here.

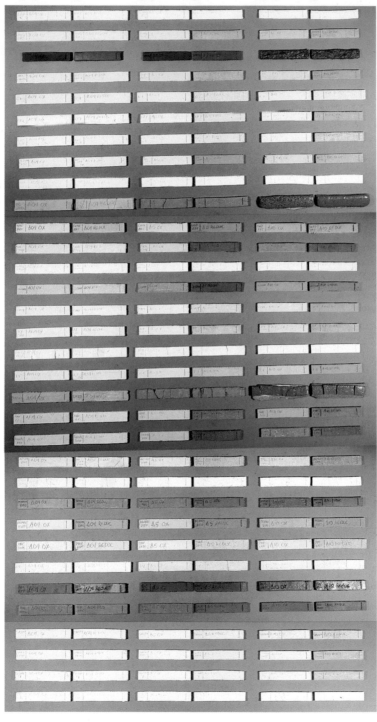

	CONE 04 OXIDATION	REDUCTION	CONE 5 OXIDATION	REDUCTION	CONE 10 OXIDATION	REDUCTION

Ajax P. Casting Kaolin

Bandy Black Ball

Barnard Common Surface

Black Charm Ball

C–1 Ball

CP–7 Ball

Champion & Challenger Ball

Dresden Ball

Edgar Plastic (EPK) Kaolin

FC 200 Feldspathic

Gold Art Fire

Green Stripe Fire

Grolleg Kaolin

Jordan Stoneware

Kentucky OM Number 4 Ball

Kentucky Special Ball

Kingsley Kaolin

L–1 Ball

LH 200 Feldspathic

Lincoln 60 Fire

Lincoln Fire

Missouri Fire

Monarch Kaolin

Newman Red Fire

North American Fire

Pine Lake Fire

PV Number 1 Feldspathic

Red Art Fire

Red Horse Fire

XX Sagger Fire

Superblend Ball

Tennessee Number 1 Ball

Number 6 Tile Kaolin

TEST RESULTS OF COMMERCIAL CLAYS

CLAY NAME	% SHRINKAGE Cone 06	Cone 5 Oxidation	Cone 5 Reduction	Cone 10 Oxidation	Cone 10 Reduction	% ABSORPTION Cone 06	Cone 5 Oxidation	Cone 5 Reduction	Cone 10 Oxidation	Cone 10 Reduction	WARPAGE IN CENTIMETERS Cone 06	Cone 5 Oxidation	Cone 5 Reduction	Cone 10 Oxidation	Cone 10 Reduction	% H₂O OF PLASTICITY	FIRED COLOR Cone 06	Cone 5 Oxidation	Cone 5 Reduction	Cone 10 Oxidation	Cone 10 Reduction
KAOLINS (CHINA CLAYS)																					
Ajax P. Casting	6	9	10	13	13	28	20	15	8	6	0	0	0	.1	.1	32	Off White	Off White	Off White	Off White	Off White
Edgar Plastic (EPK)	8	11.5	14	16	16	28	18	14	8	6	0	.3	.3	.6	.6	37.6	Light Pink	Off White	Off White	Off White	Off White
Grolleg	4	9.5	11	13.5	14	26	14	12	3	1	0	.95	.95	1.1	1.1	36	Off White	Off White	Off White	Off White	Off White
Kingsley	5.5	7	8	12.5	12.5	33	29	24	12	8	0	.2	.2	.7	.7	37	Off White	Off White	Off White	Off White	Off White
Monarch	5	6	7	12	12	33	27	23	15	11	0	.45	.45	.55	.55	37.2	Off White	Off White	Off White	Off White	Off White
Number 6 Tile Clay	6.5	8	9	12	12	25	15	11	9	5	0	.1	.1	.2	.2	26.2	Off White	Off White	Off White	Off White	Off White
BALL CLAYS																					
Bandy Black	5	10	11	13	13	26	12	8	2	2	0	.8	.8	.9	.9	34.2	Light Pink	Buff	Gray Tan	Medium Gray	Gray
Black Charm	6	10	11	13	13.5	22	13	6	5	4	0	.3	.3	.45	.45	33.4	Gray Tan	Yellow Buff	Buff	Mottled Gray Buff	Olive Gray Brown
C–1	3.5	5	5	6	7	19	14	14	10	8	0	.5	.5	.75	.75	21	Pink White	Purplish White	Speckled White	Speckled Buff White	Speckled Off White
Champion & Challenger	6	11	11	12	12.5	23	9	7	2	2	0	0	0	.3	.3	29.4	Gray Tan	Buff	Buff	Buff	Mottled Gray Tan
CP–7	5	10	11	12	12	22	10	6	3	3	0	.3	.3	.4	.4	31.6	Gray Tan	Buff	Buff	Mottled Gray Buff	Gray
Dresden	9	13.5	14	15	15.5	20	8	6	1	>1	0	.35	.35	.5	.5	34.2	Tan	Buff	Gray	Medium Gray	Gray
Kentucky OM Number 4	7	10	12	13	13	22	10	8	2	2	0	.15	.15	.25	.25	30.6	Gray Tan	Buff	Gray	Medium Gray	Gray
Kentucky Special	7	12	13	14	14	27	11	8	1	1	0	.15	.15	.2	.2	38.2	Pink Tan	Buff	Gray Tan	Medium Gray	Gray Brown
L–1	5	8.5	10	11	11	20	11	4	>1	>1	0	.35	.35	.45	.45	28.8	Gray Tan	Buff	Gray Tan	Meduim Gray	Gray
Superblend	5	8.5	10	11	11	23	12	8	5	2	0	.5	.5	1.3	1.5	30.6	Gray Tan	Buff	Buff	Mottled Gray Buff	Mottled Gray Tan
Tennessee Number 1	5.5	9.5	10	11	11	24	11	8	2	2	0	.15	.15	.35	.35	30.2	Light Pink	Buff	Buff Gray	Buff	Mottled Gray Tan
STONEWARE																					
Jordan	7	11	12	10	10	17	5	3	2	>1	0	.65	.65	1.1	1.1	29.2	Orange	Tan Orange	Dark Charcoal	Dark Gray	Charcoal Gray
FIRE CLAYS																					
Gold Art	6	10.5	10.5	11	12	13	5	>1	1	>1	0	.1	.1	.3	.3	24	Light Pink Orange	Yellow Buff	Gray	Medium Gray	Gray Brown
Green Stripe	6.5	14	15	17	18	27	5	3	2	>1	0	.13	.13	.16	.16	33.6	Tan	Yellow Buff	Medium Brown	Green Brown	Medium Brown
Lincoln	6	14	15	16.5	18	27	6	5	2	>1	0	.4	.4	.6	.6	19.6	Tan	Yellow Buff	Medium Brown	Green Brown	Medium Brown
Lincoln 60	5	11	11.5	12	14	14	7	6	4	4	0	.4	.4	.5	.5	31	Pink Orange	Yellow Buff	Walnut Gray	Medium Gray	Charcoal Gray
Missouri	7	11	12	13	13	14	7	6	4	4	0	.4	.4	.4	.4	16	Pink Tan	Light Tan	Speckled Tan	Speckled Tan	Speckled Gray
Newman Red	3.5	7	10	12	12	24	16	9	8	3	0	.75	.75	.85	.85	32.4	Orange Red	Orange Red	Pink Red Orange	Mottled Red Buff	Red Brown
North American	4	8	8	8	9	12	7	3	2	1	0	.75	.75	1	1	15	Yellow Tan	Yellow Buff	Medium Brown	Dark Gray	Walnut
Pine Lake	4.5	5.3	6.5	6	6	12	11	8	8	7	0	.23	.23	.27	.27	15	Tan	Buff	Speckled Tan	Light Tan	Tan
Red Art	6.5	9.5	10	9.5	11	11	>1	>1	>1	>1	0	2.35	2.35	2.7	2.7	24	Rust	Brown Red	Dark Olive Gray	Metallic Olive Gray	Medium Red Brown
Red Horse	6	8	9	10	10	18	12	10	7	7	0	.75	.75	.85	.85	25.2	Orange Red	Orange Red	Red Orange	Brown Red	Red Brown
XX Saggar	5	11.5	13.5	12.5	14	24	13	8	4	2	0	.31	.31	.34	.34	32	Light Pink	Buff	Buff	Mottled Gray Buff	Light Gray
COMMON SURFACE CLAYS																					
Barnard	15	16	16	19	19	7	4	2	>1	>1	0	Fused	Fused	Fused	Fused	27	Chocolate Brown	Chocolate Brown	Metallic Black	Metallic Black	Metallic Black
SPECIAL CLAYS CONTAINING NATURAL FELDSPAR																					
FC 200 (Thixotropic)	10	15	Fused	Fused	Fused	20	6	>1	>1	>1	0	Fused	Fused	Fused	Fused	24	Orange	Olive Brown	Avocado	Avocado	Avocado
LH 200 (Thixotropic)	1	10	10.5	Fused	Fused	18	12	>1	Fused	Fused	0	Fused	Fused	Fused	Fused	25.6	Orange	Tan	Walnut Brown	Caramel	Caramel
PV Number 1 Plastic Vitrox	2.5	7.5	8	11	12	22	11	8	Fused	Fused	0	1.7	1.7	2.6	2.6	27.2	Pink White	Pink	Gray White	Gray White	Gray White

CLASSIFYING FIRED CLAY WARES

The next major considerations are the basic characteristics of clays and clay-body compositions once they have been fired. Except for unfired clay art, clay is usually fired to at least "red heat" — bonfire temperature, about 1300 °F (700 °C) — or above, for hardness and durability. The greater the heat, the denser, stronger, and more vitreous the fired clay. Studio kilns range from bonfire to about 2500 °F (1370 °C) or cone 14 maximum, and many kilns cannot be fired that high. Some clays, particularly kaolins, will continue to harden beyond cone 14; at some point, each clay will soften into glass.

Finished claywork is classified into three categories, according to fired density: earthenware, stoneware, and porcelain. These terms may denote other characteristics such as workability, tactile quality, and color, but the pure definition is given according to fired density. In other words, "earthenware," "stoneware," and "porcelain" do not exist in the ground *per se*; these are names given to finished wares. The clayworker uses the basic characteristic of the natural clays, and may combine clay with other materials, to produce the following results.

EARTHENWARE

Earthenware is any claywork that has 10 to 15 percent absorption after firing, that is, when a fired piece is boiled in water, its weight increases by 10 to 15 percent (p. 136). Earthenware is relatively soft, chalky, porous, breaks easily, leaks liquids, is not acid or stain resistant, and is light in weight due to the air voids it contains. Surface clays, often iron-bearing and frequently low-fired, cause us to think of earthenwares as being reddish, like bricks and flowerpots. In reality, an earthenware body is possible at any temperature, and it can be white or almost any color as long as it fits the density definition.

The degree of density or *porosity* of fired claywork determines its strength and durability as well as the shrinkage of the body during firing. All clays shrink in drying, but shrinkage during firing depends on how dense the clay becomes; as density progresses toward *vitrification*, clay shrinks more. Earthenware, with a low shrink factor, may be the right choice for large, complicated shapes or primarily decorative work, but high absorption leaves it porous and fragile. On the other hand, earthenware pieces have some thermal shock resistance due to their porosity, making them useful for certain cookwares and outdoor sculpture in hot-and-cold climates.

STONEWARE

Stoneware is the name given to any claywork that has 2 to 5 percent absorption after firing, that is, it increases in weight by 2 to 5 percent in water. Stoneware, with its strength and durability, usually has a certain stone-like feel

Earthenware: contemporary Mexican folk pot

Stoneware: Bauhaus coffee pot, c. 1920

due to its weight and density. It is used industrially for heavy clay-product manufacture such as waterpipes and refractory brick for blast furnaces, and for sturdy kitchenwares all over the world. Clay artists are fond of stoneware bodies for the look of the dense surface without a glaze, the appeal of the stony texture, and the characteristically variegated color. Stoneware bodies are tough and can take abuse in the wet plastic stage as well as during and after firing. Stoneware is generally high-fired, but it can be made at any temperature.

PORCELAIN

Porcelain is any claywork that has 0 to 1 percent absorption. It is usually white and is translucent when it is thin: color in a porcelain body tends to lessen translucency.

Fired porcelain has strength, durability, hardness, and resistance to acid and bacteria — hence its many industrial uses. A typical porcelain clay body is made from the whitest-burning clays and fired at temperatures above 2300 °F (1260 °C) to attain the necessary density. An atypical porcelain body can be made for low-temperature firing (1900 °F, 1040 °C) by adding unusual materials (p. 137).

The purest clays are the least plastic and hardest to work with during fabrication. A porcelain body is not only difficult to work in the plastic state, but is also difficult to fire because it is brought to density nearly at the softening point. Porcelain bodies crack and deform easily and require time-consuming precautions during building and throughout the firing process. Even then a 50 percent recovery is normal in industry; that is, one out of every two pieces is thrown away, and the cost is high.

Porcelain: teapot by Susan Peterson, 1950

WHAT IS A CLAY BODY?

Most clays are not used alone, but are combined with non-clay elements into a "clay body" composition. The clay body is thought of in three parts: (1) *the plastic material —* clay or clays chosen for their workability and firing qualities; (2) a density-controlling material, called a *flux*, which lowers the melting point of ceramic material; and (3) a *filler* for lessening the characteristic stickiness and shrinkage of the clay content. Components of a clay-body batch should always be expressed as parts of 100, for comparison and ease of determining weight or volume.

Common surface clays are the only ones that should be used alone, as they are by indigenous societies and by some industrial brick and pipe plants. The impurities in these clays act as fluxes, and the dirt or sand present acts as filler.

Nature occasionally houses mixtures in the ground that are actually clay bodies, that is, deposits of clay with flux and filler in the same place. The ancient Chinese probably had a natural deposit in China consisting of kaolin, feldspathic or bone ash materials, and silica, all in the same place in the ground, so that they in fact dug a "porcelain body." Hundreds of years later in other parts of the world, alchemists like the Englishman Josiah Wedgwood (1730– 95) experimentally put together china clay, fluxes, and fillers in proper combination and "discovered" porcelain.

CHOOSING THE FLUX

Fluxes and fillers vary over the world. In the United States, the most common flux is the mineral feldspar. Feldspars that occur in nature have a predominant alkaline content such as sodium, potassium, and/or calcium, in addition to the alumina and silica that are the basic chemistry of clay. Mined feldspars have various brand names; you must always find out the composition.

A potassium feldspar is best for a flux in a clay body. However, a soda feldspar, which melts at a lower temperature and hinders plasticity, is often used in a porcelain composition to enhance translucency. Feldspars are also basic components in glazes. (Note the feldspar bars fired cone 5 and cone 10 on page 148.)

Other fluxes can be considered, but they are not used as often: bone ash, especially in areas where no feldspar exists; natural volcanic ash or pumice from the lumberyard; ground glass or cullet, usually a by-product of glass manufacture; commercially made and marketed *body frits —* glassy compositions pre-fired and re-ground; wood ash; salt; various crushed rocks of alkaline composition; or anything that will cause the chosen clay to mature (develop some density) at lower temperature than it would alone.

CHOOSING THE FILLER

The usual filler in clay body composition is silica, pure SiO_2 ground to a fine powder and bought commercially. But the filler could be crushed flint or quartz rocks or sand from beaches, deserts, or mountains. Sometimes a filler of less finely-ground particles is needed to add texture to the look of the clay, to add strength for the building method, to reduce shrinkage of the natural clay, or to give porosity for firing. In some cases, ground-up, previously fired pots or other crushed clay products serve this purpose; when bought commercially, in varying particle size, this product is called *grog.*

CHOOSING THE CLAYS

Clayworkers need to be aware of the visual and tactile look of earthenware, stoneware, and porcelain. Without glaze, earthenware often looks and feels soft and chalky or pasty, stoneware looks rock-like, and porcelain has a smooth, almost glass-like appearance, no matter what the texture or treatment.

The first decision to make is on the chalkiness or stoniness of the desired finished look. After this, determining the color of the finished fired work with glazes or other surface treatments is perhaps most important. The hue of the clay, and whether it is light or dark in value, makes a difference if a glaze is to be added. Think of rubbing white chalk over black construction paper. The black of the paper beams through the white chalk; so it is with a dark clay and a white glaze. But an opaque dark glaze will obscure a white or light clay — it doesn't make much difference what color the clay is. If the clay is to be used without glaze, then the clay color, look, and feel are paramount.

After visual, density, and color concerns are decided, workability comes to mind. Are you handbuilding or throwing? What are you making? What is the size? How will the work be fired? Fine-grained clay bodies are most plastic; coarse-grained less so. Smooth bodies are sluggish; coarser ones stand up better and take more strain. Thinness requires a smooth rather than a coarse feel; coarse bodies texture and tear easily.

Also consider the amount of clay to be used in the body. For best workability, the clay content should not be less than 50 percent of the total. It is often as high as 80 percent, with 10 percent flux and 10 percent filler. In the case of porcelain, which needs density, the clay content generally falls to the minimum 50 percent of the total batch, with feldspar and silica forming the other 50 percent, and workability suffers.

TESTING MATERIALS

Choose the clay or clays for the body composition first, according to your esthetic and fabrication criteria, and then adjust the drying and firing characteristics by adding flux and filler minerals. Test the individual clays you are likely to use if you don't already know them well.

Make tests, whether you buy individual clays commercially mined from ceramic suppliers or factories that sell clays or blended clay bodies, or whether you prospect your own materials in natural locales. Many books give clay-body batches (we never use the term "recipe"), but there is no substitute for first-hand knowledge of your own materials and your own methods. The principles I am giving you will allow you to develop your own clay bodies. Keep the results visually available for reference and for rechecking over the years.

TESTING PLASTICITY

This test involves feeling the moistened clay for elasticity and for response to pressure. Roll clay into coils and bend them; pinch clay into thin pieces to see if it holds the shape. Flatten slabs to examine stretchiness, build up the clay to see how it supports weight, and cantilever one piece off another to understand its strength. Observe each clay experiment during drying, noting warping or cracking.

Test prospected clays on location by adding enough water to make small forms so you can distinguish mud pies, dirt, or sand combinations from real clay, which is the only material that retains a formed shape when dry. Sometimes prospected clay is too sandy or too full of leaves or twigs to be workable, but if it really is clay, you can make it usable by screening out the non-plastic elements.

If the clay you want to use does not seem plastic enough as you work it, if it crumbles or tears, if it becomes dry quickly, if it is sluggish, or if it is too sticky to the touch and refuses to go into shapes easily, you will need to correct these faults. When a clay is not plastic enough, it can still be used by adding a more plastic clay with it in a body; if it is sluggish, it may need a coarser-grained clay addition; if it is too sticky, it needs filler, and so forth.

Make tests of individual clays first. Then make tests of clay bodies that you have concocted or bought commercially. Keep notes about the plastic quality of individual clays, bought or prospected. You can add to the file what you read in books or ceramic magazines about specific types or brand names of clays, and clay companies provide information about their materials.

TESTING WATER OF PLASTICITY

This is a specific test that is important in industry or in a studio where production is large and the clay body is mixed frequently in quantity. *Water of plasticity* is that percentage of water necessary to make any one clay or a clay body composition have the workability necessary to a particular method of fabrication. There is a different water content for throwing, for certain ways of handbuilding, for press molding, for slip casting, for dry-pressing, and so on. A water of plasticity test can be accomplished by measuring the amount of water added to dry material to make it plastic. Alternatively, it can be stated as a percentage; weigh a plastic bar and a dry bar and calculate according to this formula: weight of water added, divided by weight of dry clay, times 100. All data sheets from clay mines include water of plasticity figures.

TESTING SHRINKAGE

Natural clays shrink both in drying and firing; clay is the only material that has this quality. How much it shrinks depends on temperature and density. In a clay body composition, the percentage of shrinkage is altered by fillers and other materials. Know the shrinkage of each individual clay you may want to use, from wet to dry, and from dry to fired to three median temperatures of low to high fire — such as 1922 °F (1050 °C), 2150 °F (1177 °C), and 2350 °F (1288 °C), which correspond to cones 04, 5, and 10, the mean temperatures for earthenware, stoneware, and porcelain. Then test clay-body compositions the same way as the individual clays. Testing at the three temperatures gives the total range of the clay or body.

Make six test bars of each clay or clay body, with two bars for each temperature. Roll out rectangles 5 × 2 × ½ in (12.7 × 5 × 1.3 cm) thick that can be marked with identifying codes for clay names and temperatures. Carefully measure and draw a 10 cm line on the face of each tile, scoring the beginning and end of the line with a tiny perpendicular mark that will give an exact spot to begin and end the measurement (this part of the test is always done using centimeter measurements).

To measure wet to dry shrinkage: when the tile is dry, measure the line that was initially 10 cm long. Compute with this formula: line wet minus line dry divided by line wet times 100 equals percentage of wet to dry shrinkage. Measure all six tiles to see if the shrinkage is similar.

To measure dry to fired shrinkage: use two tiles for each of three firing temperatures, as described above. When the tiles are fired, compute the percentage with this formula: line dry minus line fired divided by line dry times 100. Testing two tiles for each temperature gives the opportunity to take an average between the two. A good clay body shrinks about half of its total shrinkage in the drying and half in the firing. Add the wet to dry and dry to fired percentages for the total shrinkage for that particular clay or clay body at a specific temperature.

Earthenware bodies with high porosity shrink the least — about 10 percent wet to fired. Stonewares shrink more — about 12 to 15 percent. Porcelain bodies, having the greatest density, shrink the most — 15 to 17 percent. A very broad rule of thumb relates an average total earthenware body shrinkage to 1 in in 12 (2.5 cm in 30), ½ in in 6 (1.2 cm in 15), ¼ in in 3 (.5 cm in 7.5), and so forth.

Bodies are composed of various clays for various properties. A blend of clays in the body composition allows some control of shrinkage; after testing the shrinkage percentages for individual clays you will be able to choose intelligently. If you are limited to firing at only one temperature, no matter what it is, you should make two tiles for the shrinkage test and fire at one specific heat. Otherwise, test at all three temperatures for more information.

Clay moves a lot during the shrinkage process as it dries and as it fires (see chapter 5), and large size makes it worse. The lower the shrinkage, the fewer problems in drying and firing. High shrinkage causes difficulties of structure and weight. Engineer forms skillfully and fire carefully, or accept the possibility of warping and cracks as part of the design.

TESTING ABSORPTION

To test for absorption, use the fired clay bars from the shrinkage tests, each coded separately for identification. Weigh each bar dry on a gram scale and record the amount. Boil the tiles immersed in water in a covered pan for one hour. Remove each one separately, blot it quickly, and immediately weigh it again on a gram scale. Compute the percentage of absorption with the following formula: fired weight wet minus fired weight dry divided by fired weight dry times 100 equals percentage of absorption of water by the bar.

Know the temperature range at which the individual clays you work with are porous, semi-porous, and dense. The percentage of absorption that a clay body has after a particular firing temperature determines whether it is earthenware, stoneware, or porcelain. Earthenware, because of its high absorption and low shrinkage, presents fewer fabrication and firing problems than stoneware, which is denser, but stronger on all counts. Porcelain, with no absorption, or total density just prior to melting, poses the grandest struggle in trying to keep round shapes round without warping. Achieving the fascination of translucency requires extreme thinness, and a myriad of other difficulties must be conquered.

Study the photographs and charts (pp. 130–1 and below). I have given examples of both clay and clay-body tests, with relative shrinkages and absorptions at mean firing temperatures, and other data. Remember that natural raw materials have changing variables, and test them frequently yourself. Knowing as much as possible about the clays will give you the greatest freedom.

REPRESENTATIVE CLAY BODIES

BODY MATERIALS	EPK China Clay	Kingsley China Clay	Bandy Black Ball Clay	C-1 Ball Clay	Champion & Challenger Ball Clay	Dresden Ball Clay	Kentucky Ball OM 4 Clay	Jordan Stoneware Clay	Lincoln Fire Clay	Lincoln Green Stripe Fire Clay	Red Horse Fire Clay	PV Clay	K-Spar (feldspar)	N-Spar (feldspar)	Nepheline syenite (feldspar)	Ground Glass (cullet)	D 51 Talc	Silica	Bentonite	Grog	Warping in centimeters	Shrinkage	Absorption	Fired Color: Oxidation	Fired Color: Reduction
Porcelain Cone 10	45				10										25			15	5		.7	13%	0–1%	White	Cool Gray
Porcelain Cone 5	30				15							15			25			10	5		.7	12%	1%	White	Warm Gray
Stoneware Cone 10		15	20	20				20				15						10			.4	10%	3%	Off White	Buff
Stoneware Cone 5							10	50	15				25								.4	11%	3%	Buff	Toast
Stoneware Cone 04						30	30										4			6	.2	9%	4%	Beige	Toast
Earthenware Cone 04											60			30	10						.1	8%	11%	Brown	Dark Brown
Raku Cone 04			30								40						30				.1	6%	13%	Tan	Brown
Talc "low-fire" Whiteware Cone 04	30																70				.1	8%	14%	White	White

COMPOSING A GOOD CLAY BODY

There are five basic types of clay according to geological formation (p. 128). All the brand names of mined clays anywhere in the world fall into these five categories: primary and secondary kaolins, ball clays, fire clays, stoneware clays, and common surface clays. Brand-name clays have been ground and cleaned before they reach you. Even with good quality control at the mine, natural refined clays will vary over the years; and locally found clays usually contain impurities. Different clays within the same classification will vary in subtle ways of workability, texture, and firing characteristics, but when you have tested these qualities or read the literature about your available materials you will be able to adapt accordingly.

Just as clays fall into a few basic categories, so do the types of clay bodies that can be concocted: earthenware, stoneware, and porcelain (p. 132). With only a few types of clay, every clay body is a variation of only a few basic themes. As its look and feel are usually important, you will need to test and re-test your clay body over time to see that it continues as you wish. There is no need to keep files of clay batches on hand; just understand the principles.

Proportions of ingredients. A rule of thumb is not to go below 50 percent clay in a 100 percent body batch. Almost every clay body also needs at least 10 percent flux and 10 percent filler within the 100 percent. Most clay bodies should not exceed 20 percent flux or 20 percent filler. Clay gives the body its plasticity; inert materials lessen plasticity. However, clay shrinks; inert materials reduce that tendency.

Combining clays. Try to use two or more different natural clays for the clay percentage of a given batch; the more kinds of clays, the better. This is because clays vary in particle size. Think of filling a square frame with balls of the same size, and the subsequent air voids between each ball — a picture of one clay with only one particle size. On the other hand, think of filling the frame with balls of different sizes, which fill in the voids — a picture of a mixture of clays. The combination makes a more homogeneous body, resulting in better workability and strength.

HIGH-FIRE PORCELAIN BODIES

The best basic porcelain for all-round use was developed by the electrical porcelain industry; it fires dense, and translucent where thin, at about 2350 °F (1288 °C) (cone 11). All high-temperature porcelains are variations on this theme:

China clay 25%

Ball clay 25%

Feldspar 25%

Silica 25%

The 50 percent total clay content can be spread among several china clays, or some other percentage of ball clay can be used with china clays instead of the combination above. The feldspar can vary from all potash, or all soda feldspar, to a combination of both (refer to the feldspar bar tests on page 148). Alternatively, another flux such as bone ash can be substituted (hence the name "bone china" in countries that have bone ash and not feldspars). As already stated, using all soda feldspar will lessen plasticity of the body and make it sluggish. This property, technically called *thixotropic*, is used by some artists to make slumped shapes, but most consider the body unworkable for handbuilding or sculpture. The 50 percent feldspar/silica total in the above batch can be changed in ratio; for instance, there could be more feldspar for greater density or translucency.

This porcelain clay body, or a number of variations on it, will fire relatively dense as low as 2150 °F (1177 °C) (cone 5) with most of the look and feel of porcelain, but at the lower end of the temperature range, it will not be translucent.

Elsa Rady: "Still Life Number 1," high-fire porcelain body and aluminum

LOW-FIRE PORCELAIN BODIES

A porcelain body can be developed to fire with translucency as low as 1922 °F (1050 °C) (cone 04), but the flux must be changed to a material that melts lower than any feldspar, such as ground glass (sometimes called cullet) or a commercially made body or glaze frit (p. 161). A cone 04 porcelain body looks like this:

China clay 25%

Ball clay 25%

Body frit 40%

Silica 10%

Vary this batch by trying different china and ball-clay brand names and frit compositions. A low-fire porcelain will have the difficult characteristics common to all porcelains and will require the same precautions in fabrication and firing. Only the kiln temperature will be different.

HIGH-FIRE STONEWARE BODIES

These can be composed of a variety of fire clays, depending on the desired color and temperature and keeping in mind the requirement of 2 to 5 percent absorption in the finished work. Some fire clays by themselves are nearly dense at 2350 °F (1288 °C) (cone 10), but not at 2150 °F (1177 °C) (cone 5). So the feldspar content of the body might vary from none at the higher temperature to 10 or 20 percent at cone 5. (Refer again to the clay bar tests on

Elaine Carhartt: painted earthenware body

page 130 and the chart of the same clays on page 131.) A basic batch for stoneware can be composed:

Fire clays 60%

Ball clay 20%

Feldspar 10%

Silica 10%

For a white stoneware, use 20 percent china clay at the expense of some fire clay and use only light-burning fire clays such as the American XX Sagger clay (brand name). When you have tested individual fire clays and other clays available to you at the three mean temperatures, and when you know their individual absorption percentages, you will be able to approximate the amount and type of flux that should be necessary in the body, depending on the temperature you wish to fire.

LOW-FIRE STONEWARE BODIES

As with low-fire porcelain, low-fire stonewares are possible as low as 1922 °F (1050 °C) (cone 04), but the flux will be cullet or frit instead of feldspar. You may use as much as 40

percent flux with the fire and ball clays, depending on the relative densities of the clay you choose at this low fire. (Again, consult the clay bar chart.)

EARTHENWARE BODIES

Earthenware bodies will result from any of the above batches if they are fired at cone 04. In other words, any clay body developed for high temperature is automatically an earthenware when fired at low temperature. If common surface clay is locally available, and if it is fired low, it will probably fit the earthenware classification. It is possible to make earthenware at high temperature by leaving out the flux in a regular high-temperature stoneware or porcelain body, using only clays and filler for the total batch.

ADJUSTING CLAY BODIES

Test the clay body you have arbitrarily developed to your specifications. See if you have conceived it correctly regarding workability, fired color, and density. If not, rearrange or change the materials within the 100 percent batch and try again. Always use 10 percent silica, but increase the amount of feldspar if more density is necessary, or change some of the clay content to a clay that matures at a lower temperature by itself; increase plasticity by using a more plastic clay, or adjust the filler if the body is too plastic.

TALC BODY

The so-called *talc body* is not really a clay body. Talc, steatite, and soapstone — all magnesium silicates of similar chemistry — are non-clay minerals which act much like clays in terms of plasticity, but which have low to no shrinkage and great resistance to quick thermal changes. Talc mixed with water can be worked in any method in which clays can be worked, and can be fired in minutes instead of hours, due to the low thermal shock.

The ancient Egyptians were the first to use talc and clay mixtures. In this century, a California company named Gladding-McBean reinvented the talc clay body and outlived a patent formula that is now widely used, especially in the wall tile industry. In some places, the talc body is used as a cheap clay substitute in elementary schools.

Talc can make up as much as 90 percent of the total body composition. At least 10 percent clay is necessary in the batch for plasticity and firing chemistry, but the talc content should remain high in relation to the clay, and not be less than 50 percent of the batch. No flux is used, but 10 to 20 percent silica can be included to lessen the soapy feel of talc. Industry uses four or five different talcs — which vary a great deal — to make up the total talc amount in a body,

for the same reason that we try to use two or more different clays in a clay body (p. 134).

Unlike clay, talc has a very short firing curve and will distort even before it becomes dense. A high talc/clay combination has a narrow range of density and softens suddenly at about 2000 °F (1093 °C), so is used only at low temperatures. After firing to an earthenware of 10 to 15 percent absorption at about 1900 °F (1038 °C), a talc piece will ring when tapped as if it were porcelain. The low expansion of talc makes it possible to fit glazes like a glove to this porous body, whereas glazes are likely to crackle on earthenware clay bodies. But it is best to bisque talc bodies one cone higher than you expect to glaze-fire, to rid the body of any of the gases peculiar to talc which might cause blistering in glaze if the bisque is too low.

A small percentage of talc acts as a refractory, making the body or glaze more resistant to heat. Therefore talc is not of much use in clay bodies, except in large quantities and at low fire. A small amount of talc will not act in the ways described above, including not helping to prevent thermal shock. Instead, it acts as filler. As a general rule, use talc as described above or not at all in clay bodies.

ADDITIONS TO THE CLAY-BODY BATCH

Materials that change the clay body in some way, burnout materials that form patterns within the clay, and colorants, are added as percentages to the total batch. Variables are easiest to understand when they are described as percentages added to a known quantity (100 percent) of clay-body ingredients.

COLOR THROUGH THE BODY

When colorants are added to a white-firing clay body, it will assume their exact hues, as opposed to a darker-firing clay, which is colored already.

Clays can be colored with the same metallic oxides and manufactured stains used for glazes (p. 165), but the fired result will look like clay rather than glass. Oxides and stains are both expensive, and more colorant is needed for an opaque mass such as clay than for a glassy substance such as glaze. Begin testing percentage additions for coloring clay by adding two or three times those given for coloring glazes (p. 167).

Naturally occurring colored clays can be used effectively as colorants in clay bodies or engobes. Those in the hues of the grand canyons of the world are usually from the most common and least expensive metals and earth colors, such as iron-rust reds or buffs, manganese purples, black-iron darks, or impure titanium dirty oranges. Such earth oxides are not as costly as the rarer metallic oxides or stains manufactured for use as clay-body pigments.

ENGOBES TO COLOR SURFACES

An alternative to coloring all the body is to color its surface. This is accomplished with a liquid clay — usually a white one such as ball clay — colored with natural clays or with metallic oxides or manufactured stains. I personally call this composition an engobe, rather than "slip," as explained in chapter 3 (p. 106).

Engobes can be made from the basic batch of the clay body, especially if the body fires white. Alternatively, an all-purpose engobe for all temperatures and all clay bodies is:

Ball clay 70%

Feldspar 20%

Silica 10%

Add water to make the proper liquid consistency. If you want it whiter, add 15 percent zircopax. Experiment with color additions, using colored clays, oxides, or stains at 10 to 50 percent, depending on their strength and the intensity of desired color. Engobes are used in many decorative techniques (p. 107) on wet to leather-hard clay, with or without glaze, at all temperatures. They come to their full hue under a shiny, clear glaze, and are dulled by matt glazes. The above engobe is dense at high fire without a glaze, but somewhat chalky at low fire without a glaze.

Vitreous engobes are hard and dense without glaze; they can be formulated for any temperature. The engobe described above is a vitreous engobe at cone 10, but not at cone 04. Vitreous engobes sometimes yield a fuzzy line — they fuse with the glaze — because they are so dense.

A low-fire vitreous engobe that will be both bright and hard at 1922°F (1050°C) without glaze is:

Ball clay 65%

Ground glass or frit 25%

Silica 10%

Engobe surface under clear glaze by Jun Kaneko

Low-fire engobe test, oxidation fired

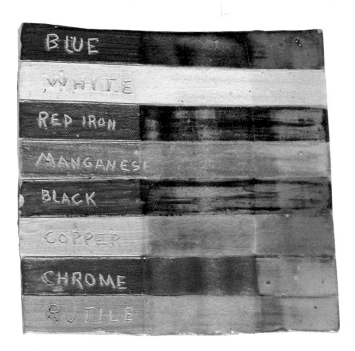

High-fire engobe test, reduction fired

Different palettes are available at cone 04 oxidation and cone 10 reduction. The 15 low-temperature engobes have clear glaze on the left, are unglazed in the center, and have translucent glaze on the right. The 8 high-temperature engobes are unglazed on the left, have clear glaze in the middle, and matt glaze on the right. Notice how the high soda matt glaze helped the copper engobe turn pink, while the clear glaze made the copper green.

Color the low-fire vitreous engobe with 10 to 50 percent addition of a variety of manufactured stains in order to achieve the bright, intense hues for which low temperature is noted.

To make a median-temperature vitreous engobe for firing at 2150°F (1177°C) (cone 5), adjust the low-fire engobe to include more clay and less flux, or use the all-purpose engobe and increase the flux 20 percent. Experiment with color additions and fire the tests both without glaze, and with clear, matt, and opaque white glazes, to see how the engobes change.

TEXTURE

Specks in a clay body result from impurities that are in the natural clay, or from deliberate additions of dirt; gravel; sands of various colors; granular metallic oxides such as magnetite, manganese, rutile, and ilmenite; tailings from an assay office or coarse overburdens on ore deposits from mines; valve grindings from an auto garage; colored grogs; cut-up kitchen scrub pads made of copper, brass, or stainless steel; and so forth. Combustible textural spots become voids after firing, leaving their own patterns. Such burnout materials include coffee grounds; rice or other grains; dehydrated pet food; dried peas or lentils; pasta; string; styrofoam [polystyrene] pellets; sawdust; the fertilizers perlite and vermiculite; ground nutshells and other animal fodder; fine nylon fibers; fiberglass cloth; nylon screen; and many others.

Some of these additions, like ground nutshells and nylon fibers, actually make the clay easier to handbuild, adding tooth to the structure and holding it up. Textural components function as inert materials in the clay body and reduce shrinkage, but the higher the percentage added to the base batch, the harder the clay body becomes to work. Up to 50 percent textural materials can be added to the basic batch (making it now a 150 percent batch), which is especially useful for large, flat, thick wall plaques or floor tiles where size, low shrinkage, and no warping are important. So much textural addition will probably make the clay unthrowable. If some of the additions you are using are very light, don't bother to weigh them; just throw them into the mixer or wedge them in by hand until it feels like enough.

Burnout materials and the voids they cause lessen the fired weight of a claywork, but too many holes reduce the strength of the fired piece. Experiment with everything you can think of, and keep fired tests as examples.

PREPARING THE CLAY FOR WORK

Once the composition has been determined, clay bodies are mixed to the plastic stage by hand or machine. If the materials have been prospected and are in chunks or are damp, they must first be dried, pulverized, and screened of foreign particles before they can be measured and combined. If materials are bought other than in bulk (as in factory purchases), they probably come in something like 100 lb or 50 kg bags ground to 200 mesh powder. Refined materials can be easily weighed and mixed in dry batches.

MEASURING AND MIXING DRY MATERIALS

Usually clay-body ingredients are weighed in pounds or kilos. Test batches might be weighed in ounces or grams, and production amounts will be weighed in tons or metric tons.

Volume blending is an alternative to weighing, provided the instrument of measurement is always the same container, to keep the volumes consistent. As the volumes of the different materials vary in weight, direct weighing and volume blending are not interchangeable in the same batch.

Dry mixing of the body components is most important before hand mixing with water. Dry mix the weighed or volume-blended materials by stirring the composition with a stick or your hands; or put the dry mix into a cardboard drum with a tight-fitting lid and roll it around on the floor (there is no need to dry mix if you are using a machine).

MAKING CLAY PLASTIC BY HAND

After thorough mixing of the dry components, one of several hand mixing methods can be used for adding water to make the clay plastic, ready for use. (1) Lay the powdered mixture out on a table, on the floor, or in a shallow container; make a hole in the center, and add water little by little, kneading the clay and water mixture into a plastic mass. (2) Slake (immerse) the dry materials in excess water, screen when wet into a porous trough, and allow the moisture to evaporate as it forms a thick slurry; stiffen it to the plastic stage on soft wood, plaster, or cement. (3) Put the mixed dry materials into a coarse-weave sack, totally soak the sack with water, and hang it up to drip until the clay is plastic. (4) Use the "soak pit" method of layering the dry blend several inches at a time in a bucket or bathtub or other container, sprinkling water between each layer; cover with moist cloths and leave it to become plastic in a few days.

MAKING CLAY PLASTIC BY MACHINE

Commercial bread-dough mixers, cement mixers, and machines with blades made especially for mixing clay are useful for amounts of clay body over 50 lb (22 kg) of dry materials plus water of plasticity. Slurry made from slaking dry, scrap clay body in water is often the base for the new mixture, but do not use it if the color or composition is important. Begin with about 4 in (10 cm) of water in the bottom of the mixer for a 100 lb (45 kg) batch; add some dry materials and turn the mixer on. Continue adding dry material and more water carefully until all dry materials are used and the clay feels plastic. It may take ten minutes to combine materials; another five minutes of mixing is sufficient to complete the process.

A *pug mill* with a de-airing chamber is useful for *pugging* (mixing and compressing) plastic clay and removing the air that is put in during the blade-mixing process. A pug mill without a de-airing chamber can be used as a mixing machine — the dry mixture is added in layers with small amounts of moisture, and the auger forces it through a chamber that forms it into a continuous plastic "pug" which extrudes from the machine. A pug mill, fitted with various dies, can also become an extruding machine for specific shapes used for handbuilding or sculpture.

Sometimes dry clay body is wet-blended into a slip, and run through a press with cloth filters, to squeeze out the moisture to a plastic state. This laboratory "filter press" can be the answer for porcelain plastic bodies, because slaking clay in a slurry and filter-pressing the liquid clay enhance plasticity.

STORING PLASTIC CLAY

It is important to keep clay airtight so that it will not change consistency or dry out. Plastic wrapping inside a plastic or metal container is an easy solution, but plastic is porous and will not keep clay moist indefinitely. Clay can be kept in old-fashioned iceboxes or laundry tubs, in zinc-lined wooden cupboards or boxes, in barrels, or — as is often done in handcraft production studios — in a huge pile on the ground. The pile is allowed to harden to a crust on the surface, which will be penetrated with a shovel to the moist clay inside when it is needed for use.

MAKING CASTING SLIP

If liquid clay cast into a plaster mold were just a mixture of clay and water, too much water would be needed to make it liquid, and after evaporation there would not be enough clay. So-called "deflocculated" casting slip is used to solve this problem. It can be made from any clay-body composition, but with a maximum 40 percent water per 100 percent dry batch. An *electrolite*, called a defloccuant — such as sodium silicate, soda ash, Darvon, or tannic acid — is used in a ratio of from two-tenths to five-tenths of 1 percent (.002 to .005) of the dry batch, as a catalyst to make the clay become liquid in a small amount of water. In addition to its use in casting, a deflocculated slip is used for dipping cloth or other combustibles before a firing that leaves the clay standing after the core is burned out. Deflocculated slip is also used for pouring on to plaster slabs to make thin, smooth clay sheets for handbuilding fragile forms.

Not all clays deflocculate in the same way, so the first batch of slip is always experimental. Commercial casting slips can be bought from ceramic suppliers or from industry. However, if you make your own, you are in charge, and it is cheaper. Keep track of test results in order to duplicate them. A 10 lb (4.5 kg) dry batch is a good sample to test in the following way.

Water ratio. For 10 lb (4.5 kg) of dry material, use 4 lb or U.S. pints (3⅓ U.K. pints or 1.9 liters) of water; for 100 lb (45 kg) of dry material use 40 lb or U.S. pints (33 U.K. pints or 19 liters) of water.

Determine the percentage of deflocculant. (1) Translate pounds to grams (454 g = 1 lb). 10 lb becomes 4,540 g; 100 lb becomes 45,400. (2) Multiply by minimum and maximum percentage of deflocculant: 4,540 × .002 and 4,540 × .005 for 10 lb (4.5 kg) of dry material; 45,400 × .002 and 45,400 × .005 for 100 lb (45 kg) of dry material = 9.08 g minimum and 22.7 g maximum amount of deflocculant for the 10 lb (4.5 kg) dry batch, and 90.8 g and 227 g for the 100 lb (45 kg) batch.

Mix materials. To re-use the scrap from casting slip, it is necessary to put dry soda ash in the water first, using half the minimum amount of deflocculant; the other half will be sodium silicate or other liquid deflocculants, added later with the dry body ingredients. Divide the minimum amount you calculated above for the given dry batch (half of 9.08 for 10 lb/4.5 kg, half of 90.8 for 100 lb/45 kg).

(Of course, you could be making a sample test of any size; the arithmetic is the same.)

When you have mixed the soda ash into the measured water, add some of the other dry materials. Mix by hand or with an electric mixer called a *blunger*. This can be nothing more than a shaft and propeller on a one-quarter horsepower motor or an electric drill, or it can be a commercial casting-slip machine.

Add the second half of the deflocculant. It will go into the mixture as sodium silicate or other liquid deflocculant, measured in cubic centimeters (1 liquid cc = 1 dry gram) in a glass beaker, as necessary. As the mixture stiffens with the addition of more dry batch, add further drops of deflocculant, but not more than the maximum amount you calculated. One or two drops make a big difference — too much will gel the mixture, and you will have to start again.

Continue the process until all the dry batch has been added. Measure the amount of liquid deflocculant it took to give the right viscosity.

TESTING VISCOSITY

There are two ways of testing a liquid casting slip. (1) By the manual method, see that it forms a long, well-draining drool with a few drops off the end of fingers. (2) The viscosity can be tested by calculation. A good casting slip has a specific gravity of 1.7, and water has s.g. of 1.00. Therefore, 100 cc of good casting slip should weigh 170 g on the gram scale. If it is overweight, add drops of deflocculant or water — whichever seems preferable; if it is underweight, add more dry batch. Keep notes so that you can repeat the procedure next time.

TESTING SHRINKAGE AND ABSORPTION

Shrinkage and absorption tests can be made for casting slips by pouring slip on to plaster, drawing a 4 in (10 cm) line when the slip stiffens, firing at the desired temperature, boiling the bars, and doing both calculations (chapter 8). Casting slips can be colored in the manner described for plastic clay or engobes, using metallic oxides or manufactured stains (p. 165).

HISTORICAL CLAY BODIES

Some clay bodies are historically famous, either because of what was done with them, or for some unusual quality. Examples follow.

Belleek porcelain pitcher, c. 1900

BELLEEK

This is famous as the most translucent of all chinas, and comes from Ireland. A porcelain body that can be made paper-thin and has almost glass-like transparency, it is composed of china clay and frits and vitrifies at low temperature.

MEERSCHAUM PIPE

It is made from an hydrous talc-like silicate of magnesia found in Asia Minor, from which pipe bowls are intricately carved of raw clay in two layers, one inside the other. The raw clay becomes more and more fired as the pipe is smoked. The name literally means "sea foam," and the clay-like material is light enough to float in water; the pipes weigh almost nothing.

A much-used meerschaum pipe

PARIAN PORCELAIN

Used for bisque doll heads in Victorian times, it is made with 65 percent Cornwall (or Cornish) stone feldspar (a calcium spar) and 35 percent china clay, fired to 2190°F (1200°C) (about cone 6). It is named for the island in the Cyclades that is famous for the marble it resembles.

EGYPTIAN PASTE

According to hieroglyphic records, Egyptian paste is the material used during and before Cleopatra's time for figurines and for the tiny extruded beads and carved necklace components that formed the yoke of garments. The so-called paste is a self-glazing clay body generally thought of as turquoise blue (achieved by the addition of copper) because it is the color of so many famous Egyptian artifacts in museums. Actually, the paste was used with many different colorants as well. It had a high content of salt (sodium), which was the basic flux in glass; it was its alkalinity and the low firing temperature that made it so bright as long as 7,000 years ago.

A good base batch for white Egyptian paste for firing from cone 010 to cone 04 (depending on the desired degree of gloss) is:

Parian ware figure of Massachusetts governor John Albion Andrew, sculpted by Martin Milmore, c. 1850

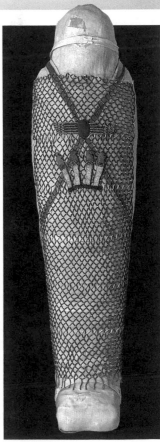

Egyptian paste beads on the *Mummy of Nesmutaatneru with Beaded Shroud*, from Deir el-Bahri, 767–525 B.C.

Ball clay 14%

Nepheline syenite (or any soda feldspar) 37%

Soda ash 6%

Baking soda 6%

Silica 37%

Store it dry, and mix wet only enough to use at one time. When the formed objects are beginning to dry, salt crystals will come to the surface. This whitish coating of salts is important; be careful not to rub it off. If the crystals do not appear, mix table salt and water or soda ash and water and paint the dried surface.

Egyptian paste can be colored with any of the earth oxides or manufactured stains. Here are some possibilities: turquoise — 3, 4, or 5 percent copper carbonate; blue — ½ to 2 percent cobalt carbonate; purple — 2 to 4 percent manganese dioxide; green — 2 to 5 percent chrome oxide; yellow, pink, maroon, coral, tan, baby blue, and most colors of the rainbow — 10 to 15 percent manufactured stains of the appropriate color (p. 167). The percentage variations above give light and dark values of the hue. Of course, the white Egyptian paste can be mixed with any colored paste to lighten it, or white can be marbleized into a color.

Although Egyptian paste is not very plastic, it can be thrown or handbuilt in addition to the traditional use for bead making, or it can be added as decoration on other clayworks. Fired at high temperature, it becomes a glaze. Even at low fire, beads will stick to each other and objects stick to the kiln shelf. To fire beads, string them on ni-chrome wire (to which nothing sticks) from the ceramic supplier, or make cradles of the wire for supports.

TERRA SIGILLATA

This is not exactly a clay body, although it can be. Usually it is a clay slip made from one natural clay ground fine over thousands of years under rocks and water. Such prospected slips can be found near wet or dry rocky creek beds. They generally contain impurities and become colored during firing. Their characteristic surface sheen, generally rusty red, is familiar from the museum exhibits of several 1,000-year-old pots of the Greeks of Attica and later the Romans. The Chinese at Yi-hsing used this kind of clay for the whole body, not just the surface coating, and made their famous Yi-hsing teapots, which have the peculiar sheen all the way through.

You can make a sigillata if you do not have a creekbed clay or want to make a white-burning sigillata base to add color to. Use any ball clay in a measured amount with twice as much water as dry material and 1 percent sodium hydroxide for a suspension agent; grind in a ball or jar mill for 24 hours. After milling, bring the liquid to a specific gravity of 1.2, which means that 100 cc will weigh 120 g on the scale (weigh the cc graduate first). Usually the slip will register 1.2 s.g. straight out of the mill; if it does not, add drops of water or clay. Let the mixture stand for about a week in a glass jar until it separates into three parts: water at the top, "semi-water" in the middle, sludge on the bottom. Siphon off the water; the middle portion is the sigillata, but sometimes even the bottom portion works, too. Apply this very thin liquid by spraying on leather-hard or bone-dry ware; it should shine immediately. Sigillata is only clay and water, so it won't stick to other pots or to kiln shelves; but as a fired surface it becomes shiny and makes a dense coating, even on earthenware.

White ball clay sigillatas can be colored with ceramic oxides and stains, in the same way as Egyptian paste or engobes. In addition to its own decorative qualities without glaze, sigillata can be used: (1) to make a smooth undercoating for high-temperature dinnerware that needs an unglazed foot, (2) to give flowerpots color and sheen without closing the pores of the pot completely, and (3) to give color and surface variety to bricks and other architectural clay products that are fired stacked together and would therefore stick if they were glazed.

FAIENCE

A term sometimes used by art historians, faience has several meanings: (1) colored clays used by the Egyptians for beads (like Egyptian paste); (2) tin-glazed decorated earthenware from Egyptian and Islamic cultures; and (3) the colorful embossed earthenwares of the 16th to 18th century, popular in middle Europe and England. Clayworkers don't use the term faience.

RAKU

Raku is a clay body that is not necessarily made up specially, but can be; it is also a process, and the name of a family dynasty in Japan. A raku clay body needs to be porous enough for heat to pass through it, with as much inert material as possible in relation to the clay content to prevent thermal shock in the raku process. Any clay body can be made into a raku body by "opening it up" with dirt, sand, or grog wedged in a ratio of about one-third to two-thirds clay body; or use half pumice from the lumberyard and half fire clay, to make a bonfire-proof body like the San Ildefonso Pueblo Indians of New Mexico do with volcanic ash and local clay. Buying a ready-mixed raku body is not necessary, even if you buy clay; just wedge some dirt into your clay. More or less any clay body works, used judiciously.

UNUSUAL CLAY BODIES

Unusual clay bodies are those that have unusual ingredients or serve unusual purposes, but are not necessarily "historical." Examples follow.

TOP-OF-THE-STOVE CERAMICS

All ceramic vessels can be used for cooking in the oven at any temperature provided that: (1) the oven is not preheated; (2) the ware is at room temperature to start with; and (3) the vessel is not empty. (If you just want to warm a dish in the oven, fill it with water first.) However, no ordinary ceramic vessel will stand being heated on the hob (on top of the stove), with the possible exception of the very porous, partly glazed earthenwares made in Mexico today.

An unusual clay body is therefore needed to withstand burner heating. Certain shock-proof lithium compounds are used in the clay body. These include lithium carbonate — the source for lithium oxide — and lithium compounds such as lepidolite, spodumene, petalite, and lithospar (see molecular formulas for these compounds in chapter 8).

Experiment with flameware body batches by using combinations of these lithium compounds, plus clay. As much as 50 to 60 percent spodumene or 70 percent petalite have tested satisfactorily, but less lithium compound and more

clay give better plasticity. Spodumene is bought in the United States as the raw "alpha" compound, chemical grade, which means 50 to 200 mesh; finer grind is available, but seems not to make a difference in bodies or glazes. The fired "beta" version appears better for flameware in research (fired above 2000°F [1093°C] to the beta stage), but you would have to make your own. Use any clay or combination thereof; research has been mainly with kaolins. Pyrophyllite is a clay-like mineral with low shrinkage which can be substituted for china clay. Test-fire flameware directly over the stove burner with and without food or water, and cool the hot pot in water; repeat several times.

At Hunter College, we have worked successfully with the following batches, firing at cone 11:

Flameware A:

Petalite 30%

Spodumene 20%

Fire clay 30%

Ball clay 20%

As reported in Dr. W. G. Lawrence's book, *Ceramic Science for the Potter*, we have found that firing temperature makes a big difference to thermal shock resistance. Lawrence states that firing flameware cone 11 to cone 12, rather than cone 10, increases thermal shock resistance appreciably. Make your own flameware tests at different temperatures, with cone packs mounted next to the tests to see the exact cone. According to our tests, however, the following body works at cone 10:

Flameware B:

EPK china clay 13%

Ball clay 35%

Petalite 45%

G—200 feldspar 5%

Bentonite 2%

The flameproof ceramic body Novarlit was developed by the Gustavsberg laboratories in Sweden to be used for part of a space rocket, and was then adopted by designer Stig Lindberg for household items. In 1955 the brown-glazed Terma line was launched, and it stayed on the market for about 20 years. Its novelty lay in the convenient hob-to-table concept

(Bentonite is used as a plasticizer in clay bodies and as a suspension agent in glaze, but it has the fault of expanding in water; therefore its shrinkage is high. It is also one of the materials that varies a great deal in the ground and is rarely the same twice when you order it from the supplier. I think it is best never to use bentonite if it can be avoided, but it is cheap. A more expensive manufactured plasticizer, which does not vary, is Macaloid.)

Glazes are difficult to bond to lithium bodies. It helps to use some of the body materials in the glaze. The following glaze works for Flameware B:

Gerstley borate 14.0%

Dolomite 8.6%

Talc 3.0%

Zinc oxide 1.9%

Lithium carbonate 1.7%

EPK china clay 30.2%

Silica 40.2%

Bentonite .4%

Arabia Factory in Finland and Gustavsberg Factory in Sweden produce flameware commercially, apparently using a local talc found only in small deposits in each country; the production is limited.

CLAY FOR WELDING AND SOLDERING

Experiment with fired clay body samples that contain variations of a 50/50 combination of any lithium compound such as petalite plus any fire clay (which seems to weld with lithium better than other clays). Test them using various welding, braising, and soldering fluxes. I personally think a clay body can be made to withstand the torch used in these processes, but only a few clay sculptors have researched the challenge, and the literature is slight.

VOULKOS SCULPTURE BODY

Many years ago Peter Voulkos, wanting the simplest body, mixed half fire clay and half ball clay, sometimes adding crystal silica, sand, or grog (p. 86). This works at cone 10; lower, it is porous. Due to the lack of clay variety and of flux, this body is more open than it is homogeneous.

NON-SHRINK BODIES

It is difficult enough to move and fire large-scale work without the further difficulty of the shrinkage characteristic of regular clay bodies. The solution is to combine inert, non-shrink materials with clay. We have discussed a few: pumice, volcanic ash, talc in high quantity, sand, grog, and organic matter. Another answer is cement, for air-setting bodies or firing. Half-and-half combinations of any clay and any cement should be tried. Lumnite (the brand name for an alumina cement) seems to work best in bodies to be fired. Many cements are available, and all companies produce data sheets on their products.

FELDSPARS: CLAY AND GLAZE FLUXES

Feldspars form a bridge between clays and glazes, in a sense, because they are such necessary elements in both, at least above 2000 °F (1093 °C). Clay with enough feldspar addition can become a glaze at a certain temperature. Feldspars are the first breakdown product in the geological disintegration from the original rocks of which clays are a further breakdown. Many feldspars contain clay or vice versa, hence the name "feldspathic clay." (See clay tests, page 130, and clay chart, page 131.)

Most feldspars in the world — and they can be found in many countries — begin to melt at about 2100 °F (1150 °C), and act as fluxes in stoneware and porcelain clay bodies as well as in stoneware and porcelain glazes.

The chemical composition of a feldspar is similar to a glaze formula. Feldspars — also called spars — can be used by themselves as high-temperature glazes (rubbed on to make the surface glisten) or as the base for glaze development at high fire; they do not melt at low fire. Theoretically, feldspars are calcium, soda, or potassium, with alumina and silica. Nature's feldspars are combinations of at least two of the above alkalies plus alumina and silica. A spar is defined as a soda, potassium, or calcium spar, according to which mineral predominates.

Test bars of non-clay minerals such as feldspars are difficult to make and handle in the plastic stage because they do not hold together. Use a mold, or form bars by hand. Draw a 10 cm shrinkage line on a feldspar tile to see whether the line will hold in the fire. My feldspar tests are fired at cone 5 and 10 only, because no melt occurs at cone 04.

Feldspars change in availability as mines and corporations change, but everyone in the world should have access to some feldspar that is similar to the ones on this chart. (Refer to the chemical analysis and formulas in chapter 8.) Look carefully, in the photographs of the feldspar tests at cone 5 and 10: at the way a bar breaks up and moves, at the relative degree of melt of each different feldspar, and at the sheen of each at the two temperatures. The variations in these bars of feldspars that are supposedly substitutes for one another, or that have similar compositions, may result just from their particle size variation (particle size makes a big difference in the melting action of a material). *Looking is the best way to assess feldspars* — it is far better than reading chemical compositions. You will use feldspars in both clay bodies and glazes.

FELDSPAR TEST RESULTS

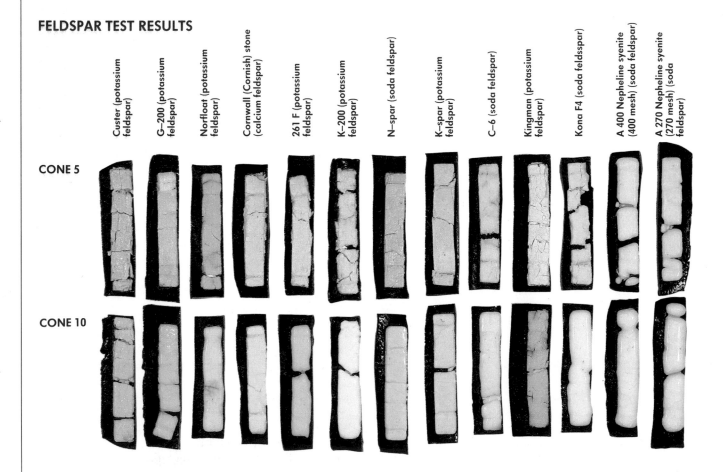

When a particular feldspar becomes unavailable, substitute one that is similar. The popular Kingman brand is no longer mined; substitute G–200.

GLAZES

Glaze is a substance that melts to a glassy state at a given temperature in a fire but does not melt enough to run off the ware to which it is applied. It is thought that glass was discovered by the Egyptians — first, before glaze — at some time between 12,000 B.C. and 3000 B.C., probably as the result of an accidental combination of sand and salt in a bonfire. The Egyptians added clay to their sand–salt combination, saw that the mixture would stay on a vertical surface during firing, and found glaze. Glaze thus differs from glass in chemical composition. Although glaze is a sort of glass, glass is formed in a molten state and stands alone, whereas glaze bonds to clay or metal.

Today, glass is made of silica, the glass-forming oxide, plus oxides that cause the refractory silica to melt at lower temperature. The fluxes used in glass are soda and lead. Glaze contains at least one more component than glass, to hold the molten glass on the vertical surface: alumina. Alumina is the chemical binder in glaze, and it also controls viscosity; its usual source in glaze is clay itself.

The Egyptians used alkaline glazes because salt (sodium) was the material available. The Chinese had developed high-temperature glazes by 2000 B.C. from using wood to fire kilns; they realized that the wood ash blowing on the ware caused a shine. In addition to wood ash, the Chinese had feldspathic rocks and lead oxide. Used in China for glazes by 500 B.C., lead yielded different colors from the metallic oxide additions — especially from copper, which produces turquoise blue in an alkaline base, but grass-green or yellow-green in a lead-based glaze. Colors are greatly influenced by glaze composition.

Glaze can be matt or glossy surfaced; transparent, translucent, or opaque; rough or smooth; colored with metallic oxides or not. Glaze provides a vehicle for decoration, an impervious surface, durability, easy cleaning, and acid and bacteria resistance; it does not make a clay body more dense than it is at a particular firing temperature, or leakproof if the body is porous.

Glazes can be calculated from an original molecular formula (chapter 8), from tests of raw materials, or from batches found in books and other sources. Glaze coloring additions do not mix exactly as paints; their chemistry under fire must be considered. Ceramic pigments are sometimes the same as those in paints, and some paints actually can be used to color glazes, particularly at low fire. Experiment with natural metallic oxide coloring additions to glazes, and commercial stain colorants — and paints if you wish — to find your own palette.

Some cultures have never used glaze as a finish. The Indians of North and South America burnished the clay body or an applied clay slip for smooth and almost vitreous surfaces. Some Central and South American tribes, as well as Africans and East Indians, discovered that ingredients such as milk would permeate and seal the pores; others found that tree resin rubbed into hot pots gave a shiny finish. These surfaces might last as long as the pots, but are not permanent, and are thus not glazes.

DEVELOPING GLAZES

Developing glazes for yourself, with supplier-bought materials including coloring oxides and stains, is the main way to exercise control of the ceramic vocabulary for nuances of color, texture, and surface quality. Even so, control is hard to maintain. Materials change at the mine, suppliers change their sources, or someone makes a mistake in packaging. Besides, ceramic engineers say that there are 1,100 possible variables in every ceramic piece!

You can be even more independent, and prospect rocks, semi-precious stones, and various mineral deposits yourself. Prepare them with the proper grinding equipment, and test them. Control found materials by keeping as many variables as possible constant in the process of prospecting and refining.

Commercial prepared glazes for the entire temperature range are available today from most ceramic suppliers. They are usually provided with instructions for use. Be aware that prepared liquid glazes react with their plastic containers and have a short shelf-life. With regard to coloring, so-called "underglazes" — equivalent to engobes — and "one-strokes" — equivalent to stains — are blended by the same companies that make and market prepared glazes. Different companies may call these products by their own brand names, but all are essentially the same, made primarily for low-temperature use (pp. 182–5). "Secret" high-fire colored glazes are also available in powder form from many companies.

Whether you buy or mix your own glaze, and whatever else you choose to do for surface treatment, are essentially factors of individual expression.

Tests should be made in the environment in which the materials will be used, under the same conditions. Always test-fire commercially prepared glazes before counting on them. Application is so important to fired result that it too must be practiced before you can achieve control.

A complete study of glaze implies learning the chemical composition of raw materials, the characteristics of each oxide contained in each material at each temperature range, and eventually the chemical and mathematical calculation of glazes that I describe in chapter 8. If you divide the glaze molecularly according to oxygen valence and work a formula mathematically this will yield an understanding of glaze composition that you cannot get any other way, but it is a complicated, sophisticated method that you may never want to learn.

We begin the study of glaze materials as simply as possible, with the relative melting capacity of 34 base glaze materials in my original tests that follow.

VISUAL SAMPLES: 34 GLAZE MATERIALS,

I recommend, especially for beginners, a simple approach to glaze development that requires only visual samples. Experiment with blends of raw materials after you know what they look like fired by themselves at various temperatures. In the photographs of fusion button tests and the charts of 1,190 tiles at two temperatures, I have arbitrarily chosen 34 materials that can be used in glazes. I have first tested and photographed them as fusion buttons, made from crucible [thimble] amounts of the dry individual materials, fired at the three mean temperatures, cone 04, 5, and 10. Secondly, the same 34 materials were applied to tiles as glaze application amounts, on each of 34 tiles, and then each of the 34 materials was blended in 50/50 combination with each other material and applied to a tile. The second test was fired at cone 5 oxidation (pp. 156–7) and at cone 10 reduction (pp. 158–9), but was not run at cone 04 because only a few materials melt at low temperature.

FUSION BUTTONS OF GLAZE MATERIALS

The following 34 materials were chosen for the fusion button and 50/50 series. (More information about the chemistry of each of these materials, the oxides they contain, and what the oxides do, can be found in chapter 8.)

1 Albany slip — a common surface clay that becomes a glaze by itself above 2000 °F (1093 °C); the deposit used to be mined in New York State but is no longer; substitute other mined clays such as Blackbird, or prospect any local iron-bearing clay

2 Barium carbonate — a low-fire matting agent; serves as a greenish auxiliary flux at high fire

3 Barnard clay — a surface clay containing manganese and iron, found in the U.S.A. as an overburden on ore deposits; it is used as a colorant in clay bodies and glazes or by itself as a metallic coating

4 Bentonite — a clay-like aluminum silicate; sometimes a plasticizer in clay bodies and a suspension agent in glaze, but a very variable natural material

5 Bone ash — a refractory (high-temperature) flux used in bodies and glazes

6 Borax — an alkaline low-fire flux used in glaze

7 Calcium carbonate — also called "whiting;" a refractory flux and whitener, which lends hardness to glaze

CONE 04   CONE 5   CONE 10

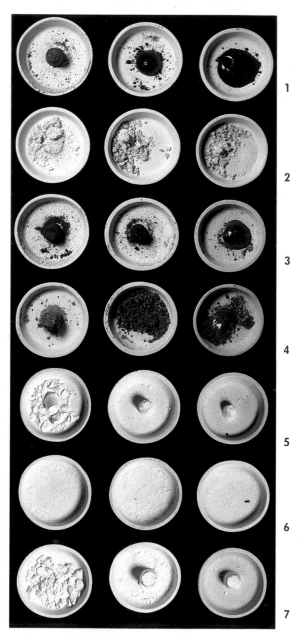

1
2
3
4
5
6
7

ALONE AND IN 50/50 BLENDS

8 Cornwall stone — a calcium feldspar from Britain; the most refractory of the three main types of feldspars

9 Dolomite — a calcium magnesium compound used to make glazes matt

10 EPK china clay — a Florida secondary kaolin

11 Kingman feldspar — has been a popular high-potassium spar (with some sodium), from Kingman, Arizona, but is not currently mined; substitute G–200 or another feldspar of similar composition

12 Gerstley borate — a calcium borate substitute for the mineral colemanite (which is too fluffy as it is now mined); an active glaze flux over the entire range of temperatures

13 Ilmenite — iron-titanium natural compound used as a colorant in bodies and glazes; can be granular

14 Lead carbonate — an active flux for low temperatures; insoluble, non-poisonous sources are lead mono- and bi-silicate, and lead frits (this test is the raw material — it should not be used for dinnerware)

15 Lepidolite — a lithium compound; lithium compounds are erratic fluxes in bodies and glazes

16 Lithium carbonate — the source for lithium oxide

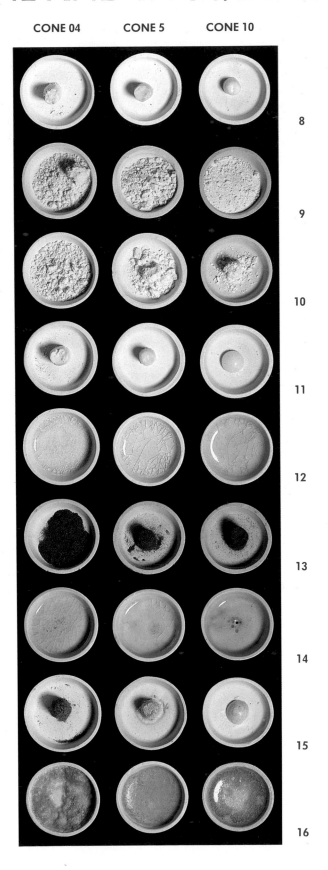

CONE 04   CONE 5   CONE 10

8

9

10

11

12

13

14

15

16

17 Lithospar — a lithium feldspar

18 Magnesium carbonate — a matting agent in glaze; the only oxide that makes cobalt purple

19 Magnetite — black iron oxide, usually granular, used as colorant or to make specks in bodies and glazes

20 Nepheline syenite — high sodium feldspar (soda spars melt more easily than calcium or potassium spars); a median-temperature flux

21 Pumice — similar to volcanic ash; used in bodies for thermal shock resistance, and can serve as a flux in glaze

22 Red clay — in this case "Red Art" from Cedar Heights, Ohio; used as an iron-bearing colorant in bodies and glazes; try any local iron-bearing clay

23 Rutile — impure titanium oxide; an orange colorant in clay bodies or glazes; also a matting agent in glazes; it can develop crystals

24 Silica — all ceramic materials contain silica or form silicates; glazes are generally 50 percent silica; it is the backbone "glass former" of the ceramic family

25 Soda ash — a soluble active flux over the entire temperature range

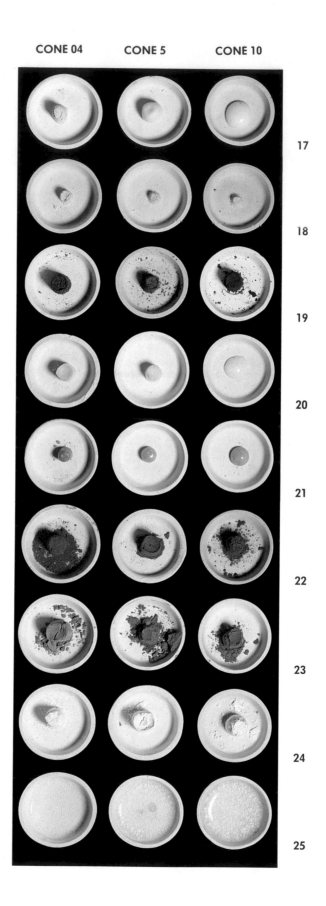

CONE 04   CONE 5   CONE 10

17

18

19

20

21

22

23

24

25

26 Spodumene — lithium compound, more impure than the others, generally with speckles

27 Talc — magnesium silicate (also called soapstone or steatite), used in clay bodies and to make glaze matt; many varied talcs exist worldwide

28 Tin oxide — an opacifier in many glazes, sometimes yielding iridescence; can give a pink cast; a reducing agent and a flux at high fire; also used in chrome-tin pink stains

29 Trap rock (this one is from the Hudson River Palisades) — a common surface clay-shale used as colorant in glaze or alone as glaze at high temperature

30 Trisodium phosphate (TSP, a cleaning compound bought in hardware stores) — a flux that can make glazes bubble like lava when used 50 percent or more and from cone 04 to cone 5

31 Wood ash (hardwood in this case) — used as a flux in ancient glazes; usage currently revived as a glaze material or as a patina in wood firing

32 Zinc oxide — a whitener in glaze; 25 percent or more will grow crystals in glaze if the firing is right

33 Zircopax — one of a family of zirconium silicates, used as opacifiers at all temperatures

34 Alkaline frit (Ferro Number 3134 in this case) — a boro-silicate frit; any frit is a group of oxides taken to melting temperature, crystallized in water, and reground to powder; primarily used in low-fire glazes

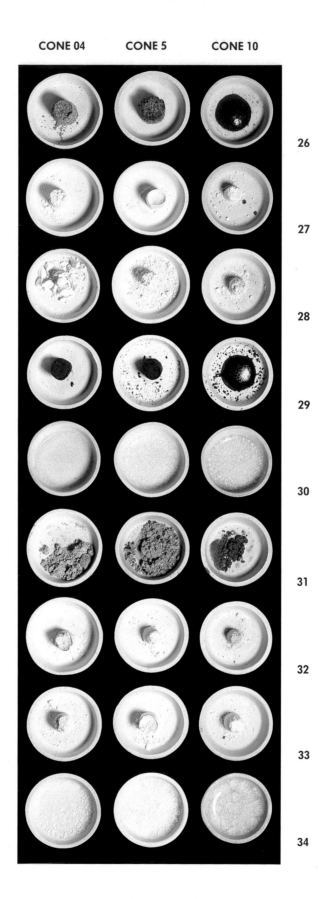

CONE 04   CONE 5   CONE 10

26
27
28
29
30
31
32
33
34

READING THE TEST PHOTOGRAPHS

Let's look first at the fusion button series. Fusion buttons are made by tamping a given material — mixed almost dry with just a drop of water — into a thimble, crucible, or other small cupped volume and inverting it onto a tile. If you make your own tests, use a flat tile made of a white clay body with sides high enough to contain a melt if one occurs. The bottom of each tile should be labeled with the name of the material and the temperature of firing. You have my photographs for reference — fired at the three mean temperatures, cones 04, 5 and 10 — but it is a good idea to make your own fusion button tests of your materials.

TEMPERATURE

Analyze the photographed results of my tests of the fired buttons. Study the three buttons of each material fired at the three temperatures. Then look (vertically) at all the cone 04 buttons to find the few materials that melt at cone 04 and the many that do not. As you see from the fusion button series, only borax, Gerstley borate, lead carbonate, soda ash, and Ferro alkaline frit melt at cone 04. You can make low-fire glazes from these samples by using the low-fire melts on the fusion buttons combined with some of the lesser melts.

The cone 5 series of 50/50 blends (pp. 156–7) gives an idea of what the lower fire cone 04 oxidation colors would look like; the cone 10 series fired in reduction atmosphere (pp. 158–9) gives an idea of what the cone 5 series would be like if fired in reduction. From the cone 5 oxidized series, it is possible to understand something of what the cone 10 series would be like oxidized.

Color is influenced by both temperature and atmosphere; surface, mainly by the fired temperature.

Now look in turn at each of the materials as a fusion button and compare it with the 50/50 blends tests. The fusion buttons will serve as a form of visual dictionary, with the concentrated quantities of raw materials used there showing how large amounts of each substance react at the three mean temperatures. Here is a simple and unique visual basis for developing glazes.

Do the same with cone 5 and cone 10, to familiarize yourself with what melts and what does not at those temperatures. Make your own notes as you analyze the photographs of these tests. Try to see combinations you might want to use. You will see that all glazes melt more readily at high fire than at low fire. More materials and also blends on the 50/50 charts are melting on the cone 10 series than on the cone 5 chart. The cone 10 "glazes" seem more mellow while the cone 5 "glazes" appear to stay on the surface rather than meld with the clay tile. This is the effect of the higher temperature (or it can be the effect of a vitreous body that melds with the glaze). Looking at these charts, along with other material information, will help you to plan glazes visually for any temperature.

Notice that heat-resistant refractory elements, such as silica, EPK china clay, zinc oxide, and a few others, stay dry and unmelted through low to high temperatures except when they are combined with very active fluxes such as borax that melt at low temperature.

QUANTITIES

Look back now at the fusion buttons, which were made with concentrated raw materials; think of the fusion-button results as a guide for using a large percentage of the material in a glaze. The 50/50 blends tests use glaze application quantities of the 34 materials; think of this as a guide for using a smaller amount of the materials in a glaze. Compare the buttons and the tiles.

ATMOSPHERE

Now study the effects of oxidation and reduction on the 50/50 blends of those 34 materials, on the big charts of sample tiles. *Oxidation* atmosphere in a kiln or open fire is one in which all materials receive their full complement of oxygen; *reduction* atmosphere is one of reduced oxygen where not all clay and glaze materials receive their full complement of oxygen atoms. Some colorants change in different atmospheres, and even some surfaces change (see p. 196 for a fuller discussion of oxidation and reduction). Use the cone 5 series for information about oxidized color of the 34 materials and the cone 10 series for information about reduced color, comparing the results. Notice that some materials have distinctive colors, such as barium carbonate and lithium compounds, and some make unusual colors when blended with other materials.

COMBINING MATERIALS

The photographic charts show the 34 individual materials reading on the diagonal from the top left downwards, 1 to 34 (34 is the single tile at the bottom of the diagonal). The numbers of the same materials are written across the top of each chart. The 50/50 blend of each pair of these materials is shown where they intersect. For instance, the number 1 tile in the top row on the left side is Albany slip by itself; the second tile in the top row to its right is a 50/50 blend of tiles 1 + 2 (Albany slip plus barium carbonate); the third tile in the top row is a blend of 1 + 3 (Albany slip plus Barnard clay); and so on, to 1 + 34. The same is true through every line (2 + 3, 2 + 4, 2 + 5, etc., to 2 + 34).

OPACITY

The clay tiles for this series were made with a dark left side (at cone 5, red iron oxide engobe, and at cone 10, an iron-colored clay body) and a white right side (white clay body at cone 5, and white engobe at cone 10) to show relative transparency or opacity of a glaze material over light and dark clay.

LAYERS OF GLAZE

The glazes were dry-mixed. To make the 50/50 blends, the substances were volume-blended with a measured teaspoon of each material in the pair. Water was added to make the proper consistency of glaze application. Tiles were then dipped in the liquid, with the dip starting below the top edge of the tile so that the dark and light clay body was left showing alone at the top. Then the bottom half of the tile was dipped a second time, over the first dip, so that a thin and thick application of each glaze could be seen after firing.

In making your own glaze tests, instead of dipping tiles, you might use a long, wide spatula to pick up the liquid glaze and run it halfway down the tile, which you should hold at an angle. Then overlap that layer with the next load of glaze, letting it coat the second half of the tile; this gives the double-glaze thickness in the middle of the tile.

You might also prefer to weigh the materials instead of volume-blending them, but this will give you a different constant, and so your results will probably look different from mine. If you do blend by volume, be consistent, and always use the same container as a measuring device. Batching by equal volumes is not troublesome here because these are simple glazes; it would be more difficult if there were three or four components. All of the two-member blends shown could in fact be run as three- or four-member blends at varying temperatures and/or atmospheres. Yet without more tests, a great number of the two-member surfaces in the photographs here are usable as shown.

SURFACE EFFECTS

Notice that some materials produce crystalline surface effects (such as zinc, rutile, and dolomite), some cause bubbling (such as TSP at cone 5), some cause crawling (magnesium carbonate), some cause crazing (soda ash), and some do not even bond to the tile. As you look, be aware of the surface changes caused by certain materials; see whether these changes occur at both cone 5 and cone 10, and in the fusion button series of thimbleful as well as in glaze application amounts. Make your own notes from these photographs.

SURFACE ANGLE

The test melts are on flat tiles. Try what suits you on a vertical surface before making absolute judgment; no glaze is the same on flat surfaces as it is on round or tall shapes. Study everything for similarities and differences, and refer back to the fusion buttons to see how sluggish or fluid the material is in a larger quantity.

Working by looking will give you a basic knowledge of glaze ingredients by themselves and in elementary compositions. However, these two-member combinations are not technically glazes; they do not follow the basic tenets of a good glaze. Just as a good clay body needs the plastic material, flux, and filler, so a good glaze needs three components.

50/50 BLENDS OF 34 GLAZE MATERIALS

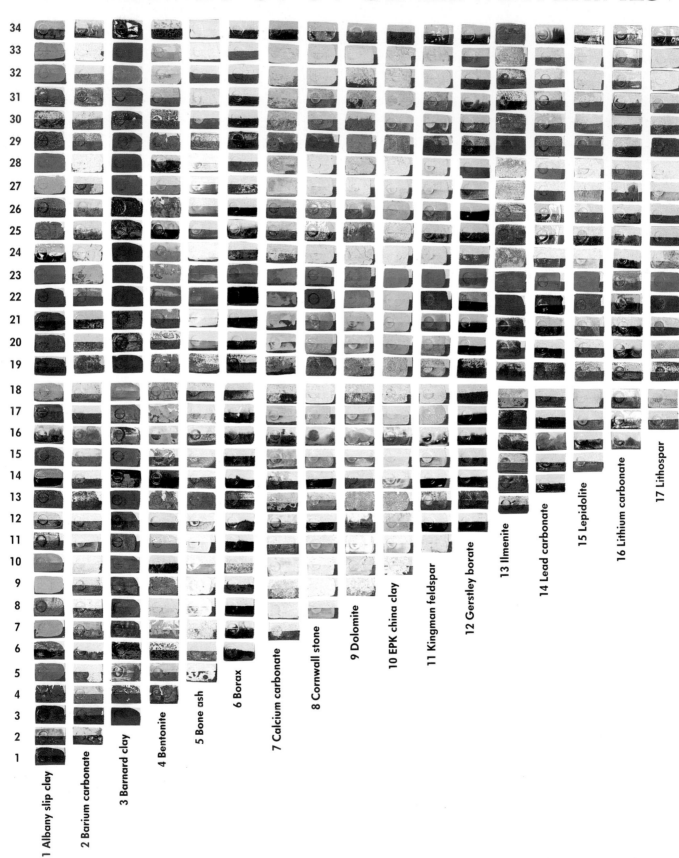

34
33
32
31
30
29
28
27
26
25
24
23
22
21
20
19
18
17
16
15
14
13
12
11
10
9
8
7
6
5
4
3
2
1

1 Albany slip clay
2 Barium carbonate
3 Barnard clay
4 Bentonite
5 Bone ash
6 Borax
7 Calcium carbonate
8 Cornwall stone
9 Dolomite
10 EPK china clay
11 Kingman feldspar
12 Gerstley borate
13 Ilmenite
14 Lead carbonate
15 Lepidolite
16 Lithium carbonate
17 Lithospar
18 Magnesium carbonate

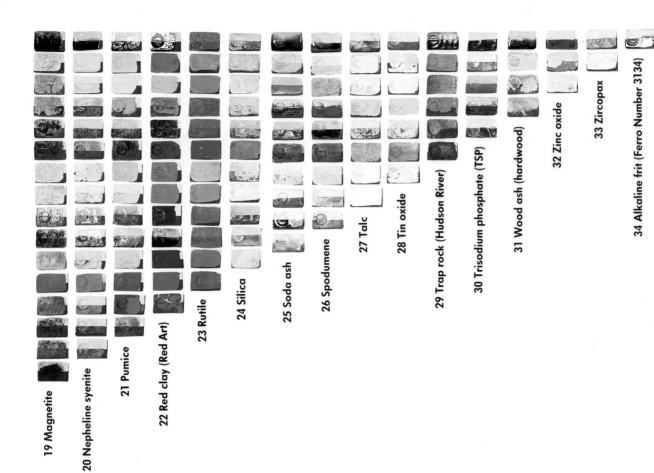

19 Magnetite

20 Nepheline syenite

21 Pumice

22 Red clay (Red Art)

23 Rutile

24 Silica

25 Soda ash

26 Spodumene

27 Talc

28 Tin oxide

29 Trap rock (Hudson River)

30 Trisodium phosphate (TSP)

31 Wood ash (hardwood)

32 Zinc oxide

33 Zircopax

34 Alkaline frit (Ferro Number 3134)

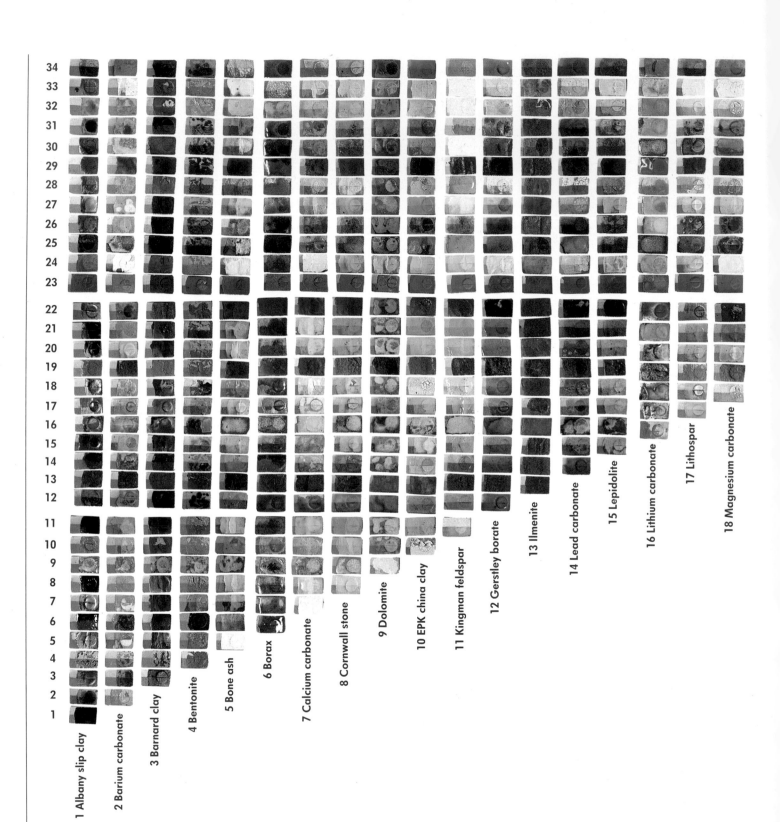

34
33
32
31
30
29
28
27
26
25
24
23

22
21
20
19
18
17
16
15
14
13
12

11
10
9
8
7
6
5
4
3
2
1

1 Albany slip clay
2 Barium carbonate
3 Barnard clay
4 Bentonite
5 Bone ash
6 Borax
7 Calcium carbonate
8 Cornwall stone
9 Dolomite
10 EPK china clay
11 Kingman feldspar
12 Gerstley borate
13 Ilmenite
14 Lead carbonate
15 Lepidolite
16 Lithium carbonate
17 Lithospar
18 Magnesium carbonate

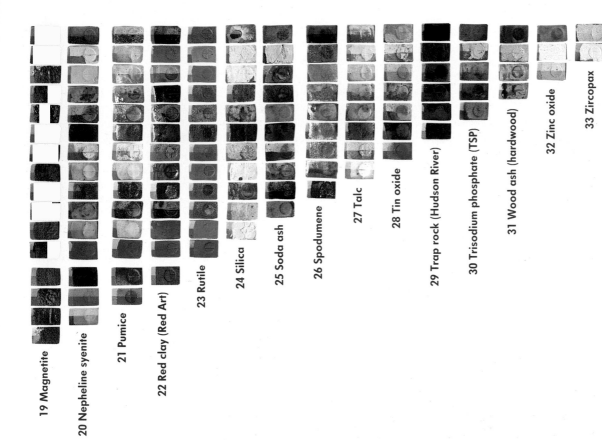

19 Magnetite

20 Nepheline syenite

21 Pumice

22 Red clay (Red Art)

23 Rutile

24 Silica

25 Soda ash

26 Spodumene

27 Talc

28 Tin oxide

29 Trap rock (Hudson River)

30 Trisodium phosphate (TSP)

31 Wood ash (hardwood)

32 Zinc oxide

33 Zircopax

34 Alkaline frit (Ferro Number 3134)

CONE 10 REDUCTION

COMPOUNDING A COMPLETE GLAZE

Some materials melt by themselves, as you can see in the fusion buttons and on the tiles. These melts of the individual materials or their 50/50 blends can be used just the way you see them in the photographs, but a more classic glaze formulation will bring better results.

Bonding agents. Glaze needs a binder — the alumina that we get from clay — to hold it on a surface during firing; most glazes also need about 50 percent silica as the chemical glass-former. Fluxes, or melters, are used to bring down the basically high-temperature (cone 32) melts of clay (or alumina) and silica alone. Complete glazes, then, consist of fluxes (see p. 148), bonding agents, and the glass-former. Glaze batches usually contain 10 percent clay as the binder and 10 percent silica as the glass-former; they may also contain more molecules of alumina and silica from other ingredients in the chemistry of the glaze.

If you want to know the chemistry of the melts on the photographic charts — or the chemistry of the changes of new blends you may invent — while you are visually creating glazes, turn to chapter 8. Follow the steps in calculating from a batch to a formula and a formula to a batch until you think you know the method. Use the batches from the 34-member line-blend photographs, or create your own oxide formulas, to practice the chemical and mathematical calculation of glazes.

To make a more complete glaze from the 50/50 charts, add 10 percent clay for the binder and 10 percent silica to any of the one- or two-member blends that you may choose from the photographs, to improve the glaze quality. (The fired look may not remain exactly as it was on the 50/50 blend tile.) The batch will now read 40 parts "X," 40 parts "Y," 10 parts clay, and 10 parts silica, to keep the glaze on the basis of 100 percent. It is probably easier to weigh it on a gram scale than to volume-blend it.

Suspension agents. You may want to use a material to help suspend the glaze slip. Glaze materials are heavy, and some will tend to drop to the bottom of their container or even harden in it over time. Commercial glazes are suspended with gums and other bonding or wetting agents (which can also make brushing easier). C.M.C. (methocellulose) is a synthetic gum that does not deteriorate and can be used to suspend your own glaze mixes and to aid application.

To make a saturated solution of C.M.C., add the dry gum to water until small amounts of it float on the surface; repeat daily until the gum solution is the consistency desired (possibilities range from liquid to cream to gelatin). The thickest consistency helps if you want engobes to form three-dimensional decoration. Add thin gum solutions instead of plain water to glaze ingredients or stains to make suspension and application easier.

With most glazes, the thickness or thinness of glaze application also creates many visual variations. In fact, the variations of a particular glaze due to application or to clay body, engobe, or stain underneath or over it, is one of the great enigmas in ceramics. One glaze can be handled in many ways with many different results. If your test of a mix selected from the 50/50 charts does not react as it did in the photograph, find out why. Experiment again with the two materials alone and together. The answer may simply lie in the way it was applied.

COMPOSITE GLAZE FLUXES

Another way to experiment with glaze is to begin with a composite material known to melt at a given temperature, such as a frit for low fire or a feldspar for high fire. Often low-fire glazes consist only of frits as the flux, plus 10 percent clay and 10 percent silica; feldspars are often the most important component of high-temperature glaze development. (Please refer to the feldspar test bars on page 148 and the frit fusion buttons on page 163.) Organic ash can also be used in glaze as the basic material, instead of feldspar or frit.

FRITS

Fritting is the process of pre-melting materials together, either in a laboratory crucible in your own kiln, or commercially in big batches. This renders poisonous oxides non-poisonous and soluble oxides insoluble. The molten mass is crystallized (*sintered*) when poured into cold water and reground into fine powder. You can buy frits commercially

manufactured by a number of companies (such as Ferro and Pemco), code-numbered according to their composition, from your ceramic supplier.

As we have seen, glaze melts are hardest to make at low temperature. Pre-melted materials melt better the second time; frits are pre-melted, so their use helps in low-fire glazes. Different frit compositions melt differently, as do glazes of different composition. Most frits will fall into a lead-frit or a boric-frit classification, as those are the active fluxes at low fire (see chapter 8 for chemical formulas of representative frits).

Lead frits give good gloss and active melt, but lead is yellowish in color; alkaline frits are transparent or translucent and colorless. The classic two-frit glaze is 40 percent lead frit, 40 percent alkaline frit, 10 percent clay, and 10 percent silica. Special frits are made for glass and china paint colors, as well as difficult colors such as fire-engine red, lemon yellow, and true orange. These colors burn out at high fire and should be used primarily at low temperatures — up to 2150°F (1177°C). Potters often buy red, yellow, and orange glazes readymade, instead of stocking the frits and the cadmium-selenium oxides that make these colors. Otherwise, it is simple to color frit glazes with regular metallic oxides or manufactured stains.

Frits can be used for high as well as low fire, although some will burn out or *devitrify* (bubble and blister) at temperatures higher than 2000 °F (1093 °C). Experiment, because the results can be interesting.

The frit fusion-button photographs on page 163 show the color variations and the variety of melts of a number of Pemco Corporation frit compositions, fired on red clay tiles in oxidation to cone 04 and to cone 5. All frit manufacturers make similar compositions to which you can refer for substitutions (chapter 8). The composition of a frit or a glaze makes a great deal of difference to color. This is especially evident in the glaze color chart on pages 176–7, which shows the effects of different Ferro frits on a variety of colorants.

FELDSPARS

Feldspars can be considered as nature's frits. Experiment with them as the basis for a high-fire glaze: spar 80 percent plus 10 percent clay and 10 percent silica. Anticipate the results by looking at the three types of feldspars — sodium, potassium, and calcium, which translate to the materials nepheline syenite, G–200, and Cornwall stone respectively — as they appear in the fusion button tests and the single ingredient tiles (tiles numbers 20, 11, and 8), and the feldspar bar tests on page 148. The composition of the feldspar makes a difference to the various colorants that are added to the glaze, whether at low or high fire. The earliest Chinese glazes were probably feldspathic. Eventually, more materials were added to vary the surface as well as the color.

ORGANIC ASH

Organic ash is one of the world's oldest glaze materials. It was probably discovered thousands of years ago when the first kilns were fired with wood. Wood ash that lands on unglazed clayworks during a fire can cause a sheen or a shine, depending on the amount of wood used, the temperature, and the length of firing time. The ash patina formed on unglazed wares in a kiln is a random glaze. More control can be assumed by mixing ash with water and applying it like glaze, or by laying the greenware in wood ashes.

Wood ash glaze. Wood ash can be used as the basic material in glaze. Look at the wood ash tile, number 31 on the 34-material tests, and the 50/50 blends of wood ash with all the other materials. Different wood ashes make different surfaces at different temperatures; of course, you should experiment.

Wood ashes contain alkali and silica and have most of the properties necessary to make a glaze, but not the requisite binder, clay. Begin your ash tests with a 50/50 wood ash and clay mix for firing at cone 5 to cone 10; then change to 75/25, and 25/75. Try varying the kind of clay to vary the color of the glaze.

Shoji Hamada was the last Japanese potter to fire all bisque, glaze, enamel, and salt kilns with wood, and use the resulting ash to make more glaze. Most traditional potters in Japan and elsewhere use oil or gas for part of the firing, and wood at the end. Wood is too expensive in many countries to be a viable fuel or a base ingredient in glaze, but wood firing is a practice now being revived with gusto by many clay artists, some on a grand scale.

Other organic ash glazes. Ash from any organic material can be used for glaze. The Bizen pottery village in Japan is famous for laying and wrapping rice stalks, and other straws, on raw pots to give a shiny patina and pattern after firing. Organic materials work as glazes because of their chemical composition and also because of the chemistry of their habitat. In Iran, a turquoise glaze is made from a particular cactus that grows on copper-ore deposits.

Porcelain jar with apple-tree ash glaze by Tom Coleman. This typical appearance of ash glazes — broken, runny, variegated surface — is not the only possible result. Wood ash glazes can be transparent or opaque white, depending on the ash and the glaze composition. Perhaps the characteristic ash look is the most interesting.

ORGANIC MATERIALS FOR GLAZES

Ashes of plant materials mixed with water should be tested at several temperatures by themselves (see illustration) and then tried out in the ratios 50/50, 40/60, and so forth, with single glaze components or with glaze mixtures. Try all plant ashes with various clays — red ones, china clays, ball clays, fire clays, in 50/50 blends and other ratios. Ashes are difficult to keep in suspension in water so clay additions help, as will bentonite, commercial suspension agents, or Epsom salts.

Test organic materials, such as seaweeds or flowers, raw as well as burned. All ash burns into different colors; Hamada tried to use only the white ash, not the black, from burning red pine. His white glaze, called "nuka," was made from smoldering rice husks in a particular manner, from one end of a mound to the other. Washed ash is different from unwashed ash, as the impurities are lost if the ash is slaked in water. Most clayworkers prefer unwashed ash for its impurities, but impurities mean lack of control. Ash glazes are thought to have a characteristic fluidity, greenish color, and textured surface, but these factors depend on what is mixed with the ash; ash glazes can be colorless and non-fluid.

The organic tests I have made for the photographs show various plants available in southern California, tested raw and burned by themselves, rather than with glaze ingredient mixtures. The tiles were made of iron-bearing clay with a diagonal of white engobe. Each raw plant has been tested alone, laid on the tile, and fired only at cone 10. Then the ash of each plant was mixed with water, applied to a tile, and fired in oxidation and reduction at both cone 5 and cone 10 (not much happens with ash alone at cone 04). The many varieties of weeds found in fresh or salt water make some of the most interesting patterns wrapped raw on clay pieces or used ashed as glaze ingredients. Analyze the photographs of my tests, and try your own local plants.

In chapter 5, you will find discussion of firing with organic and inorganic materials to develop patinas, colors, and textures on clayworks.

(See also the wood ash results on pp. 153, 157, and 159.)

	Raw plant Cone 10 Oxidation	Ashes and water Cone 5 Oxidation	Ashes and water Cone 5 Reduction	Ashes and water Cone 10 Oxidation	Ashes and water Cone 10 Reduction
Charcoal					
Eucalyptus					
Marigold					
Pine needle					
Rose					
Sea grass					
Bamboo					
Bougain-villaea					
Bird of Paradise					
Sea kelp					
Sea lettuce					
Soft wood ash (sawdust)					
Straw					

FUSION BUTTONS OF FRITS

Use frits as beginning points for simple glazes; test them with colorants

LEADLESS FRITS

PEMCO Leadless Frits, Cone 04, Cone 5 Oxidation

1 P 25: high soda, high boric oxide, medium alumina
2 P 54: high calcium, boric oxide, no alumina
3 P 64: barium, zinc, boric oxide, low alumina
4 P 311: high calcium, boric oxide, alumina
5 P 609: lithium, calcium, magnesia, strontium, boric oxide, low alumina
6 P 626: soda, high barium, boric oxide, alumina
7 P 760: cadmium, potassium, soda, high boric oxide, alumina
8 P 786: high calcium, strontium, boric oxide, low alumina
9 P 830: high soda, calcium, boric oxide, no alumina
10 P 926: high calcium, high boric oxide, medium soda, low alumina
11 P 930: high strontium, high boric oxide, low alumina, zirconia

LEAD FRITS

PEMCO Lead Frits, Cone 05, Cone 5 Oxidation

1 Pb 41: high lead, zinc, boric oxide, no alumina
2 Pb 63: lead, calcium, soda, boric oxide, low alumina, zirconia
3 Pb 83: lead, zinc, high boric oxide, no alumina
4 Pb 349: high calcium, lead, boric oxide, low alumina
5 Pb 716: high lead, calcium, no boric oxide, no alumina
6 Pb 723: high lead, no boric oxide, low alumina
7 Pb 740: high lead, high zinc, no boric oxide, low alumina
8 Pb 742: lead, calcium, soda, high boric oxide, low alumina
9 Pb1038: high lead, high zinc, low boric oxide, low alumina
10 Pb1307: lead, zinc, calcium, low boric oxide, low alumina
11 Pb1K75: lead, calcium, high boric oxide, low alumina

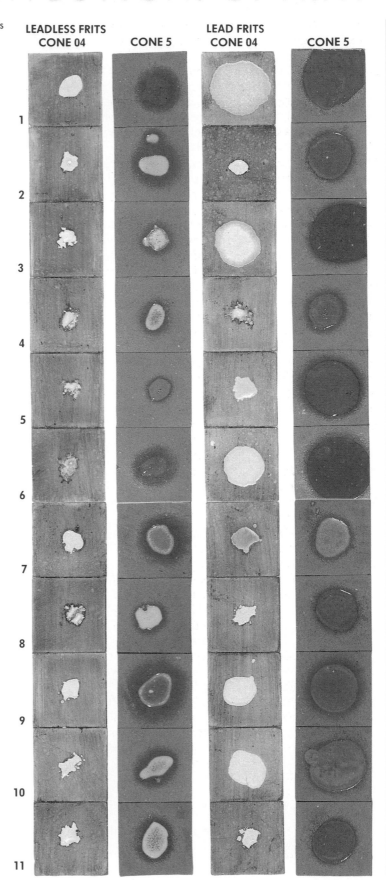

| | LEADLESS FRITS CONE 04 | CONE 5 | LEAD FRITS CONE 04 | CONE 5 |

GARBAGE GLAZES

Interest in firing organic materials, found objects, and grocery and drugstore items probably stems from artistic interest in prospecting, finding, and testing natural materials, but also from the heritage of ancient cultures and folk art, which traditionally used what was at hand.

Saggar firing and *pit firing* prompt the use of anything in and around the ware. Mounds of food, either garbage waste or whole, new foods, piled on and around pieces, will give varying patinas to the ware, which vary further according to temperature. Cactus, plant materials in various stages of flowering, pine needles, roots, and seaweed in all its forms are particularly interesting raw, especially if they have grown somewhere near ore deposits.

Drugstores and grocery stores also yield bonanzas. Read labels to find substances containing minerals with which glazes are associated, but try unfamiliar ones, too.

Things such as potassium, sodium, magnesium, calcium, dolomite, zinc, copper, pumice, and kaolin are also found as chlorides, nitrates, phosphates, carbonates, and sulfates in many products. Try them alone and in combination; boil crystals in water to make a solution. Try each one over and under glazes, and even in glazes, remembering that they are not concentrated 100 percent minerals like regular glaze ingredients are.

In the illustration below, various found materials were fired to 1900°F (1038°C). Notice that something happened to everything in the fire; sometimes only patina was left, and some substances changed the coloration of the buff stoneware on which they were placed. A higher-temperature fire would have made most of the materials volatile, leaving only glistening marks or pattern patinas on the clay.

Raw found materials include fruit, string, wire, nuts and bolts, copper pennies, screen, weeds, nails, glass bottle, and broken glass

Fired found materials, cone 04 (1922°F, 1050°C)

COLORS

Colorants are always additions to any clay, engobe, or glaze batch. We saw how to add color to engobes and clay bodies at the beginning of this chapter; now we are concerned with how to color glazes. Simply make the glaze correct in every way — look, viscosity, fit (see p. 114) — and then add colorants to the 100 percent batch.

All batches of anything in ceramics are colored with the same coloring agents, which are natural metallic oxides from the earth and the manufactured stains made from these oxides, with the addition of other chemicals that change the color of the basic metal oxides.

DEVELOPING A PERSONAL PALETTE

Clayworkers need to develop a color palette for the one or more temperatures they use. This must be done with glaze test pieces, but it is a more complex task with manufactured glaze preparations than with natural colorants, for the ingredients are published by only a few companies. All commercial preparations and manufactured stains are artificially colored to look similar to the color they will fire. The natural metallic oxides from which they are made either have no color or are a different color raw. All must be tried in the user's own firing situation.

Make tests at the proper temperature and atmosphere on the clay body to be used; then try variations. Commercial underglazes can be mixed successfully.

METALLIC OXIDES

Natural metallic oxides that withstand kiln temperatures are few, so the color palette is limited.

Some metallic oxides are available as metals with different oxygen valences, such as red iron oxide — Fe_2O_3 and Fe_3O_4 — and black iron oxide — FeO.

Some metallic oxide molecules come to us in the form of carbonates; for example, manganese carbonate is $MnCO_3$ as opposed to the dioxide, MnO_2, and copper oxide is CuO as opposed to the carbonate, $CuCO_3$. Carbonates are weaker in color than oxides because they have an added atom of carbon and three atoms of oxygen per atom of metal. (Carbonates accordingly cost less, usually.) You can use more of the carbonate or less of the oxide to equal the same color. You can use the oxide because you want the color stronger, or the carbonate because you want the color weaker.

Salts of the metals, such as chlorides, sulfates, and nitrates, can also be used as colorants. These are even weaker forms of the metals because of the higher oxygen valence and the amount of acid per atom of the metal — for instance, $FeSO_4$ is the molecular formula of iron sulfate. Salts are primarily used as fuming agents, luster producers, or washes on top of or under glazes.

The percentage of colors for the oxides overleaf are for glazes. (To color engobes, start by multiplying these figures by 3; go up or down from these results after testing.)

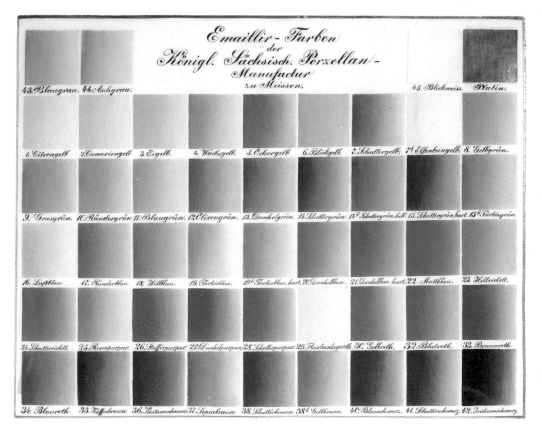

17th-century Meissen palette: a factory's method of testing china paint color variation by brushing light to dark and, I assume, by varying the amount and type of flux added to the color

Chrome. 1 to 2 percent chrome oxide, Cr_2O_3, is enough; use no more than 5 percent. Color is unaffected by oxidation or reduction, but if zinc is present in any glaze the oxide will change from forest green to pink-brown or coral. All chrome green percentages of chrome stains are more yellow in the presence of lead, darker in an alkaline glaze. Chrome and tin with lead combinations yield a variety of pink and red glaze stains (many of which are stable at high fire) and a variety of oranges and reds in glazes containing high lead and very low alumina and silica if fired at low temperature — around cone 010. Lead chromate gives varieties of yellow-oranges and yellow-greens. Chrome oxide is refractory, never a flux.

Copper. There are three copper colorants: black copper oxide, CuO, is the most frequently used; red copper oxide, Cu_2O, is reduced already; the third is copper carbonate, $CuCO_3$. Use a 3 to 6 percent average; larger amounts produce metallic green-black, sometimes called gun-metal. The most common colors are grass green in lead-based glazes, and turquoise in alkaline glaze with no lead or zinc. In reduction atmosphere, copper turns red, used from $1/2$ to 2 percent in an alkaline glaze base (i.e. a high soda and boric oxide base). Somewhat volatile over cone 04, copper may "jump" around and land on other glazes during firing.

Cobalt. Its two forms are black cobalt oxide, Co_3O_4, and cobalt carbonate, $CoCO_3$. The strongest of the colorants, $1/2$ to 1 percent gives medium blue, 2 to 4 percent midnight blue. Zinc intensifies cobalt, magnesia makes it purple, boric oxide influences it toward red. It is good over the entire temperature range but can be a flux in large amounts.

Ilmenite. An iron-titanium compound, $FeO-TiO_2$, it comes powdered or in granular form. Use 1 to 6 percent powder for warm tans and browns in glaze or as clay body colorant. Use the grains for warm brown speckles in glaze, engobe, or clay body; generally 10 percent is enough, and too much may cause runny streaks.

Iron. As mentioned above, there are two forms: red iron oxide, Fe_2O_3, and black iron oxide, Fe_3O_4. 2 to 4 percent produces amber, 5 to 8 percent rusty red-brown, 8 to 15 percent dark brown in oxidation and *tenmoku* (the rich reddish brown-black famous from Chinese and Japanese glazes) in reduction. Alkalis and potash intensify rust-red shades, calcium fades and yellows the color, zinc makes it browner. In reduction atmosphere, $1/2$ to 1 percent yields celadon green, 4 percent olive green. Use as medium flux in large amounts; it is good over the entire temperature range. (Both synthetic and natural iron oxides are sold; try all forms that your dealer supplies.)

Manganese. Manganese dioxide, MnO_2, and manganese carbonate, $MnCO_3$, can be used from 2 to 10 percent in either oxidation or reduction. Large amounts are needed to show at low fire and smaller amounts at high fire; it is a decided flux at high fire (cone 10). Manganese used as a "stain" (mixed with water) by itself, thick, at high temperature (cone 10) produces gold-metallics, but runs fiercely; try adding clay or another refractory to retard this. The natural color is claret brown; purples are brought out in a boric oxide glaze high in soda; zinc has no effect. If manganese is not well mixed, specks result; it can be bought crude and granular to give definite, intentional specks. Both iron and manganese are good, inexpensive ways to color glazes and clay bodies.

Nickel. Nickel oxide comes in black (Ni_2O_3) and green (NiO). $1/2$ to 2 percent is usually enough to use. Not a very pleasant gray — gray-green or blue-gray — by itself, it produces nice, muted colors when used with other coloring oxides. It can produce blues in glaze and a peculiar "nickel-blue" with zinc in a high soda glaze; a good variant is to run it with rutile. It is refractory, not a flux. Chrome and nickel are not used as often as other oxides as glaze or engobe colorants, but they are both worth experimentation.

Praseodymium. Not generally used in the oxide form, PrO_2, this relatively new stain made from the oxide is used for yellows and oranges in 10 to 15 percent amounts. It is apparently stable over the entire temperature range and in oxidation and reduction atmospheres.

Rutile. Pure titanium dioxide, TiO_2, produces stark whites at 5 to 10 percent. Rutile — impure titanium (also TiO_2) — at 10 to 15 percent yields yellow-orange to tan-orange in most glazes over the entire range; it tends to change to gray in excessive reduction. Rutiles vary around the world; some, "cleaner" than others, give better colors. They opacify, have a matt surface, and contribute to the development of elongated crystals in glaze or when used as a stain over a glaze.

Tin. Tin oxide (also called stannic oxide), SnO_2, was discovered by the Persians about 1,000 years ago. It is a popular oxide for developing a creamy white, despite its expense, and is used especially at low temperature. Tin can develop a pink tinge in some glazes, and at times a lustrous finish; it is used in chrome-tin pink stains. 5 to 10 percent is sufficient to opacify; too much tin causes crawling and pinholes. Tin oxide at 1 percent is a useful reducing addition at high temperature, where it also acts as a flux rather than as a whitener.

Vanadium. Before the atomic age, uranium oxide, U_3O_8, gave us a range of reds, yellows, and oranges. It is currently not possible to use any metallic oxide alone for yellow, except small amounts of iron oxide for amber or iron-yellows. Vanadium pentoxide, V_2O_5, bought as a stain, gives yellow-to-mustard colors in 10 to 15 percent amounts over the entire range; it usually goes gray in reduction.

Zirconium. Zirconium oxide, ZrO_2, is used in zircon-silica combinations with trade names such as zircopax, ultrox, and opax. 10 to 15 percent creates the color white. Zirconium opacifies, and stays white in reduction.

MANUFACTURED STAINS

Stains are manufactured colorants made from the basic oxide colorants combined with other elements that stabilize the metals or broaden their color range. They are usually used in higher percentage than metallic oxides because their added ingredients reduce the proportion of colorant.

Stains mixed with water are used for both underglaze and overglaze decoration. They can be used alone, or be added to basic batches of engobes and glazes. Stains are usually bought in pound weights or more, but can be purchased in fractions of a pound. The chemical composition of the stain is sometimes on the label of the bag. If it is not, write to the company — you need the chemical information to use the stain in a proper glaze base. It may be preferable to buy stains directly from manufacturers such as Mason, Pemco, Ferro, Drakenfeld, Harshaw, Blythe, and O. Hommel in the U.S., the U.K., and Europe. The addresses of these companies are listed in the materials issue of the *American Ceramic Society Journal,* or *Ceramics Monthly* magazine, which has international circulation, or the *Source Book,* published by Craft Report, Seattle, Washington, or other ceramic periodicals in other countries (see chapter 8).

The percentages of stains below are calculated for glazes. (Multiply by two to three times or more for coloring bodies and engobes.)

Blue stains

Cobalt types 1 to 2%

Alumina pale blues 8 to 10%

Chrome-cobalt blue-greens 2 to 4%

Vanadium turquoise 8 to 10%

Copper blues 4 to 6%

Green stains

Victoria greens 10% used in zinc-free base with zircopax

Chrome olive-greens 2 to 4% in zinc-free glaze (zinc makes chrome brownish)

Vanadium copper greens 4 to 12%

Yellow stains

Naples yellow, antimony 10%, only at low fire; best in lead and zinc base

Lead chromate yellows 10%, only below cone 5

Tin-vanadium lemons, mustards 8 to 10%; gray, not yellow, in reduction

Praseodymium yellows, oranges 4 to 12%, stable to cone 10

Vanadium-zirconium yellows 10%, stable to cone 10, best in low boric glaze

Maroon stains

Chrome-tin maroons and blue-pinks 10%, use in zinc-free base with tin or zirconium opacifier; many are stable at high fire

Manganese maroons and pinks 10%, stable at high fire to cone 12

Peach stains

Chrome-tin pinks 10 to 12%, zinc-free glaze; use tin opacifier

Manganese pinks, violets 2 to 10%, stable to high fire

Chrome-alumina pinks 10 to 12%, best in high-zinc glazes

Brown stains

Iron red-browns 2 to 4% for amber, 10% for dark brown, good in any base glaze; these stains will not promote a tenmoku-style glaze, but give a leather-brown color

Chrome, alumina, zinc tans 5 to 10%; zinc in base improves color

Black stains

Iron blacks 2 to 10%, brownish-black

Cobalt blacks 2 to 5%, blue-black

Cobalt-chrome blacks 2 to 5%, greenish-black

Cobalt-free blacks 2 to 10%, usually gray-black

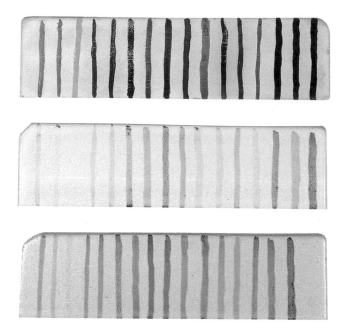

Stains can assume different looks with different glazes. The top tile shows various stains mixed with water, brushed over an opaque white glaze. On the middle tile the same stains were brushed on bisque, and covered with the opaque white glaze. The bottom tile shows the same stains brushed on bisque and covered with a matt glaze. All the tiles were fired at cone 10 oxidation.

Cadmium red and yellow stains

Cadmium-selenium 10 percent, various reds, yellows, oranges, with special frits; most artists buy these as glazes in bulk, dry or wet, from companies producing prepared glazes; best at low temperature, some are stable to cone 5; they must be fully oxidized

LOW-FIRE ENAMELS

These are not stains or china paints but very low-fire "enamels," made in your studio or commercially available. (Enamel is a term for low-fire glazes used on metals; the term applies to glazes that fire very much below the normal glaze-firing temperatures, and to glass colors.) Made for use on metals such as copper or silver, they consist of stains or oxide plus flux, and have a composition somewhat like glaze. Their colors are brilliant, and they are useful alone or on glazed claywares at temperatures from 1300 °F (704 °C) to 1900 °F (1038 °C); above cone 04 most of them burn out. As an alternative to buying them ready-made, you can make your own enamels by using a glass frit as flux plus a metallic oxide or a stain and grinding the mixture very fine.

The procedure for using low-fire colored glazes or low-fire stains or enamels on porcelain or stoneware is to bisque the body at high temperature and glaze at low fire. Alternatively, use a vitreous high-fired piece that is already glazed, apply the low-fire enamel or glaze, and fire the piece again at the low maturing temperature for what you are using — luster, china paint, enamel, or low-fire glaze.

Rose medallion overglaze enameled tea set — China's exhibit at the Chicago World Fair, 1893

SUMMARY OF USES FOR COLORANTS

- Mixed in engobes for color
- Mixed in clay bodies for color
- Mixed in glazes for color
- In serigraph and decal work over glaze
- Using photo emulsion technique
- Making glaze stain crayons, chalks, and pencils
- Decorating slumped glass at 1300 °F (704 °C), used with glass frits
- Brushed or sponged over bisque to highlight a texture; with or without glaze
- Sprinkled dry on clay and pressed in; used on a slab roller and rolled in
- Under and over glaze
- Making colored grogs to be added to clay, engobe, or glaze

SUGGESTIONS FOR CHANGING COLORED GLAZES

- Fire copper oxide in small amounts — ½ to 1 percent — in clear base glazes in reduction for reds, at any temperature
- Fire iron oxide in large amounts — 10 to 15 percent — in clear base glazes in reduction for tenmokus, at any temperature
- Fire iron oxide in small amounts — ½ to 2 percent for celadon colors in clear base glazes in reduction, at any temperature
- Add 10 to 15 percent rutile to any colored glaze for crystals
- Try ½ percent chrome oxide with all stains for gray glaze colors
- Add manganese dioxide from 4 to 10 percent to various glaze bases for violets and purples
- Use stains in 20 to 50 percent amounts as additions to color engobes
- Use nickel oxide at ½ to 1 percent with any other colorant for glaze gradation
- Mix 5 to 10 percent rutile with other colorants; try other two-member oxide or stain combinations to color glazes
- For specks in glaze, do not stir stains or oxides much and do not screen them

CERAMIC COLORING IMPLEMENTS

Some artists make their own drawing and coloring implements to mark bisque or dry clay, and use under or over glaze. Water-color-type kits, crayons, pencils, chalks, tubes, and spray cans can also be bought readymade from ceramic suppliers. These ceramic pigment tools are made from the metallic oxides and manufactured stain colorants discussed above. Frequently, ceramic drawings and coloring treatments made from these implements are left unglazed; glazes can also be applied under or over the "tools."

If you want to make your own tools, begin with a basic white clay body to which colorants will be added and from which the tools will be formed. Jeanne Otis uses the basic electrical porcelain with added ingredients.

50% ball clay
25% feldspar
25% silica
Plus:
3% macaloid plasticizer
1% sodium silicate for hardener
Coloring oxides and stains in amounts up to 15%

Make pencils by putting the colored plastic clay body into a ceramic extruding or a decorating clay gun (from your ceramic supplier). Extrude from different orifices for variable widths and cut into lengths; fire at 1500 °F (815 °C) to 1700 °F (927 °C) — enough to give strength but still allow marking quality.

Make chalks by hand-forming the colored clay body into chunks comfortable to hold, and fire at 1500 °F (815 °C) to 1700 °F (927 °C).

Make crayons by adding wax resist to the colored clay bodies without water; let them air-dry before use (do not fire them).

Colored pencils made by Jeanne Otis from colored porcelain, extruded, and fired low; for drawing on dried clay or bisque

STAINS FOR COLORING IMPLEMENTS

CONE 8 OXIDATION

Top row, left to right:
Mason 6134 Red Brown, 5%;
Mason 6190 Deep Brown, 5%;
Mason 6274 Nickel Silicate, 5%;
Pemco GS (glaze stain) 815 Black,
5%; Mason 6500 Sage Gray, 5%

Row 2, left to right:
Pemco GS 44 Blue, 5%; Mason
6388 Mazarine, 4%; Mason
6371 Dark Teal, 3%; Mason
6266 Peacock, 3%; Pemco GS
100 Blue Green, 7%

Row 3, left to right:
Mason 6242 Bermuda Blue
Green, 5%; Harshaw S 500 Blue,
10%; Mason 6363 Sky Blue, 5%;
Mason 6302 Cadet Blue, 5%;
Mason 6319 Lavender, 10%

Row 4, left to right:
Ferro C 440 Yellow, 10%; Mason
386 Titanium Yellow, 10%;
Mason 386 Titanium Yellow, 7%
plus Mason 6020 Pink, 7%;
Harshaw F 444 Pink, 10%;
Mason 6020 Pink, 10%

Row 5, left to right:
Harshaw G 5100 Yellow, 10%;
Mason 6236 Chartreuse, 10%;
Mason 6280 Avocado Green,
10%; Mason 6201 Celadon, 5%;
Mason 6202 Florentine Green,
5%

Mason Color and Chemical Company, Pemco, and Harshaw stains used in the photographs of colored bodies
and pencils

COLOR BLENDS

Color variations in glaze can be tested and studied in several ways.

1 50/50 LINE BLENDS

Basic percentages of coloring oxides or stains (as discussed above, pages 165–8) can be added to a base glaze which can then be used as a 100 percent member of a line blend. Each member will be blended 50/50 with each other member, as in the 34-member blends of all the raw glaze materials on pages 156–9. The reason to run a line blend test is to show all the 50/50 possibilities of the 100 percent members, no matter how many members are used.

In my photographs of this type of test a base glaze plus six colorants is tested at three different temperatures. When a small number — such as six — 100 percent members will suffice; they can be represented as the top "line" of an inverted stair-step pattern. With six colorants, for instance, they would be the tiles numbered 1, 2, 3, 4, 5, 6 across the top line of the diagram. The 50/50 blends among them begin stair-steps down on the next row. Row two is blends of glaze-plus-color of tile number 1 with numbers 2, 3, 4, 5, and 6 (1+2, 1+3, 1+4, 1+5, 1+6); the third row down blends colorant tile number 2 with 3, 4, 5, and 6 (2+3, 2+4, 2+5, 2+6); the fourth row down blends tile number 3 with numbers 4, 5, and 6 (3+4, 3+5, 3+6). The fifth row blends tile number 4 with tiles 5 and 6 (4+5, 4+6) and the sixth row shows the only remaining combination possible, 5+6.

To make a 50/50 blend of six 100 percent members, use six tiles — bisqued tiles if you bisque fire, raw tiles if you once-fire. Mark their backs with the numbers 1, 2, 3, 4, 5, and 6 by scratching or by brushing them on with engobe or stain. Place the tiles in a horizontal line on the table to indicate six original members — the base glaze batch plus colorant. Use six different colors in average percentages, or six different percentages of the same colorant, or whatever.

Dry-mixing. Begin mixing the glazes for this test by weighing out a 600 gram dry batch of your chosen base glaze, and mix it thoroughly. Divide the dry mixture into 100 gram amounts, and place each 100 grams in one of six marked containers. Then add to each container the weighed percentages of colorants you have chosen, such as 5 grams for 5 percent added colorant. Mix the color thoroughly with the dry batch and screen if necessary, or if you normally screen your glazes.

What I call the 100 percent top members of the diagram are in fact more than 100 percent — they are actually 100 parts glaze batch plus the colorant. The exception is the base batch, which you may have chosen to run in the blend with no added colorant.

Application. To put the glaze on tile number 1, take one teaspoon of dry colored glaze from container number 1, put it on a saucer, add water until you reach glaze consistency, and then dip the face of the tile into this glaze. Rinse the plate thoroughly. Put one teaspoon from container number 2 on the dish, add water, blend, and dip tile number 2 into the new glaze, rinse, and continue until all six marked tiles have been dipped.

50/50 blending. The second row, stair-stepping down, will include four tiles to be marked on the back: 1+2, 1+3, 1+4, 1+5, for the 50/50 blends with tile number 1. To coat test-tile 1+2, place a teaspoon from container number 1 and a teaspoon from container number 2 on the saucer and dry mix. Add water to glaze consistency; dip the tile face down or apply the glaze to the tile with a spatula. Do the same with a teaspoon from container number 1 and a teaspoon from container number 3 dry-mixed on the plate: add water, and dip or spatula the glaze onto tile 1+3; and so on.

(The use of teaspoons indicates volume blending. You will have weighed the top members of this test — glaze batch plus colorant — whereas you will have been using teaspoons to make the 50/50 blends. This is adequate, but you can be a little more particular by weighing your 50/50s, dry, on the gram scale — say 5 or 10 grams of each member, depending on the size of your tile. Always use the same scale or measuring device throughout the tests.)

The third row will begin with tile 2+3, that is, a teaspoon or weighed amount from container number 2 and a teaspoon or weighed amount from container number 3; then 50/50 blends of 2+4, 2+5, 2+6. Continue this way until you reach the bottom row, which in our example is a half-and-half blend of top members 5 and 6.

Firing. Fire the tests at the appropriate temperature for the glaze that was used as the base batch, or make several sets and fire in both oxidation and reduction, or try several temperatures. Each glaze has some variation; the only way you find what it is and how it looks at different temperatures is to try it. Make a cone pack and set it beside each test in the kiln to know exactly what the cone reads at the test spot.

Using larger quantities. If you choose one of your test results to use in a larger quantity on claywork, decide first how much glaze to make. Remember that a U.S. pint is 1 lb, 1 lb is 454 g, and a pint is 16 oz of fluid. (A U.K. pint is 1¼ lb, or 567 g – 20 oz of fluid.) When you have decided the number of base grams to weigh, take half the percentage of color in each of the two top members (100 parts glaze batch plus X percent colorant) in your blend, multiply each by the total number of grams in your base batch, weigh, and add to the base. Mix dry, add water, and apply. Transposing a small test to a gallon of glaze has its own variables; works glazed from a large batch and the test tile seldom look exactly alike.

Color variation. Look at the six-member line-blend glaze-plus-color test on pages 174–5, which I have made and photographed to indicate color variations at the three mean temperatures, cone 04, 5, and 10, in both oxidation and reduction atmospheres. Notice the radical differences in some of the colors at oxidation and reduction. The copper tile is some shade of red in reduction at each temperature. The color additions to the base batch were constant at all temperatures; but notice that cobalt varies with the composition of the glaze and yields more purples in the cone 10 series, where the base glaze is high in magnesium. (The base glazes had to vary in this series due to the requirements of the three mean temperatures, but were constant for both the oxidation and reduction firings at each temperature.) In the oxidation series, notice the effect on color of barium in the cone 04 glaze, zinc in the cone 5 mixture, and magnesium from talc and dolomite at cone 10. These chemicals act particularly on copper, iron, and cobalt. Make your own notes from the visual examples and use them as a basis for further tests.

In my example, the top members — tiles 1, 2, 3, 4, 5, and 6 — are common metallic oxides added in average percentages to the base glazes; but they could have been base glaze stains or other metallic oxides or other percentages. If you want to test a variety of blues, for instance, blend different percentages of cobalt, or different percentages of cobalt and copper, or cobalt and chrome, or cobalt and manganese, or make a longer line of top members to include some of each.

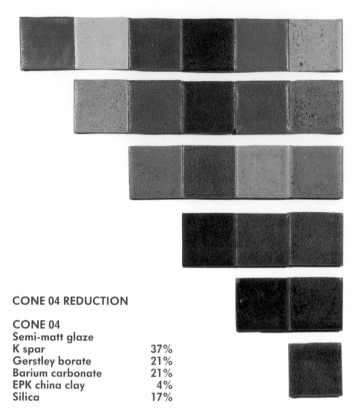

CONE 04 REDUCTION

CONE 04
Semi-matt glaze

K spar	37%
Gerstley borate	21%
Barium carbonate	21%
EPK china clay	4%
Silica	17%

1	2	3	4	5	6
	1 + 2	1 + 3	1 + 4	1 + 5	1 + 6
		2 + 3	2 + 4	2 + 5	2 + 6
			3 + 4	3 + 5	3 + 6
				4 + 5	4 + 6
					5 + 6

Line blend top members
1 **Red iron oxide** 4%
2 **Rutile** 6%
3 **Manganese carbonate** 3%
4 **Copper oxide** 3%
5 **Cobalt carbonate** ½%
6 **Nickel oxide** 3%

CONE 04 OXIDATION

CONE 5 REDUCTION

CONE 5
Matt glaze
K spar	51.6%
Whiting	18.8%
Zinc oxide	8.6%
EPK china clay	15.4%
Silica	5.6%

CONE 10 REDUCTION

CONE 10
Matt glaze
G–200 feldspar	27.0%
Gerstley borate	12.0%
Dolomite	8.8%
Talc	19.5%
Tennessee ball clay	7.5%
Silica	25.2%

CONE 5 OXIDATION

CONE 10 OXIDATION

2 CHANGING COLOR PERCENTAGES

Study this variable by changing oxide or stain percentages in a base glaze formula while keeping the base glaze elements constant, as shown in the examples here. In this series, red iron oxide, black nickel oxide, vanadium stain, copper carbonate, rutile, cobalt carbonate, and manganese dioxide have been added to a base glaze in varying percentages and fired in oxidation to cone 5. Two base matt glazes were used, both highly alkaline, but the glaze marked "H" was calculated to give more warmth to the colors and the glaze marked "A" to give brilliance to the blues and purples. Two clay bodies — one porcelain, one high in iron — are used to show color over a dark and light ground.

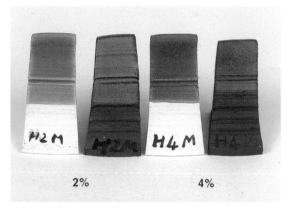

2%   4%

Manganese dioxide

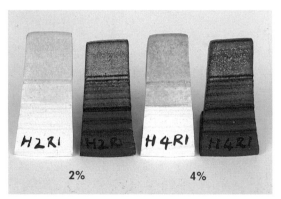

2%   4%

Red iron oxide

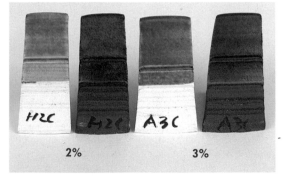

1%   2%   3%

Black nickel oxide

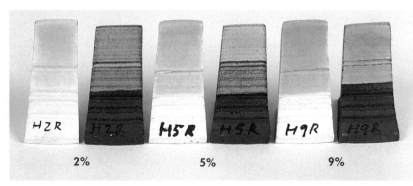

2%   5%   9%

Rutile

2%   3%

Copper carbonate

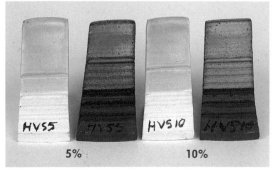

5%   10%

Vanadium stain

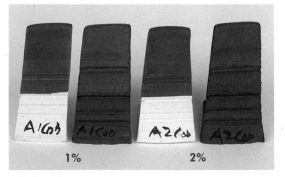

1%   2%

Cobalt carbonate

The batch for "H" glaze was:

F4 spar 50%

Barium carbonate 10%

Lithium carbonate 5%

Whiting 5%

Frit 3110 5%

China clay 10%

Silica 15%

The batch for "A" glaze was:

F4 spar 52%

Barium carbonate 16%

Zinc oxide 12%

China clay 10%

Flint 10%

3 CHANGING BASE GLAZE ELEMENTS

Study this variable by changing basic glaze elements, while keeping color constant, as shown visually on the Ferro frit-plus-stain test on pages 176–7. In this test, 25 different glaze compositions were used – some lead-based frits and some non-lead frits. The colors ranged through the basic stain compositions for yellows, greens, pinks, blues, browns, and blacks. The firing temperature varied from 1800 °F (982 °C) to 2200 °F (1204 °C) because of the different glaze compositions. Stain colors always read most true in oxidation atmospheres, so this test was electric-fired in oxidation.

It is easy to see the range of differences in color with the glazes of varying compositions (Ferro frit compositions are listed in chapter 8). If the glazes had not been fritted the differences would have been about the same, but the glazes would not have been as stable. Lead should always be fritted for use on functional pottery.

4 TRIAXIAL BLENDS

Blends of three glazes can be represented as blends from three points in a triangle. You can test combinations of three basic glazes or colors, as shown here where three

colors on the same base are blended and fired in cone 04 oxidation. The chart in chapter 8 shows how to read a triaxial blend. This method is complicated, but it shows slight color changes and subtle variations in color better than a 50/50 blend does. Triaxial blends are primarily used in industry where a precise color dictionary is needed.

The base glaze for cone 04, especially formulated for cadmium colorants, is constituted:

Frit PG–IV–48 78%

Frit P–830 20%

Bentonite 2%

The yellow corner of the triaxial is Drakenfeld stain number 21–2128 at 2 percent; the red corner is Drakenfeld stain number 21–1284 at 2 percent; the blue corner is Drakenfeld stain number 4053 at 1 percent.

Most clayworkers buy the low temperature red, yellow, and orange glazes already prepared, wet or dry, and do not stock the special frits or the cadmium-selenium stains necessary to compound these glazes in the studio; this triaxial could have been blended with commercial preparations.

FERRO FRITS-PLUS-STAINS

				1 SnV C420	2 SnV C409	3 ZrV F4988	4 ZrV P478	5 ZrV P437	6 PrZr C412	7 CrAlZn F1862	8 CrAlZn P818	9 CrAlFeZn F10568	10 CrAlZn P810	11 CrAlZn P813	12 MnAl C808	13 ZrFe C830 (Opacified)
	GLAZE KEY NO.	**FERRO FRIT NO.**	**FIRING TEMP.**													
LEAD FRITS	A	3403	1800°F													
	B	3457	1800°F													
	C	3496	1900°F													
	D	3417	1800°F													
	E	3482	1900°F													
	F	3470	1800°F													
	G	3435	1800°F													
	H	3481	2000°F													
	I	3497	1900°F													
	J	3467	2000°F													
	K	3509	2000°F													
	L	3300	2000°F													
LEADLESS FRITS	M	FB103A	2200°F													
	N	3124	1900°F													
	O	3134	1800°F													
	P	3288-A	1900°F													
	Q	3286	2000°F													
	R	3257	1900°F													
	S	3278	1800°F													
	T	3110	1800°F													
	V	3299	1900°F													
	W	FB168J	2000°F													
	X	3293	1900°F													
	Y	5301	1900°F													
	Z	3289	1800°F													

| 14 ZrFe C830 (w/o Opacifier) | 15 CrSn F2821 | 16 CrSn F1875 | 17 CrFeZn F2184 | 18 CrFeZn F6176 | 19 CrFeZn C107 | 20 CrFeZn F6140 | 21 CrFeZn F10134 | 22 CrCo F3624 | 23 CrCo F3664 | 24 CrCo F5691 | 25 CoCrFe F3794 | 26 CrFe F3786 | 27 ZrCo F3704 | 28 ZrCoNi F3708 | 29 SnCoNi F2753 | 30 ZrCoNi F3706 | 31 SnSb F4791 | 32 ZrCoNi C717 | 33 CoAl F3225 | 34 CoAl F202 | 35 CoAl P200 | 36 CrSnCo F6252 |

MAKING GLAZE MATT OR OPAQUE

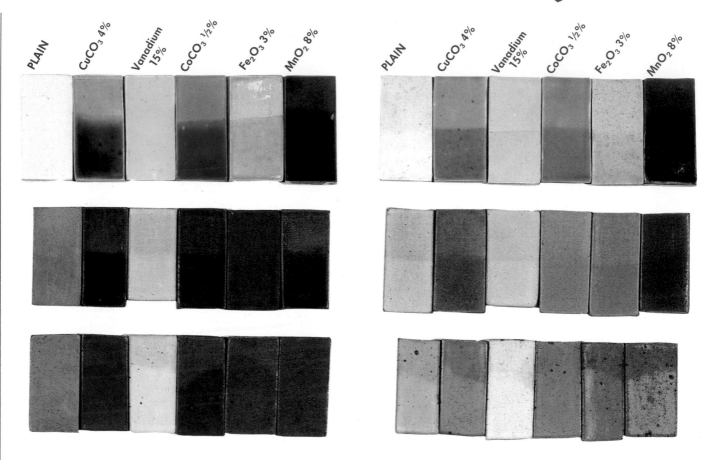

CLEAR GLAZE

MATT GLAZE

The fewer base glazes an artist uses, the more intuitive the handling of glaze can become.

It is useful to know how to make any basic clear glaze opaque or matt at any temperature. In each case this is possible with the addition of just one ingredient. Whether it is the best way to make a glaze to your specifications is another matter. Choose the three median cones to experiment with: 04, 5, and 10 (unless you know you will always standardize at one temperature, in which case make the tests only at that temperature).

Matt glaze. Look first at the 34-member 50/50 blend charts and fusion buttons (pp. 156–9, 150–3) to determine materials that are refractory (heat-resistant), dull-surfaced, or unmelted, for an indication of matt choices. From the chart it is apparent that whiting, zinc, magnesium carbonate, dolomite, and china clay are possibilities at all temperatures. Some of them may affect color. Study the metallic oxide and stain colorants, and then decide how to make your own tests. You could use a basic clear glaze you already know, or choose a clear blend from the chart, and add substances to make it matt.

Opaque glaze. At low fire (to cone 5), a 10 percent addition of tin has been a universal choice for centuries; however, it is expensive, not now available everywhere, can produce a lustrous surface with a pinkish cast, and in reduction atmosphere it goes gray and does not opacify. The term "opaque" is normally used to denote a white opaque glaze; however, it is possible to add color and retain opacity. Zirconium opacifiers stay white in any atmosphere. Add 10 to 15 percent zircopax to a base glaze for low to median temperatures; 10 to 15 percent ultrox or opax at high fire.

To make the above tests I first developed the clear glaze to use at each of the three median temperatures.

CONE 04 The classic two-frit glaze is the basic low-temperature clear, shiny glaze. With variations, it is also the norm for a clear glaze in industry at low temperature. Here the base is 45% lead frit number 3403 and 45% alkaline frit number 3195 plus 5% clay and 5% silica.

To make it matt. Add 40% whiting to the above batch. (If you are learning to calculate glaze formulas, as explained in chapter 8, while creating glazes visually, you will see that this is a calcium matt according to the limit formulas because the calcium in the RO column of the unity molecular formula of this glaze is a high .75 equivalents.)

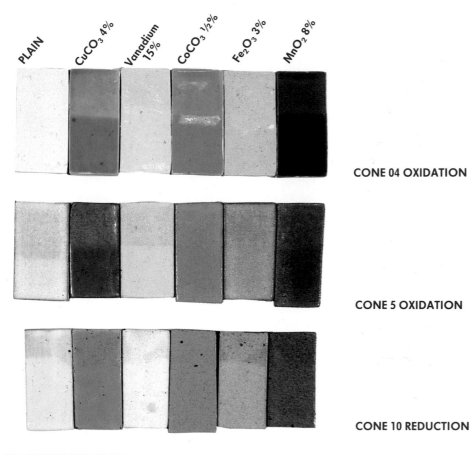

PLAIN CuCO₃ 4% Vanadium 15% CoCO₃ ½% Fe₂O₃ 3% MnO₂ 8%

CONE 04 OXIDATION

CONE 5 OXIDATION

CONE 10 REDUCTION

OPAQUE WHITE GLAZE

To opacify. Add 15% zircopax to 100% of the two-frit base clear glaze.

CONE 5 A lead-alkaline base, similar to the cone 04 composition, was desired for a base cone 5 clear, shiny glaze. Experimentation with the 34-member blend melts led to the following combination: lead silicate 20%, Gerstley borate 15%, soda ash 15%, clay 18%, silica 32%.
  To make it matt. Add 30% dolomite to above 100% batch.
  To opacify. Add 10% opax to above 100% batch.

CONE 10 A feldspathic clear glaze for high temperature will turn matt or opaque in the same way. From the 34-member charts and the feldspar bar tests, my material choices and experiments resulted in this clear, shiny glaze: Kona F4 (sodium) feldspar 44%, whiting 18%, china clay 10%, silica 28%.
  To make it matt. Add 15% magnesium carbonate to above clear 100% glaze.
  To opacify. Add 15% ultrox.

Similar changes for making any clear glaze matt or opaque

with one ingredient will work for any temperature from cone 010 to cone 14.

Color changes. To show the effect of these base glazes on colorants, each plain glaze was line-blended with five constant colorant percentages: copper carbonate 4%, vanadium stain 15%, cobalt carbonate ½%, red iron oxide 3%, manganese dioxide 8%. At cones 04 and 5 they were oxidized; at cone 10, reduced. The clay body at low fire was a white-burning talc body; at cone 5 and cone 10, it was a buff stoneware. The influence of the clay color can be seen particularly in the clear and the matt series; in the opaque series the opacifier keeps the number 1 tiles white at all three temperatures, and makes the clay color less evident.

Color is brightest at cone 04, whether clear, matt, or opaque; ultrox retards copper-red most, as seen in the cone 10 opaque line fired in reduction. Vanadium yellow stain does not hold in reduction; in the cone 5 oxidation test, a small percentage of iron (3%) yields amber, but it turns celadon green at cone 10; the zirconium opacifier particularly lightens cobalt. Spend more time looking at these visuals and make your own generalizations.

LOW-FIRE TREATMENTS

A technique slightly different from regular glaze application is needed for painting greenware and bisque with commercial preparations such as "one-strokes," "underglazes," or "art glazes." The readymade substances are generally sold in small plastic bottles containing 4 oz or 100 g or even less, and painting is the only possible method of application.

PAINTING PROCEDURE

Learning to paint glaze on ceramic ware is difficult even if you make your own glaze by the gallon. Cleanliness is always important for greenware or bisque, particularly for low-fire colors; sponge the ware with alcohol, which evaporates as it cleans. The studio should be kept clean, too — do not sweep the floor with bottles open; do not use sandpaper or grit cloths on greenware or bisque; never use hand lotion unless you wear surgical gloves. These factors can be problems at high fire, too, but high-temperature glazes have a different color palette and a different chemistry, and are not so sensitive.

To load the brush for painting commercial preparations, first wet it in water and blot it on a clean, damp natural sponge. Pour a puddle of liquid from the bottle onto a plate. Hold the brush at a 15-degree angle and pull it through the liquid, or lay the brush in it and twist it right around until full, shaping the brush as you float it and, lastly, making a point at the tip.

Brush strokes that are important to the design can be applied to the ware so that they will show after firing. It is possible to coat evenly so that strokes do not and will not show, but it takes skill. Brush shapes — sides, ends, fans, and tips — are different; and the hairs from which brushes are made vary the stroke. Different brushes make different marks; you can float or pull or dabble onto the ware. The famous British potter, Bernard Leach, said that a brush stroke was made in three parts — put down, pull across, lift up — making three perceptible changes in the line. Glaze can be applied evenly by painting on three or four coats going in opposite directions, floating the liquid, taking care not to let the bristles touch the clay.

Practice strokes using water or India ink and different brushes, against newspaper. Hold the brush lightly; use a full arm swing for broad strokes, and try small, gentle strokes with the brush held flexibly. Go to the clay after

Commercial china paints and gold on a Limoges chocolate set, 1925, painted by my mother, Iva Harnly

Elena Karina: luster glazes on porcelain, high-fired with stain and oxide accents; lusters fired at cone 022

practicing on the paper. These directions apply to brushing for high-fire engobes, stains, and also glazes.

COMMERCIAL LOW-FIRE PRODUCTS

Many companies make commercial products for low fire. Here I have chosen the MayCo line of "underglaze colors" (really engobes), "one-strokes" (really stains), "art glazes," and "special glazes." They were tested on 20 × 24 in (50 × 60 cm) whiteware bisqued slabs: color was applied evenly to each tile, which was then half glazed on the diagonal. To show textured color, a small brush stroke was made underneath each tile (these were also glazed). The tests were fired to cone 06 (see pp. 182–5). The "art glazes" were tested in cone 10 reduction as well, and most of them worked, although the colors and textures differed. Commercial preparations change rather often, due to material alterations, pricing, availability, and demand; so if a number appears here that is no longer on sale, there will be a substitute for that color. All companies have similar colors and textures. I have found the MayCo ceramic engineers at their headquarters in Columbus, Ohio, to be very helpful with technical questions.

COMMERCIAL LUSTERS AND CHINA PAINTS

These expensive commercial products fire at cone 022 to 013 and are different from the low-fire (cone 06 to 04) commercial undercoats and glazes just discussed. They absolutely must be applied in a totally clean, metal-free area, with immaculately clean brushes. The best of them, including the precious metals gold and platinum, come from just one or two companies worldwide (Hanovia is best known). They can be purchased ready-mixed with a medium in the vial, or in a tube or dry, needing to be mixed with a medium and/or a flux. Try varying these components and experimenting with firing temperatures around 1150 to 1500 °F (625 to 825 °C); the technique allows for almost endless multiple firings. Electric kilns contaminate all low-fire glazes if the elements flake, but unfortunately gas kilns project impurities, too. The photograph of the 1925 vintage china-painted chocolate set shows a traditional use of china paints; the shell sculpture shows the use of commercial luster-glazes. Study the photographs of Margaret Ford's and Ralph Bacerra's china-painting process techniques in various layers and firings (pp. 186–8); the methods of using china paints and lusters are among the most meticulous in all ceramics.

MAYCO "ONE-STROKES" (STAINS)

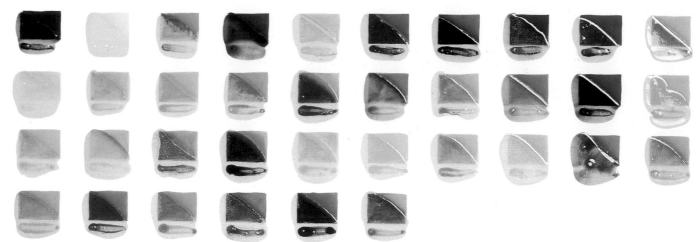

CONE 06 OXIDATION

1	2	3	4	5	6	7	8	9	10
Mirror black	Snow white	Lip red	Chinese blue	Citron yellow	Foliage green	Victory green	Briarwood	Auburn	Shell pink

11	12	13	14	15	16	17	18	19	20
Skin tone	Bamboo	Aquamarine	Tangerine	Apple green	Eggplant	Pearl gray	Princess blue	Night blue	Chartreuse

21	22	23	24	25	26	27	28	29	30
Petal pink	Lilac	Peach	Pea green	Fiesta rose	Buttercup	Orchid	Orange	Delft blue	Amber gold

31	32	33	34	35	36
Wedgwood blue	Shamrock green	French blue	Sienna brown	Avocado	Umber

MAYCO "UNDERGLAZES" (ENGOBES)

CONE 06 OXIDATION

1 King's blue	2 Sea blue	3 Baby blue	4 Turquoise	6 Lavender	7 Purple	8 Violet	9 Powder blue	10 Crimson	11 Ruby red
12 Deep rose		14 Baby pink	15 Coral pink	16 Salmon pink	17 Sandalwood	18 Ice blue	19 Electric blue	21 Leaf green	22 Spring green
23 French green	24 Jade green	25 Lime	26 Myrtle green	27 Pomona green	28 Avocado green	30 Sand	31 Chocolate	32 Cocoa	33 Redwood
34 Chestnut brown	35 Carnation pink	37 Suntan	38 Pink flesh	39 Light flesh	40 Oriental flesh	41 Orange	42 Light yellow	43 Lemon yellow	44 Chartreuse
45 Golden yellow	46 Bright yellow	50 Jet black	51 China white	52 Pepper gray	53 Silver gray	54 Beige	55 Hazelnut	56 Rustic red	57 Spice brown
58 Harvest gold	59 Golden bluff	60 Art brown	61 Art yellow	65 Art seaweed	66 Art gray	67 Ivory	68 Apple green	69 Green olive	70 Medium green
71 Wisteria	72 Wedgwood blue								

MAYCO "ART GLAZES"

CONE 06 OXIDATION

112 Spectaclear	**110** Golden clear	**641** Imperial yellow	**212** Party pink	**244** Chartreuse	**224** Aztec jade	**204** Alpine blue	**404** Golden amber	**117** Rusty clear	**421** Pepper pot
119 Eggnog	**423** Palomino	**643** Tangerine	**213** Blossom pink	**425** Golden mist	**454** Holly green	**206** Egyptian blue	**453** Old English	**115** Smoky black	**460** Empress white
116 Golden spectaclear	**242** Canary yellow	**640** Poppy orange	**215** Reef coral	**225** Parrot green	**400** Luster green	**202** Persian blue	**414** Tawny birch	**253** Twilight gray	**462** Emperor green
114 Pale lime	**243** Golden-rod	**645** Flame	**214** Tropical rose	**227** Kelly green	**429** Silver jade	**203** Flame blue	**407** Olde pine	**424** Sparkle	**463** Emperor bronze
118 Green spectaclear	**241** Mango orange	**642** Vibrant red	**210** Burgundy rose	**226** Olive green	**205** Blue green	**403** Gold dust blue	**401** Cordova white drape ®	**430** Burnt copper	**461** Emperor blue
111 Scandia blue	**411** Speckled amber	**644** Poppy red	**408** Sirocco red	**412** Russet green	**420** Autumn green	**201** Royal blue	**235** Mahogany	**405** Gun metal	**251** Black beauty
113 Blue spectaclear	**413** Autumn gold	**600** Dragon red	**216** Orchid bouquet	**426** Antique brass	**402** Foliage green	**207** Royal purple	**409** Bronze	**605** Gold filigree	**410** Black luster
101 Blu-white (clear glaze)	**105** Dual tone (special clear)	**234** Ebony	**601** White drape ®	**602** Marbleizer	**603** Clear spill	**604** Black lace	**630** Opaque white		

MAYCO "SPECIAL GLAZES"

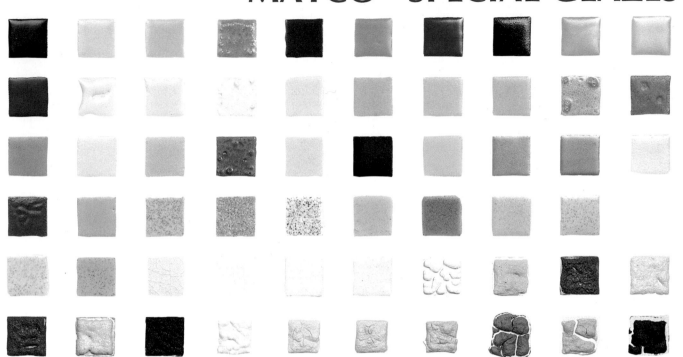

CONE 06 OXIDATION

S–1 Black **A**	S–3 Ivory **A**	S–4 Light flesh **A**	S–7 Flamingo **A**	S–8 Wine red **A**	S–10 Nile green **A**	S–11 Avocado **A**	S–12 Navy blue **A**	S–13 Leprechaun **A**	S–14 Honey blond **A**
S–15 African brown **A**	S–17 White **A**	300 Matt transparent **B**	301 Antique white **B**	302 Flesh **B**	303 Tawny flesh **B**	304 Angel pink **B**	305 Rose tan **B**	306 Silver teak **B**	307 Cedarwood **B**
308 Dutch blue **B**	309 Soft yellow **B**	310 Nymph green **B**	311 Teal green **B**	312 Dawn gray **B**	313 Congo black **B**	315 Turquoise **B**	316 Pumpkin **B**	317 Olive matt **B**	340 Clear satin **B**
341 Burnt orange **B**	406 Mojave sand **B**	450 Dotte citron **C**	451 Dotte orchid **C**	452 Carousel **C**	550 Robin egg **C**	551 Jasper green **C**	552 Blue granite **C**	553 Indian yellow **C**	
555 Stone gray **C**	556 Stone pink **C**	500 Transparent crackle **D**	501 White crackle **D**	502 White matt crackle **D**	503 Pink matt crackle **D**	610 White foam **E**	611 Turquoise foam **E**	612 Green foam **E**	613 Yellow foam **E**
614 Brown foam **E**	615 Pink foam **E**	616 Black foam **E**	620 White **F**	621 Sky blue **F**	622 Light green **F**	623 Golden red **F**	624 Brown **F**	625 Pink **F**	626 Black **F**

"A" group – Satina R glazes (set of 12)
"B" group – Satin matt glazes (set of 20)
"C" group – Stone Age glazes (set of 10)
"D" group – Crackle glazes (set of 4)
"E" group – Foam glazes (set of 7)
"F" group – Hesitation glazes (set of 7)

CHINA PAINT PROCESS

PERSIAN-STYLE LUSTER

This is developed in the glaze (commercial lusters are developed on top of the glaze) and in a special firing that uses reduction atmosphere on the cooling side. Unlike the commercial luster preparations just discussed, in texture and color, Persian luster is also absolutely permanent; commercial preparations, although fired on, can wash off in time. Colors for Persian-style luster are developed by using the "salts" of the metals, that is, chlorides, nitrates, and sulfates. Probably discovered accidentally by the Persians nearly 1,000 years ago, this type of luster is complicated but beautiful.

Persian luster basic batch:

Boric frit or borax   90%

Ball clay   10%

Add 10% tin oxide for a more opaque, white glaze.

Color additions to the base batch: red, 1 to 2% copper sulfate; mother-of-pearl, 1% silver nitrate (silver can be added to any of the other colorants to give more luster); gold, 4% bismuth subnitrate; purple, 4% manganese chloride; blue, 1 to 2% cobalt sulfate. Alternatively, the glaze can be applied as the plain white that it is, with the metallic salts brushed over in pattern.

Try salts of more metallic oxides than I have listed, from a chemical supplier. Fire in an electric or gas kiln to cone 04 (1922°F, 1050°C) to mature the glaze. Cool the kiln to 1300°F (704°C) on the pyrometer reading, and hold your kiln at that temperature for 30 minutes while continuously reducing the atmosphere; use mothballs or newmown grass or oil-soaked rags thrown into the peephole or directly into the kiln, for the reduction necessary to develop the luster. Turn off the kiln and allow it to cool. You can apply more silver nitrate over the whole piece and fire again in the same way, if the luster is not sufficient.

Commercial lusters contain a reducing agent to develop luster, so the kiln is fired oxidizing. The only way to develop true glaze luster that is permanent is as described here.

Margaret Ford paints china paints over underglaze, using Amaco, Willoughby, and Hanovia products.

1 The piece bisqued, with one coat of underglaze fired cone 06

2 Pattern is masked and china paint airbrushed on

3 Masks are removed before firing china paint at cone 020; another china-paint coating is planned

4 The piece ready for a last china-painting fire

Ralph Bacerra china paints a platter.

1 Cobalt and copper engobes applied, lines drawn in greenware, bisque fired cone 05; cobalt oxide inlaid in line, clear glaze over center, crackle glaze on rim; glaze fired cone 06

2 Yellow, red, green, pink Blythe and Ceramichrome china paints applied to develop solid shapes; fired cone 014

3 Hanovia gold and platinum luster to define larger shapes; fired cone 019

4 Black and white enamels (p. 168) to define individual shapes and pattern; fired cone 019; this platter had at least five firings

GLAZE FAULTS

The following are the primary faults that occur in or after glaze firings (mainly from cone 04 to 10). Almost all faults in ceramics can be corrected. Try to intellectualize the problem and the solution. Often, so-called glaze faults are really the fault of poor clay-body composition, or incorrect firing technique. Sometimes they can be caused by a bad batch of material from your supplier. Check each possible element to find the reason.

CRAZING

A problem of glaze "fit." When the glaze expands more than the clay body, the result is a series of tiny to large craze marks on the glaze surface. When crazing is intentional and used decoratively, it is called "crackle." Most porous earthenware bodies are hard to fit, and glazes tend to craze; they do the same on vitreous bodies like porcelain. The body and glaze have to have the same expansion. If crazing occurs, the cure is to increase the expansion of the body or decrease the expansion of the glaze. This adjustment is always possible, but takes some testing.

Silica has one of the lowest coefficients of expansion of all glaze materials. Silica added to the clay body increases expansion; silica added to the glaze decreases expansion relative to the other glaze oxides. Begin with additions of 10 percent silica to either body or glaze — not both at the same time — and continue until the problem is solved. Alternatively, work another way: of all glaze oxides, soda has the highest coefficient of expansion and magnesia the lowest; maneuver percentages of these without working on the silica or in addition to the silica changes.

If crackle is desired, increase one or more of the high-expansion oxides, such as soda and potassium. A large crackle means a near-fit; a small one means the fit is farther away. Enhance your crackle by rubbing India ink into it, or use sugar syrup and bake the pot in the oven to carbonize the sugar. Crackle on an earthenware body will pick up dirt and bacteria; on a vitreous body it is sanitary.

CRAWLING

This too can be either a problem or a decorative effect. Crawling can be a physical or a chemical difficulty. Dust on the bisque, fingerprints, oil from hand lotions, and other surface impurities cause crawling. Sponge bisque lightly with water if it has been sitting for weeks on the shelf; clean oils off with alcohol on a sponge. To induce chemical crawling, add a "fluffy" material like magnesium carbonate to any glaze, beginning with a 10 percent addition and continuing until the bond is lost, to see what degree of crawling matrix occurs. The mounds of the crawl can be controlled by the rest of the composition and, to some extent, by the application of the glaze (thick or thin).

DUNTING

Dunting is a cooling crack, a sharp crack through the glaze and the clay, sometimes with a "Y" at the beginning. Shock-cracks usually develop in the ware on the cooling side of the firing cycle. If the crack occurred on the way up, as firing temperatures increased, this is not called dunting, and is probably due to a fabrication strain of some kind. You will be able to see that the glaze has melted over a crack. Some people think dunting is caused by cooling too fast at the "silica inversion" of the firing (chemists say silica expands and contracts at 500°F [260°C] and 1000°F [538°C], both on the way up and on the way down). My years of experience tell me that this is not a problem. I think dunting is caused by the clay-body composition — some bodies are simply prone to dunt, and it occurs most frequently on fine, dense ones with no grog. Avoid thermal shock by slowing down the cooling or opening up the clay body.

PINHOLES

These are tiny or large blisters still in the glaze after firing, which can be broken open, healed over, or left in the glaze surface. All are caused by one of the following factors: (1) air bubbles resulting from application that have not been "dusted down" before firing; (2) too low a bisquing temperature, resulting in poor clay-glaze interface; (3) bisquing too low for gases to be eliminated from the clay before the glaze melts; (4) too high a glaze content of materials that boil during firing (for example, boron); this can be controlled by the addition of 5 percent zinc oxide. Intentional blisters and bubbles can be made by using large amounts of highly active materials like trisodium phosphate, calgon, or antimony in the glaze.

SHIVERING

This is the opposite of crazing, with the glaze compressing too much and popping off or squeezing the body so much that it cracks. If glaze shivers off the surface at the lip or the edge of a handle or another sharp spot, over-finishing or over-sponging during fabrication may be the fault. It is thought that silica or grog coming to the surface generally causes shivering. Carbon-core, developed by reduction too early in a firing, will cause glaze to shiver from a poor bond; the carbon ion is larger than the iron ion, so if too much reduction takes place during firing, carbon displaces iron and pushes the glaze off the surface, or dunts the ware. Too much fire clay in a body composition, or too much free silica, can also cause shivering. There is almost no way to call this a decorative accident; it is an undesirable fault.

5

FIRING THE WARE

Paul Chaleff's wood-burning kiln firing

Clay bodies and glaze cannot be discussed without consideration of firing. Nor can we talk about fabrication processes and design and decorative techniques without being aware of firing capability. If work is to stay within the traditional ceramic vocabulary, firing must be considered from the start.

Room temperature "glazes" are the exception — these are surfaces that are not fired on, for example paint pigments of all kinds, shoe polish, paste wax, epoxies and polymers, lacquer, flock or other methods of applying fabric finishes. They do not have firing to contend with, unless the unfired colors are to go on already fired surfaces. Work is usually bisqued for room-temperature glazes, for strength, but does not have to be. Substances such as paints can go on raw ware; this may well be the best way for artists as well as youngsters to achieve quick color.

Firing clay is an age-old process. The difference between a white translucent porcelain teacup and a common red brick is created not only by the type of clay, but also by the temperature to which it was fired. Simple firing in the open, practiced by indigenous societies with wood or dung as fuel, does harden clay, but the durability of the brick or pot may be counted in days, because the firing is not sufficiently long or hot to give it permanence. This fact no doubt helped to build the artforms associated with early civilizations: because of breakage, more pots or effigies were continually needed, which enlivened the artistic spirit and refined the skills.

At some point, the bonfire was contained in a cave or a pit, or by covering the fire with shards or cow dung. Containment produced a hotter fire and harder ware, whether the fuel was wood or dung. With liquid petroleum fuels — kerosene, oil, gas — high temperatures became easier. Later, electricity, globar elements (carbon rods), and the esoteric gases of the space industry allowed heats of up to 6000 °F (3300 °C) or more, depending on the furnace capability.

The Chinese were the first to build kilns that would reach 2400 °F (1300 °C). They were also the first to understand the control of heat by reading the color of the fire, probably by the 1st century B.C. Thousands of years later, the principles of firing have not changed, but the materials and structures have evolved. It is still necessary to fire most clay wares somewhat slowly and evenly, on a progressive curve to the top temperature, and to cool them for approximately as long as it has taken to fire. How long the cycle takes is determined by the size of the ware, the kiln space, the kind and style of furnace, and sometimes by the clay body.

Burning pots under cow dung, Lucy Lewis, Acoma Pueblo, New Mexico

Carrying bonfired vessels to market, Timi, Nepal

TEMPERATURE

Heat treatment is so important to the development of clays and glazes that intelligent firing of claywork must include controlling, managing, measuring, and recording temperature and atmosphere throughout a firing.

For centuries, kilns were fired by specialists who read the heat; the wise clayworker still reads heat and learns to see if the kiln is red all over inside, and the same color of red top and bottom with no black corners. The kiln-firer also notices how the color of the heat changes, and sees whether the atmosphere is clear or opaque during the fire. Firing is a mystical adventure; experience teaches.

Ceramic kiln temperatures are loosely defined as low, medium, and high heats: respectively about 1900, 2100, and 2300°F (1037, 1148, and 1260°C) (much hotter than an ordinary oven). Temperatures lower than 1900 (1037) are used for bisquing ware to red heat — about 1600°F (870°C) — and for glass melts, china painting, overglaze enamels, and porcelain enamel for metals, all generally fired between 1300 and 1500°F (700 and 815°C), sometimes higher. Most floor and wall tile in the United States is made of talc body and fired about 1900°F (1037°C) (cone 04); temperatures higher than 2300°F (1260°C) are used in making high-temperature refractory brick and for various pure alumina and pure silica bodies for the space and transistor industries. Commercially produced tableware ranges from low-fire earthenwares, talc bodies, and semi-vitreous whiteware — median-fired around cone 3 — to fine porcelain, hotel china, and bathroom fixtures fired at 2300°F (1260°C) (cone 10). Some porcelains are bisqued high and glazed low. Artists need to understand the whole range and utilize the differences.

CONES

In 1886, Hermann Seger at the Royal Porcelain Factory in Berlin devised the original Seger cone system — primarily used now in Europe and Asia — which was the first accurate temperature measurement inside a kiln. In 1896, Edward Orton, Jr., Professor of Ceramic Engineering at Ohio State University, developed the Orton cone system and began cone manufacture in the United States. These 2½ in (6.5 cm) tall cone-shaped combinations of clay and glaze materials are put into the furnace raw. They bend according to the temperature reached in the chamber and thus give a method of measuring heat absorbed by the ware inside a kiln that can be duplicated.

Numbering. Cones were ingenious inventions, using various material combinations that melt at specific heats from cone 022 (about 1250°F or 675°C) to cone 42 (about 3800°F or 2093°C); the average interval between cones is 32°F (17.5°C). Cones for the low-temperature range have a zero preceding the number; in the high-temperature range they do not. The dividing point in the scale (cone 01 and cone 1) occurs at 2000°F (1093°C), the melting point

of cast iron. As discussed in chapter 4, one can learn to remember important places on the cone chart, such as mean temperatures for earthenware, stoneware, and porcelain (cone 04, 5, and 10), and the basic distinction between cones with or without a zero. Full cone charts for both Orton and Seger systems are given in chapter 8. The references in this book are all based on Orton cones.

Making cones. To allow cone packs to dry, make them in advance of firing. Use clay mixed with grog, sawdust, etc., for the cone-bed, and poke holes in the wet clay to allow moisture to escape. Use only enough clay to hold the cones, not a great wad. Disaster occurs when cone packs blow up in the kiln because they are not dry enough; this means that the final temperature cannot be read, and the cone shards will stick to the glazed pieces. (Suppliers sell clay casts into which cones fit; they can be re-used many times, but in fact making cone packs is enjoyable.)

Positioning. Cones are used inside the chamber to indicate temperature because they are the equivalent of materials in the clay and glaze; only they "know" the actual heat absorption of the ware. A number of cone packs can be used to record the temperature in various parts of the kiln, or to assess the evenness of firing; but a pack of three cones is always placed in front of each viewing hole, or at least on decks at the bottom and top of the firing space.

It is important to set the cones in the pack correctly, a fact that many kiln-firers overlook. Cones are fabricated in a shape that produces an angle; put each one on a flat surface to see that angle, then set it in the pack of three *facing forward* in the direction it wants to bend. This will keep the cones from hitting each other during melting; if they touch, they give a false reading. The center one is the cone to which the kiln is to be fired; the side ones are for slightly lower and higher temperatures (one or two cones down and one or two cones up) — they are used as an advance warning and to determine over-firing. (The average difference between neighboring cones represents about ten minutes of firing time, so choosing temperatures two cones apart allows about 20 minutes' initial warning.) Place the pack in the kiln at a right angle to the viewing hole, so the profile of each cone can be seen as it falls. When it bends to 3 o'clock position, it is equivalent to its rated temperature.

Firing. Proper firing is tricky. Cones help to cut down the variables, but you must try to keep them consistent, at least in terms of how and where they are set. Keep and review cone packs from particularly good firings, coded with the written schedule of that firing; analyze the cones, checking the exact degree of bending of all three, and fire next time to that exact look.

A "cone-sitter" is standard equipment on many electric kilns. It is a mechanism geared to turn the kiln off when the cone bends, and uses tiny cones that do not register in the same way as the larger cones that are always placed inside the kiln. The cone-sitter cone can blow up or register falsely; use it only as a guide, and always try to fire a kiln when you can be present continuously to watch it.

SETTING CONES

Set cones in clay mixture with side facing you that will bend in firing

Set all three at the same angle, facing forward

Poke holes in the wet clay

Cones bend under heat

DRAW TRIALS

Sometimes it is necessary to see the action of heat on the clay body or the glaze during the firing. Cones bend only when they reach a given temperature, they tell us nothing else. Draw trials — coiled rings or other shapes made from the same clay body and glaze as the wares in the kiln — are used for pulling out of the kiln and checking at intervals during firing. Use them especially in firings that cause cones to be less reliable, such as salt or wood, when you want to watch the development of a color or a glaze, or when you need to record a specific glaze development, so it can be repeated later. To use draw trials, you need a large enough hole in the kiln door or bricked-up opening to allow you to pick up the trial on an iron pole or metal shovel, or with a raku tong. If you own the kiln, you can cut a brick-sized, or partial brick-sized, hole in it with a saw. Alternatively, see that a hole is made when the kiln is built or when bricking up a door. A sizable viewing hole is anyway preferable to allow you to observe the atmosphere and anything else that is going on inside the kiln during firing. Use a removable brick or other plug for the hole.

MECHANICAL MEASUREMENT OF HEAT

For some years, there have been excellent mechanical methods of measuring specific temperatures at specific spots in the kiln during firing. The simplest is a *pyrometer* — a temperature-calibrating device measuring in degrees F and C, placed outside the kiln. It is attached by lead-wires to a *thermocouple* — two twisted wires placed inside the kiln — on which the heat registers. A pyrometer-thermocouple arrangement is absolutely necessary on every kiln in addition to cones inside; it allows you to use time and fuel efficiently, to know what the heat in the kiln is at all times, and to have a method of duplicating temperature rise and time factors. I believe that no kiln should be fired without a pyrometer and thermocouple; further reasons will be discussed later in this chapter.

Thermocouples. For high-temperature measurements, it is preferable to have a platinum-rhodium thermocouple with a pyrometer calibrated for platinum. Below cone 5, a chrome-alumel thermocouple can be used with the appropriate pyrometer calibrated for chrome-alumel. For low temperatures, a fairly cheap pyrometer and thermocouple will do. Remember, though, that cheap instruments are not as accurate as expensive ones. But in this case accuracy is not as important as consistent measurement.

Platinum-rhodium thermocouples never wear out, but they are initially very expensive. As a less expensive option, some of us use chrome-alumel ones, with a pyrometer calibrated for chrome-alumel, for high-temperature firing (to cone 14). Used this way, the low-temperature chrome-alumel thermocouple must be encased in a heavy-gauge "inconel" (nickel alloy) protection tube, with a metal connector head attached to the lead wire going to the pyrometer. An inconel tube is the *only* complete protection for a

Shoji Hamada checks the firing of the kiln by looking at a hot draw trial just extracted by a worker during firing of the five-chamber kiln, 1970. (Hamada used no cones or other temperature devices, but checked the "fire reading" of each chamber by pulling draw trials)

chrome-alumel thermocouple used in high firing. Neither the small pieces of porcelain-cover that come readymade on it, nor the high-alumina tube sold by some ceramic suppliers, will keep a chrome-alumel thermocouple from burning out in a few high firings. Even in an inconel tube, the low-fire thermocouple will need replacing every few years if the kiln is frequently fired at high temperature, and accuracy will diminish as it wears out. The tube will last longer than the thermocouple, but eventually it will also need to be replaced. Most kiln manufacturers do not sell inconel tubes (in fact, many have never heard of them). The best source in the U.S.A. is the Thermocouple division of Honeywell Corporation in Anaheim, California, and Houston, Texas. In the U.K. they can be obtained from Wiggin Alloys in Hereford.

Another measuring device that has come into recent use is a "platinel" thermocouple, a name-brand product of Engelhard in Carteret, New Jersey, with its own instrument calibrated specifically for platinel, as well as a special lead wire. Platinel, a combination of platinum, paladium, and gold, is definitely more accurate than chrome-alumel and less costly than platinum-rhodium (in which the rhodium accounts for the high price) for high-temperature firings. Platinel must also be encased in an inconel tube, and it will eventually deteriorate at cone 10 temperatures, especially in reduction. Different instruments read differently; just be consistent in the use of one.

Digital pyrometers. Large, expensive pyrometers are usually elaborately encased and hang on the wall or the kiln, but most people use the inexpensive, small gauges such as that shown here. Better are the rectangular digital pyrometers now available. They have a large red number for every degree of temperature, showing instantly whether the kiln temperature is rising, holding, or dropping.

Left to right: connector head, inconel protection tube, inexpensive pyrometer, thermocouple, and lead wire

The digits are easy to read, unlike the tiny numbers and lines on a regular pyrometric gauge. If several kilns need instrumentation, a single "roving" digital pyrometer and thermocouple attachment can be moved carefully from kiln to kiln and slowly inserted into each fire. It can then be left there or removed slowly to take a reading on another fire.

More than one thermocouple-pyrometer set is usually necessary on large kilns, or different thermocouples and their wires can be attached to one large pyrometric instrument that can be changed to monitor several places or several kilns. Other electronic temperature devices that are taken for granted on industrial furnaces can be added to studio kilns. For instance, temperature-controlling instrumentation that will run the kiln according to a program, hold temperatures, and start and shut off kilns is available. These instruments are attached to every burner or switch and are expensive.

Optical pyrometers. These devices are the only accurate method of reading heat during a salt or wood fire. They are self-contained "eye-ball" instruments that register after red heat is achieved in the kiln, for they read color. They are particularly valuable where many different kinds of firing take place, and where glass is being fined in a furnace. One optical pyrometer, without thermocouple, reads any kiln; the best are available from Honeywell and from Bausch.

For advice on measuring temperature as well as other information, make use of the knowledgeable ceramic engineers employed by almost every large ceramic manufacturing corporation and mining company in the world. In my experience, these experts give telephone information readily and send available printed data. Keep your own file, and keep it updated.

Detail of draw trial pulled during glaze-firing of Hamada's wood-fueled five-chamber kiln, 1970. He used it to determine whether the kiln had fired to completion

ATMOSPHERE

Atmospheres in the kiln are as important as temperatures causes of variations in claywork. Glaze coloring oxides change considerably according to how much oxygen they do or do not receive at specific times during the firing (pp. 172–3). Clays alter color measurably if they are smothered or smoked. Special contaminants inserted in the kiln during firing change atmosphere and cause color change. Other ingredients thrown into the kiln during the fire create a variety of marks, halos, colors; even residues from previous firings lodged in the brick can affect the kiln atmosphere.

OXIDATION

As mentioned in chapter 4, an oxidizing atmosphere occurs when carbonaceous fuel receives the full amount of air or oxygen it needs to burn well. All energy sources for firing ceramics contain carbon, except for electricity. When carbon and oxygen unite in combustion, the by-product is carbon dioxide (CO_2), one carbon and two oxygens. In this oxidation atmosphere, heat rises easily and all the oxides in the clay body and glaze receive the number of oxygen atoms needed to achieve their regular colors; white is white, iron red is iron red, and so forth.

REDUCTION

When something happens to smother or smoke the fire, or somehow robs the kiln chamber of some oxygen, reduction – a condition of reduced oxygen – takes place; that is, the carbon atoms do not receive all the oxygen atoms they need for normal combustion. When some oxygen is taken away, carbon monoxide (CO) results; if too much oxygen is taken away, pure carbon (C) results. In this reducing atmosphere, heat rise is more difficult to achieve. Smothering causes clays to become jet black, as happened accidentally in early cultures or deliberately in certain American Indian and Mexican pottery villages or in Japanese raku firings.

In an atmosphere of reduced oxygen, the chemical elements other than carbon are not allowed to have their full complement of oxygen either; the clay changes color, and some glaze coloring oxides become radically different, notably copper and iron.

The Chinese discovered the difference between oxidation and reduction firing in about the 8th century A.D. Perhaps the reduction of oxygen was achieved in the oxidizing climbing kiln when something – an animal? – fell into the kiln and burned, robbing the atmosphere of oxygen, changing some of the usual glaze colors. At about the same time, the Persians developed luster glazes by reducing on the cooling side of the firing.

The wonderful reduction glazes of the Sung Dynasty, the "Golden Age" of ceramics, have had a worldwide effect. The low-fire oxidized color palette of European peasant wares, currently popular with many clay artists, is the opposite in brilliance of color.

In an electric kiln, reduction can be achieved by inserting materials that will smolder and rob the atmosphere of oxygen: moth balls, oil-soaked rags, asphalt, fresh grass cuttings, or leaves, for example. Make a metal or clay trough to put through the peephole, or open the kiln lid or door. Alternatively throw the reducing material into an empty receptacle inside the kiln. Specific timing will create specific colors and effects. It is very important that no reducing agents should touch the electric elements. To prevent toxic fumes, the kiln room should be well-ventilated.

In a petroleum-fueled kiln (natural gas and propane are the easiest of these fuels), reduction is achieved by controlling the air intake – increasing or decreasing it with a damper or with blowers – or by raising or lowering the amount of fuel. Wood-fired kilns can be handled similarly, but there is a danger of choking the kiln and causing an explosion. If air cannot be shut down enough for reduction, and carbon cannot be increased by adding pure fuel, then burn-agents such as those used to reduce electric kilns can be thrown in.

Reduction can cause *carbon core*. At low temperature, smoking causes clays to turn black, and does not harm the ware. At higher fires, smoking can cause the center core to blacken, resulting in a brittle body that may burst open or crack after the firing. This happens because the larger carbon ion has displaced the smaller iron ion in the clay. The fault seems to be caused by too early or too much reduction in the firing. Some clays cause worse carbon core than others, according to their chemistry. Adding iron oxide as a clay colorant increases the problem, so it is best to make terracotta-colored clay bodies with naturally iron-red clays. Try never to allow a kiln to "smoke" (emit black smoke) during reduction firing.

Porcelain bodies remain white in oxidation, but are inclined to turn gray in reduction unless the reduction atmosphere is held to the end of the firing cycle, and used only to reduce the glaze.

Neutral atmosphere is neither oxidizing nor reducing, and is in fact bad. Ware resulting from a neutral atmosphere will look washed out, under-developed, or undeveloped. Neutral-fired work doesn't have the same feel, or the same ring, as fully oxidized or reduced ware. A neutral atmosphere – not enough oxygen, and yet not reduction – can happen in a gas kiln, but more usually happens in an electric kiln where the kiln is totally enclosed, with no air circulation at all. A remedy is to leave the peephole plugs out, the door slightly open, or the lid propped up slightly during the entire fire.

Here are two important concepts: (a) oxidation and reduction atmospheres produce different colors from the same oxides, and (b) oxidized color has a different palette at low and high temperatures, whereas high- and low-temperature reduction have the same palette.

KILNS

The first kilns were a simulation of caves, built into the ground; next came a tubular structure which went up along the angle of a hill, or was constructed flat along the ground, or rose vertically above ground like a dome. All of these kinds of kilns are still used somewhere in the world.

In the Asian "hill kiln," the fire is at the lower end of the long tube and the heat naturally rises to the higher end of the chamber, escaping through the top flue. Such kilns can be called *anagama*, or *Korean kiln* or *bamboo kiln*, or *split bamboo kiln*. When the hill kiln has chambers that can be stoked from the side, it may be called a *noborigama*. Flat tubular kilns are many feet long but only about 18 in (46 cm) above ground. They have an underground fire box at the mouth, with the heat proceeding horizontally through the wares, and a short stack at the far end; in early colonial America, they were called "ground hog"

kilns. The vertical tube-shaped kiln took many forms, from the simplest dome above ground with a fire box underneath, still seen today in Greece, Egypt, and Mexico, to the beehive and Hoffman kilns used internationally in industry for heavy clay products.

Lightweight refractory materials that do not need to be mortared can be used to make portable kilns which are relatively easy to build or move. Generally these kilns follow the age-old principle of a container with the fire underneath. The relationship between the amount of heat input and the shape and size of the kiln is important; how it will fire is partly determined by where the fuel enters the kiln and the course it takes prior to exiting. Kilns may have several chambers with a single fire box. Each chamber reaches a different temperature according to its distance from the heat, and can be used simultaneously for different purposes.

Cave kiln for firing bricks, China

Six-chamber *noborigama*, Shigaraki, Japan

Eric Nelson's *anagama*

Woodburning tubular hill kiln built by Paul Chaleff in Pine Plains, New York (above and below)

GAS FIRED UPDRAFT AND DOWNDRAFT KILNS

In *updraft* kilns, the heat develops under the floor, enters and surrounds the ware, and rises to exit through a hole in the top. *Downdraft* kilns are built with burners at the front or back; the heat travels horizontally before rising full circle around the chamber, down again, and out through a damper hole opposite the burners. A *cross-draft* kiln is similar to a downdraft one, except that the burners are on the sides. The heat comes across under the floor, goes in two directions around the chamber, and out of a hole in the side wall.

What makes the best kiln is a never-ending argument. The most portable design is an updraft kiln built of soft, refractory brick called "insulating brick," encased in metal

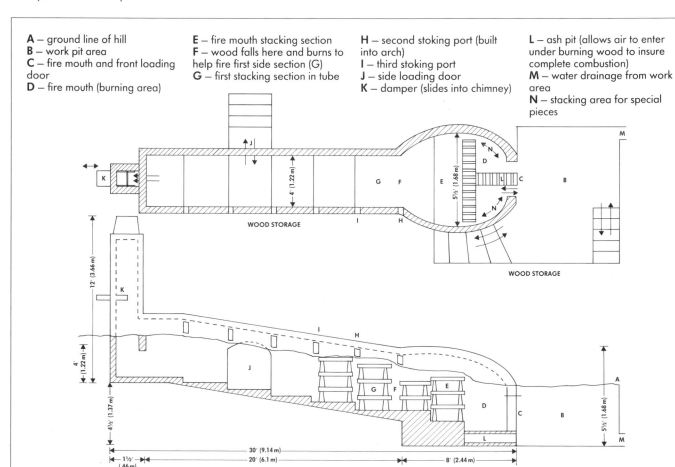

A – ground line of hill
B – work pit area
C – fire mouth and front loading door
D – fire mouth (burning area)
E – fire mouth stacking section
F – wood falls here and burns to help fire first side section (G)
G – first stacking section in tube
H – second stoking port (built into arch)
I – third stoking port
J – side loading door
K – damper (slides into chimney)
L – ash pit (allows air to enter under burning wood to insure complete combustion)
M – water drainage from work area
N – stacking area for special pieces

It takes three to four days to load the kiln. The firing process is six to nine days of continual stoking, consuming about eight cords of wood (one cord is usually 128 cubic ft or 3.62 cu m). It will take three to five days for the kiln to cool down enough to be unloaded, and another three to four days to unload it, sort the ware, and scrub the pottery. The total firing cycle will last for 16 to 20 days.

The walls of the tube section are built of 6 in (15 cm) of high-heat duty firebrick below the ground line of the hill.

The arch of the tube section is built of 4½ in (11.5 cm) of high-heat duty firebrick covered with a layer of insulating brick 2½ in (6.5 cm) thick. The arch is then covered with a layer of clay-sand-straw mixture 1 to 2 in (2.5 to 5 cm) thick.

The fire mouth is built of a 9 in (23 cm) layer of high-heat duty firebrick covered by a layer of 2½ in (6.5 cm) of insulating firebrick (K–20) and then a layer of mixed clay, sand, and straw 1 to 2 in (2.5 to 5 cm) thick.

with a burner grid under its floor. If the construction inside the kiln is "open fire" — meaning that there is no muffle-wall or bag-wall (a secondary wall between the chamber and the stacking area) — and if the combustion space between the wall and the ware is 4 in (10 cm) all around, the updraft is the fastest and most efficient firing kiln for oxidation and reduction atmospheres. At least 12 burners should be used on the bottom of the kiln for quick, efficient firing. I am partial to this type of updraft, which is the kiln I developed in California in 1952. (My statements do not apply to up-draft kilns with two to four burners on the front with small blowers which are not as efficient or as fast-firing.)

Downdraft and cross-draft kilns are generally considered to fire more evenly than updraft ones, because the atmosphere is propelled across, up, and around before exiting via the flue; however, this movement can cause the firing to take longer. Downdraft kilns are usually non-portable. They are generally built from hard firebricks, which are durable, but take longer than soft brick to heat; they can also be built of soft brick with insulation.

ELECTRIC FURNACES

Electric kilns are firing enclosures powered by electricity, which thus do not need combustion space or flues; electric elements in the wall of the kiln go around the sides and sometimes the door. Glazes do not fire the same in electric as in gas kilns.

Electric kilns can be made of insulating brick or fiber, in

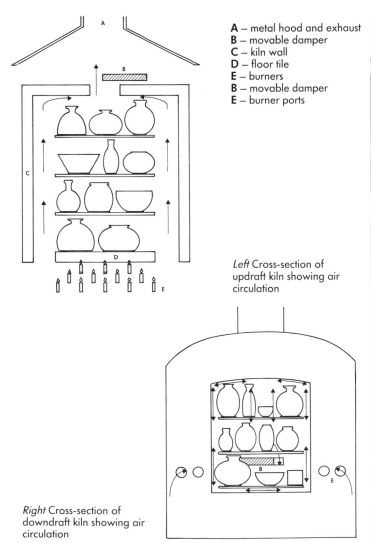

A – metal hood and exhaust
B – movable damper
C – kiln wall
D – floor tile
E – burners
B – movable damper
E – burner ports

Left Cross-section of updraft kiln showing air circulation

Right Cross-section of downdraft kiln showing air circulation

Robert Turner's woodburning downdraft kiln

Richard Hirsch's fiber raku kiln

Lisa Larson's electric side-loading, high-temperature kiln in Sweden

Extendible rings for unlimited height electric firing

Jun Kaneko's downdraft car kiln for large wares

Throwing salt into the outdoor downdraft kiln at the University of Southern California

Open-fire pit kiln, Toluca, Mexico

Building the "Tree of Life" kiln over the ware at Metapec, Mexico

any shape, and designed for side or top load; they can also be bought in multi-sectioned rings that stack. Low-fire electric kilns have ni-chrome elements good to 2000 °F (1093 °C); high-fire temperatures need Kanthal-A1 elements that fire to cone 8 (or cone 10, but not for long).

In using an electric kiln, learn to manipulate the low-, medium-, and high-temperature switches to allow even firings. Never go by the hour timer that comes with some electric kilns; always use cones and a pyrometer-thermocouple device. Small kilns firing only to low temperature (cone 04) can be plugged into most domestic electricity supplies. Large kilns, and all kilns firing to high temperatures, must be fitted with fuses capable of carrying a current load of 60 amps. In the U.S.A. they must be specially installed on a 220-volt system using 6 gauge copper wire.

OTHER TYPES OF KILN

Salt and various specialized *firings* will be discussed later in this chapter. Salt kilns are usually hard-brick downdrafts; since salt is deleterious to brick, these kilns need frequent rebuilding. For *raku kilns*, and fuming techniques at low temperature, soft brick serves the purpose.

Pit firing is done in a hole in the ground. It may be lined with brick or with a few inches of wet clay that will harden in the first firing, and covered with a piece of metal or kiln shelves.

Sawdust firing can be done in a regular galvanized metal garbage can. The ware is buried in sawdust or other materials that will smoke, and is smoldered and smothered; punch holes in the can for air. Sawdust can also be a component in a *saggar*.

Saggar firing is done in a handbuilt or wheel-thrown lidded clay box, or a bricked-up box (a saggar), in which the materials for fuming or smoking are placed (pp. 213, 214). Other ware can be stacked as usual in the kiln without harm from the closed saggar, and the kiln can be fired normally. A piece set in the saggar can be fired in a kiln to any temperature, with the look and density differing from low to high fire.

Loose-brick kilns can be built up without mortar around the claywork, or completely without mortar so as to be more movable. They can then be left up for long periods, or taken down when the firing is finished. A loose-brick kiln can be fired with any fuel, or have a simple burner grid, or use a portable gas burner.

Solar kilns have been built experimentally with some success on small works at various temperatures, but cannot be considered a viable method for normal firing; too much superstructure is needed to yield high temperature for average-sized pieces.

Gravity-feed kilns are interesting, but are probably not viable for studio ceramics. Industry uses them for talc-body tiles where the ceramic piece drops through the firing and cooling cycle in minutes.

PLACING KILNS

Altitude is important in designing a kiln if the fuel is carbonaceous — with electricity, altitude doesn't matter. At sea level, there are no problems, but at elevations of 5,000 ft (1,600 m) or more, gaining temperature is difficult. More burners, a tall shape, or updraft rather than downdraft provide solutions. Blowers do not enhance firing at high altitudes because oxygen is scarce. A delicate balance is always important between the factors of kiln size and shape, burner placement, and orifice size; the dimension and flow of the combustion or flue space inside the chamber are especially critical at high altitude.

Outside installation insures adequate ventilation, but may cause rapid cooling. Down-firing can be used to slow the cooling process, and the air ports can be blocked after firing.

Inside installation should be in a fireproof room with a high ceiling, and windows and doors that can be kept open. There should be plenty of space surrounding the kiln. In some situations, a hood at least 18 in (45 cm) above the kiln and a stack to exit the building 7 ft (213 cm) above the roof line are required by law; if legal restrictions do not apply, the kiln can be vented directly out of a window or the roof. Once it is installed and firing patterns that work are established, it is not prudent to move the kiln.

Clayton James builds loose-brick kilns around his large, handbuilt vessels

KILN MATERIALS

The material from which a kiln is built influences its firing. Hard, dense, refractory bricks need more time to heat up, hold the heat longer, and are slow to cool; lightweight insulating bricks heat and cool quickly. You can use one course of brick plus insulating material, or several courses of brick, to achieve approximately the same heating and cooling time. Buy bricks that will withstand several cones more than the highest you will fire.

New ceramic fiber blankets and blocks are a lighter, but not cheaper, alternative to brick. If you use them you will have to change your firing schedules, because fiber does not absorb and hold heat the way brick does. Fiber kilns may need to be fired down slowly on the cooling side to prevent thermal shock.

Japanese folk potters make the brick for their stoneware kilns out of fire clay and straw. Many cultures still make bricks for low-firing kilns by hand from their pottery clays. Today, refractory bricks are available in a variety of shapes for every structural form, and in many compositions according to temperature and atmospheric requirements, for the building of any chamber. There are also good manufacturers of readymade and made-to-order kilns.

Kiln construction can be simple or complicated, depending on the desired life expectancy for the furnace, protection from the elements, and the degree of controllability. At the simplest, refractory fiber blankets can be used to make a kiln anywhere — on the ground, in a pit or a garbage can. One course of brick, hard or soft, can be covered with

Chip Garner built this solar kiln at the University of California, Santa Barbara

refractory insulation such as vermiculite, or can be backed or fronted with fiber. Conventional kilns may have two or three courses of brick to make them more durable, or one layer can be insulated and encased in metal.

Burners can be temporary units made portable with plastic tubing or flexible conduits attached to the fuel source; they can be constructed from beer cans or pipes, or can be bought readymade from reliable companies and installed permanently.

Kiln shelves must be level, or pieces warp even in the bisque fire. Silicon carbide shelves hold up well, but are expensive. Clay shelves do not last at high fire; cordurite does not hold up as well as silicon carbide, but is better than clay.

Consult thoroughly before you build or buy a kiln.

Carrying greenware for packing in the largest *noborigama* (chamber-style hill kiln) in Japan; Otani, Shikoku Island

Students at Valley College, Ridgecrest, California, building a salt kiln

A catenary arch kiln is easier to build than a sprung arch. Drop a chain from two points to the proper height for the kiln, draw the curve the chain makes, transfer it to plywood, and then cut and use the form for the brick laying. Burners here are on the side for cross draft; salt ports will be in the front

Raku tongs, for putting pieces into a hot kiln or fire, and removing them hot

STACKING KILNS

BISQUE

Greenware is bisque-fired to red heat, 1500 °F (815 °C) or above, to facilitate handling for the glazing process and to prevent blow-ups on glazed pieces. Talc bodies should be bisqued one or two cones higher than the planned glaze firing because of impurities. Clay bodies are usually bisqued much lower than the glaze firing to keep them porous; 1600 °F (870 °C) is sufficient. Porcelain bodies can be bisqued high and glazed low when it is desirable for the body to be dense but the glaze is to be low temperature.

All kiln firings should be as rapid as is expedient for the sake of energy conservation and economy; *stilting* helps the speedy bisquing of thick and even damp greenware. For fast bisque firing, put all greenware on stilts, off the kiln shelf, to improve air and heat circulation. Large vessels bisque best on the side, on tripod stilts or broken kiln shelves, levelled with clay wads. Stilting also facilitates even heat treatment of dry ware, and lessens accidents.

It is preferable to stack individual items singly in a fast-firing bisque (four to six hours), when pieces are very large, or when they are of precarious weight or profile. If pieces are stacked inside or on top of each other, weight distribution and shrinkage must be taken into account. The best rule is: don't do it if you think it is unreasonable to expect a successful outcome.

Electric kilns are problem glazers; Dorothy Hafner's fiber kiln "taught" her how to fire

Bisque-stacking in a large electric kiln; ware must not touch elements; pile it lip to lip or foot in foot, lids askew

Refractory fiber cradles broad shapes; powdered silica or sand can be used instead

Leather-hard ware bisques quickly if stilted; air circulates underneath, and few blow-ups occur

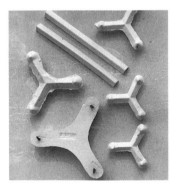

Clay stilts for bisque and low-fire glaze

Self-leveling three-point shelf suspension gives most space; use clay or silica pads between them

A glaze kiln at Hunter College, New York City, is loaded to the top to help hold heat

Dora de Larios loads her car kiln with large sculpture and plates

Bisquing and high firing large flat works is difficult, but some helpful generalizations can be made: very thin cross-sections are hardest to keep flat; firing the kiln evenly helps; and elevating the tile from the kiln shelf with zirconia sand (very refractory), a bed of kaolin, bar-stilts, or a fiber blanket is necessary. Standing tiles upright if the dimension is not too great works best in the bisque, but not always at high temperature. If large slabs have been dried evenly they will fire better. Big flat tiles can be evenly supported among ceramic fiber blankets or ceramic fiber board and will fire well in a pile. In other words, there is a reason most commercially manufactured floor and wall tile is only 4 in (10 cm) square; not much is manufactured flat with dimensions of over 12 in (30 cm). Make large slabs 1 in (2.5 cm) or more thick; thickness limits warpage, but extends drying and firing time.

Huge sculptures should be built on $\frac{1}{2}$ in (1 cm) thick plywood board on which sand can be placed for movement if the piece is heavy; the board is loaded on a forklift into the kiln and burned out in the fire. Building on a 2 in (5 cm) thick pad of newspapers is an important possibility for medium-sized, broad shapes and for drying extra-large platters; newsprint absorbs moisture slowly and evenly and can be burned out in the kiln.

Greenware that is bisquing should never be fired with low-fire glazed pieces; raw ware robs the glaze of oxygen.

GLAZE

Glazed pieces must not touch in the kiln. Molten glaze bubbles like boiling water and attaches itself to nearby objects or shelves. A finger's distance between wares is not enough; 1 in (2.5 cm) is better. In gas kilns, stack to the muffle- or the bag-wall if there is one; in open-fire kilns, stack to within 4 in (10 cm) of each wall. In electric kilns, glazed ware should be 2 in (5 cm) from the elements; stacking work too close to them causes burns or devitrification; elements also flake off and drop into glaze. Stack pieces apart for air circulation, and leave 3 to 4 in (7.5 to 10 cm) above the tallest item on each shelf before loading the next shelf. Gas or other petroleum or organic-fueled kilns have natural air circulation; still, the more space there is between shelves and among works, the better the kiln will fire. Lids should be fired on pots, and feet in stoneware and porcelain firings should be free of glaze.

As previously mentioned, kiln shelves must be level. Place pads of plastic silica-kaolin between posts and shelves for stability; three-point posting of shelves keeps them level. *Kiln wash* — 50 parts silica to 50 parts kaolin — is often painted on shelves to protect them from glaze drops, and keeping posts and shelves clean also helps them to stay level. (You may decide not to kiln-wash shelves, in order to turn them over for alternate firings to discourage warping. Without kiln wash on the shelves to protect them, be certain to glaze in proper thickness and to wipe each foot clean $\frac{1}{4}$ in [.6 cm] up from the base.)

Stack evenly to the top. If only three pieces are fired, give each of them one third of the space. Mass, volume, and weight all hold heat; so, to stack the mass evenly, create an arrangement that mixes the sizes together, rather than grouping all small wares in one place and all large ones in another. Leaving a chimney up the center of the kiln, using shelves staggered or not butted together, helps in fast firing. The quality of a kiln firing depends largely on how well it is stacked.

FIRING

The principles and methods of firing are the same whether it is bisque or glaze, high or low temperature, salt or fume, or whatever, with the possible exception of bonfire. All clayware goes through four stages during firing: *water smoking, dehydration, oxidation,* and *vitrification.*

Bisque firing includes water smoking and dehydration, when physical and chemical water is removed from the ware in the initial stages. Physical water is the tapwater added to dry clay, and it evaporates at boiling point in the process of water smoking. Chemical water is the H_2O in the chemical composition of clay; it is driven off up to 900 °F (485 °C) in the dehydration process.

Fire during the day or the night, but stay close to the kiln. Do not simply leave it on low heat overnight — sometimes called *candeling* — for the first firing stages, as that is wasteful and dangerous. Using just one setting, any kiln, gas or electric, gets as hot in a few hours as it does in 12 hours; the settings for burners or elements need to be changed gradually but steadily for heat to rise evenly.

With greenware, use stilts, leave the door or lid open a crack to insure that all moisture can escape from the chamber, and slowly raise the temperature on the pyrometer — 50 to 100 degrees per hour for large ware, faster but evenly for small ware — to 900 °F (485 °C). Not controlling a kiln, no matter what kind, not raising the temperature little by little, will draw out the cycle. A mirror held close to the peephole or door (which is a fraction open), to "fog up," will tell you whether moist air is still being emitted; if not, danger is past.

When 900 °F (485 °C) is reached, the ware is no longer liable to blow up. The open door or lid can be closed, and the kiln heated as fast as it will fire — perhaps another hour to bisque temperature, 1600 °F (870 °C), or whatever is necessary for your work. The shorter the firing cycle, the closer the kiln must be watched and manipulated, but the more economical it will be in time and energy.

Once the ware has been bisqued, in the glaze fire the kiln passes quickly through the first two stages of the firing cycle, and slows according to a prescribed schedule for the next oxidation and vitrification stages, from about 1100 °F (600 °C) to top temperature. This oxidation period is not to be confused with oxidation atmosphere; it is called oxidation because impurities burn off or unite with oxygen (some of this will in fact already have taken place during bisquing) at 1100 to 1600 °F (600 to 870 °C). Beyond this, glaze firing progresses toward vitrification rather fast, before slowing down to rise the last 100° (F or C) in 45 minutes to an hour to allow the glaze to mellow and mature. Without this slow-down, it can look harsh and underfired, even if the proper cone is achieved. But be careful not to "soak" glazes or clays in heat by holding them at the same temperature, which causes other visual changes to occur; the firing should reach maximum heat and then begin to cool.

FIREPLACE FIRING

Stoked with wood gathered from the streets of New York, Robert Segall's kiln for miniature fireplace work is nearing temperature; note the plug to watch low-temperature cones; salting is possible toward the end of the firing

Kiln opened and found to be underfired after firing a ten-hour stoke; next time, stacking will be more open to create more draft, and draw trials will be pulled during the fire to monitor progress

PRINCIPLES OF KILN FIRING

1 BALANCING FIRING FACTORS

All firing is a balancing act between time, temperature, and atmosphere. The longer the firing time, the less important is the way you get through the firing; in other words, time heals. If the firing is short, how you fire is much more important — how fast, how slow, and at what points, with what rates of temperature change. The longer the firing time, the less reduction is needed; the shorter the whole cycle, the more reduction is needed. Keeping a clean oxidizing atmosphere may mean allowing more time for oxidation to take place. Oxidation is not as complicated an atmosphere as reduction; on the other hand, some kilns and some fuels do not oxidize well.

The factor of time does not necessarily apply to the whole firing cycle, just to crucial points; study time and temperature as they apply to each of the clays and glazes you use. Some low-fire glaze colors, such as reds, oranges, and yellows, are critical in their demands to be fully oxidized; their oxidation depends on time rather than temperature, yet a slightly higher temperature sometimes gives a better surface.

Temperature heals, as does time. At low fire, it is harder to achieve quality surfaces; everything melts better at high temperatures. Low-temperature firing can be shorter simply because the temperature developed is lower, but be sure to observe the one-hour slowdown at the last 100 degrees of the firing, to mature the glazes fully.

2 FIRING SPEED

Firing speed varies, according to the kind of kiln and the fuel — the way the kiln is constructed and the *BTU* (British Thermal Unit, a unit of heat by which fuels are rated) of the fuel. In general:

A. Downdraft kilns take longer than updraft kilns to fire

B. Gas kilns are more controllable than electric ones

C. The more burners a gas kiln has, the faster it fires and the more controllable it is

D. The more electric elements and switches an electric kiln has, the faster it fires, and the more controllable it is (the newer the elements, the faster the kiln)

E. Size of burner, gas pressure, orifice size, and size of gas line are all variables that pertain to speed of fire

F. Propane is faster than natural gas (it provides more BTUs)

G. Oil and other impure petroleums take longer to fire than gas

H. Proper combustion space in the kiln speeds firing

I. Stacking of the bisque or glaze kiln makes a great difference to firing time

J. Altitude affects firing speed, except with electric kilns: sea level is fastest, and firing takes longer as elevation gets higher

K. Hard brick kilns take more time to heat up than soft brick ones, but hard bricks hold the heat longer

L. Ceramic fiber kilns do not fire like brick kilns, and they cool very fast.

3 RECORDING FIRINGS

Keep records of each firing, bisque or glaze; eventually cull them and keep the best and maybe the worst firing records. Firing requires experience, almost more than anything else in ceramics. Sometimes, it is so exciting that you forget to keep records or think you will remember. I cannot overemphasize the importance of written records of every firing, no matter how much experience you have. Write an analysis after unpacking each kiln-load.

Firing records are of two kinds: *anecdotal* and by *firing curve* plotted on a time-temperature grid.

Anecdotal record. Log the kind of day or night it is, rainy or dry (moisture in the air aids firing, dry days make it more difficult, nights are best), windy or still (even if the kiln is indoors); whether the ware is dry or moist; the time the kiln is started; how the burners or switches are set, how the damper is set (if there is one), whether the door or lid is open or closed; the temperature the pyrometer is registering (before the kiln is turned on it should be room temperature); and anything else that needs to be recorded. Watch the kiln and make new entries at least every 30 minutes, under each of these headings. (See Bernard Leach's kiln log, p. 208, for his method of recording a firing.)

Firing curve. Plotting a firing curve is almost more important than anything else in learning to fire, but it is the one aspect that seems to be difficult for all of us. Make a graph of even squares or rectangles covering a page (and photocopy it so you have a stack of forms for future firings). Mark degrees up the left-hand side from 100° to 2500°F (38° to 1371°C), and across the bottom in hours from 1 to 9 hours.

Begin by putting a point where starting time and temperature intersect; an hour later, mark another point for both time and temperature; connect the points with a line and the curve begins. In some complicated firings like high-temperature reduction, you may want to record every 10 to 15 minutes; make a graph with more markings to allow this.

4 VARYING TEMPERATURES FOR REDUCTION

As you have seen in some of my glaze tests in chapter 4, glazes appear the same in reduction from cone 04 to cone 10. If you want to fire at a low temperature to save fuel, it is possible to duplicate all the cone 10 reduction results with similar types of glazes and the same copper and iron percentages; it is especially easy at cone 6.

5 KNOWING YOUR KILN

Built exactly alike and installed next to each other, still no two kilns will fire alike. Every kiln has variables and foibles. Principles will help in analyzing and solving firing problems; specific knowledge of your kiln will help you to duplicate results. Gas varies, pressure varies, even if there are two off-shoots to two kilns in the same line; bricks are made individually, and individually they vary; stacking is always a variable in how a kiln fires.

6 THE DAMPER

Closing the damper at the end of firing is approved procedure, but try not doing it. Leave the damper open as the pyrometer drops by 400 to 500°F (200 to 250°C), then close the damper. Record what you do. Fast-cooling at top temperature can set glaze effects such as crystals. Try various amounts of degree drop or time of leaving the damper open. Nothing is so precious that you cannot experiment.

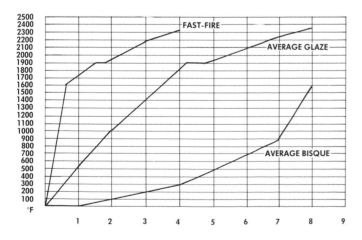

Fast-fire and average firing curve for glaze cone 10, and average bisque firing curve. Damper and burner (or switch) settings can be written in along the curve

7 NECESSARY GAS PRESSURE

In the United States, residential and commercial gas pressure is measured in inches of water column (the number of inches that a column of water in a tube is moved by gas pressure, usually read on a water-column gauge now). High-pressure gas, such as propane, can be measured in pounds. Gas companies in the U.S.A. are allowed to give 8 to 10 in of water column in the line in the street or at your meter, and the pressure is similar in the U.K. Firing with natural gas is best when you have 8 in water-column pressure at the kiln when all burner valves are open. Propane needs the same; 8 in of water column equals 1/4 pound pressure. If you lack inches of water column pressure, as we do in New York City (which has 3 to 4 in maximum in the street) then you need a larger diameter gas line than the usual 1 to 1 1/2 in pipe; use 2 to 3 in diameter pipe for the gas-line installation. Most natural gas companies give 8 to 10 in pressure at your kiln by installing a larger meter free of charge. Propane pressure can be regulated at the tank.

8 FIRING LARGE WARE

Kilns vary in what needs to be done to fire large work slowly and evenly. Downdrafts (as compared with updrafts) heat more slowly, and theoretically have more even heat circulation, both of which are better for large work. Updraft kilns have fire at the bottom or on the sides, and a hole at the top; usually, they are hotter at the bottom than the top. Control this tendency by understanding which burners or burner valves control the bottom, and which the top, of your kiln. In my updraft, the four middle burners on a 12-burner grid control the bottom, and the other eight (two on each side of the grid) control the top. There are two gas-burner control valves, one for the center four burners, one for the eight outside burners. I vary them at different inches of water-column pressure to keep the heat even, adjusting continuously by watching the color of the heat in the kiln, top and bottom. Updrafts can fire large work much faster than downdrafts if the kiln heat is kept even.

Electric kilns can be controlled if at least three switches can be manipulated. The tendency is to think electric kilns fire themselves; they can, but they ought not, and they should be controlled with the same attention as gas kilns. The key for big work is evenness of fire; time helps but, as mentioned before, not a long time at the same temperature — instead, raise the temperature consistently by a few degrees over a long period. Sometimes kilns should be fired down to retard cooling and keep it even: turn burners or elements on and off on the cooling side.

"REBIRTH THROUGH CLAY"

Bernard Leach, living link between East and West, with his colleagues Shoji Hamada (p. 49) and Soetsu Yanagi, Buddhist scholar and esthetician, founded a movement called "mingei" in the 1920s. It was a synthesis of work and life with roots in tradition and involving a "rebirth through clay." The movement spread in Japan to an awareness of all village crafts. Internationally, it was exemplified by individuals working with their hands as a way and a means of life. In 1920, Leach began his own pottery at St. Ives in Cornwall, England, with the help of Hamada.

Hamada and Leach became renowned artists, exhibited in museums in many countries. Leach wrote many books, and traveled the world, lecturing and counselling clayworkers. *A Potter's Book*, published in 1940 by Faber and Faber in England, is a lively and sensitive discussion of the craft of clay, with an introduction entitled "Towards a Standard" which is still valid today. Leach describes the recording of a firing, then the unpacking:

"Altogether it was one of those days which make a potter's existence worthwhile; nevertheless at the end of it, when the pots were all out and the best of them assembled in groups, I experienced a sudden depression. This may have been partly due to enervation from the heat and general tiredness, but I think every artist and potter will know what I mean. At any rate it is counterbalanced by realistic self-criticism and various practical suggestions as to future efforts, which always arise during the unpacking."

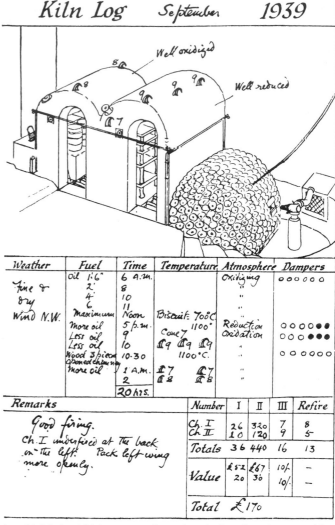

Leach's kiln fired 20 hours, as indicated on the log, from 6 a.m. until 2 a.m. the next day

SPECIAL FIRING TECHNIQUES

Clayworkers now use a number of challenging approaches other than these standard firing methods. They can be so exciting that some people tackle a special technique first, before or instead of learning the standard ways. However, it is usually best to begin with the standard methods, as they develop an understanding which can only help when special techniques are tried.

FAST-FIRING

I learned about fast-firing the hard way. Having been trained at New York State College of Ceramics at Alfred University to do 18- to 24-hour downdraft kiln firings to cone 10, I began to cut firing time in the 1960s when I had three young children. By then, I had built the first open-fire multiburner updraft kilns that would permit fast-fire, but I had not recognized how much potential difference in firing time existed between updraft and downdraft kilns. I gradually chopped hours off firing time, over several years, until the fastest was cone 10 reduction in three and a half hours, start to finish. Along the way, I learned that the bigger the pieces, the more care was needed to keep the kiln even. In fact, after a great deal of breakage, I settled on a six-hour firing when the piece was as tall as the interior chamber of my kiln (4 feet, 120 cm). Cooling was definitely a problem; the kiln is outside and has 12 burners underneath it — the temperature fell too quickly for big work when it was fast-fired. Part of the solution was to close the damper and board up around the base with kiln shelves as soon as the kiln was turned off.

Firing at this rate means watching the kiln continuously — hardly leaving it for a minute. I plot points on the firing curve every three to four minutes, noting every possible variable. With reduction, I record how high the flame is out of the damper, how long the lick of flame is at the peephole, how much feathering of the burners there is under the kiln, and what color all of the flames are. Damper movement is crucial to fast-fire. I measure how much I tap the metal ends of my damper slab in tiny fractions, and record the movement to the last 1/32 of an inch. It may seem ridiculous, but this degree of accuracy is essential to fast-firing.

I glaze a whole kiln-load at once, recording the glazes (which takes about 12 hours), and then fire immediately. I used to blow the sides out of wet-glazed ware in fast-fire before I learned to pre-warm the ware. I turn one set of burners on as low as possible and stack the warm kiln as I glaze; only the last piece goes in really wet but, by then, the kiln is hot enough to dry it.

Another imperative of fast-fire is to get to 1600 °F (870 °C) on your firing curve in the first half hour, or 45 minutes at the most. If you do not manage this, forget a three- to four-hour firing. It is essential, after getting the temperature up fast, to slow down the curve for the rest of the firing.

For me, fast-firing has been a challenge, once I realized it was possible. I researched by trying different maneuvers

Susan Peterson, copper red bottle, cone 10 reduction, kiln schedule three and a half hours

Pulling a draw trial to check the accumulation of salt glaze on the ware (p. 211)

during each firing. I also coupled firing control with control of copper reduction reds. I have spent many years perfecting varieties of blues, turquoises, reds, pinks, and purples, by slightly varying the amounts of copper in the same glaze and by varying the application techniques, meanwhile controlling the reduction atmosphere and the firing cycle as much as possible. Without a strict firing curve on each firing, and much consideration of where the differences occurred, I could not have achieved such control.

Peterson fast-fire schedule. This is a schedule with a top temperature of cone 10, in a reduction atmosphere for copper reds and celadons, using my Peterson-style updraft open-fire 24 cubic foot (.68 cu m) kiln chamber with 12 burners underneath it, installed outdoors.

Raise the temperature to 1600 °F (870 °C) in the first 30 to 45 minutes, with damper half-open. The center four burners, on one valve, should begin at 1 in (2.5 cm); the eight side burners, on one valve, should be at ½ in (1.25 cm).

Move the outside burner valve upward and/or adjust the damper to get a rise of about 50 degrees per minute. Leave center burners on 1 inch (2.5 cm) until close to the end of the fire.

Next, go from 1600 to 1900 °F (870 to 1037 °C) in another 30 to 45 minutes; your hand should feel some back pressure (heat-flow) at the peephole, and the damper may have to be moved in slightly to keep the temperature rising. The side burners will have increased a few inches. Continue from now on to adjust the outside burner setting, and the damper, to keep the heat rising — too much fuel causes the temperature to stall; too open a damper causes heat loss, as can too closed a damper.

At 1900 °F (1037 °C), begin reduction by turning on excess-gas jets — small tubes on your burners for gas without air — if you have them. Turn them to a 1 in (2.5 cm) flame (or to 1 to 3 in of water column if you have a gauge, as I do). Probably push damper in slightly, and hold 1900 °F (1037 °C) for 15 minutes; back pressure at the open peephole will increase, and some flame will project there. (Scientists say that iron and copper reduce best at this temperature and at 2150 °F (1175 °C).) You should now be one to one and a half hours into the firing.

Take 1900 to 2000 °F (1037 to 1093 °C) in one hour and 2000 to 2200 °F (1093 to 1204 °C) in one hour, but pause a few minutes at 2150 °F (1175 °C) to give a bit more reduction by closing the damper a fraction. From 1900 °F (1037 °C) onward, the flame from the open peepholes extends about 6 in (15 cm), and the flame at the top (at the damper) extends about a foot. Try for blue and yellow transparent flames, with a sprinkling of copper green (if there is copper in the glaze); flames should not be orange and smoky.

Allow 30 minutes or an hour from 2200 °F (1204 °C) to cone 10 bending (about 2350 °F [1300 °C]). Inside the kiln there should be minor turbulence and a slightly clouded atmosphere. Keep the reduction flames and the heat rising

by continually adjusting the damper as the outside burner gauge is raised to the maximum inches of water-column pressure. When necessary, increase the center burner gauge to get to top temperature in the proper time. Turn the burners down to read the cones, then back up.

To create moist steam, I use a stream of water from a garden hose or from bucketsful of water thrown under and over the top of the kiln every 15 minutes or so after 1900 °F (1037 °C) (see below). If the kiln refuses to move upward in temperature, reduce the fuel input slightly by lowering the burner settings, or provide more air intake by opening the damper slightly, or water it more frequently. Too much fuel without enough air cannot combust, and combustion is essential to raise temperature. Throughout the firing, do one thing at a time, and make each change very slight, recording as you go.

This schedule is more or less three and a half hours to four hours, depending on how patient you are at maneuvering the varying kiln factors in order to keep on target. To elongate it to a normal eight to ten hour length, increase the initial time to 1600 °F (870 °C), give extra time at 1900 °F (1037 °C), and stretch out 2150 to 2300 °F (1175 to 1260 °C); the curve will still go at a steep angle to 1600° (870°), arch to 1900° (1037°), and flatten to cone 10.

Stacking for fast-fire. Stacking is more crucial in fast-fire than for normal eight to ten hour firings because of the speed of heat treatment. Leave more space than usual between the ware and the kiln shelves, and stagger the shelves where you can; think of "channeling" or "pulling" the atmosphere as well as the heat in and around the ware. To enhance this effect, I use 6 to 8 in (15 to 20 cm) kiln posts hanging over the edge of each shelf in any direction, and into the flue.

Watering the kiln. Another fast-firing tip is to water the kiln after red heat and on to peak temperature. Some years ago I realized this, because my outdoor kiln was firing better in the rain. The firing went more smoothly and easily; reduction was accomplished with less use of the damper; and the ware was stronger after firing. I remembered that some used-brick manufacturers shoot water into a kiln at various ports to change the color of the brick, and that Shoji Hamada always tried to fire in the rain. I find it best to use a water hose to "make rain" on top of the kiln, and also shoot it under the kiln, to cause billows of steam, every 15 minutes or so, even on gas kilns that are indoors.

Silica inversion. Chemists refer to the *silica inversion* as a point of strain; this is when silica expands and contracts from alpha to beta quartz, in all four times during the firing and cooling cycle — at 500° and 1000 °F (260° and 540 °C) on the firing side, and again at 1000° and 500 °F (540° and 260 °C) on the cooling side. As students, we were advised to go slowly at each of these temperatures upward and downward. But if silica inversion were much of a factor, I could not be firing as fast as I am. The only conclusion I can draw is that silica inversion may occur, but it does not seem to be a problem.

SALT GLAZING

This dramatic firing is accomplished in a hard-brick down-draft kiln by throwing rock salt into the atmosphere at the maturing temperature of unglazed raw clay, in a kiln used only for salt. It produces a characteristic clear, glossy, orange-peel texture on unglazed clay as sodium from the salt unites with silica in the clay. Developed in middle Europe in the 16th century, salt glazing was used, as it is today, as an alternative surface for functional, sturdy engobe-decorated claywares. It has quite a different appearance from ordinary glaze, but in fact glaze can also be used for patterning in a salt kiln.

Low-fire salting prior to the maturing temperature of a clay body gives brighter colors, but less shine, than high-fire salting. Bisqued ware can be post-fire salted in a fire-proof bucket or in a kiln in which salt has been placed from the start, or into which the salt is inserted at red heat.

The best orange-peel texture is produced from cone 5 to cone 10 on stoneware and porcelain by throwing shovels-ful of wet rock salt or salt bundles (newspaper-wrapped and soaked in water) into the firing chamber at peak temperature. Pull draw trials after each addition of salt to watch the orange-peel gloss develop (p. 209). Cones are invalid in salt firings, but use them anyway for consistency; to chart your firing, note the fire color and pull the draw trials.

Firing a salt kiln at night is beautiful, and darkness seems to enhance the popping sound of the salt as it hits the fire. You can use from a few pounds to several hundred pounds of rock salt (100 lb or 45.4 kg is average). Kilns that have been salted many times accumulate salt; it is deleterious and eventually they need to be rebuilt.

A salt kiln should be outside for ventilation. Chemists agree that gases resulting from the use of sodium chloride are not hazardous above 2000 °F (1093 °C), which is the lowest temperature used for low-fire salt glazing. Some clayworkers use sodium bicarbonate (baking soda) instead of sodium chloride because it is chlorine-free and they thus do not have to worry about safety concerns; this gives brighter colors, but not as much of an orange-peel effect as rock salt.

All clays salt differently, but sodium makes most colors in the engobes brighter. As salting is a form of reducing, copper may give reds and pinks. White porcelain bodies and china clay engobes develop orange tinges. Grog and the amount of free silica in the clay body cause variations.

The *kiln furniture* (shelves and posts) will salt too, as will the bottoms of pots and flanges of lids. To prevent this, paint those surfaces with alumina oxide and water or with aluminum paint that becomes alumina oxide in the fire. Use plastic china clay, mixed with alumina oxide, for wads between posts and shelves for stability, and under ware as well, to prevent sticking. Hamada used wads of china clay/alumina filling under seashells as stilts; the shell turned to ash, but the clay mixture supported the piece, leaving seashell impressions on the pot feet.

CRYSTALLINE GLAZING

Crystalline glazes require high zinc and low alumina in the composition. Firing is usually to cone 10 with a drop to cone 5, where the temperature may be held several hours to "grow" the crystals in the glaze.

FUMING

This technique, which comes from glass technology, is usually associated with a silver patina, a colored silvery shine, or randomly patterned marks developed on un-glazed or glazed clay. It is accomplished in a saggar, by using various thin-gauge metals like copper, brass, or aluminum, or salts such as stannous (tin) chloride for silvery tones. They are either placed in the saggar in the kiln chamber with the work, or are added later. Fire from 1500° to 2300 °F (815° to 1260 °C) to observe the differences temperature makes. Fuming can either be a post-firing process after the work has been taken to another temperature with other color treatments, or the entire coloration can be developed on raw clay in one firing.

RAKU

This process has been enthusiastically adopted worldwide since its origination in Japan in the latter part of the 16th century. "Raku" means happiness and it is also the name of a dynasty of Japanese potters whose works were often chosen by tea masters for the tea ceremony. Raku earthenware pieces and their fascinating quick-firing process were brought to the U.S.A. in 1947 by Warren Gilbertson, and caught the imagination of many clayworkers.

Clay, glazed or unglazed but preferably bisqued, is put into a hot (1800 °F, 982 °C) kiln for a few minutes. If it is glazed, a glassy surface shine like melting ice will appear. The work is pulled out hot, then smoked in a metal container of leaves, brush, pine needles, or similar, and finally quenched in cold water to stop the heat action. For large pieces, it is wise to make a kiln that moves off the ware, pulled like a drawer or lifted on a winch; the work can then be smoked, if desired, and quenched in place.

Raku glazes can be any low-temperature glazes that you already use; or make new ones from frits, clay, and silica (chapter 4) or simple Gerstley borate, soda ash, and borax bases (our low-temperature melts from the fusion button and 34 raw material 50/50 blend tests). Add colorants to raku glazes as usual; silver nitrate and other salts can be added to give lustrous finishes. The kiln can be any type — electric side loading, gas, propane, loose-brick, or fiber blanket. An electric kiln can be equipped with a thermostatic control, allowing it to climb to temperature fast and hold the heat, even with repeated door openings and closings to insert and take out ware.

Laura Andreson achieves lively colors with nitrates of metals in low-temperature fuming

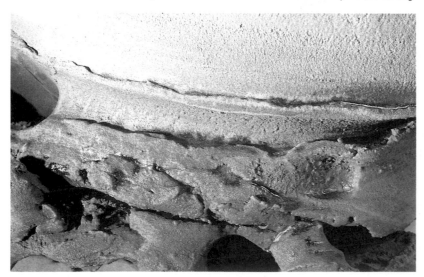

Ken Hendry's fumed colors from a charcoal post-firing

David Middlebrook's loose-brick kiln for fuming holds metals like brass, steel, aluminum, and salt — with the burnished greenware — for coloration during low-temperature firing. Finished pieces of a sculpture cool outside the kiln

Joyce Clark's post-firing magazine and salt smoking is accomplished with a more-or-less portable kiln moved outside and a portable burner on a portable propane tank (see bottom photograph). She stuffs magazines, which smoke better than newspapers, in and around all pieces, also sprinkling rock salt in and around them. The kiln is fired in oxidation for one and a half hours to about 1800 °F (982 °C), and reduced for 30 minutes. If the atmosphere does not seem smoky enough, the top can be opened to insert materials such as green grass, plants, tar paper, or even moth balls (generally used for reducing electric kilns)

Bill Davis saggar-fires in a regular kiln, building a brick housing around the vessels and the garbage, metals, salt, and organic materials. The kiln's own fuel is the fire for this saggar; other pieces can also be firing outside the saggar in the conventional manner. Alternatively, this is an appropriate method for sawdust fire. Either firing works at low or high temperature

Paul Soldner, an experimenter in raku firing and surface development, has built a kiln that moves on tracks for ease in moving ware into and out of the fire

CHARCOAL FIRING

Philip Cornelius' saggar is built in an updraft kiln on the top bricks to elevate it; it is not quite closed during firing. Charcoal drips into the firebox and leaves a residue of carbon and color

Kaolin bodies tend to turn orange under this charcoal firing, as they do in salt firing. These finished handbuilt porcelain teapots are white, orange, gray, and black

Cornelius adds charcoal briquets to the saggar to patina porcelain greenware. He fires the kiln to cone 11 and then dumps about 100 lb (45.4 kg) of charcoal into the saggar; sometimes charcoal goes in at the beginning and not the end

WOOD FIRING

Associated with oriental-style climbing kilns of one sort or another, wood firing is a highly physical technique which can be used two ways: (1) to develop a patina or a glaze directly on greenware or bisqued clay from the dropping and piling up of wood ash during the wood firing (p. 161); and (2) just as fuel, for conventional glazes or glazes made with wood ash as the primary flux (in this case, it is not obvious what kind of fuel was used when looking at the glazed results).

Wood-fired kilns exist all over the world. Japan and Korea probably have more built in the hill-kiln style than other countries; today, the traditional pottery villages that are still in existence usually begin firing with petroleum and only end with wood. In England, this style of kiln is short, with perhaps two or three chambers, while oriental *nobori-gama* have five to eight chambers. Traditional updraft wood kilns abound in central Europe, India, Mexico, and South America.

Wood kilns have become popular in recent years in the United States — where they have not always been so traditional — for a variety of reasons, including living near a wood supply, being enamored of the look of wood-fired patina, or the remarkable challenge of the spontaneity of wood-stoking. Below are some comments of a few of the many artists who wood-fire; they illustrate some of the effects of wood-firing methods.

Color variations. Over long periods of firing, ash builds up and causes color variations, as seen in the wood fire of Paul Chaleff in New York state, whose 30 ft (9 m) long *anagama* (p. 198) uses eight to ten cords of wood per firing. The kiln is stoked for warming at the fire mouth for about two days. Then, when the front of the firebox has reached kindling temperature, it is stoked with smaller pieces of wood. At the end of the third or fourth day, cone 11 is reached in the mouth; stoking of the first port begins with thin wood, and Chaleff continues stoking at the mouth. On day five, all side ports are being stoked. On the sixth day, many draw trials are pulled throughout the kiln to monitor color. Stoking continues for another two to three days — it takes about nine days in total. When the firing is finished, the kiln is sealed very well and cooled for five to six days, which is particularly necessary if the work is big.

Chaleff says that yellows form in the early build-up of ash that later melts or blows through the kiln at high temperature. Reds and browns result when very little ash falls on the clay; this can be effected by covering areas with other pieces or shards. Water sprayed into the kiln at cone 6 produces oranges and yellows. Gray-blues and soft reds come from charcoals building up and smothering ware, or from putting charcoal over pieces before the firing. "Once the clay is at high temperature," says Chaleff, "you are painting the ware from the chemistry of the wood, and by continually stoking, you are building depth."

Peter Callas' *anagama* in New Jersey is 18 ft (5.5 m)

Kiln god offering of saki on the wood-burning kiln in Kawaii Kanjaro's studio museum in Kyoto

Large updraft wood-burning kiln built into a hillside, and its firing mouth, Old Town, Cairo

long and about 4½ ft (1.3 m) tall and wide, with nearly straight sides. His cycle of seven days to fire and another seven to cool (with a team of three taking eight-hour shifts) uses eight cords of soft and hard wood. The first few days of firing use wood calculated to spread fine ash randomly over all the work. When the kiln is hot, coals are tossed onto the ware, which causes melting. Stoking of the side ports does not begin until cone 12 is reached at the front. Callas has been firing Peter Voulkos' wood-fired work since 1978.

On unglazed work, color changes in wood-fire are effected by manipulating the method of firing to produce more or less ash, changing the body or colorants in the body, injecting oxides and other materials into the kiln during the fire, covering areas so they are not exposed to the ash or other substances, placing bowls of rock salt in the kiln, wrapping the clay with seaweed or other plants, or changing the maturing temperature or length of firing.

Surface effects. Karen Karnes and Ann Stannard wood-fire in a Bourry box kiln in Vermont, based on a concept originally devised by Emile Bourry, a French engineer who worked in the early 20th century. The technique utilizes a downdraft firebox in which sticks lie at right angles to the direction of the line of draft (the opposite of most wood-firing kilns); a tall chimney is important. Two and a half cord of softwood fire the kiln to cone 11 in 18 hours; shorter firing does not yield the effects of fly ash burned into the unglazed surface that these two artists want. Karnes and Stannard reduce the atmosphere about ten hours into the fire and say that there is music as the river of fire is pulled through, and a visual sensation of being at one with it.

In contrast to those who fire unglazed ware (mostly for many days and nights of exuberant stoking to achieve the natural effects of almost indescribably mellow colorations that ash deposits give), there are those who glaze the work before it goes into the kiln and fire relatively fast.

Glazed ware. Todd Piker's Connecticut production of commercially sold thrown and glazed pots, casseroles, and dinnerware, is wood-fired about every three weeks in a 35 ft (10.5 m) long, 5 ft (1.5 m) wide Korean-style hill kiln to cone 12 in 17 hours, with four people working in shifts; cooling takes three to five days. The fairly rapid firing, for a 600 cubic foot (17 cu m) kiln, is accomplished with scrap lumber (red or white pine). Piker's innovation is in stoking all ports together to keep the temperature even over the entire single chamber. His clay body contains feldspar and two stoneware clays; he believes that ball clays and fire clays in wood firing cause crystobolite formations that are deleterious, at least to ovenware bodies.

Malcolm Wright glazes his work and wood-fires a split bamboo kiln 20 ft (6 m) long, 6 ft (1.8 m) wide and 4 ft (1.2 m) high, in Vermont, in 18 to 20 hours, to temperatures varying from cone 5 to 15. He uses the secondary air port between the after-burning chamber and the chimney to control the fire; his porcelains fire best in the second chamber. In all woodburning kilns, air controls the nature of the flame; the greater the draft speed, the shorter the flame will be, and the more oxidizing the atmosphere. To achieve a reducing atmosphere, a faster stoking cycle and more fuel are used. Too much air prolongs the firing; too little produces carbon.

TORCHING

You can use a small refillable propane torch, purchased in a hardware store, or an oxyacetylene jeweler's soldering tank torch, or a 25 gallon (100 liter) propane tank with a flexible tube and burner attached, for spot melting, or for an all-over swishing heat treatment. Torching can be tried with fluxes and china paints, frits plus colorants, scrap glass and metals, or low-fire glazes, on both vertical and horizontal work. A clay body with pumice, volcanic ash, or lithium compounds, or filled with grog to let heat through easily is best in terms of thermal shock resistance, but ordinary clay bodies work with careful torching.

Joan Campbell uses an acetylene torch to reoxidize a post-fired smoked sculpture, for another variation in the coloring process

PATINAS DEVELOPED IN FIRING

Robert Piepenburg: stannous chloride fuming

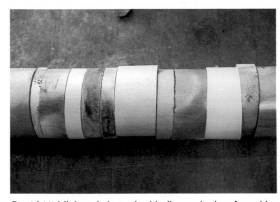

David Middlebrook: burnished hollow cylinders fumed by metals and salt

M. C. Richards places raw seaweed in and around pots for efflorescence during firing

Kris Cox: potassium dichloride fuming

6
HIGHPOINTS IN CERAMIC HISTORY

This ancient *haniwa* fragment shows the early sophistication of ceramic art

Ceramics has an extremely long and varied history. Neanderthal hunting and gathering groups who roamed across Eurasia 70,000 to 35,000 years ago had fire and may have made clay vessels hardened in fire, but the first evidence of true carving and artistic use of clay does not appear until the development of *homo sapiens* about 35,000 years ago during the last Ice Age. A prehistoric drawing found at an excavation site in China leads archeologists to believe that, at least in this area, twig baskets, mudded with clay to make them hold water or food, were one day put on a fire — with the discovery that the basket burned out, leaving a hardened clay vessel.

In about 30,000 B.C., clay animals and figures emerged, modeled in the round as well as carved in clay walls and floors. Ruins of prehistoric kilns have also been found from this period. It has been discovered that the North American Indians were burning clay pots in bonfires 25,000 years ago; to this day, they do not use kilns. All early cultures that fired clay had knowledge of different clay pigments, of metallic oxides that would resist temperatures of red heat and could be used for decoration, and of methods of hand fabrication and structure.

Fragments from clay vessels and objects have been the chief remnants left from prehistoric human activities. Ancient peoples are studied mainly through the clay artifacts — or shards thereof — that remain. From the ceramic fragments that have survived, we draw inferences about cross-cultural borrowing, trade, migrations, and the degree of sophistication of different societies. For instance, cultures with potters' wheels were no doubt somewhat industrial and production-oriented, whereas handbuilding cultures may have been isolated and more spiritually oriented. Some cultures had trained potters or communities of potters, while in others all members of the community made clay forms when necessary for everyday or ceremonial use. Indications of whether potters were only men or only women, whether decorations were elaborate or minimal, and whether high technologies were developed or traditions continued unchanged for thousands of years have been used as clues to the lifestyle of ancient peoples, their political and governmental development, and their degree of communication with other societies.

Decorative motifs often seem to be universal and timeless. Buff-colored clay pots recently excavated in China and dated thousands of years old are painted with black designs that are very similar to Peruvian and Southwest American Pueblo pots from about A.D. 1000. Archeologists have no evidence of communication between these cultures so widely separated in time and space except these pots. Perhaps the motifs are repeated in different cultures because processes are similar and because the universal forms demand certain kinds of graphics. Or perhaps, as some leaders of surviving indigenous groups maintain, there were long-term, long-distance migrations and communications between distant peoples.

Tradition prevails in ceramics more than in other arts, probably because there are so many variables to be controlled in the materials and firing. Potters tend to stick to what they do and not to change anything, for fear of having to change everything. Often the processes are secret, handed down from generations; the knowledge is refused to outsiders. In this case, traditions are finally lost.

It is interesting to speculate why some cultures were ceramic pioneers. For instance, why did only the Chinese develop porcelain, when the natural kaolin plus feldspar and silica combination existed in the ground in Japan and Korea as well? Why did South American tribes burnish clayware so assiduously for hundreds of years instead of discovering glaze? Part of the answer lies in the surrounding circumstances, in attention-demanding situations such as wars, and in the value placed on manual accomplishments. In some cultures, working with the hands made the person socially untouchable. And in some cases, materials other than clay met people's needs. Much of Africa, for instance, has not had a clay tradition; wood and gourds were plentiful for ritual pieces and functional vessels.

Although new ways have been adopted by whole cultures, evolutionary stages of clay art have always originated with individuals. Innovators secure enough in vision to chart new directions emerge infrequently from traditional backgrounds; yet when they do, they tend to be steeped in their own cultures, skilled in their craft, and brilliant in perception. In contrast to often anonymous folk artists, these innovative individuals are usually known by name. On the other hand, in our culture, the breaks with tradition initiated by contemporary clay artists in their search for new ways have liberated claywork, sending it crashing into the art world and allowing not only technical innovations with space-age applications, but also such non-traditional uses of clay as unfired clay art and site-specific installations.

In every culture and every time, there have been truly outstanding works — sometimes anonymous, sometimes signed — as well as mediocre, mundane objects. Historically, certain cultures have reached greater artistic heights than others, a tendency that continues today. In the pages that follow, I will note some highpoints in ceramic history and compare what was going on in different parts of the world at the same time. The dates given are approximate, derived from the sometimes controversial carbon-dating of objects found near clay artifacts (fired clay contains no carbon and does not change over time). Furthermore, there has been relatively little historical research into the ceramic arts *per se*. Unfortunately, much of the ceramic record was obliterated in China — one of the greatest of all ceramic centers — by 20th-century Cultural Revolutionaries bent on destroying everything old in order to start afresh. This overview of highpoints in ceramic history is based partly on my own observations in museums and at archeological digs around the world. It is followed by a survey of some surviving examples of traditional ways of working with clay.

HISTORICAL OVERVIEW

11,000 TO 2000 B.C.

Crude clay pieces appear in very ancient sites, including works of unusual esthetic interest. Throughout the Japanese islands, archeologists have found earthenware objects of great antiquity and artistic exuberance. Some have been carbon-dated as old as 12,000 B.C., though current estimates place them somewhat later, and spanning many millennia. They are referred to as *Jomon* (6.1), which means "cord pattern," for the early pieces are characterized by overall surface decorations apparently created by pressing cords into the damp clay or incising it with sticks, shells, or tools. It is likely that the porous Jomon ware was handbuilt by some coiling technique, but the coils have been smoothed and obscured by the texturing, which was often highly elaborated into sophisticated designs. Urns had narrow bases and flared openings, perhaps to facilitate settling them into the embers of a fire or holes in the ground. Later Jomon ware was shaped into fantastic forms, with low-relief designs in clay added to the surface.

Except for this early work, Japan was not the center of clay innovation in East Asia. Instead, claywork became highly developed in China. The cradle of civilization in China appears to have been the Yellow River valley of the north. In the western part of this region, Neolithic potters made simple coiled earthenware (6.3), apparently rotated on a mat or a flat stone. They fired it, not in an open fire, but in a compartment separate from the fire, at temperatures possibly up to 1870 °F (1020 °C). To the east, the Lungshan culture developed a rapidly turning potter's wheel, on which a fine-grained plastic clay was skillfully used to throw thin-walled black ware and complicated multiple-piece constructions.

Early kiln development is hard to trace because kilns do not last forever, or even for very long, especially when they are fired with wood and other organic materials. At some point, pits in the earth and caves gave way to the built tube or hill kilns. Essentially updraft, they were stoked from the base and heat rose to the top (p. 198). Innovations resulted eventually in chambers and side stoking. Many other kinds of kilns existed and were developed over the following thousands of years, thus eventually enabling sophisticated clay bodies and glazes to be formulated.

Another area of elegant claywork was the Middle East. Pottery dating back to about 6000 B.C. has been found in Çatal Hüyük, a Neolithic village in what is now Turkey. The earliest clay objects were unpainted, often shaped into cattle heads and female goddess figures; somewhat later pieces are made either of red clay decorated with white engobes or vice versa (6.2).

What seem to be the earliest glazes have been discovered in the Nile Valley of Egypt, dating from about 5000 B.C. Before glazes were developed, the Egyptians and many other peoples used burnishing to decrease the

11,000 TO 2000 B.C.

Many of the dates on this time chart have been rounded up or down to give a broad picture rather than the exact dating

6.2 Mother Goddess, Çatal Hüyük, Neolithic village in Turkey, 6000 B.C.; Museum of Anatolia Civilizations, Ankara, Turkey

6.3 Prehistoric, natural oxide painting, China, 3000 B.C.; Asiatic Museum, Stockholm

6.4 Clay figure of potter wedging clay, 3000 B.C.; National Museum, Cairo

6.1 Jomon, coil-built, Japan, 10,000 B.C.; Brooklyn Museum, New York

porosity of a clay piece, polishing it to an esthetically pleasing shine. The potter rubbed the leather-hard clay surface with something like a smooth stone or bone; sometimes, the piece was first painted with a thin slip of fine-grained clay. In about 5000 B.C., Egyptians began using "Egyptian paste" to make small pieces such as beads, in which glaze materials were mixed into the clay (p. 144). Mourners also made small *ushabti* figures to be buried with the dead (6.6). Egypt's deserts contained sand and salt in great abundance, and someone must have discovered that glass could be made by heating the two together (p. 149). Then came the discovery that mixing clay with the ingredients of glass — soda and silica — produced a low-temperature glaze that would bond with clay. Copper, cobalt, or manganese were used as pigments to color it. These brilliant glazes were not as stable as later glazes using lead as a flux, and they flaked off the clay.

Some pre-dynastic Egyptian communities also developed separate-compartment vertical kilns. They allowed slow, controlled firing and the use of light-colored clays painted with reddish engobes, free from the blackening smoke of an open fire (6.4).

By 4000 B.C., work thrown on a slow wheel seems to have appeared in Mesopotamian sites to the south. Some of the first known glazes capable of bonding with clay pots were created in ancient Mesopotamia, perhaps as early as 4000 B.C. A recipe dating back to 1700 B.C. lists glass, lead, copper, saltpeter, and lime as ingredients; it also describes techniques for preparing greenware so that it will bond with glaze.

In what is now Pakistan and northwestern India, a highly developed ancient civilization has been found in the Indus River valley, with major metropolitan centers called Harappa and Mohenjo-daro dating from about 3000 B.C., according to archeologists (but as old as 10,000 to 25,000 B.C., according to some Indian museums). Along with other sophisticated technologies, the Indus valley residents seem to have had potters' wheels set into pits. As in other early arrangements for a wheel, the potter seems to have sat on the edge of the pit, pushing the lower flywheel by foot, thus turning a smaller wheelhead connected to it by an axis. Pots from this era are finely thrown and undecorated. The effigy figures are fat and simple, probably pinched, with easy daubs of clay for features like eyes (6.5).

One of the earliest civilizations in Europe began on the island of Crete, in about 3000 B.C. The early Minoan culture there made pots distinguished by their lively stylized or naturalistic drawings of plants and sea creatures on relatively simple, unglazed forms. At Knossos, the Cretan metropolis, there were pits lined with flattened, polished stones, with a carved hole in the center that was probably used to insert a pole to go under a potter's wheelhead (6.7).

2000 TO 1000 B.C.

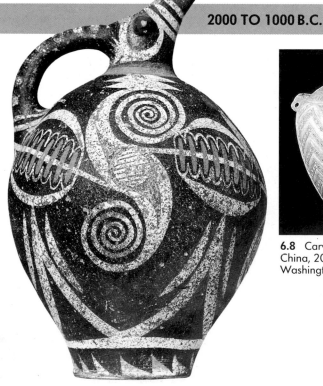

6.5 *Above* Figure, Harappa/Mohenjo-daro excavation (Pakistan), 3000 B.C.; National Museum, Madras

6.6 *Ushabti* figure, talc body, glazed, Egypt, 2000 B.C.; author's collection

6.7 Engobe decorated pot, Knossos, Crete, 2000 B.C.; Herakleion Museum, Crete

6.8 Carved jar, Shang Dynasty, China, 2000 B.C.; Freer Gallery, Washington, D.C.

2000 TO 1000 B.C.

The Late Minoan culture in Crete, which was ended suddenly in 1400 B.C. by invasion or earthquake, produced huge thrown or coiled and turned jars — a testimony to the potters' skill — as well as straightforward smaller pieces. The pottery is distinguished by freely painted, ornate polychrome designs (6.11), and wonderful toy-sized figures and animals.

During the 16th century B.C., the Hittites of Anatolia advanced clay art with their distinctive carinated (keel-like) forms. Some historians speculate that the claywork copied metalwork, but visually it has an exuberant life of its own (6.10).

In China, as well, clay technologies continued to develop during the Shang period (about 1600 to 1027 B.C.). Very thin leadless glazes appeared, as did earthenware pieces of fine-grained white clay, probably fired at about 2000 °F (1100 °C). This was not quite hot enough to produce stoneware or porcelain, and although the china clay needed for porcelain existed in the ground, it had not at this stage been incorporated into the clay body. It seems that the innovative kilns of this era allowed a kind of downdraft reduction firing. Despite these advances, bronze, rather than clay, was treated as the highest of arts. Some clay pieces were actually carved in the leather-hard state to look like the cast bronzes of the time (6.8).

The Amlash of Luristan in ancient Persia created marvelous burnished pieces. They used fat, luscious volumes for simple, stylized animals. Details were minimal, with attention paid only to the most salient features, such as a creature's great horns or a hunter's drawn bow (6.9).

The earliest examples of pottery found in pre-Columbian South America have been carbon-dated to about 3200 B.C., and during the second millennium B.C. ceramics began to reach remarkable heights in Peru, Ecuador, and Mexico. Clay was used not only for functional wares, but also for toys, musical instruments, and religious objects such as deity figures. These were usually constructed by relatively simple technologies — coil, hand modeling, and mold techniques, with burnishing or decorations of colored clays — employed with a fine sense of design (6.12).

While these other cultures were developing increasingly exquisite clayworks, northern Europe still had a very simple approach to clay. Pieces were utilitarian low-fired earthenware, with no decoration at all (6.13).

6.9 Hollow-built animals and pots, Amlash culture, Luristan dig, Persia, 2000 B.C.; Los Angeles County Museum of Art

6.10 Pinched figure, Hittite, Anatolia, 1600 B.C.; British Museum, London

6.11 Late Minoan engobe painting, Crete, 1500 B.C.; Herakleion Museum, Crete

6.12 *Above* Burnished handbuilt pitcher, Chavin culture, Peru, 1200 B.C.; author's collection

6.13 Utilitarian pots, Viking, Scandinavia, 1000 B.C.; Viking Museum, Stockholm

1000 TO 500 B.C.

Potters of the Chou dynasties in China (1122 to .255 B.C.) developed the first pots fired hot and hard enough (at approximately 2200 °F [1200 °C]) to be called stoneware. Another distinguishing characteristic of Chou ware is its sophisticated decoration of wheel-turned grooves and incised or applied geometric patterns (6.18).

Historians disagree as to when true porcelains first appeared in China. In 1981, I visited recent excavations of ancient mounds in the north-central desert plateau of China and saw what appeared to be near-porcelains. By definition, porcelain is fine-textured ceramic material fired to absolute vitrification (p. 133); the glaze is usually matured with the body at 2400 °F (1300 °C) to create a thick and strong vitreous layer. Porcelain was, and still is, highly valued as the apex of the clayworker's art. The excavations I saw included ware made of porcelaneous materials — china clay, feldspathic stone, and silica, which exist together naturally in the earth in China. The pieces — fired rather hard, glazed, but without the translucency of later porcelains — suggest that the Chinese may have made a type of porcelain in about 1000 B.C.

Abstract patterns were also highly developed in Greece. The Attic Geometric clay period is notable for its large vessels decorated with elaborate patterns (6.14), and for its development of the shiny surface of terra sigillata (p. 145).

By about 550 to 530 B.C., late in the Classical Attic period of Greece, black-figure ceramics reached their peak. The early emphasis on geometric patterns had given way to marvelous studies of the human figure (6.16), painted in black onto red clay, with fine lines scratched through the black. A few decades later, the reverse also appeared: figures in the original red clay, with background and details painted in black (6.17). The Greeks were very skillful wheel throwers, perhaps more so than the Chinese at this period.

Exquisite large forms in clay were produced by the Etruscans, the ancient pre-Roman people of Italy, whose art reached its culmination from 700 to 400 B.C. The beautiful piece shown here (6.15) is about 5 ft (1.5 m) tall and was probably a lamp. The Etruscans buried their dead in clay sarcophagi topped with life-size figures of the tomb occupants — often a whole family of them. These phenomenal handbuilt clay works ceased to be produced when the whole Etruscan civilization vanished, leaving a record in clay, but no written language.

1000 TO 500 B.C.

6.14 Attic geometric patterned vase, Dipylon dig, Greece, 800 B.C.; National Archeological Museum, Athens

6.15 Black-smudged lamp, intaglio decoration, Etruscan, 700 B.C., Italy; Etruscan Museum, Rome

6.16 Achilles slaying the Amazon Penthesilea, black-on-red figure vase, terra sigillata, Greece, 540 B.C.; British Museum, London

6.17 Red-on-black figure vase, terra sigillata, Greece, 500 B.C.; Louvre, Paris

6.18 Incised jar, Chou Dynasty, China, 300 B.C.; Victoria and Albert Museum, London

500 B.C. TO A.D. 300

The Romans, who supplanted the Etruscans in Italy, were not artistic innovators. They seemed to imitate Greek work, but without its spontaneity. Roman forms were slick and crisp, and this esthetic tradition, rather than the Etruscan or Greek one, was carried throughout Europe by conquest during the period of the Roman Empire (31 B.C. to A.D. 500). The early Roman influence was later counteracted by the light-hearted peasant earthenwares of Italy and Middle Europe.

Lead-fluxed glazes, with their yellowish influence on greens, blues, and browns, appeared in Roman culture and also in Han Dynasty China (206 B.C. to A.D. 220). Since raw lead is potentially toxic, it is as well that the Chinese lead-glazed pieces were used primarily as funerary pieces. Many were figures depicting naturalistic scenes from everyday life (6.22). For more than 2,000 years, Chinese clayworkers have used both low-fired lead glazes that fuse with the clay body at 1475° to 1650°F (800° to 900°C), and high-fired ash and feldspathic glazes that require temperatures of 2200° to 2400°F (1200 to 1300°C) for fusion. The latter was first used in eastern China by the late Han period to produce a brownish-green celadon known as Yueh ware.

The most astonishing early Chinese works found so far are the 6,000 life-size terracotta figures unearthed near Xian (6.21), the ancient capital. Buried in about 200 B.C. with the powerful first emperor of China, Ch'in Shih Huang Ti, these figures are stylized yet realistic representations of real warriors, servants, and horses, each apparently fired in a single piece in temporary kilns that were built around them. It is thought that, in this case, the emperor was accompanied into death by clay effigies of his retinue. The earlier practice would have been to bury everyone in his entourage.

Japan's ceramics were less advanced. The Yayoi culture that replaced the Jomon in about 300 B.C. used coil-building techniques to create minimally ornamented but elegantly shaped vessels, finished on a rudimentary wheel, with wide bodies supported on narrow bases (6.20). Japanese clay deposits are not nearly so fine as those found in China; before the Japanese learned how to refine their clay by elaborate slaking processes, it was sandy, coarse, and not very plastic. The ware was fragile and crumbled easily. Ancient Japanese pots in museums have usually been pieced together from shards; whole pots are very rare.

Undecorated but textured ware reminiscent of the Jomon was created on the other side of the world by the ancient Hohokam culture of what is now the southwestern United States. The people seem to have been great basket makers, and their squat, functional pots were built by a coiling technique similar to that used for baskets (6.23).

500 B.C. TO A.D. 300

6.19 Head, fragment from a hollow-built life-size figure, Nok culture, Tsuni Camp, Jemaa, Nigeria, 500 B.C.; National Museum, Lagos

6.20 *Left* Coiled-and-thrown pedestal vase, iron painting; Yayoi, Japan, 300 B.C.; Ueno Museum, Tokyo

6.21 *Below* Life-size warriors and horses, Xian, China, 200 B.C.; Xian excavation, China

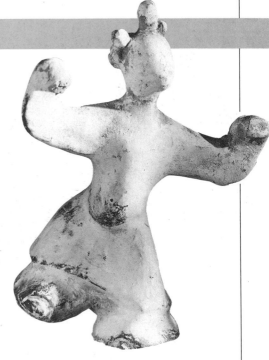

6.22 Dancer, Han Dynasty, China, A.D. 200; National Gallery, Prague

Historians have long assumed that the pot imitated the basket, but it is possible that the reverse is true.

In Africa, as well, a strong ceramic tradition has been unearthed in northern Nigeria, where it has been named for the village of Nok. Among the 150 sculptures found, there are strongly modeled earthenware heads which may have been part of nearly life-size statues (6.19). Although this culture disappeared from the archeological record after the third century A.D., the style — reminiscent of woodcarving — was found in West Africa for centuries.

A.D. 300 TO 1300

During this period, Korea and Japan began to use technologies imported from China. The Silla period in Korean ceramics (4th to 6th century A.D.) and the Tumulus period in Japan (beginning about A.D. 400) saw the adoption of high-firing techniques in *anagama* kilns climbing up the slope of a hill, similar to the Chinese "climbing kilns." We are fairly certain that the kiln cycle (from warming through firing to cooling) took a week or two in order to achieve and control temperatures of 2200° to 2400°F (1200° to 1300°C).

Japan also adopted the hand-turned potter's wheel from China and a type of kickwheel from Korea which allowed more rapid and symmetrical production. Ceramics were now used not only for cooking pots, but also for braziers to hold the cooking fire (6.24). In Japan, there was a continuing tradition of producing handbuilt *haniwa* figures (6.25). These stylized, hollow-built warrior and animal pieces had high bases or exceptionally long legs that were set into the ground around tombs. *Haniwa* figures have inspired many 20th-century sculptors, including Henry Moore.

Meanwhile, Chinese clayworkers continued to push the frontiers of ceramics forward. During the T'ang Dynasty (A.D. 618 to 906), contacts with the Middle East brought brightly-colored lead frits from Persia to make polychrome glazes, and Greek ideas to influence forms. Some of the

A.D. 300 TO 1300

6.24 *Left* Pot on brazier, Silla Dynasty, Korea, A.D. 400, Ueno Museum, Tokyo

6.25 Horse fragment, Haniwa, Japan, A.D. 400; British Museum, London

6.23 Coiled and smoked vessel, Hohokam, southwestern United States, A.D. 200; author's collection

6.26 Horse and rider, lead glazed, T'ang Dynasty, China, A.D. 600; Freer Museum, Washington, D.C.

most notable clay creations during the T'ang period were large horses and human figures placed in tombs (6.26).

During the Sung Dynasty (A.D. 960 to 1279), Chinese ceramics entered a golden age that seems not to have been surpassed even today. It combined the highest technical ability with simplicity of form to create works of exceptional beauty. Chinese court potters clearly achieved their goal of a thin white translucent porcelain, shaped into classically simple, hand-carved, clear-glazed Ting ware, during the early Sung period. It was also the Sung ceramists who somehow discovered reduction firing, reducing oxygen in the kiln chamber just at the point where small amounts of copper change radically from green to luscious reds such as peach bloom or oxblood or flambé, and iron turns to celadon (6.31) or jade green or, if overloaded with iron, to hare's fur or oil-spot black. Transparent green celadon glazes were often used over low-relief floral carvings. At the same time, clayworkers from Tz'u-chou in northern China and elsewhere were applying vigorous designs to everyday stoneware by freely painting and carving through engobes on to light gray clays (6.32).

Around the Mediterranean, Muslim ceramists elaborated on the Egyptian and Mesopotamian traditions and were inspired by imported porcelains and stonewares from T'ang and Sung China. The Persians must have been mining ores, for they began putting tin oxide into clear glaze to create an opaque white glaze. This first opaque glaze gave a porcelain-like white surface to the local clays. It was then overglazed with local pigments, particularly stunning blues from cobalt oxide (6.27) and brilliant turquoises from copper (6.28). To a certain extent, these clayworkers were guided by sayings of the prophet Muhammad, who reportedly forbade representations of humans or animals, as well as use of precious metal for tablewares. It is thought that the latter prohibition was partly responsible for the development in A.D. 700 or 800 of lusterware (p. 186), in which an already-fired glaze is repainted with metallic salts and refired in a reducing atmosphere to a metal-like brilliance.

In the Americas, ceramic arts were reaching new heights in the same period. Although the various cultures did not have potters' wheels, the Mayans of Central America exercised their genius in marvelous handbuilt clay sculptures (6.29). Farther north, the mysterious Anasazi ("Old Ones") of the southwestern deserts developed the exquisite abstract and stylized designs referred to as *Mimbres* (6.30). These unique patterns have influenced many contemporary artists.

In contrast to these various forms of artistic sophistication and technological innovation, the potters of medieval Europe were still making simple functional clayware. Thanks to the Romans, they did have closed kilns and wheels, which they used to create strong, earthy forms, usually not very well fired (6.33). Contemporary potters admire their sturdy simplicity.

6.27 *Above* Tin-opacified white glaze, cobalt design, Persia, A.D. 700; author's collection

6.28 Copper-turquoise clear glaze and cobalt design, Persia, A.D. 900; Brooklyn Museum, New York

6.29 Warrior with jaguar head and claws, Mayan culture, Central America, A.D. 900

6.30 *Above* Ceramic bowl with hole punctured on death of owner to help release vessel's spirit, white clay, black iron oxide decoration, Mimbres, southwestern United States, A.D. 950; Maxwell Museum, Albuquerque, New Mexico

6.31 Porcelain ewer, celadon glaze, Sung Dynasty, China, A.D. 1100; Freer Museum, Washington, D.C.

A.D. 1300 TO 1600

Trade between countries led to new combinations of resources and technologies. In China, potters of the Ming Dynasty (1368 to 1644) imported cobalt from Persia for blue painted decorations on their fine clear-glazed white porcelain bodies (6.35). They also must have discovered and used contaminated ores to yield subtle glazes such as apple green, Ming yellow, and Ming lavender. Clayworkers have never since been able to duplicate these hues.

Marco Polo carried blue-on-white Ming porcelains to Europe in the 14th century. They became popular items of commerce, inspiring a search for a porcelain-like smooth white surface among European potters, although Europe seemed to have no natural deposits of china clay combined with the other ingredients of porcelain. The Arab art of opaque tin-glazing for this purpose spread north through Spain into Renaissance Italy, where it formed the basis for Italian majolica wares (6.36). After the pieces were coated with a light-colored opaque glaze, designs were painted in metal oxides directly onto the raw glazed surface; then the whole piece was coated with a thin layer of clear glaze.

By the 16th century, clayworkers in the Delft area of Holland were using majolica technique to imitate Italian ware (6.38) and later the Ming blue-on-white porcelains, with an emphasis upon fine decorative techniques. Wares glazed in numerous bright colors became popular in France, where the master potter Bernard Palissy (1510–90) delighted the king and queen with his "rustic" pottery, using reliefs cast from natural forms (lizards and frogs, shells and leaves), with brilliant polychrome glazes (6.41).

During the 12th and 13th centuries, Muslim ceramics reached new heights under the influence of the conquering Seljuk Turks of Central Asia. They introduced a white composite body of powdered quartz and alkaline frit, which could be shaped into thin, fine, white, porcelain-like ware. For centuries, Persians had been developing sgraffito techniques of incising designs through colored engobe coatings to reveal the clay body; often, the incised lines were painted, with the incisions helping to contain the pigment as well as creating a low-relief effect. Under the Seljuks, sgraffito, carved, or molded patterns — as well as luster-painting techniques — became extremely sophisticated and were applied not only to vessels, but also to wall tiles placed over bricks for prayer niches in mosques (6.40).

Although the Muslim civilization in Spain was gradually overrun by Christian kingdoms, Arabic influences remained in pottery traditions such as the lusterware of Valencia (6.37).

In the Americas, before the 16th-century conquests by Spain, the Aztecs had developed a strong civilization in which ceramics was a major art form used for everything from cooking vessels to musical instruments. Spanish ex-

A.D. 1300 TO 1600

6.32 Stoneware jar, engobe decorated, Tz'u-Chou, China, A.D. 1200; Royal Ontario Museum, Toronto

6.33 Functional ware, pitcher, medieval Europe, A.D. 1250; British Museum, London

6.34 Earthenware, hollow-built figure, Aztec, Mexico, A.D. 1300; Royal Ontario Museum, Toronto

6.35 Porcelain, cobalt, clear glaze, Ming Dynasty, China, A.D. 1400; Asiatic Museum, Stockholm

6.36 Majolica, tin-opaque white glaze, Italy, A.D. 1400; author's collection

plorers reported seeing marketplaces filled with pottery of a thousand different forms. Much of the work that has been found seems to have served religious purposes (6.35).

Japan began to develop stoneware production centers during the 14th century. Each village had its own communal style and tradition, making distinctive pottery from local clay and high-temperature firing. The Shigaraki ware (6.39), for instance, is thick-walled and coarse-grained, with some feldspar visible in the body, and often a simple incised latticework design around the neck of jars.

A.D. 1600 TO 1900

During this period, clay traditions evolved in two different directions. On one hand, the search continued in Europe and Japan for porcelain-like fineness. Appropriate clay was found in Japan at Arita in the 17th century. Japanese clayworkers began mass-producing high-quality Imari porcelains at Arita, using transfers to duplicate patterns for matched place settings (6.42). The Imari potteries are still in existence today.

At the same time as fine decorative porcelains were being created in Japan, Zen Buddhist monks inspired an extraordinary appreciation for quietness, simplicity, and earthiness in the arts. In their tea ceremonies, great attention was paid to each element of the tea service, including the ceramic vessels used for storing, preparing, and serving the tea, the incense-holder, the vase for a single group of flowers, the cake dish, and the brazier. Decorations were minimal, and were produced with "artless" spontaneity, or at least the appearance thereof.

Raku firing (p. 211; 6.47) was first used for tea-bowls by a Korean roof-tile maker in Kyoto. But according to legend, the discovery was made by a group of Zen monks who were making their own tea-ceremony bowls. As they were sitting at work, they decided to throw the pots into a hot fire to see what happened. Some of the pieces survived. Nowadays, the word "raku" is applied to the

6.38 *Right* Cobalt over tin-opaque glaze, earthenware, Delft, Holland, A.D. 1500; author's collection

6.37 *Below* Plate, copper luster glaze, Valencia, Spain, A.D. 1500; author's collection

6.39 Stoneware, wood ash fired, Shigaraki village, Japan, A.D. 1500; Victoria and Albert Museum, London

6.40 *Left* Majolica-decorated, luster glazed, tiles over brick, Persia, A.D. 1500; Mosque, Isfahan, Iran

6.41 "Dream of Polyphilus," Bernard Palissy, polychrome glazes, France, A.D. 1550; Louvre, Paris

process of placing an unfired or bisqued glazed piece directly into a hot fire, waiting a few minutes for the glaze to fuse, and pulling the piece out hot. In contrast to the ordinary, more elaborate ceramic technologies, raku firing takes place in a matter of minutes.

The vitality of this simple attitude toward clay appears in many folk traditions around the world. In England, during the same period, it was found in peasant ware, the pottery of the people, hand-produced in small home industries, generally of local buff or red clay. Decorations were often added by means of colored clay engobes finished with clear glazes (6.43).

In the Middle East, with its much older and more developed ceramic tradition incorporating so many decorative techniques, even the peasant earthenware of this period was sophisticated (6.44). Both the esthetic and technical prowess were highly advanced.

In Switzerland and northern Europe, clay was used exuberantly to fashion decorative furnaces (6.48). Almost every room in a house had one of these fabulous stoves, some of which are still in use today. They must have been handmade, though with industrial molds and jigs, for I have never seen two alike.

While serving the needs of the people well, ceramics also became the art of the European royalty. In 1760, the Englishman Josiah Wedgwood won the patronage of Queen Charlotte for his delicate, thin-bodied ware, some

of which had translucent, molded applied reliefs of neoclassical subjects (6.45). Wedgwood developed industrial production methods to a high standard of technical excellence, shifting ceramics from small local potteries to large-scale industrial concerns producing quantities of cheap but high-quality wares for export as well as home use.

On the European continent, the desire to discover the secrets of making porcelain was finally fulfilled in Meissen, Germany, under very peculiar circumstances. The king of Saxony, Augustus the Strong, had imprisoned a famous young alchemist, Johann Friedrich Bottger, and ordered him to produce gold from lesser metals. In the process of testing and heating various earths and minerals, Bottger first succeeded in making a hard red stoneware, which he treated as semi-precious stone. Then, in 1708, using a white clay from the Meissen area instead of red clay, he created a fine "hard-paste" porcelain. After a period of copying Chinese and Japanese forms and motifs, Bottger developed a uniquely European porcelain style, imitating fine metalworking and often set in precious metals. His successors added brilliant detailed enamel paintings and then elaborate porcelain sculptures to the Meissen line, which became the envy of Europe (6.49).

French clayworkers had already discovered an expensive process for making "soft-paste" porcelain. The aristocracy enhanced their social standing by supporting the porcelain factories, whose output reflected the growing

A.D. 1600 TO 1900

6.42   Porcelain, overglaze enamel and gold, Imari, Arita, Japan, A.D. 1600; author's collection

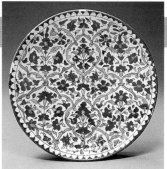

6.44   Cobalt and copper over tin-opaque glaze, A.D. 1800, Iran; author's collection

6.46
Porcelain, overglaze enamels and gold, Sèvres, France, A.D. 1800

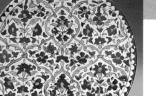

6.43   Slipware, engobe, red clay, England, A.D. 1700; Victoria and Albert Museum, London

6.45   Cobalt-colored porcelain with sprigged (relief applied) design, Wedgwood, Stoke-on-Trent, England, A.D. 1800; author's collection

French preference for romantic, flowery designs. The most important of the factories was that of the king, at Sèvres (6.46). The soft-paste porcelain enhanced colors, so, to make full use of this quality, the fine white glazes were often nearly covered by paintings in blues, yellow, apple green, and bright pink — Madame de Pompadour's favorite. Wares became more and more luxurious, and were commonly used as gifts to royal heads of state.

When suitable kaolin deposits were discovered at Limousin and Limoges, Sèvres switched to more plastic, higher-firing hard-paste porcelain, as did many ceramics works throughout Europe. Some in the British Isles, however, used an off-white Parian porcelain body (p. 144) that achieved a marble-like look at stoneware temperatures, allowing a greater range of colors than hotter-fired porcelain bodies. The Irish Belleek factory used an iridescent glaze over its low-fire porcelain (p. 144), the most translucent ceramics in the world.

European ceramics became increasingly mechanized, with cheap duplication by molds. Industrial factory organization meant that a series of workers performed separate, repeated functions; a single artisan did not create a piece from start to finish. Some lovely ornamental Victorian pieces were created in this way (6.50). But a late-19th-century reaction to the showiness and depersonalization of this approach arose, called the Arts and Crafts Movement. An English designer, William Morris, and others, tried to promote a return to small-scale fine craftsmanship. However, one-of-a-kind pieces were often designed by an artist and then executed by someone else with technical skills. This movement spread to the United States, where ceramics had consisted mainly of sturdy functional wares (6.51) and kitsch knick-knacks, industrially produced. One short-lived exception was the Willets Manufacturing Co. of Trenton, New Jersey, which produced exquisite Belleek-type porcelain from 1883 to 1890 (6.52).

In 1880, an exhibition of international ceramics in Philadelphia inspired the opening of the famous Rookwood pottery in Cincinnati, Ohio. Early Rookwood pieces had asymmetrical flower-like abstractions showing a strong Japanese influence, from the chief designer, Kataro Shirayamadani (6.53). Rookwood unique or limited-edition pieces soon won international praise, but unfortunately the factory closed early in the 20th century.

6.48 Room furnace, Switzerland, A.D. 1800; National Museum, Zürich

6.49 Porcelain condiment centerpiece, Meissen, Germany, A.D. 1800; Victoria and Albert Museum, London

6.47 Raku tea-ceremony bowl, Kenzan style, Japan, A.D. 1800; Ueno Museum, Tokyo

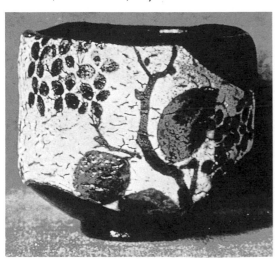

A.D. 1900 TO THE PRESENT

At the beginning of the 20th century, small-scale art potteries were struggling to survive against cheap, mass-produced ware. Nevertheless, the studio pottery movement began to catch on, a development for which the British potter Bernard Leach and his counterpart Shoji Hamada in Japan can be credited (p. 49). After studying ceramics in Japan, Leach returned to start a studio pottery at St. Ives in Cornwall, where he found local clays to suit his functional domestic ware (6.54). He usually made the prototype, to be copied by skilled throwers; pieces that he made himself were stamped with his own imprint. Hamada, who revived a 400-year-old folk tradition in Mashiko, Japan, also exhibited in Ginza, London, and Paris. The Zen scholar Soetsu Yanagi, ascetic and author, traveled and spoke around the world, spreading the philosophy of Leach and Hamada — that the work of the anonymous craftsman of all ages was the ideal. The paradox that the work of Leach and Hamada was exhibited and in demand worldwide did not belittle their ideals nor tarnish the influence they will exert for generations to come.

In identifying with specific craftspeople, the studio pottery movement differed from the folk pottery traditions found in many parts of the world. The true folk tradition is that of the truly anonymous craftsperson, whose unsigned pieces stand on their own merits, as in the folk potteries of Mexico and elsewhere (6.56). A growing appreciation for contemporary folk art, however, led to recognition of the people behind the pots. In Pueblo Indian ceramics, the work of Maria Martinez and Lucy Lewis (6.57) was discovered and so highly valued that their pieces now sell for thousands of dollars. Their extended families returned to specializing in ceramics, reviving time-consuming traditional methods that require great skill.

European painters who were inspired by the vigor of folk and studio pottery began to use ceramics as an art medium. Some picked up clay merely as a sketch material, but others, most notably Picasso (p. 233), carried clay into museum sophistication. Only now are we beginning to recognize what a contribution these artists — including Giacometti, Miró, Chagall, Leger, Rouault, Matisse, and many others — made to the use of clay as art. Miró had his own potter, Artegas, who executed the works from Miró's maquettes. Recognizing that it would take a lifetime to learn to throw and glaze well, Picasso utilized glaze chemists and the throwers of the Madoura pottery at Vallauris. He reshaped the thrown plastic forms, or used the shapes of heavy clay products like waterpipes; incised and painted them with enamels and experimental engobe colors; and applied glaze selectively, not always as an all-over coating. Picasso's lively efforts broadened the boundaries of what could be conceived and executed in clay.

6.51 *Left* Salt-glaze stoneware, cobalt design, New England, A.D. 1850; Wichita University Museum, Kansas

6.52 *Below* "American Belleek" porcelain basket, Willets Manufacturing, Trenton, New Jersey, A.D. 1883–9, only production of this ware; author's collection

6.53 Porcelain, one-of-a-kind jar by Kataro Shirayamadani, Rookwood factory, Cincinnati, Ohio, A.D. 1900; Everson Museum, Syracuse, New York

6.50 Porcelain bisque, glaze, and overglaze enamels, France, A.D. 1850; author's collection

On an industrial scale, some European ceramic factories employed artists who were also craftspeople. At Gustavsberg in Sweden, Royal Copenhagen in Denmark, and Arabia in Finland (6.55), the worlds of the artist and of industry coincided. Artists were hired because their input was valued; their individual works were often sold bearing their signatures and exhibited in galleries and museums around the world, perhaps creating a synthesis of art and industry.

The world's only college of ceramics was established in 1850 by the state of New York at Alfred University, and, since the 1950s, the U.S.A. has been the chief stage on which clay has come of age and been honored as art in museums and galleries. In 1952, Jack Peterson and I developed the first heavy-duty variable-speed potter's wheel at Chouinard Art Institute in Los Angeles. With Mike Kalan of Advanced Kilns, we also built the first fast-firing high-temperature open-fire periodic oxi-reduction kilns in the country, making the whole ceramic palette quickly accessible.

A.D. 1900 TO THE PRESENT Ceramic art by famous painters, c. 1950

Fernand Leger; Maeght Museum, St. Paul de Vence

Alberto Giacometti; Maeght Museum, St. Paul de Vence

Pablo Picasso; Picasso Museum, Paris

Joan Miró; Chicago Art Institute

Marc Chagall; Maeght Museum, St. Paul de Vence

Georges Rouault, Potiche, 1907; Musée National d'Art Moderne, Paris

This equipment was a crucial step toward the explosion of West Coast clay art in the 1950s. Peter Voulkos came to Otis Art Institute near Chouinard, and together we all continued to improve the equipment we used, freeing the scale and scope for clay ideas so that equipment itself again became unimportant. Voulkos' monumental thrown and altered forms (p. 86) were unlike anything else. John Mason's monumental handbuilt works of the early 1960s (pp. 46–7) evoke the same awe and emotion today. Ken Price was then, and still is, in an innovative class by himself (6.58).

At the end of the 20th century, the range of clay vessels, sculptures, images, and installation pieces is so rich as to be nearly incomprehensible. The newest work includes large site-specific installation pieces, often created as temporary displays in which a rapid process of weathering or transformation by other elements is part of the visual experience. In such works, idea and visible process are often more important than the ceramic object. A coexisting trend is narrative work, which is more traditionally object-oriented, but which uses ceramic techniques to create fantastic, playful, surreal, or anguished statements about modern society.

Not only has the state of the art exploded, but also the market for both functional and sculptural ceramics has become a dizzying showplace. Clay art can be seen everywhere — in books, magazines, galleries, and museums. There is even a renaissance of expert analysis and appreciation of historical clay works and surviving folk traditions. There are magazines dealing only with clay, and art critics who write about clay. This has all happened within my lifetime. I can remember being treated as a voice in the wilderness when I wrote articles in 1950 claiming that clay should have the same status as any other art material. Now art periodicals regularly publish important articles on individual ceramic artists.

Process is still an obstacle to use of the medium. Working clay so that it will stand up through drying and firing is truly difficult. Compared to other visual media, I think that process makes clay the most difficult art material in which to realize concepts. We clay artists are struggling with our material to make a statement, and some of that struggle is visible. On the other hand, great feats have been achieved, overcoming the obstacles to scale, color, exquisite control of form, decoration, and fire. And to some tastes, the simplest brush stroke on a piece of red clay may be the best. We each do what we want to do, what we must do.

In the pages that follow, we will look at some examples of revived historical approaches and then present a portfolio of some of the exciting work of contemporary clay artists. As in all the arts, there is no one prevailing esthetic. The field is wide open for exploration and evolution. There is now no leading edge, but rather a horizontal expansion. That we all follow a very ancient tradition in which a great deal is still new, still to be done, is absolutely regenerating!

6.57 *Right* Bonfired, polished clay, black iron oxide with wild spinach, "fine-line" decoration, Lucy M. Lewis, Acoma Pueblo, New Mexico, 1983

6.55 Porcelain, rice kernel pattern, designed by Friedl Kjellberj, Arabia Factory, Helsinki, Finland, 1969; author's collection

6.54 Stoneware bottle, iron decoration by Bernard Leach, England, 1950; Victoria and Albert Museum, London

6.56 Tree of Life, painted earthenware, Mexico, 1990; Mexico City

6.58 Ken Price, c. 1970; Los Angeles County Museum of Art, Los Angeles, California

SITE-SPECIFIC INSTALLATIONS I

Elsbeth S. Woody: "Misty Formation," stoneware

Tony Hepburn: "St. Louis Gate," interior installation

George Geyer and Tom McMillin: "Surface Erosion," Laguna Beach, California; clay, wood, steel, water, and sand

SITE-SPECIFIC INSTALLATIONS II

Robert Segall: "Arc Configuration," stoneware

Peter Kuentzel: "Miami Garden," clay fence in a pond

Judy Onofrio: interior installation; wood construction washed with porcelain

Berry Matthews: burning fence of porcelain squares, wax, wire, and string

Jeff Schlanger: "Chile New York," section of a wall with 400 faces, about war and oppression

NARRATIVE

Yiannes: "Still Life Number 10," ceramic mosaic

Randall Schmidt: "Private Shrine," stoneware, wire, and low-fire glazes

Rober M. Winokur: "Long Table II," salt-glazed stoneware with engobes and ash glaze

David Furman: "It's Knot for Me to Say," earthenware, stains, and luster

Judy Moonelis: "The Hold," earthenware and engobes

Jack Earl: small porcelain figure

Frederick L. Olsen: earthenware and porcelain with stains

ANCIENT TRADITIONS

Primitive clay art that existed thousands of years ago in most cultures still exists today in many. Fabrication techniques vary from handbuilding to some form of wheel-throwing. The potter's wheel is not used by North or South American Indians, Eskimos, or the peoples of the West Indies or the South Pacific; all these cultures maintain traditions of handbuilding and firing in the open or in semi-structures. People in Egypt, the Middle East, Africa, China, India, Greece, and Mexico are still pressing clay bricks, making sewer pipes and functional pots of ancient design on crude potters' wheels or by hand, and hardening them in bonfires or simple kilns. Glaze is unknown in most of these traditional cultures, even today.

Much can be learned from those who have for so many millennia practiced this craft: prospecting for natural materials, preparing clay, freeing it from impurities, controlling particle size and color, slaking it to plasticity, adding shards, crushed bark, or powdered bones to control shrinkage and volcanic ash to control thermal shock, using vegetable matter for colored decoration at bonfire temperatures, burnishing; firing in the open or in kilns and gauging temperature by the color of the fire and height of the flame, using animal dung for fuel, using methods of smothering for reduction firing; and making forms for particular functions or ceremonies. It would be rewarding to study any indigenous, non-industrialized culture's ways of pot-making. If it is impossible to travel, the work of these cultures can be studied in museums. Serious scholarship is now being applied to documentation and conservation of the anonymous folk art of all ages worldwide.

Many of these peoples have not changed their methods of handmaking pottery at all in thousands of years. The Jivaro Indians of South America quickly fashion a water jar $\frac{1}{4}$ in (.6 cm) thick and 3 ft (91 cm) tall when the previous one breaks. Bricks are made by hand and carried, one in each hand, to a deserted spot to build a "skove" kiln with fireboxes. When the brick structure is about as big as a house, it will be fired. If one suggests carrying a number of bricks at a time on a sled or a skid in order to speed the process, one is usually answered with an incredulous look and the exclamation, "What would we do if we didn't do this?"

Some traditions are newer, but still unchanged over the years. In the southeastern United States, there are a number of folk potters who work in exactly the same manner, using the same materials, as several generations of their families have. Burlon Craig of Lincoln, North Carolina, is purportedly the last to be firing a real "ground-hog" kiln, adapted from the design of European settlers. Every few weeks, he crawls into a burrow in the ground 18 in (45.7 cm) high — just tall enough in which to place his face jugs upright — about 80 ft (24.4 m) long. The jugs are glazed with wood ash from previous firings, mixed with ground glass from broken bottles he collects along the road. At the front of his kiln is his "firebox" — a deep hole in the ground, into which he shoves long, thin planks of

Ladie Quali, traditional potter (brought to United States to demonstrate in the early 1970s by Michael Cardew), in her native village, Nigeria

Pottery village, Timi, Nepal, 1962 (but no different today)

Traditional Thai storage vessels and bowls, food vendors on the river, Bangkok, 1982

Glazed kimchi pickle jars stacked, ready for the market, 1981; Seoul, Korea

"Mary's House," built of clay, rice-paste decoration, north Ghana, Africa, 1975

Spanish folk pots, Toledo, Spain, 1975

Pottery in the market, Toluca, Mexico, 1980

Village potter near Quito, Ecuador, 1970 (his black raw clay fires red)

wood when firing the kiln. Craig thinks his work will be carried on, by nephews or whoever, but yes, it will go on, he told me, like his daddy, and his daddy before him.

In some cases, people from traditional cultures that have been changed by contact with industrial societies have researched and returned to earlier ways of working. In New Mexico, the influence of the Spanish conquistadores on pottery traditions was strong until Maria Martinez of San Ildefonso Pueblo and then Lucy M. Lewis of Acoma Pueblo rediscovered the value of earlier indigenous ceramic traditions.

When Martinez was only 13 years old, she was approached as the best potter in the area by archeologists from the Smithsonian Institution who had unearthed some 2,000-year-old black shards and wanted to know what the vessels might have looked like. Martinez obligingly reconstructed the shapes and learned to burnish beautifully. Setting aside her Spanish-influenced poly-

chrome painting, she began to look for iron-rich clays that would produce a vibrant black when smothered during the firing. She found that wild-mountain-horse manure worked best for smothering, and eventually she became very famous for her black-on-black work. Martinez gave all her secrets to the people of her pueblo; the community was saved from its economic decline as many of them adopted these techniques.

Similarly, Lucy Lewis found old fine-lined black-on-white Mimbres motifs on shards in Chaco canyon. Her pueblo — the high mesa called "Sky City" — was no longer working in the older tradition, but Lewis revived it, painting highly stylized geometric black designs onto burnished white clay, using the chewed end of a yucca frond as a brush with which to make fine, precise lines. She, too, saved her pueblo economically as other potters began to copy the fine-lined work, for it drew considerable interest from collectors and museums.

Lewis coiling a seed pot

Lucy Lewis texturing a "corrugated" vase

Above Acoma Pueblo, "Sky City," Southwestern New Mexico, a 500 ft (150 m) rock mesa with no water supply, no electricity — the oldest inhabited village in the U.S.A.

Below Lewis: wedding vase with traditional parrot pattern

Right Martinez' famous black-on-black ware (smothered with manure during firing), decorated by Santara

Left San Ildefonso Pueblo, near Santa Fe, New Mexico

Above Maria Martinez pinching a pot a few years before her death (she was nearly 100)

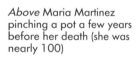

Martinez' red polished and painted pots stacked for bonfiring; they will turn black when smothered with horse manure

There are some "folk" potters who have been trained in technological societies, but who attempt to adopt more ancient values and techniques. Two of my students, Deborah Smith and Ray Meeker, moved in 1970 to Sri Aurobindo Ashram in Pondicherry, South India, where they built a pottery called Golden Bridge. They use local materials, but not local methods. In Pondicherry, there was no strong clay tradition, as local artisans tended to do metalwork. Instead, Smith and Meeker have ingeniously combined a Californian pottery vocabulary with Japanese methods Smith learned at Bizen, and with me at Hamada's, using the simplest techniques and the most natural ways to refine the clay, grind the grog, and chop the wood. To give the ware strength and to use the stoneware color palette, they fire to high temperature.

Golden Bridge is staffed by four throwers, seven clay, glaze, and firing workers, and four support crew members, all Tamil villagers. Clay is mixed and slaked in concrete tanks with the slurry hosed into drying tanks in the middle courtyard. Grog is ground from old broken saggars. 1,500 pieces a month are made and fired in the 300 cubic ft (8.5 cu m) three-chamber kiln that Meeker built. He fires to cone 10 with kerosene and water dripped by gravity flow on to hot iron plates; casuarina wood is used at the end of the firing. The finished ware is packed in plaited palm leaf bags for sale throughout India.

Why have some folk ways lasted? On one level, the people may seem to take their traditional methods for granted. For the Pueblo Indians of the American Southwest, pottery is just another thing to be done at certain times, like hunting coyotes. That does not make it unimportant. Hamada believed that the same attention should be given to anything one did, whether it was growing rice or making pottery. The human concerns and integrity associated with artistic traditions, the need for continuity, and the feeling that ceremony and spiritual values can be maintained by keeping an art tradition alive are some of the justifications for wanting to preserve folk crafts, even when the life may have ebbed from the culture and deterioration already taken hold. Only a few folk crafts are practiced in pure form today, uninfluenced by the market. When we find the genuine thing, we should nurture it and keep it safe. If it no longer exists, documentation may allow the craft to live on and nurture us.

Burlon Craig, throwing in his studio

Right Stoking the fire-mouth of his ground-hog kiln

The flue-end of the ground-hog kiln

Unsigned *mishima* (engobe-inlaid) pot by Tzaro Shimaoka, with the box made for it bearing a description and the artist's name — preserving a tradition of anonymity; author's collection

Screening clay

Clay is slaked in water, screened many times in the big vats, and ladled into the cement troughs to become plastic

One of the Tamil workers trimming teacups

Glazing pots for a firing

Casuarina wood is used at the end of the firing to cone 10; initial firing is with kerosene and water dripped by gravity

Deborah Smith, who with Ray Meeker built the Golden Bridge pottery, Pondicherry, South India, sorting ware from the firing

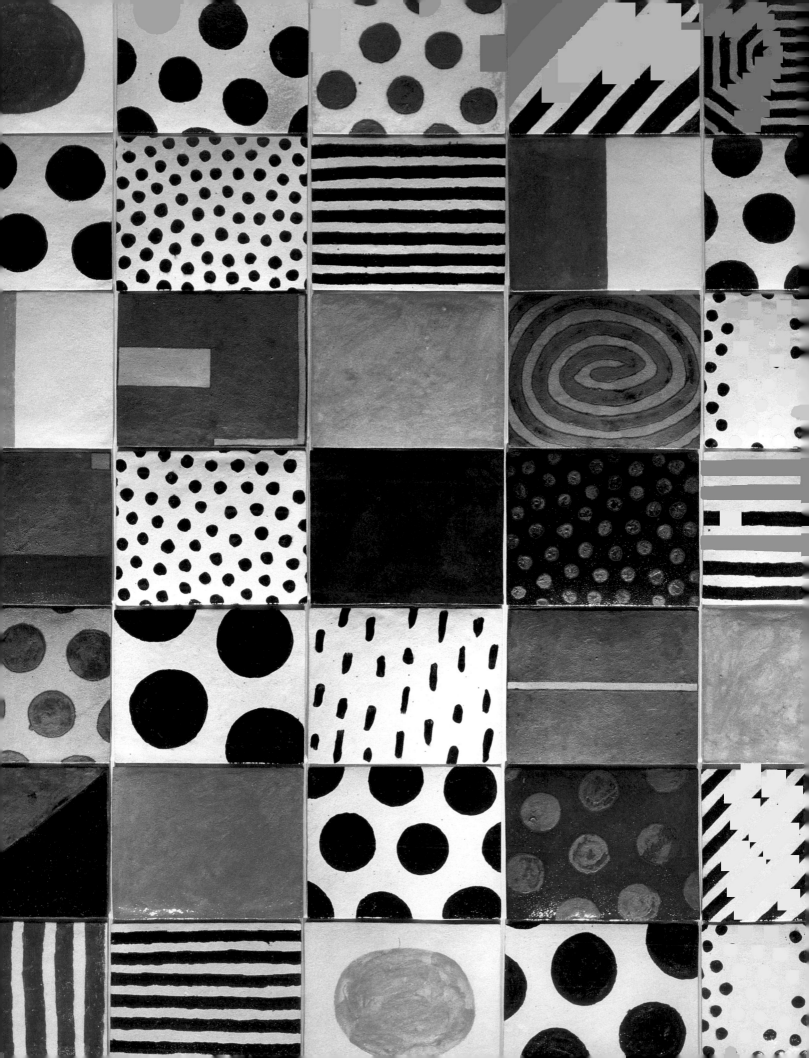

PORTFOLIO

Detail of Jun Kaneko's "Nagoya Wall"; the whole wall is
225 in (571 cm) wide and 105 in (227 cm) high

The international portfolio grew from my wish to illustrate the best of the contemporary art of clay. It began with requests for photographs to clayworkers I know personally, and was then supplemented by responses to advertisements in ceramic and craft magazines, and various recommendations. Submitted transparencies and black and white photographs were chosen according to their esthetic quality and representative techniques. Many more artists around the world would equally qualify, and I hope that you will recommend others and will send me photographs of your latest work for future editions.

The artists' statements are intended to help you to understand their commitment to clay and their feeling for it as a material.

About half of the artists teach fulltime; in this case, the institution is named. Otherwise just the studio location is given. In chapter 8 there is a further list of all other artists mentioned in the book but not in this portfolio, with similar information.

Ann ADAIR
Studio: Berkeley, California

Clay allows a spontaneity through which an idea can take form.

Above "Alligator Holding Painting"; porcelain, oil on canvas; w 12 × l 19½ in (30.5 × 49.5 cm)

Laura ANDRESON
Teaching: Retired, University of California, Los Angeles
Studio: Los Angeles, California

I am pragmatic. My pots are made for use — each one works.

Left Bottle; low fire, nitrate, luster fired; 6 in (15.2 cm)

Robert ARNESON
Teaching: University of California, Davis
Studio: Benecia, California

I like art that has humor, wit, irony, and playfulness. I want to make high art that is outrageous while revealing the human condition, which is not always high.

Right "Last Gasp"; glazed ceramic; head: 17½ × 17 × 19½ in (44.4 × 43.2 × 49.5 cm); pedestal: 34½ × 9½ × 9½ in (87.6 × 24.1 × 24.1 cm); overall h 51 in (129.5 cm)

Arne ASE
Studio: Oslo, Norway

I don't know why I work in clay. It is more or less a coincidence. Among my concerns when I work in porcelain is musical metaphor, the natural non-verbal parallel to combining the color and shape of porcelain. One technique I use is to strip the porcelain object bare and to create its esthetic expression in a washing technique. I layer shellac on areas to be thick, wash the greenware, then shellac and wash again until new lines are "painted" on the thinnest part of the piece.

Right Porcelain bowl; unglazed, wash and lacquer technique; h 9⅘ in (25 cm); 2372 °F (1300 °C), oxidation

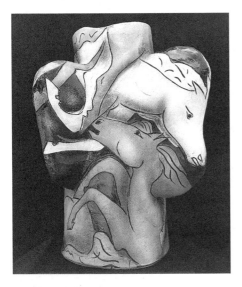

Rudy AUTIO
Teaching: Retired, University of Montana
Studio: Missoula, Montana

There are always new possibilities in ceramics. You have to let them happen. I usually handbuild. I've used a variation of slab and coil building for the past twenty years. It's fast for me. I like to use engobes wet on soft clay, then sgraffito draw through.

Above "Remuda"; 33 × 30 × 21 in (83.8 × 76.2 × 53.3 cm)

Costel BADEA
Studio: Bucharest, Romania

A fine line separates the humor of the impossible from the wonder of what lies just beyond what already exists.

Left Earthenware; 28¾ × 5⅙ in (73 × 13 cm)

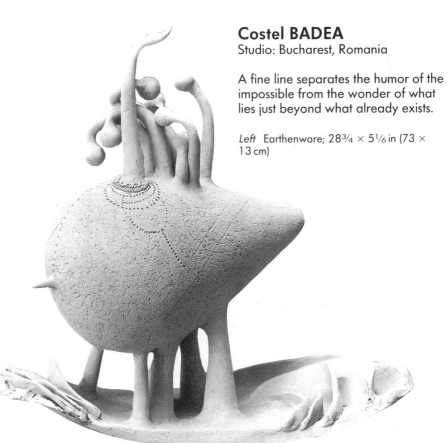

Clayton BAILEY
Teaching: California State University, Hayward
Studio: Benecia, California

I like the "magic" of converting mud into stone.

Above "Demon Dog"; stoneware; h 24 in (61 cm)

Douglas BALDWIN
Teaching: Maryland Institute Art College
Studio: Baltimore, Maryland

I like to make fun of faculty, students, staff, and administration.

Above "The Great Duck Ceramic School"; terracotta; d 45 × h 22 in (114.3 × 55.8 cm)

Bingul BASARIR
Studio: Sadikbey, Izmir, Turkey

I am working on natural shapes, stones, analyzing their physical properties, trying to discover the secrets of their origins.

Left Refractory clay, lignite coal, engobe, and glaze; $12\frac{3}{5} \times 11 \times 9\frac{2}{5}$ in (32 × 28 × 24 cm); cone 03, oxidation

Bennett BEAN
Studio: Johnsonbury, New Jersey

For me, these pieces are about control and accident. At each step in the process, I react to what is there, produced by all the previous steps. After years of consigning pieces to the kiln and accepting what is given back, now I am involved with a process of painting after the firing, which gives me the last word.

Above Vessel; burnished low-fire clay, pit fired and smoked, acrylics; 10 in (25.4 cm)

Jeroen BECHTOLD
Studio: Amsterdam, Netherlands

I sublimate my thoughts on ancient ruins into my porcelain — once walls, now fallen apart. I think of today's big concrete and glass walls and how they will one day look. Porcelain, because it is clean, pure, translucent, almost not of this earth. A porcelain piece which can live much longer than us, need only be dropped once. . . .

Left Vessel; eggshell porcelain, textures under color; 11⁴⁄₅ × 9 in (30 × 23 cm); oxidation

Karin BJORQUIST
Studio: Gustavsberg, Sweden

The two most important pieces of furniture in the home are the bed and the set table. About beds I need say no more. At the table one meets one's friends, who enjoy sitting at a well-decorated, functional table. And since the world today is so full of products, it is important that designers create meaningful articles. Above all, it is important to accept the age one lives in, to be neither nostalgic nor hypnotized by passing fashions!

Right Studio-produced bowl; glazed porcelain, silver decoration

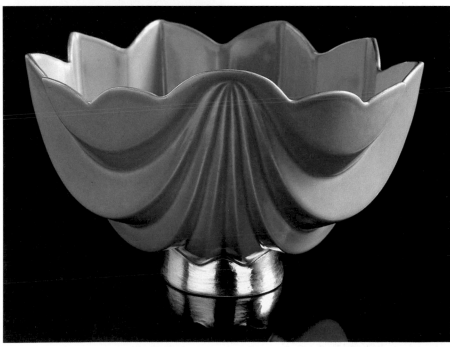

Joe BOVA
Teaching: Louisiana State University
Studio: Baton Rouge, Louisiana

I'm of the persuasion that no particular technique is superior, but I do like the wheel – and I come back to it rather often. Most of all, I like to squeeze the clay in my hand.

Left "Alligator Head"; white stoneware, china paints; cone 6

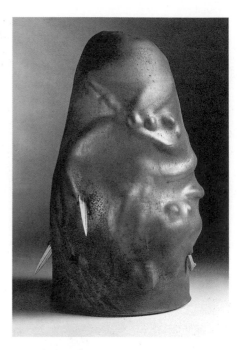

Frank BOYDEN
Studio: Otis, Oregon

One day last fall as the wind shifted, the sky over the sea was full of long wisps in the shapes of cormorant heads and backs and beaks. The sky was full of bird lines, like trails of ghost birds. I do not go out of my way to find symbols like this, they happen upon me from time to time.

Above "Heron Heads"; stoneware, porcelain; h 30 in (76.2 cm); wood fired, cone 13

Robert BRADY
Teaching: California State University, Sacramento
Studio: Berkeley, California

I've done a lot of drawing through the years that has always been figurative. I'd always wondered why my drawings contain people and my clay work is abstract, and I thought it would be interesting if they came together. I wanted my work to have a kind of life of its own. I didn't want to get into a pitfall of just being able to design nice objects one after another. I did a big series of drawings that were full of imagery. I started making some small objects again, and all of a sudden I was making the things I was drawing.

Left "Mum"; earthenware; 38 × 27 × 24 in (96.5 × 68.6 × 61 cm); oxidation

Peter G. CALLAS
Studio: Belvidere, New Jersey

Although I travelled to Japan and feel that wood-firing ceramics was my starting point, my influences come in waves. I vacillate now with Dogon and Senufo African work. Their references come from the stories of heat, age, and being overexposed to the elements.

Left Untitled Slab; stoneware; 22 × 22 × 3 in (55.8 × 55.8 × 7.6 cm); wood-fired

Nino CARUSO
Studio: Rome, Italy

My work is architectural, but concerned with myth and mind.

Below "The Traxonda Door"; terracotta; 96 × 72 in (243.8 × 182.8 cm); cone 06, oxidation

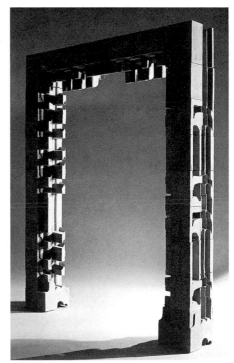

Above left Stoneware; 47¼ in (120 cm); cone 8–9, reduction

Claudi CASANOVAS
Studio: Girona, Spain

Some pieces I search for; others come to meet me. I have a recurrent memory of walking on a spiral staircase, on which at any given moment I have the feeling of treading again where I have already trodden before. For me there is no lift to go up.

Paul CHALEFF
Studio: Pine Plains, New York

I am concerned with impurity, chance, the fundamentals of earth, water, fire, and air — basically risk and the skill it takes to create ideas from these elements. Some of my works are wood-fired objects which refer to function. Their strength comes from being rough, gestural, split, and impure. My sculptural work — cauldrons, cogs, and drum forms — talk about primitive industry, man's endeavor to control nature.

Above   Jar; firemouth piece

Kari CHRISTENSEN
Studio: Oslo, Norway

My work is based on my "fuglefolket," the myth of the bird people.

Above   "Birdpeople"; dark stoneware; 11⅘ × 10¼ in (30 × 26 cm); 2192 °F (1200 °C), reduction

Jerry CHAPPELLE
Studio: Watkinsville, Georgia

Most recently I've largely worked in clay reliefs utilizing the spontaneous surface embellishments that only clay can offer.

Left   "Lovers"; stoneware; 36 × 48 in (91.4 × 120 cm); cone 10

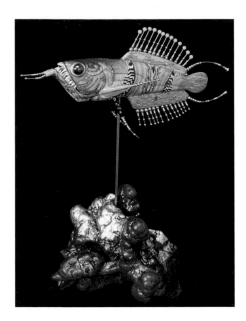

Cynthia and Erh-Ping Tsai CHUANG
Studio: Taipei, Taiwan

Although we are influenced by Matisse, Picasso, and Kandinsky, perhaps our greatest inspiration has been from nature.

Above "Arawana Fish"; porcelain, brass wire, millefiore technique, underglaze, overglaze; 10 × 5 × h 2 in (25.4 × 12.7 × 5 cm); cones 7, 06, 016, oxidation

Barbara CICHOCKA
Studio: Olesnica, Poland

My clay art is about a woman torn to pieces between affection, languishing, anticipation, and everyday exigences.

Right "The Harlequin"; ceramic, colored clays; 62³⁄₅ × 35²⁄₅ in (159 × 90 cm); 2282–2318°F (1250–1270°C)

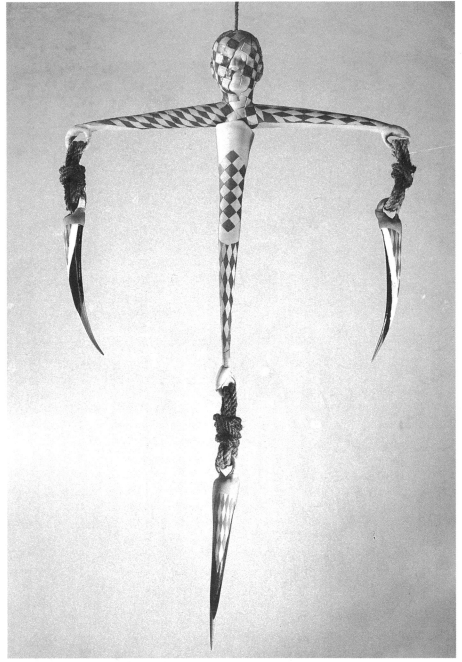

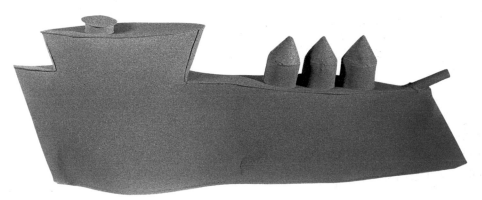

Philip CORNELIUS
Teaching: Pasadena City College
Studio: Pasadena, California

Working in clay is like having a conversation with your maker.

Left "Three Sisters"; porcelain; 19 × 8 × 3 in (48.2 × 20.3 × 7.6 cm)

Charles COUNTS
Studio: Atlanta, Georgia

When I left Berea College in Kentucky in the 1950s, it was not clear to me then that the ceramic arts would unify my life. The California (U.S.C.) experience was intense. I was shocked at what was being done in clay. It made me want to know more about my own particular heritage. I returned to the southern highlands and made over 100,000 pots, wondering all the time about being a human being. As I work I feel the universal order of things. I go on strengthened by this clay language of form and life.

Below "The alphabet is in the trees; Tribute to Robert Graves; and the White Goddess"; stoneware, engobe; h 15 in (38.1 cm); cone 6, oxidation

Tony COSTANZO
Studio: Niskayuna, New York

No matter how well you have your technique down, no matter how well you know the material, you can be sure of the results only 90% of the time! It's that other 10% that keeps me excited about clay.

Above "Pink and Poppin"; low-fire slip, wood; 34½ × 19½ in (87.6 × 49.5 cm)

Val CUSHING
Teaching: New York State College of Ceramics
Studio: Alfred, New York

I want to make pottery that communicates a feeling of warmth and sensitivity. I want it to speak something of humanity and of the common origins shared by the user and the maker. I hope it has values and implications for others to contemplate, but it is for myself that it holds its deepest meanings.

Right "Serving Platter" (Sherd series); stoneware; 24 in (61 cm); cone 9, reduction

Willis Bing DAVIS
Teaching: Central State University, Ohio
Studio: Dayton, Ohio

The rich artistic heritage of African art with its religious, social, and magical substance is what I select as an esthetic and historical link.

Left "Ifa-Divination Platter Number 13"; stoneware; 20 × 20 in (50.8 × 50.8 cm)

Mario Ferreira da SILVA
Studio: De Gaia, Portugal

Since the ceramic piece is the result of the chemical transformation of the material by the fire, giving form to the material that the fire will transform into ceramic is enjoying the sublime pleasure of the four basic elements of life: earth, water, air, and fire.

Above "Circlo Erotico"; stoneware; 33½ × 15¾ × 7⅘ in (85 × 40 × 20 cm); 2192 °F (1200 °C), oxidation

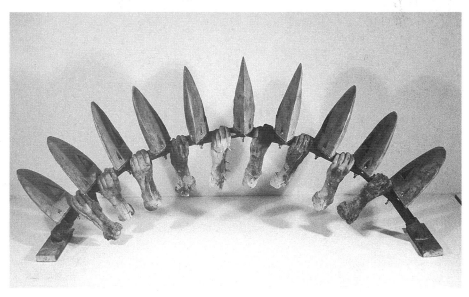

Bruce DEHNERT
Studio: Lander, Wyoming

My work is driven by political, social, and personal events much as stories are. Presently I am placing these dynamics in an architectural context.

Above "Evolution I"; press-molded earthenware, engobes, oxides; 120 × 36 × 18 in (304.8 × 91.4 × 45.7 cm); cone 04

Stephen de STAEBLER
Teaching: California State University,
San Francisco
Studio: Berkeley, California

Clay is quite remarkable in its
susceptibility to force — yet after firing it
is vulnerable to breaking. It is this
range that intrigues me.

Above "Standing Woman With Flared Base";
stoneware; 87 × 17 × 19 in (221 × 43.2 ×
48.3 cm)

Jugo de VEGETALES
Teaching: Moore College of Art,
Philadelphia
Studio: Chalfont, Pennsylvania

Clay is the basic sculpture medium. Its
history is rich. It has soul.

Right "Vida Eterna"; painted ceramic; h 65 ×
w 16 × d 22 in (165 × 40.6 × 55.8 cm)

Richard DeVORE

Teaching: Colorado State University
Studio: Fort Collins, Colorado

Regarding aspirations, John Fowler
said it very well — "All serious scientists
and artists want the same: a truth that
no one will need to change."

Right Bowl; h 9½ × w 12½ in (24.1 ×
31.7 cm); cone 8, cone 04 overlay, oxidation

Mike DODD

Studio: Boltongate, Cumbria, England

I am deeply interested in actualizing
the "dance of life," not in its
conceptualization. Form is the vehicle
of its expression, not the "self."

Below Bottle vase; stoneware, brick clay slip,
local river iron over local granite glaze;
h 10¼ in (26 cm); wood and oil fired, cone
10–11, reduction

Rick DILLINGHAM

Studio: Santa Fe, New Mexico

No one is a master of ceramic arts; it's
just a matter of how much you can
cooperate with the elements at the
time. That's a humbling sort of thing
that I like to keep in mind because it
gives me the freedom to experiment.

Above "Gas Can"; low-fire glaze; 23 × 16
× 3 in (58.4 × 40.6 × 7.6 cm)

Ruth DUCKWORTH

Studio: Chicago, Illinois

I try to nourish.

Above Porcelain bowl; cobalt clay inlay;
d 25 in (63.5 cm)

Vladimir ELISEER
Studio: Sochi, U.S.S.R.

I have been working at Sochi art works for 20 years as a ceramist. I make ceramic work in decoration in public and resort buildings.

Right "The Night Park"; fireproof clay, iron oxide; h 32¼ in (82 cm); 1742 °F (950 °C), oxidation

Raymon ELOZUA
Studio: New York

I believe in time as my grandparents did and in the life chronological rather than the life existential. We live in time and through it, we build our huts in its ruins and we cannot afford all these abandonings.

Above "Number 17 Western Sawmill"; ceramic with oil; h 32 × w 50 × l 98 in (81.3 × 127 × 249 cm)

Bill FARRELL
Teaching: School of Art Institute of Chicago
Studio: Oak Park, Illinois

My work follows a series of related form types that change direction from year to year or idea to idea. The best ideas are parked in the mind's eye and appear in a spontaneous way throughout the work.

Right "Vatican Twist"; clay, rubber, found objects; 73 in (185.4 cm)

Christine FEDERIGHI
Teaching: University of Miami
Studio: Miami, Florida

My work is narrative, maybe a kind of waking dream state.

Above "Little Night Rider"; earthenware, stains; 18 × 12 × 12 in (45.7 × 30.5 × 30.5 cm)

Ken FERGUSON
Teaching: Kansas City Art Institute
Studio: Shawnee, Kansas

I want my pots to be direct. I will continue to seek after gesture, the pot that almost went its own way.

Above Rabbit bowl; black stoneware, green slip; h 15½ × w 16½ in (39.4 × 41.9 cm)

Cathy FLECKSTEIN
Studio: Rosdorf, Germany

Myriad experiences have been my launching point for work on its way to simplicity and formal austerity.

Right "Cornerprint"; stoneware, engobe, iron oxide; approx. 19⅔ × 14 × 5⅝ in (50 × 36 × 15 cm); 2336 °F (1280 °C), reduction

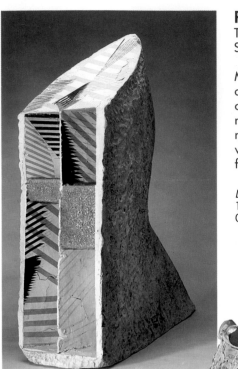

Ron FONDOW
Teaching: University of Miami
Studio: Miami, Florida

My work focuses on memory of ancient and recent past — I am trying to challenge what we know about the relationship of mass to the ground, to make ambiguous the time in which my work exists, to blur the scale and function of what I make.

Left "C-Scape"; clay, Egyptian paste; 42 × 14 × 27 in (106.6 × 35.5 × 68.6 cm), cone 01, cone 07

Michael FRIMKESS
Studio: Venice, California

I've never been without clay. At age 19 I received a vision depicting the throwing of a small "s" shape profile off the hump. The following day I went to re-enroll to study with Pete Voulkos. Usually it takes a lot of experience to get the thing to be the profile I'm aiming for. As far as a complete understanding, reproduction of the historical act of throwing a panathenaic amphora requires a certain amount of practice, that is akin to learning to play a violin perfectly or becoming a prima ballerina.

Above "Casa Gloria"; stoneware, china paints; h 28½ × 9 in (72.4 × 22.8 cm); cone 11

Viola FREY
Teaching: California College of Arts and Crafts
Studio: Oakland, California

Clay is by its very nature (not only in terms of what it is as material) non-hierarchical. That position promotes it.... You paint, you do sculpture, you draw, you do functional things, you make a mess, and it is all part of the clay. Also I think if you use the word "ceramic" you are denying that there is sculpture, or painting or architecture involved. It's all clay — it's all one. Further, you can say "clay is art," and that becomes a battleground for breaking down art-historical designations. No one ever said what clay is. It just became what it needed to be.

Right "Self Portrait with Vase"; low-fire white clay, underglaze, overglaze; 69 × 25 × 22 in (175.3 × 63.5 × 55.8 cm)

Ron GALLAS

Teaching: Saint Olaf College
Studio: Minneapolis, Minnesota

I am working with slab elements that
are fired before construction.

Left "J M B"; earthenware, underglazes,
glazes, paint; 42 × 16 × 10 in (106.6 × 40.6
× 25.4 cm)

Andrea GILL

Studio: Alfred, New York

I want my work to have a sense of
drawing and animation, with each
piece giving several different solutions
to the same set of problems.

Below "Vine Handle Vase"; red earthenware,
majolica glaze; 30 × 20 × 8 in (76.2 × 50.8
× 20.3 cm)

Filiz GALATALI-OZGUVEN

Studio: Istanbul, Turkey

My form has traditional pots on it
which symbolize germination and the
wealth of Aegean culture.

Above "Anatolia"; porcelain; steel and
cement, made in sections, assembled on site;
205 × 165 × 25½ in (520 × 420 × 65 cm);
cone 13, reduction.

David GILHOOLY

Studio: Dayton, Oregon

Anything that might concern you about
a life can be corrected by expressing it
in clay. The more pure creativity in
your life, the more joy.

Above "Vic and Al in the Tub"; 17 × 15 ×
18 in (43.2 × 38 × 45.7 cm)

John GILL
Studio: Alfred, New York

My work consists of historical references and my own incorrigible attitude.

Above   Vessel, stoneware; 15 × 13 × 10 in (38 × 33 × 25.4 cm) oxidation

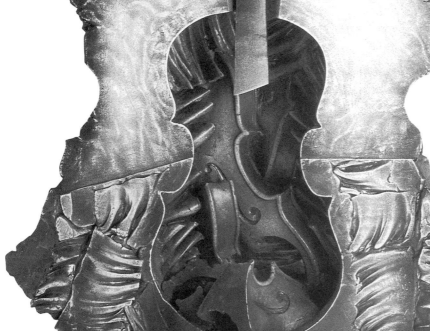

Maurice GROSSMAN
Teaching: Retired, University of Arizona
Studio: Tuscon, Arizona

My current work has been involved with the vessel as reliquary for spiritual space or social statement.

Above   "Spirit Vessel"; handbuilt; h 9½ × w 11 in (24.1 × 27.9 cm); primitive-fired

Sergio GURIOLI
Studio: Faenza, Italy

Title and image both reflect duplicity and levels of meaning.

Left   "Impronta"; stoneware; 27½ × 27½ × 11⅘ in (70 × 70 × 30 cm); 2192 °F (1200 °C), oxidation

Chris GUSTIN

Teaching: Southeastern Massachusetts
University, North Dartmouth
Studio: South Dartmouth,
Massachusetts

My work has dealt with a variety of
ideas: color, volume, light, geometry,
line, and weight. Another issue which is
constant to us all is the transformation
of one's own personal energy into the
making of an object. I believe that the
transformation of that energy is what
making pots is about.

Right Teapot; stoneware; h 9 × w 15 ×
d 6 in (22.8 × 38 × 15.2 cm)

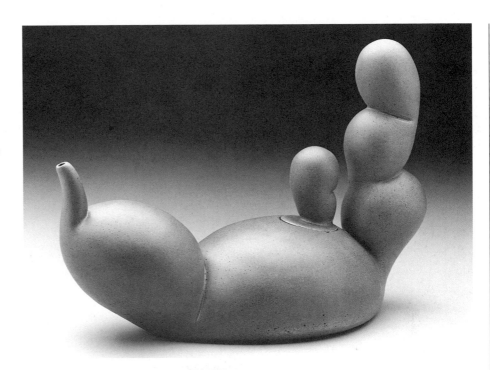

Ernst HAUSERMANN

Studio: Lenzburg, Switzerland

My relationship to clay is a very free
one. Clay is a material that doesn't set
limits, that doesn't have a given surface
or a constant structure; it knows
practically no borders in its ability to
adapt to my ideas and designs. These
qualities hide the danger of loss of
creative direction. Working in clay, I
have to set boundaries for myself; it
demands the search for reduction, self-
discipline, and simplification. The
apparent creative freedom therefore
becomes a creative trap. Only after
years of confrontation with clay does
one begin to know its true character.
One must learn to respect clay as an
independent medium of expression.

Left "Sans Titre Series Number 1"; coil-built,
unglazed, unfired oxides; 17 × 23³⁄₅ × 3½ in
(43 × 60 × 9 cm); cone 05, oxidation

Dick HAY
Teaching: Indiana State University
Studio: Brazil, Indiana

I use symbolism to build a personality.

Left "Susan"; earthenware, handbuilt, press molded, underglazes; h 37 in (94 cm)

Vivika and Otto HEINO
Studio: Ojai, California

We both are interested in the thrown pure form, enriched by a fine glaze.

Below Vase; wood-fired porcelain, fly ash, black slip decoration; 13 × 14 in (33 × 35.5 cm); cone 11

Tony HEPBURN
Teaching: New York State College of Ceramics
Studio: Alfred, New York

My work is rarely "hollow." It is to do with mass and mind.

Above "Past Past Present"; h 57 in (144.8 cm); soda-fired

Wayne HIGBY
Teaching: New York State College of Ceramics
Studio: Alfred Station, New York

I have been involved in an effort to create an emotionally charged balance between the decorative art of pottery and the fine art of painting, drawing, and sculpture.

Left "Tower Lands Winter"; landscape containers; five boxes; earthenware, raku technique, wheel-thrown and corrected; 14⅞ × 33¼ × 9 in (37.8 × 84.4 × 22.9 cm)

Hertha HILFON
Studio: Stockholm, Sweden

Dough rises, and clay shrinks. I substituted clay for dough and went on baking.

Above "Kir"; stoneware; 48 × 22 in (121.9 × 55.8 cm); electric-fired

Chuck HINDES
Teaching: University of Iowa
Studio: Iowa City, Iowa

I am infatuated with clay's ability to record movement and gesture.

Above "Saggar Jar"; stoneware, coil, paddle, and anvil; 28 × 24 in (71.1 × 61 cm); cone 7 saggar-fired, cone 9

Richard HIRSCH
Teaching: School For American Craftsmen, Rochester Institute of Technology
Studio: Churchville, New York

Raku captivates me. The variables are extensive, which makes individual firings distinctive. Thus, each piece seizes and reflects that specific period of action.

Right "Vessel and Stand"; Coper-Metti series; low-fire glazes; h 17¼ × 8 × 8 in (43.8 × 20.3 × 20.3 cm)

Curtis HOARD
Teaching: University of Minnesota
Studio: Minneapolis, Minnesota

I suppose the interesting aspect of the process I am employing is that all drawing, painting, glazing, et cetera, is done on either wet or leather-hard clay. I have always been drawn to diametrics. This latest work deals with opposing sensibilities in the painting of a somewhat formal, shape-oriented background and the literal/figurative aspects of the floral painting. Colour is of great importance also.

Left "The Little Things in Life"; handbuilt, earthenware, engobes, underglazes, overglazes; 53 × 29 × 12 in (134.6 × 73.7 × 30.5 cm); cone 02–01, oxidation

William HUNT
Studio: Columbus, Ohio

When travelling in Japan two years ago, the potters I met kept mentioning the importance of materials as one of the essential keystones for good work. For me, perlite clay is the end of a long search for this element of something special. My objects are more sculptures of containers than actually containers themselves, but I remain tied at least to vestigial function in my work.

Left Bowl; stoneware, melted-out perlite, salt-glazed; d 7 in (17.8 cm)

Jun KANEKO
Studio: Omaha, Nebraska

I just bumped into clay. It felt good. The decoration was subconscious too.

Above "Wall Slab"; stoneware, red low-fire glaze, gold luster; 31 × 21 × 1¼ in (78.7 × 53.3 × 3.2 cm)

Karen KARNES
Studio: Morgan, Vermont

Clay is a totally expressive material, making permanent the most immediate, the most profound, or the most trivial image of the maker.

Right Stoneware, engobe; h 168 in (426.7 cm); wood-fired

Susan and Steven KEMENYFFY
Teaching: Edinboro University of Pennsylvania
Studio: McKean, Pennsylvania

My primary interest is in seeing how the raku process improves or destroys my drawings.

Left "After Passing III"; raku; approx. 22 × 24 in (55.8 × 61 cm)

Evelyn KLAM
Studio: Berlin, Germany

Through my work with the clay, I have been able to express my close connection to the earth strongly. When I am at work, I can completely forget myself, and the possibility of playfulness brings me over and over again to new results.

Above Two boxes, porcelain, engobes, slips; 8 × 8 in (20.3 × 20.3 cm) each; 2282 °F (1250 °C)

Karen KOBLITZ
Studio: Los Angeles, California

I have always favored the use of color and pattern in art and in craft. This decorative quality has become a focus for me.

Left "Art Deco Still Life in Black and White"; low-fire clay and glaze; 11¼ × 19 × 19 in (28.6 × 48.3 × 48.3 cm)

Bo KRISTIANSEN
Studio: Copenhagen, Denmark

I mix my own clay which contains china clay, feldspar, flint, and a special clay from Bornholm. I cut two sizes of letters into wet clay overlapping the characters, then paint on and polish as many as 12 different slip colors.

Above Ball; stoneware, gold leaf, silver leaf; h 13½ × 16 in (34.3 × 40.6 cm); cone 9, oxidation

Albert KRYSTYNIAK
Studio: Warsaw, Poland

Here I used a photo technique to place a da Vinci drawing on one surface and a trace of fern-leaf fossil on the other.

Below "Memento" series; stoneware, photo process; 27½ × 35²⁄₅ × 11⁴⁄₅ in (70 × 90 × 30 cm); 1832 °F (1000 °C), oxidation

Michail KOPYLKOV
Studio: Leningrad, U.S.S.R.

Ceramics is not a tradition in Leningrad, as it is not in many colder, northerly areas. I think that ceramics is a transfiguration of human material. I like the theatrical elements of life, and can infuse these and the life force of the clay into the most simple object.

Above "Vita Nova"; clay, grog, glazes; h 62 in (158 cm); gas-fired, 1832 °F (1000 °C), oxidation

Lisa LARSON
Studio: Nacka, Sweden

To work with ceramics is most fascinating but also the most frustrating work that one can undertake. I think of the excitement when I open the kiln and see the results. It is something that I cannot live without. Surprises and disappointments. Next time there will be a masterpiece. Thousands of years ago pieces of art were made that cannot be surpassed, but knowing this does not stop this lust. The greatest happiness is to wake up in the morning and to know that I may use the whole day on clay.

Above   Figure, stoneware; h 4¾ in (12 cm); cone 7, oxidation

Patricia LAY
Teaching: Montclair State College
Studio: Jersey City, New Jersey

The work is concurrently structured and intuitive. The steel elements provide a counterpoint to the sensual and symbolic qualities in the clay forms.

Left   "Untitled Number 3"; fired clay and steel; h 10½ × w 20 × d 4 in (26.6 × 50 × 10.2 cm)

Elisabeth LANGSCH
Studio: Zürich, Switzerland

The priority of my work lies in the architectural field — to shape structures that reach over the mere functional by the play of forms, colors, and textures that create beauty.

Above   "Fussfigur" with wings; earthenware; 25⅗ × 7 in (65 × 18 cm); 2102 °F (1150 °C)

David LEACH

Studio: Bovey Tracey, Devon, England

Having started from a basis of functional pottery, mostly repetitively made in large number, I now make pots of an individual character in much smaller numbers.

Right   Stoneware pot; tenmoku, wax resist, dolomite; h 14 in (35.6 cm); 2370 °F (1300 °C), reduction

Janet LEACH

Studio: St. Ives, Cornwall, England

I became interested in the philosophy and techniques of Japanese pottery in 1952. All my pots are individually designed fired reduction stoneware.

Below   Slab-built vase; dark red stoneware, white glaze poured decoration; h 14 in (35.6 cm); reduction

Jim LEEDY

Teaching: Kansas City Art Institute
Studio: Kansas City, Missouri

There is a legend that Michelangelo nursed marble dust from his mother's breast which led to his life's work as a carver. When my mother was pregnant with me, she suffered from anemia and she craved clay in her diet. She would sneak into her secret hiding place and eat clay, so I was literally fed mud as a baby. Like a moth that is drawn to light (and like most children), I was drawn to every mud hole in my youth. The difference was, I ate mud. I came into this world eating clay and no doubt will leave the same way.

Above   "Baroque Forms"; stoneware; h 42 in (106.7 cm)

Marilyn LYSOHIR
Teaching: Washington State University
Studio: Pullman, Washington

The nucleus of my attitudes is an ability to retain a strong, visual memory of the past and a creative energy.

Above "Maiden America"; 17 × 68 × 18 in (43.2 × 172.7 × 45.7 cm)

Jennifer LEE
Studio: London, England

Whilst dealing with formal issues, my work is also informed by a knowledge of ancient and contemporary ceramics and through extensive travel.

Above Handbuilt colored bowl; dark stoneware, angled elipses, vanishing amber bands; h 9½ × d 11¾ in (24 × 30 cm)

Warren MACKENZIE
Teaching: Retired, University of Minnesota
Studio: Stillwater, Minnesota

Clay is marvelous, so responsive. Everything you do to a piece of clay changes it.

Right Teapot; stoneware; 10 × 8 in (25.4 × 20.3 cm)

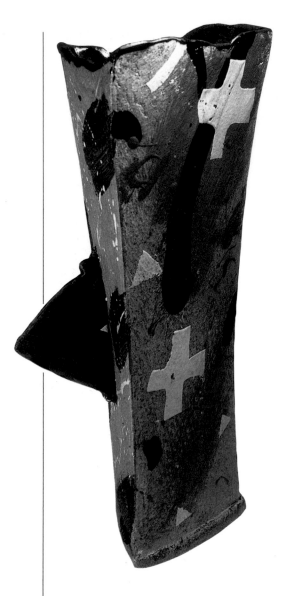

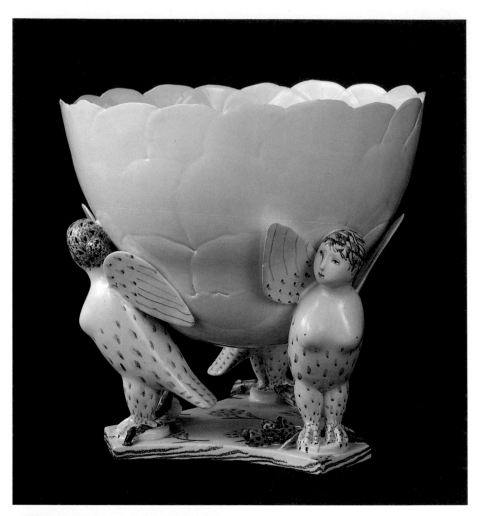

John MALTBY
Studio: Stoneshill, Devon, England

My pots are about the essential "Englishness" of my life and work: they are all individual, are all handbuilt — and, as far as I am aware, are as unconcerned with fashion or notoriety as it is possible to make them!

Above "Wells Cathedral"; tall vase; stoneware; h 16 × w 9 in (40.6 × 22.8 cm); oxidation

Heidi MANTHEY
Studio: Berlin, Germany

Functional but not functional, I want my work almost to fly but still to stand.

Above Porcelain, polychrome decoration; 9⅘ in (25 cm); 2372 °F (1300 °C), oxidation

Joe MARISCAL
Teaching: Alan Short Center, Stockton
Studio: Stockton, California

Clay is, by nature, in a perpetual state of rest … yet, in this inert, unassuming mass of earthy materials lies the incredible potential for activity and life. When tempered by fire, it becomes an immortal substance continually transmitting images of countless cultures: past, present, and future.

Left "Frank"; low fire; 16 × 7 × 8 in (40.6 × 17.8 × 20.3 cm)

Jean MAYER
Studio: Ein Hashofet, Israel

Contrasts. The softness of amorphous clay, made into basic abstract forms, yet suddenly taking on the form of natural objects. Then the firing process which changes it all.

Above   Flower form; porcelain, white matt; 8²/₃ × 7 in (22 × 18 cm); cone 9, reduction

John MASON
Teaching: Retired, Hunter College, City University of New York
Studio: Los Angeles, California

For some time I have been aware that often the most important things are overlooked because they seem to be too simple.

Above   "Torque Vessel"; high-fire ceramic; 34¼ × 20¾ × 20¾ in (87 × 52.7 × 52.7 cm)

Ron MEYERS
Teaching: University of Georgia
Studio: Athens, Georgia

My surface techniques or processes are all old standbys, because I like the simplicity, directness, and immediacy.

Right   Serving platter; earthenware, engobe; 5 × 14 in (12.7 × 35.6 cm)

David MIDDLEBROOK
Teaching: California State University, San Jose
Studio: Los Gatos, California

What interest me now are the colors and the shapes and the forms of what I discover. So I've gone the gambit, full circle, coming to grips with what the material does. I don't feel dishonest in this attempt at making clay a sophisticated expression of man's statement because I have taken it through the whole rap. Art is an active decision. You come to it after a lot of research and thinking. To quote someone, art is to life as the Richter scale is to an earthquake — only a system to measure what's shaking. Most people don't see that, but most people are a dying race.

Right "Newlum Boy"; 18 × 6 × 18 in (45.7 × 15.2 × 45.7 cm); salt- and carbon-fired, cone 06

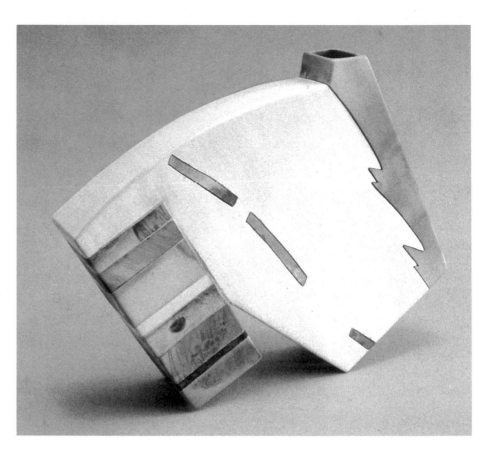

Yvette MINTZBERG
Studio: Montreal, Quebec, Canada

When I work with clay the material itself is my greatest motivation. I like to show its natural properties by using no glaze or a simple transparent glaze on the inside of vessel forms. The influence of my travels in the desert and years of mountain climbing also show in the cracks and crevices I incorporate into the final pieces.

Left "Erosion"; stoneware, unglazed, manganese oxide; 13 × 11½ × 2½ in (33 × 29.2 × 6.3 cm); cone 9, oxidation

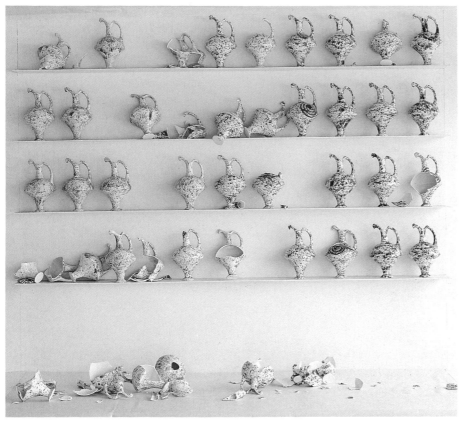

Martin MÖHWALD
Studio: Halle, Germany

An intriguing tension results from reassembling shards from a completed thrown piece which has been shattered. The form is the same form but the surfaces completely realign.

Below Teapot; thrown, deformed, painted; 10 × 8 in (25.4 × 20.3 cm); 2120 °F (1160 °C), oxidation

Juanita Jiminez MIZUNO
Studio: Los Angeles, California

I am attached to the figurative nature and function of this Hittite pitcher form.

Above "Hittite Series Number 1"; earthenware, white with cadmium; 120 × 120 × 8 in (304.8 × 304.8 × 20.3 cm); cone 04

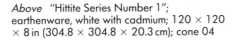

Mineo MIZUNO
Studio: Los Angeles, California

Perspective of function and forms....

Left Plate and cup; earthenware, underglaze; plate: 15 × 15 × 2 in (38.1 × 38.1 × 5 cm); cup: 2½ × 2½ × 6½ in (6.3 × 6.3 × 16.5 cm); cone 04

Jens MORRISON
Teaching: Palomar College, San Marcos
Studio: San Diego, California

I've never wanted to make "big" ceramics, but for small-scale sculpture I love the way you can carve clay or paint it "Mexican" colors or get an active surface with slips.

Right "Casa de Yolotepec"; earthenware, engobe, luster; 20 × 15 × 12 in (50.8 × 38 × 30.5 cm); cone 05

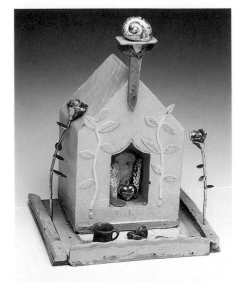

Emily MYERS
Studio: London, England

My ceramics are bold yet simple. I make the basic forms on the wheel, adding rims and handles to allow me to explore sculptural possibilities. The work shares certain qualities with metal: clean, uncompromising lines and a matt surface. It is, however, finished with vibrant stoneware glazes of deep aquamarine blue and turquoise.

Below Lidded jars; porcelain; h 8 in (20.3 cm); 2282 °F (1250 °C)

Gifford MYERS
Teaching: University of California, Irvine
Studio: Altadena, California

I think three dimensionally, and clay is a quick, malleable material to realize concepts physically.

Above "Neo/Neo"; acrylic and glaze on ceramic; 3 × 4 × 2¼ in (7.6 × 10.2 × 5.7 cm)

Ron NAGLE
Teaching: Mills College, Oakland
Studio: Oakland, California

My music and art have similarities: they're both emotional, warm, and romantic.

Right Cup; low fire, multifired; 5 × 4 × 3 in (12.7 × 10.2 × 7.6 cm)

Kimpei NAKAMURA
Studio: Tokyo, Japan

The play between the natural and the artificial that occurs from when a work is just begun until its completion is, for me, a provocative event.

Above "An Exploration of Japanese Taste"; h 19²/₃ × w 20⁴/₅ × d 16¹/₂ in (50 × 53 × 42 cm); cone 10, reduction, cone 017, oxidation

Richard T. NOTKIN
Studio: Myrtle Point, Oregon

Making things is a game with myself. I'm not purely visual; there's running commentary through the work.

Below "Heart Teapot Ironclad"; stoneware, luster; 6¹/₈ × 11⁵/₈ × 4⁵/₈ in (15.5 × 29.5 × 11.7 cm)

Magdalene ODUNDO
Studio: Bentley, Hampshire, England

Each pot is made to have the stillness of a dancer, frozen at a particular moment in the dance, with balance secure, yet full of tension.

Above Untitled piece; earthenware; 14²/₅ × 10⁴/₅ in (36.5 × 27.5 cm); oxidation

Borghildur OSKARSDOTTIR
Studio: Reykjavik, Iceland

Working in art is coping with life and coping with life is finding new ways ... to be able to survive. Clay is like life; it has many different sites and possibilities. Clay can be everything and nothing. In clay, as in life, people are not always expecting art ... but art is often where it is not expected.

Above Stoneware, slumped glass; 16 × 20 in (40 × 51 cm); stoneware: 2300 °F (1260 °C), oxidation; glass: 1976 °F (1080 °C)

Jeanne OTIS
Teaching: Arizona State University
Studio: Tempe, Arizona

I am intrigued with the interplay of actual and illusory depth with color and the rich nuances of light and shadow that can be achieved only with the extraordinary qualities of porcelains.

Above "Spectral Dance"; porcelain wall piece with colored slips, extruded clays, underglaze pencil; 38 × 35 × 1½ in (96.5 × 88.9 × 3.8 cm); cone 5, oxidation

Shiro OTANI
Studio: Shigaraki, Japan

I have tried to rediscover the expressions of the clay, its color, and the mysterious designs imparted by the fire.

Left "Shigaraki Vase"; natural ash glaze; h 13 × d 10 in (33 × 25.4 cm); wood fired, cone 10

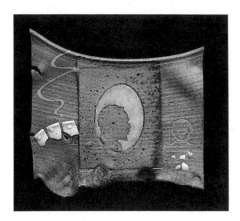

Dennis PARKS

Teaching: Tuscarora Pottery School
Studio: Tuscarora, Nevada

I work in clay metaphorically, like a snake might track a toad. All my work except that made in Poland is done single-fired in kilns fueled with crankcase oil. Copper reds on platters are produced from copper I obtained from an abandoned mine nearby. The exposed clay surfaces have been beautifully vapor-glazed, blushed by the contaminants in the drain oil fuel.

Above   "Clay Tablets"; thrown and altered, dry porcelain powder, Choke Cherry wood ash, sagebrush ash, broken pyrometric cones, ancient square nails; 15 × 15 in (38.1 × 38.1 cm); fired with crankcase oil, cone 10

William PARRY

Teaching: Retired, New York State College of Ceramics
Studio: Alfred Station, New York

It is as much man's way to divide and subdivide as it is nature's way; this has become a preoccupation in my work.

Below   "Off Butterfly Number 33"; stoneware clay, slip, underglaze color, glazes; w 20 × h 16 × d 11 in (50.8 × 40.6 × 27.9 cm)

Colin PEARSON

Studio: London, England

I work with variations of fairly traditional thrown forms. The torn and tattered rims and edges have become a necessity — my pieces look unfinished to me without them. The added attachments or "wings" enable me to broaden the language, invoking images from outside the usual ceramic experience.

Left   Untitled piece; stoneware thrown slab body with two combed and carved attachments each side, dark slip with porcelain slips, semi-matt glaze painted and sprayed; h 13 × w 20 × d 6 in (33 × 51 × 15.5 cm); electric-firing, cone 7–8, oxidation

Jan PETERSON
Studio: South Pasadena, California

I work with the metals in jewelry and porcelain in ceramics by using similar techniques, overlaying patterns and defining them with textures and colors to bring a sense of joy and humor.

Right Plate; porcelain, low-fire glaze

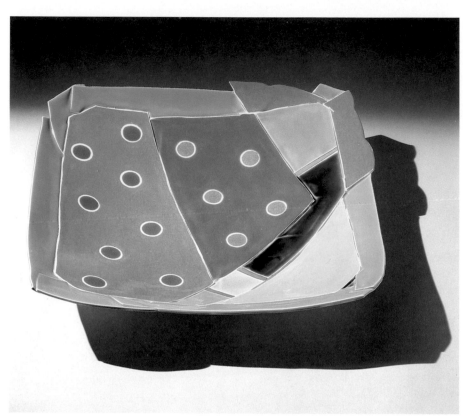

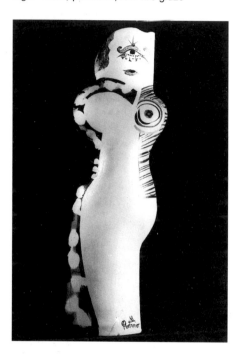

Gilbert PORTANIER
Studio: Vallauris, France

If I draw an arabesque on a piece of faience it immediately comes to life, whereas on a canvas it appears lifeless and gratuitous.

Above "Femme"; earthenware, enamels; 33²/₅ in (85 cm); 1832 °F (1000 °C), oxidation

Ken PRICE
Studio: Venice, California

Making is just the beginning. There has to be content over professionalism; the functional side can be metaphorical. I am always involved with color, color with form.

Right "Gomo"; fired clay, acrylic; h 9 × w 2½ × d 2½ in (22.8 × 6.35 × 6.35 cm)

Judith PUSCHEL
Studio: Berlin, Germany

The sewing machine, a form-pattern without its own value or meaning, a sign between an animal body and a technical monument, which has lost appreciation as an expensive commercial article, carefully protected in special housing, kept in the household, but ends on the scrap pile. There she is, shining with pearl-inlays, gold-scroll on black laquer, iron filigree-works, her nickel wheel, spools and polished bobbin feeders, which were once taboo for children to touch, who were to play instead outside in snowfields or rain. The variety of the machine's rich decor is always surprising to me.

Left "Sewing Machine Red"; raku, montage; 18 × 14 × 8 in (45.7 × 35.6 × 45.7 cm)

Juan QUEZADA
Studio: Casas Grande, Mexico

When I was about 15 I wanted to make something beautiful so I started making pottery resembling the shards from the ruins near my village which are prehistoric Casas Grandes ceramic. Then I developed my own style. Now even my brother and sisters work making their own pots, and also pottery in our village has grown to 300 potters.

Right Double vessel; local clay, pinch and coil, local oxides inlaid, burnished, cow dung fired; 15 × 6 in (38.1 × 15.2 cm)

Ingegerd RÅMAN
Studio: Stockholm, Sweden

The three basic earth colors — red, black, and white — are the most important thing to me. I work in a very Scandinavian tradition and I am a purely functional potter. My art is the functional piece. I make my own black glazes with oxides and try to mix black with almost imperceptible shades of color, shades which give life.

Left Black pot; stoneware; 3⅝ × 6⅔ in (10 × 17 cm); cone 8, oxidation

Paula Jean RICE
Teaching: Northern Arizona University
Studio: Flagstaff, Arizona

One of the problems of raku can be retaining color, lightness, and detail from underglaze and oxides on unglazed surfaces during the process of post-reduction. One way to solve this is to cover those areas, after the piece is bisqued but before it is raku-fired, with clay slip. After the raku fire, the slip falls off and reveals what has been protected. This works best on flat surfaces that are fired horizontally in the kiln.

Left "Genesis Sleeping"; raku; 23 × 27 × 4 in (58.4 × 68.6 × 10.2 cm)

Jerry ROTHMAN
Teaching: California State University, Fullerton
Studio: Laguna Beach, California

My work is any statement that continually changes with my changes, the society's changes and how the two relate.

Below "Ritual Vessel Coffee Pot"; porcelain; h 16 in (40³/₅ cm)

Lucy RIE
Studio: London, England

I work in a completely unorthodox manner, no longer using any form of scientific method. I glaze my pots raw, often using a number of glazes on top of each other and sometimes between one glaze and the next layer of slip.

Above Bowl; porcelain, brown sgraffito; d 3¹/₈ × 8¹/₄ in (7.9 × 21 cm); 2282 °F (1250 °C)

Antonia SALMON
Studio: Sheffield, England

"Unfolding" probably best describes the process I use to find new forms. I generally work in series, throwing, handbuilding, and then burnishing the work as it becomes drier and firmer. All the work is fired in sawdust, which creates the smoked finish.

Left "Double Piece"; slab sculpture; fine white stoneware; h 9⅞ in (25 cm); pit-fired in sawdust, 1940 °F (1060 °C), reduction, then wax-polished

Maurice SAVOIE
Studio: Longueuil, Quebec, Canada

Working with clay has been an "affaire de coeur" ever since I started making ceramic in the 1950s. After experimenting extensively with other materials I still find clay the most sensitive, and coming back to its contact is like a mystic experience. Clay, for instance, can incorporate architectural considerations which are free from the real architectural constraints. Thus the piece comes alive with a new, previously unimagined perspective.

Right "New York"; porcelain, overglazes; 20⅘ × 13 × 7⅝ in (53 × 33 × 20 cm); cones 8–9, 018–019, oxidation

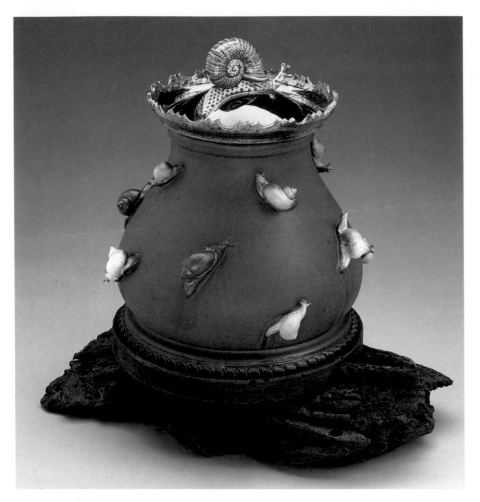

Adrian SAXE
Teaching: University of California, Los Angeles
Studio: Los Angeles, California

I use pottery as a very accessible vocabulary of means to introduce more difficult and dicey engagements with questions about what we consider art, how we value art in our society, and what the role of the decorative arts might be in our culture. I also groove on the empirical pseudo-science of applied ceramic research which approaches the sensual rewards of the culinary arts.

Left "Untitled Covered Jar (Blue, with Snails)"; porcelain, lusters, raku base; h 16½ × w 16 × d 11 in (41.9 × 40.6 × 27.9 cm)

Imre SCHRAMMEL
Studio: Budapest, Hungary

I work in clay because I work in clay.

Left "Ladies"; stoneware, grog; h 21⅔ in (55 cm); 2012 °F (1100 °C), reduction

Lilo SCHRAMMEL
Studio: Vienna, Austria

Energy – inside – movement; energy – outside – movement; inside – movement – outside; energy – movement – grasping, reducing to one symbol; energy – movement – transforming, creating a new form; everything is energy, everything is movement; everything transforms – nothing decays.

Right "Two Parts in Movement IV"; oxides, acrylic; 15¾ × 17¾ × 15¾ in (40 × 45 × 40 cm); 2120 °F (1160 °C), oxidation

Hein SEVERIJNS
Studio: Reuver, Netherlands

Porcelain fascinates me due to its extreme degree of difficulty, which keeps me humble as a potter. A porcelain potter must be more or less a fool because if he were wise, he would have been better to close the door of his kiln forever. The heart's desire in my life – to make the perfect pot – keeps me going on!

Above Vase; porcelain, matt crystalline glaze; h 9 × 7⅝ in (23 × 20 cm); electric-fired, 2300 °F (1260 °C), oxidation

David SHANER
Studio: Bigfork, Montana

I have always been interested in naked form, especially in what the form does when it meets a horizontal plane.

Below "Kiva Form"; 15 × 18 in (38.1 × 45.7 cm); wood-fired

Richard SHAW
Teaching: University of California, Berkeley
Studio: Fairfax, California

I consider myself a sculptor even if I do say that I am a ceramist. But the mood or presence in a work is equally important to me.

Below "Pile de Paniers"; porcelain, decal overglaze; h 8½ × d 8 in (21.6 × 20.3 cm)

Sandy SIMON
Studio: Berkeley, California

I make pots to maintain my avenue of communication. A good pot can touch so many senses that to experience it is to really celebrate the communions of food, friends, and conversation. To present the knowledge and experience of today while keeping a reverence for what has gone before is extraordinarily challenging.

Left "Teacup and Saucer"; thrown dinnerware, engobes, low fire; 5 × 4 in (12.7 × 10.2 cm)

Richard SLEE
Studio: Brighton, Sussex, England

My early pieces were generally symbolic, but the symbolism was becoming more and more gloomy; I began making flower forms as something more optimistic.

Above "Flower"; handbuilt, glazed earthenware; h 18½ in (47 cm)

Paul SOLDNER
Teaching: Scripps College, Claremont
Studio: Aspen, Colorado

In my work, I use any technique I can think of: smoke, manganese, wheel thrown, off wheel, slips and glazes, no slips and glazes, a welding torch — anything and everything.

Above Piece for bronze; earthenware, thrown and altered for casting, salt-finished; 24 × 33 × 10 in (61 × 83.8 × 25.4 cm)

Victor SPINKSI
Teaching: University of Delaware
Studio: Newark, Delaware

I work in super realism and illusion.

Above "Wrath of Samson"; handbuilt and cast water fountain; self-contained recyclable water system; earthenware, ceramic photo decals; h 114 × l 96 × w 54 in (289.6 × 243.8 × 137.2 cm); cones 04, 018

Susanne STEPHENSON
Teaching: Eastern Michigan University
Studio: Ann Arbor, Michigan

I am continually exploring the container form and its many relationships.

Below "Untitled"; porcelain, engobes, extruded and thrown; 25½ × 10 × 8 in (64.8 × 25.4 × 20.3 cm); cone 10

Jack TROY
Teaching: Juniata College, Pennsylvania
Studio: Huntingdon, Pennsylvania

I am a potter who reads and writes about ceramics but would much prefer being articulate *with* clay than *about* it.

Above "Winged Form"; stoneware; 8 × 15 × 4 in (20.3 × 38.1 × 10.2 cm); *anagama*-fired

Toshiko TAKAEZU
Teaching: Princeton University
Studio: Quakertown, New Jersey

I just enjoy working in clay.

Above "Bottle"; stoneware; 24 in (61 cm)

Robert TURNER
Teaching: Retired, New York State College of Ceramics
Studio: Alfred Station, New York

Absorption in the process of making brings things together for me — from thoughts, memories, readings jumbled in the intuitive.

Above "Lidded Vessel"; stoneware, high fire, sandblasted

Peter VOULKOS
Teaching: Retired, University of California, Berkeley
Studio: Oakland, California

Clay is a very intimate material. It's very fast-moving, it has silence, and it is immediately responsive to the touch. When I want to work more slowly and I want more resistance and noise, I turn to bronze. Working in the form of pottery is very demanding. It's like music: you have to know the structure and how to make sound before you can come up with anything.

Above "Stack"; stoneware; 29 × 16 × 17 in (73.7 × 40.6 × 43.1 cm); wood-fired

Heidi van VEEN-KIEHNE
Studio: Eindhoven, Netherlands

I am fascinated by the colors on ceramics.

Above Teapot; copper handle; 7 × 11 in (17.8 × 27.9 cm) soda-raku fired, 2156 °F (1180 °C), grass reduction

Ken VAVREK
Teaching: Moore College of Art, Philadelphia
Studio: Hilltown, Pennsylvania

Clay can be moved and formed many ways. It can have so many surfaces with subtleties of tactile differences. The mood of high-fire clay alone creates deep responses which expand with the inclusion of low-fire slips and glazes.

Right "Desparado"; glazed stoneware; 8 × 21½ × 11½ in (20.3 × 54.6 × 29.2 cm)

Patti WARASHINA

Teaching: University of Washington
Studio: Seattle, Washington

Sometimes the fascination of the unknown is overwhelming and electrifying. One's compulsiveness to continue this "making of Art" is a mystery to me, but I find that to keep peace of mind, it has become as necessary as eating and sleeping.

Left "Deck Paint"; earthenware, underglaze, paint, mixed media; h 18½ × l 60 × d 14 in (47 × 152.4 × 35.6 cm)

Stan WELSH

Teaching: California State University, San Jose
Studio: Oakland, California

I use low-temperature commercial glazes in conjunction with sandblasted terracotta surfaces. By using small amounts of glazed color against rough surface, I can enhance a form or strengthen a composition. I like using soft material to make a hard-edged shape.

Right "A Question of Balance"; terracotta clay; 45 × 47 × 16 in (114.3 × 119.4 × 40.6 cm); cone 04

Gerry WILLIAMS
Studio: Goffstown, New Hampshire

My esthetics in pottery are based on ethical principles which relate both to culturally inherent as well as observed judgments. Three basic principles by which I work are: (1) the belief in function as a tenet of the humanist tradition which is the root of our society, (2) reverence for materials and process as the organic connection between ourselves and the cosmos, and (3) faith in mutual aid as the obligation and support for all artistic activity.

Above "The Battle of Grant Park"; stoneware, white slip, iron stain; h 18 × w 24 in (45.7 × 61 cm); cone 10

Paula WINOKUR
Studio: Horsham, Pennsylvania

I am currently concerned with images of landscape from various points of view. I equate porcelain with the "mother-flour" of clay and find its whiteness and sensuality suits my needs. Porcelain is by its nature an intimate material. It does not allow for grand scale, but wants to remain within the bounds of personal contact.

Above "Site for Three Bowls" (Mantle); porcelain, slab constructed, assembled thrown and altered bowls; w 60 × h 56 × d 12 in (152.4 × 142.2 × 30.5 cm)

Lisa WOLKOW
Studio: Guildford, Connecticut

Now I'm working in clay with paper parts. I put white slip and stains on the clay and fire to cone 04, then epoxy drawing paper or newspaper different places and add color with pastels, paint, oil sticks, then fixative. I like to draw a lot.

Above left "Untitled Piece"; four sided, cloverleaf shaped; terracotta; 12 × 21 × 17 in (30.5 × 53.3 × 43.2)

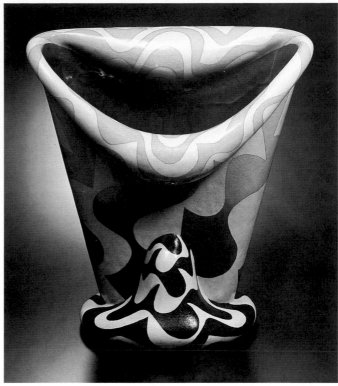

Beatrice WOOD
Studio: Ojai, California

My interest is in luster.

Above "Tall Footed Vessel"; earthenware;
h 10 × w 5 in (25.4 × 12.7 cm)

Betty WOODMAN
Teaching: University of Colorado
Studio: Boulder, Colorado, and New
York City

Function has become less important in
my work but has remained an
important symbolic factor. I don't want
to obliterate the line between pottery
and sculpture.

Below right "Twisted Handle Pillow Pitcher";
26 × 25 × 16 in (66 × 63.5 × 40.6 cm)

Mutsuo YANAGIHARA
Studio: Kyoto, Japan

I try to blend natural glaze colors with
humorous forms to create a unique
expression, breaking completely with
the concept of ceramic vessel so that
my pieces make a clear statement of
exactly what they are.

Above "Big-Mouth Laughing Pot"; 17 × 13
× h 20 in (43 × 33 × 51 cm); cone 9,
oxidation

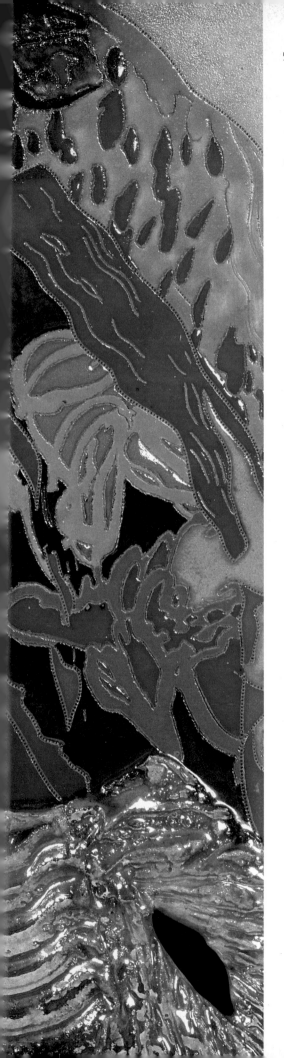

8

COMPENDIUM

Detail of Susan and Steven Kemenyffy's wall plaque "A Portrait of Linda," showing low-temperature raku glazes with sgraffito, resist, and luster

This chapter presents information that will enhance the life-long study of ceramics. Firstly, a concern for safety is expressed, with suggestions for avoiding possible hazards. The general statements will need to be supplemented in areas where the environment or regulations impose further restrictions.

A technical section follows, explaining the classic method of compounding glazes by mathematical and chemical calculation; this complements the 50/50 34-member glaze blend charts and the fusion buttons of the same 34 materials in chapter 4. It is backed up by a discussion of ceramic oxides and their raw material sources, chemical formulas of representative frits and feldspars, and glaze "limit" formulas. If you practice these procedures — calculating from formula to batch, and from batch to formula — you will learn to formulate glazes quickly, to understand them

better, and to predict results. When relying on chemical analyses of raw materials, be certain that they are not out-of-date. Reference charts are provided, including drying and shrinkage percentages, melting points of various substances, a diagram showing how to read triaxial diagrams, an example of a data sheet from a clay mine, and temperature, weights, and measures conversion tables. The charts are useful in many ways for experimentation, as are the favorite surfaces and hints from a number of ceramic artists.

Finally there are three reference lists: details of artists mentioned elsewhere in the book; addresses of the major international ceramic magazines, which are a good source for researching ceramic suppliers as well as offering up-to-date news and opinion on the craft and art of clay; and a unique museum compilation, documenting some of the wealth of the world's best ceramic collections.

SAFETY ISSUES

Ceramics is a field with recognizable problems of health and safety, which need to be handled with an awareness of the law, but, above all, with common sense. Recently, legislation and publicity have coupled to highlight some of the main dangers. Studies show that ceramic artists work longer hours per week and therefore have greater exposure to problem areas than do workers in industry. On the other hand, if we become too burdened with fears, we shall risk losing the full scope of this ancient craft.

VENTILATION

This is the number one precaution against ceramic hazards. Protection from toxic chemicals and dust is more effectively provided by adequate open-air ventilation than by closed-air systems that operate with fans, flues, and air recirculation. Unfortunately all-encompassing ventilation systems often fail to function or function faultily; it is much better to be able to open windows.

DUST

Dust is an ever-present problem. Clay is "clean dirt," but the 200-mesh particle size of most ceramic materials can affect the lungs. It is wise to have respiratory check-ups every three years if you work regularly in ceramics. Masks specifically for dust can be purchased; alternatively, use the disposable masks available in pharmacies when mixing clay, sweeping, or spraying glaze. Floors should be wet-mopped frequently.

MECHANICAL HAZARDS

The level of danger is commensurate with the machinery you have. Use caution and common sense. The flywheel on a potter's wheel can harm feet and legs; and propellors of a casting-slip mixer or the blades of a clay mixer wait to chop fingers; the fan on the spray booth can cut; slab rollers can flatten you too; and extrusion machines have sharp edges.

TOXIC MATERIALS

There is greater concern about toxicity now than some years ago, as more is known about chemicals. Again, keep your wits about you. Don't eat glaze ingredients, wear a mask when mixing glaze if the dust is bothersome, wear surgical gloves to stir glaze if you have a cut on your hand (if you have skin problems, always work in gloves), use a ventilated spray booth, and melt paraffin for wax-resist in a thermostatically controlled electric frying pan. It is a good idea to get a breath of fresh air periodically by walking outside, rather than staying in a confined studio for long periods.

The danger of lead may be overrated, but it is controversial and currently the subject of legal discussion in the United States that may totally ban its use in ceramics as well as in other fields. Lead is one of the most active fluxes, especially at low temperature, and influences color in ways that no other known material does; it is in fact irreplaceable. Raw lead compounds such as lead oxide (red lead and litharge), white lead (lead carbonate), and galena (lead sulfide) are soluble and possibly poisonous (if ingested) until fired above 2000 °F (1093 °C). The process of fritting complex lead-bearing compositions (p. 162), or the simple frits lead mono- and bisilicate, renders the poisonous ingredients insoluble and non-poisonous. If raw lead is fired above 2000 °F (1093 °C) as a component of a glaze, theoretically the same thing occurs.

Some countries such as Mexico commonly use raw lead in glazes fired at very low temperatures; it is probably not a good idea to eat and drink from these vessels. The United States has a law against the use of raw lead in glazes for functional ware that is sold commercially. A simple test for lead precipitate can be performed on any lead-glazed and fired pot: allow sulphuric acid to stand overnight in the vessel; if a white powder forms in the liquid, the lead is still soluble and might leach into any less strong acid such as citric (lemon or orange juice) or acetic (vinegar).

KILN SAFETY

It is best to install kilns fueled with gas or oil outside, if possible; adverse weather does not damage them. An up-draft kiln needs a metal hood mounted 18 in (45.7 cm) above the top, with a vent that may rise a few feet (a meter or so) above the hood. If the installation is interior, the vent may need to clear the roof, depending on local regulations. Downdraft kilns that are built inside are constructed with tall stacks which usually protrude from the building. Indoor kilns should be installed in fire-proof rooms or at least 4 ft (1.2 m) away from any existing wall. Electric kilns are manufactured with good insulation and have no burning fuel to evacuate, but some communities have rules about venting them due to potentially harmful fumes that may burn off from glaze ingredients during firing. All electric kilns should be equipped with a rubber pad on the floor in front of them to prevent shocks under damp conditions, and it is essential that all wires should be encased.

On petroleum-fueled kilns, safety mechanisms for igniting burners — and shutting them off if the supply fails — are required in some areas. However, the problem may lie more with the kiln-operator than the furnace itself. It is important to know how to light any kiln, and vital that natural gas or propane fueled burners be lit only when the kiln door or lid is open, to prevent an explosion from a possible leak in the line. As stated in chapter 5, the best safety rule is never to leave a kiln during its operation.

Propane or other "bottle gas" has more B.T.U. than natural gas, requires different burner orifice sizes, is under higher pressure, and is more dangerous if not properly vented. Liquefied petroleum gases are heavy and fall to the floor if allowed to leak; during construction, slant the floor if possible, so the invisible vapor will be able to run off, and cut open-air vents at floor level to evacuate any leaks. Periodically clean all gas burner ports and orifices with a vacuum cleaner and a jet of compressed air, and occasionally get a plumber to check the pipes for leaks.

All kilns except electric ones have open fires, at the burners or at the fire-box, and possibly elsewhere. Long hair and fluffy clothes are hazardous near flames. Some ophthalmologists warn against prolonged looking at fire without dark or cobalt lenses, lest retina problems develop. When pulling brick or refractory peep plugs out to check the cones inside the kiln, remember that the plugs may be as hot as 2300 °F (1260 °C), more than enough for bad burns. No material for gloves has so far proved as heat resistant as the now discredited asbestos.

FUMES

During firing, glaze fumes can be produced by certain ingredients such as metallic salts, reducing agents like moth balls, chlorine from rock-salt used in salt glazing, luster materials such as silver nitrate, or oils from decal firing. Ventilation in the room, or working outside, is the best answer; or else leave the work area until the fumes subside. Excessively reducing a kiln — which is unwise — produces carbon monoxide, which first causes headaches and then loss of consciousness and death if allowed to continue.

FURTHER PRECAUTIONS

Be sure to keep children away from any of the hazards discussed above. If you experience a health problem that could be connected to your ceramic activity, do tell the doctor what you do, in what environment you work, and what materials you handle in the course of a day; physicians tend not to be as aware of occupational hazards as we may be.

Detailed discussion of safety precautions to be taken in ceramics is available in *Safe Practices in the Arts and Crafts, A Studio Guide*, from the College Art Association, 149 Madison Avenue, New York, NY 10016; and from Center for Safety in the Arts, 5 Beekman Street, New York, NY 10038.

GLAZE OXIDES

Although different glazes may contain different combinations of chemicals, basically the composition of all glazes is the same. In the next section you will see how glaze formulas are written down: each formula is divided into three columns (p. 302). Each column represents elements of a particular oxygen valence (i.e. the ability that element has to combine with oxygen atoms).

Some oxides have one oxygen atom no matter how many atoms of the element they have (e.g. Na_2O and PbO). These oxides fall into the first of these three columns — the $RO–R_2O$ group. Other elements use two atoms to combine with three of oxygen. They fall into the middle column — the R_2O_3 group. Some elements combine with two oxygens, to form the right column — the RO_2 group.

The $RO–R_2O$ column is called the fluxing column because the oxides in this group act primarily as fluxes in the glaze. They lower the melting point of the glaze, and combine with the silica and other heat-resistant materials, helping them to fuse. Some of these oxides work better in their capacity as fluxes at low temperatures, others at high temperatures.

The R_2O_3 column is called the viscosity-controlling column because the most important member of this group, alumina (Al_2O_3) is responsible for the viscosity of the glaze (its ability to resist running or flow). The RO_2 column is called the glass-forming column after its most important member, silica (SiO_2) — the prime constituent in glaze.

It must be remembered that other, less abundant members of these two columns do not perform viscosity-controlling or glass-making roles. Boric oxide (B_2O_3) is really a flux, and oxides of tin (SnO_2), zirconium (ZrO_2), and titanium (TiO_2) are opacifiers rather than glass-forming oxides.

The three columns, with materials and their oxide formulas used to make up glaze, look like this:

$RO–R_2O$		R_2O_3		RO_2	
Barium oxide	BaO	Alumina	Al_2O_3	Silica	SiO_2
Calcium oxide	CaO	Boric oxide	B_2O_3	Tin oxide	SnO_2
Lead oxide	PbO			Titanium oxide	TiO_2
Lithium oxide	Li_2O			Zirconium oxide	ZrO_2
Magnesium oxide	MgO				
Potassium oxide	K_2O				
Sodium oxide	Na_2O				
Zinc oxide	ZnO				

From these oxides come glazes for all temperatures. Alumina and silica are always used; the rest of the composite is chosen according to visual and temperature requirements.

THE RO–R₂O GROUP OF OXIDES

	ACTION	SOURCES
1 THE METALS		

Lead oxide (PbO)

One of the most important oxides in glaze technology. It can constitute the entire RO column of a glaze formula or be as little as .3, which is the lowest practical amount for ordinary temperature ranges.

ACTION

- Combines with other glaze-making oxides very easily.
- Is a very active flux.
- Gives a high brilliance.
- Lowers the coefficient of expansion more than the alkalies.
- Increases the stretching ability of the glaze.
- Decreases the viscosity of the glaze.
- Melts easily at 1625°F (885°C).
- Can be used from cone 015 to 6.
- With one equivalent of boric acid or silica per equivalent of lead, it forms an insoluble glass that cannot be attacked by acids.

Contraindications

- Raw lead is highly toxic, and can be released from glazes under certain conditions — it should not be used on containers for food or drink.
- The oxide is quite volatile, especially at high temperatures.
- When fired at too high a temperature it gives a dull effect.
- Glazes high in PbO give a yellowish color.
- Glaze is soft and easily scratched.
- PbO is easily reduced, giving a gray color, and is difficult to re-oxidize.

SOURCES

Fritted lead (insoluble)

- Lead silicate — a fritted lead silica. A common lead monosilicate is 84% PbO, 16% SiO_2 — good in low temperature glazes; forms a liquid at 1346°F (730°C).
- Lead bisilicate — 65% PbO, 33% SiO_2, 2% Al_2O_3 with a fusion temperature of 1652°F (900°C).
- Complex lead-containing frits manufactured by various companies.

Lead compounds (soluble)

- Litharge (PbO) — this reduces most easily and is unsuitable for use in colorless glazes.
- Red lead (Pb_3O_4) — good for making frits because of high oxygen content which makes reduction less likely.
- Lead carbonate ($2PbCO_3 \cdot Pb(OH)_2$) — also called white lead — this is most commonly used because its specific gravity is less than the other lead materials and it stays in suspension much longer.

(White and red lead decompose before melting and change to PbO.)

	ACTION	SOURCES
Zinc oxide (ZnO)	• Functions as a flux but less actively than lead oxide over the entire range of temperatures. Small amounts (3–4%) will be just about as active as lead oxide. Excessive amounts will render the glaze too refractory and too viscous, without greatly lessening the glassiness. • Has nearly the lowest coefficient of expansion of the basic oxides. (MgO is lower.) It increases the elasticity of the glaze, and corrects crazing to some extent. • Increases the strength and durability of the glaze and its resistance to attack by solution. • Tends to opacify glazes but not as well as tin; the whiteness has a pinkish tone. It gives glazes a greater brilliance. • Affects some colors adversely, particularly chromium oxide which it turns a dirty brown. Cobalt is enhanced by zinc oxide. • A glaze saturated with zinc oxide often gives a crystalline texture. For large crystals the glaze must be heated above 2012 °F (1100 °C) and cooled to 1922–1382 °F (1050–750 °C), where it is held for three hours. The following glaze will behave in such a way: ZnO .65 Al_2O_3 .05 SiO_2 1.8 Na_2O .30 B_2O_3 .30 CaO .05 • In alumina and barium matt glazes, softens the matt texture, about .35 equivalents of zinc oxide can be used. • Heavy zinc or calcined zinc (sometimes called lead-free zinc or Denzox) works better in glazes than the fluffy or light variety. Cracking of the dry glaze and crawling in firing is corrected by the use of calcined zinc. • Is used in large quantities in stoneware glazes. Sometimes .4 equivalents are used in a "Bristol" glaze (glaze on greenware) at cone 5 to 8.	**Insoluble** • Zinc oxide or zinc zirconium silicate

2 THE ALKALIES

	ACTION	SOURCES
Sodium oxide (Na₂O)	• An active flux, increasing the fluidity of a melt. • Has a strong influence on the development of color depending on the coloring oxide used. • Has the highest coefficient of expansion; therefore it decreases the tensile strength and elasticity of the glaze and causes crazing. • Is similar to potassium in many chemical characteristics but should not be substituted for it unless the amounts are small. • Fuses at cone 4.	**Insoluble** • Feldspars — especially soda feldspars. • Frits. • Cryolite (Na_3AlF_6) can be used but is not in general use as the fluorine is volatile. Cryolite is also an opacifier. **Soluble** These are nearly always used to make frits and only used occasionally in raw alkaline glazes. • Sodium carbonate (Na_2CO_3) — commonly called soda ash. • Sodium nitrate ($NaNO_3$) — commonly called soda niter. It is expensive and is a powerful oxidizing agent. • Borax ($Na_2O \cdot 2B_2O_3 \cdot 10H_2O$) — a strong flux and solvent for all glaze materials. It has a definite effect on color; it reduces the viscosity of glazes.

	ACTION	SOURCES
Potassium oxide (K₂O)	<ul><li>A powerful flux; acts in a similar way to sodium but is different in chemical form and behavior so that it cannot be substituted for sodium, except in small quantities. This is especially true where colors are involved.</li><li>Fuses at cone 8 or 9.</li></ul>	**Insoluble** <ul><li>Feldspars — especially potash.</li><li>Frits.</li></ul>**Soluble** <ul><li>Potassium carbonate (K_2CO_3) — commonly called pearlash, is a source of K_2O and can be used in frits or raw glazes.</li><li>Potassium nitrate (KNO) — called potash, saltpeter, or niter, is a powerful oxidizing agent and can be used in making frits or raw glazes.</li></ul>
Lithium oxide (Li₂O)	<ul><li>Very powerful flux and has chemical properties similar to Na_2O and K_2O.</li><li>Can be used in place of Na_2O and K_2O with beneficial results and eliminates crazing to some extent. Lithium is very expensive, but regardless of price, it is sometimes more useful than the other alkalies.</li><li>1% addition of Li_2O to a glaze increases the gloss and mechanical strength.</li><li>Because it is such a strong flux, more calcium, alumina, and silica can be used in raw alkaline glazes, promoting stability and helping to produce more beautiful copper blues and better colors with other chromophores.</li><li>.5% of lithium oxide makes glazes more fluid and reduces pinholing.</li><li>The addition of spodumene to either a soda or potash spar, if it does not exceed 20%, lowers the P.C.E. (pyrometric cone equivalent) of a glaze as much as six cones below the feldspar temperature.</li></ul>	**Insoluble** <ul><li>Lepidolite ($LiF \cdot KF \cdot Al_2O_3 \cdot 3SiO_2$) — commercial lepidolite contains about 3% Li_2O.</li><li>Amblygonite ($Li \cdot AlF \cdot PO_4$) — a commercial material, has about an 8% Li_2O content. It promotes fluxing and high gloss content. The fluorine and phosphoric oxide contents are useful in opaque glazes.</li><li>Spodumene ($Li_2O \cdot Al_2O_3 \cdot 4SiO_2$) — commercial material, has about 6% Li_2O content. It is quite refractory.</li><li>Lithium carbonate (Li_2CO_3) — a very desirable source for Li_2O; it reduces the maturing temperature and greatly increases the fluidity and gloss of glazes.</li><li>Lithospar (see feldspars) — the purest form of lithium; it begins to soften at cone 5.</li></ul>

3 THE ALKALINE EARTHS

Calcium oxide (CaO)	<ul><li>Acts as a flux within a range of temperatures. Small quantities are used for low temperatures and large quantities for cone 4 and above.</li><li>Used in nearly all glazes and combines readily with other materials and oxides.</li><li>Gives a glaze whiteness, hardness, and durability and lowers the coefficient of expansion.</li><li>Bleaches iron oxide to quite an extent, causing more yellow coloration.</li></ul>	**Insoluble** <ul><li>Whiting or enamel white calcite ($CaCO_3$) — the most important source of CaO.</li><li>Fluorspar (CaF_2) — used in limited quantities, gives a lower fluxing temperature, is an opacifier and brightener, and is best at the lower temperatures. Use with extreme caution, as it is very deleterious to kiln brick, and fluorine gas is poisonous.</li><li>Dolomite ($CaCO_3 \cdot MgCO_3$) — can be used for CaO but generally thought of as a source for MgO.</li><li>Colemanite ($2CaO \cdot 3B_2O_3 \cdot 5H_2O$) — also called Gerstley borate — is a source for CaO but generally regarded as a source of B_2O_3.</li><li>Bone ash ($Ca_3(PO_4)_2$) — not commonly used and if substituted for whiting will be more refractory and frequently causes bubbles.</li><li>Wollastonite or calcium silicate ($CaSiO_3$) — recently has been used to give a good glaze at high temperatures.</li></ul>

	ACTION	SOURCES
Barium oxide (BaO)	• A flux in the same category with CaO; in some combinations is more and in others less active than CaO. • Gives more brilliance than other alkaline earths but not as much as lead. • If introduced into a frit it has better fluxing action because it goes into solution reluctantly. This is advantageous in using it to produce matt glazes. • Used as a matting agent, more so in lead glazes than in boron glazes. • Not susceptible to reduction action.	**Insoluble** • Barium carbonate ($BaCO_3$) — best and most common material. • Barium sulphate ($BaSO_4$) — or barytes — can be used in a glaze but is impure; it is used in amounts of 1% or more in clay bodies to remove the whitish scum from calcium salts.
Magnesium oxide (MgO)	• Functions as a flux but at higher temperatures than barium or calcium; glazes from cone 4 to 10 can use MgO. • At the lower temperatures it acts as a refractory. • Lowers the coefficient of expansion more than any other base. • Functions as an opacifier in some cases. • Depending on the type of glaze used, the quantity of MgO varies from .1 to .3 molecular equivalent. • Will affect color development, especially with cobalt blue, giving magentas and red violets.	**Insoluble** • Magnesium carbonate ($MgCO_3$). • Dolomite ($CaCO_3 \cdot MgCO_3$) — a natural double carbonate of calcium oxide and magnesium oxide. It is cheap and convenient for introducing both, and contains about 44% of magnesium carbonate. • Steatite and talc ($3MgO \cdot 4SiO_2 \cdot H_2O$) — these minerals are practically the same, with steatite being less pure and containing less water. Talc can be used to produce textures with crawling.
Strontium oxide (SrO)	• Similar in action to calcium oxide, but a more active flux — it increases fluidity and slightly raises the thermal expansion when used in place of calcium. • There is not much advantage in using it, and it is expensive.	**Insoluble** • Strontium carbonate ($SrCO_3$).

THE R_2O_3 GROUP OF OXIDES (NEUTRALS)

Alumina (Al_2O_3)	• Refractory, has a high melting point. • Promotes matt textures. • In the form of clay, it keeps glaze materials in suspension while glaze is in storage and acts as an adhesive in holding the unfired glaze on a pot. • Makes glaze more viscous (i.e. stops it from running). • In the form of calcined clay, when high alumina is necessary, it prevents the unfired shrinkage or cracking on drying that usually causes crawling on firing.	**Insoluble** • Feldspars. • Cryolite. • Clay ($Al_2O_3 \cdot 2SiO_2$) — ball clay or china clay is preferable but surface clays will work in some cases. Some calcined clay — as part of the total clay content in a glaze — is best for matt glazes, or any glaze where high clay content will be used.
Boric oxide (B_2O_3)	• An active flux — as active as lead oxide. • A better flux than lead oxide for some uses — it is whiter, goes into combination easily, and forms low-melting compounds. • Has a low coefficient of expansion that gives less difficulty with crazing. • Does not crystallize from fusion and tends to hinder the crystallization of other compounds. • Has a strong solvent action on color oxides. • Boric oxide and alumina used in excess harm underglaze reds and greens.	**Insoluble** • Colemanite ($2CaO \cdot 3B_2O_3 \cdot 5H_2O$) — slightly soluble but can be used in raw glazes. Gerstley borate (calculated for practical purposes with the same formula) is a more stable substitute. Raw leadless glazes at cone 04 can be made successfully if cryolite is used with colemanite for brilliance. **Soluble** • Borax ($Na_2O \cdot 2B_2O_3 \cdot 10H_2O$) — used in frits and in raw glazes. • Boric acid ($B_2O_3 \cdot 3H_2O$) — used chiefly in frits.

	ACTION	SOURCES
Antimonious oxide or antimony trioxide (Sb_2O_3)	• An "old fashioned" oxide not common today. • Used in low temperature glazes with lead, tin, and zinc. • An opacifier, but may make glaze blister or bubble (is often used to create this texture). • With lead and tin it gives a good yellow color at low temperatures.	**Slightly soluble** • Naples yellow ($Pb_3(SbO_4)_2$) — a paint pigment that can be used by potters as a source of antimony. • Sodium antimonate ($2NaSbO_3 \cdot 7H_2O$) — used as an opacifier in enamels. It does not work well in glazes fired over 1832°F (1000°C).

THE RO$_2$ GROUP OF OXIDES (ACIDS)

	ACTION	SOURCES
Silica (SiO_2) With the exception of oxygen, silicon is the most important element in all glazes. In most glazes the SiO_2 content will constitute approximately 50% of the batch.	• Has a fairly low coefficient of expansion. If the SiO_2 content is increased in a glaze, it has a tendency to decrease crazing. • If the SiO_2 content is too low, the glaze appears too dry; it is the glass-former in glaze. • If the SiO_2 content is too high, the glaze is more refractory and may appear immature. • To increase viscosity and correct crazing, add clay. • Raises the melting temperature, decreases the fluidity of the melt, and increases the hardness and strength.	**Insoluble** • Flint, quartz, and pure SiO_2. • Natural silicates — these include clays, feldspars, and some ordinary glaze materials already mentioned. **Soluble** • Sodium silicate (Na_2SiO_3) — rarely used as a source for silica.
Tin oxide (SnO_2)	• Considered the strongest opacifier in glazes, it is used in amounts from 1% to 10%, preferably at low temperature; at high temperature it can act as a flux. • Can be used as a reducing agent, added as 1% to a glaze, for cone 5 and above. • An important ingredient in colors (yellow, pink, red, crimson, etc.), in underglazes, overglazes, and glazes.	**Insoluble** • Tin oxide.
Zirconium oxide (ZrO_2)	• An opacifier, but three times the amount of ZrO_2 is needed to equal the opacity of tin oxide. • Is a substitute for tin oxide over the entire range; is particularly good at high temperature; stays white in reduction.	**Insoluble** • Zirconium silicate ($ZrO_2 \cdot SiO_2$) — Zircopax and other brand names such as Ultrox and Opax. • Calcium zirconium silicate. • Barium zirconium silicate. • Zinc zirconium silicate. • Magnesium zirconium silicate. • Lead zirconium silicate. • Zirconium spinel.
Titanium oxide (TiO_2)	• A strong opacifier, pure titanium oxide gives the best whiteness of all opacifiers. • Has an action similar to silica. • Affects some colors. • Gives textured effects and crystals in glazes.	**Insoluble** • Rutile — a crude mineral form of titanium having iron as an impurity. There are light, medium, and dark rutiles and a granular variety. Rutile gives a dusty orange color, and promotes crystals and matts. Blue colors may result from a reduction firing. Rutile and cobalt together produce a green color; rutile yellows other colorants. • TiO_2 — can be purchased in pure form.

CHEMICAL COMPOSITIONS

Glazes can be "composed" and written down arbitrarily before they are mixed up and tested, much the same as music can be notated and then played. Before you can do this it is necessary to know the chemical symbols for each oxide and then to know the way each ceramic material, made up of these oxides, is written as a chemical formula. With practice you will remember the materials and their

oxide formulas. Meanwhile, refer to the following charts.

The first chart shows the atomic weights of individual elements. When atoms of these elements are combined to form molecules, add the atomic weights of each atom to find the molecular weight of the molecule. The charts on pages 301–2, 307, and 310–11 show the molecular weights of various materials you may meet in ceramics.

ATOMIC WEIGHTS OF ELEMENTS USED IN CERAMICS

ELEMENT	SYMBOL	ATOMIC WEIGHT
Aluminum	Al	27
Barium	Ba	137
Boron	B	11
Calcium	Ca	40
Carbon	C	12
Hydrogen	H	1
Iron	Fe	56
Lead	Pb	207
Lithium	Li	7
Magnesium	Mg	24
Oxygen	O	16
Phosphorus	P	31
Potassium	K	39
Silicon	Si	28
Sodium	Na	23
Sulphur	S	32
Tin	Sn	119
Titanium	Ti	48
Zinc	Zn	65
Zirconium	Zr	91

CERAMIC RAW MATERIALS

Chemical composition and molecular weights, for use in glaze formula calculations

MATERIALS	COMPOSITION	MOL. WT.
Alumina	Al_2O_3	102
Barium carbonate	$BaCO_3$	197
Borax	$Na_2O \cdot 2B_2O_3 \cdot 10H_2O_3$	382
Boric acid	$B_2O_3 \cdot 3H_2O$	124
Calcined clay	$Al_2O_3 \cdot 2SiO_2$	222
China clay (kaolin)	$Al_2O_3 \cdot 2SiO_2 \cdot 2H_2O$	258
Colemanite	$2CaO \cdot 3B_2O_3 \cdot 5H_2O$	412
Cornwall stone	(see feldspar chart)	
Dolomite	$CaCO_3 \cdot MgCO_3$	184
Flint (silica)	SiO_2	60
Fluorspar	CaF_2	78
Lead bisilicate	$PbO \cdot 2SiO_2$	343
Lead carbonate (white lead)	$2PbCO_3 \cdot Pb(OH)_2$	775
Lead chromate	$PbCrO_4$	323
Lead monoxide (litharge)	PbO	223
Lead oxide (red lead)	Pb_3O_4	685
Lithium carbonate	Li_2CO_3	74
Magnesium carbonate	$MgCO_3$	84
Nepheline syenite	(see feldspar chart)	
Niter (potassium nitrate)	KNO_3	101
Pearl ash (potassium carbonate)	K_2CO_3	138
Plastic vitrox	(see feldspar chart)	
Soda ash	Na_2CO_3	106
Talc (steatite)	$3MgO \cdot 4SiO_2 \cdot H_2O$	378
Tin oxide	SnO_2	151
Titanium oxide (rutile)	TiO_2	80
Whiting (calcium carbonate)	$CaCO_3$	100
Wollastonite	$Ca \cdot SiO_2$	116
Zinc oxide	ZnO	81
Zirconium oxide	ZrO_2	123
Zircopax (zirconium silicate)	$ZrO_2 \cdot SiO_2$	183

COMMON CERAMIC COLORANTS

Chemical composition and molecular weights, usually not used in glaze formula calculations but as additions to glaze batches

COLORANT OXIDE	COMPOSITION	MOL.WT.			
			Iron oxide (black, ferrous)	FeO	72
Chromium oxide	Cr_2O_3	152	Iron oxide (red, ferric)	Fe_2O_3	160
Cobalt carbonate	$CoCO_3$	119	Manganese carbonate	$MnCO_3$	115
Cobalt oxide (black)	Co_3O_4	241			
Copper carbonate	$CuCO_3$	124	Manganese dioxide	MnO_2	87
Copper oxide (black)	CuO	80	Nickel monoxide (green)	NiO	75
Ilmenite	$FeO·TiO_2$	152	Nickel oxide (black)	Ni_2O_3	166
Iron chromate	$FeCrO_4$	172			

CALCULATING GLAZE BY FORMULA

It is hard to imagine that the chalky dry raw materials we mix with water and call glaze will turn to glass in a fire. It is also hard to think of these powdery materials as being made up of a number of chemical molecules, each one acting and reacting with the other to give a prescribed surface treatment, depending on the composition.

Learning to think in terms of $RO–R_2O$, R_2O_3, and RO_2 columns, and having a working knowledge of what individual oxides and raw materials do, give the freedom to make changes in a formula, re-calculate, fire, and generally be close to the desired mark. The batching method, or parts by weight experimentation, has wider parameters and is not a system for being specific.

Calculation of glaze from a molecular formula is the method used to be absolutely specific about relative proportions of glaze oxides. It embodies a precise technical means of drawing up a glaze, or changing one. It requires the molecular equivalent of the glaze oxides to be worked out mathematically.

As has been said, glazes are chemically written in a formula in three columns according to the oxygen valence; $RO–R_2O$ on the left, R_2O_3 in the middle, and RO_2 on the right side. A sample formula looks like this:

$$K_2O \quad .15 \qquad Al_2O_3 \ 2.5 \qquad SiO_2 \ 6.0$$
$$Na_2O \ .10$$
$$CaO \quad .40$$
$$MgO \quad .35$$

This is a "unity" formula — it shows in simplest form the ratio of molecules in the glaze, rather than the actual amounts. The ratios, or molecular equivalents, are based on the left or $RO–R_2O$ column, on what is called "unity" — the numbers in this column always add up to 1. As discussed in the previous section, the oxides in this left column act as fluxes, lowering the melting point of the glaze and controlling fusion.

Alumina is the most important oxide in the middle column, in which the oxygen valence is 3 (Al_2O_3). This column does not add up to anything, but proportionally it can be related to the first ($RO–R_2O$) column. Usually, although not always, the alumina amount is more than one molecular equivalent. This will vary as the temperature goes up or down. Because alumina is a refractory oxide, more of it can be used in high-fired glazes than in low-fired ones. High alumina content, or more than average for the heat treatment, will cause opacity and mattness and, in consequence, stiffness of melt. Low alumina is needed when great fluidity is desired, such as in crystalline glazes, or where alumina is deleterious to color, as in chrome reds.

Silica is the most important oxide in the third column, in which the oxygen valence is 2 (SiO_2). Depending on the temperature of the glaze, silica usually varies between 4 and 8 whole molecular equivalents. Again, you can compare these figures proportionately with the $RO–R_2O$ column, which always totals 1 whole molecular equivalent.

Alumina and silica, the basic needs in glazes and enamels, have individual melting points around 3000 °F (1648 °C) — much hotter than kilns fire for earthenware, stoneware, or porcelain. Alumina, the binding oxide that keeps the glaze on the clay or the enamel on the metal, and silica, the glass-former that sets up the glassy matrix, would be sufficient alone if we could fire hot enough. Since we can't, the fluxing oxides found in the $RO–R_2O$ column are necessary, reducing the melting points of Al_2O_3 and

SiO₂ as low as necessary (not lower than red heat, 1300 °F [704 °C]), and determining to a great extent the character of the glaze. Some of the RO–R₂O oxides are very fluid melters, some sluggish, some contribute to opacity, some to transparency, some to mattness, some to glossiness, and they are chosen for these qualities needed in a given glaze. The one whole equivalent that the RO–R₂O totals — "unity" — is divided into parts of one whole according to the function of the oxides chosen. For instance:

.3 Na₂O (fluidity, clearness, helps make colors
 brilliant)
.2 CaO (hardness, whiteness)
.2 MgO (opacity, mattness)
.3 K₂O (fluidity, gloss)

1.0 comprising the total RO–R₂O column.

The alumina and silica amounts in the formula will further modify the look of the glaze.

Glazes are compounded to mature at the temperature that is chosen for the clay body being used, or the temperature chosen to make the clay body porous or dense, as desired. More specifically, glazes are designed to work at the temperature necessary to make the clay body into earthenware, stoneware, or porcelain.

The clay artist learns the functions of the oxides that fall into each of the three columns, and the approximate amounts or proportions of molecules that give certain results at different heats. Then the oxides must be translated into the materials in which they occur in nature. Each oxide generally has more than one possible material source, although materials can differ in character (pp. 296–300). The same chemical formula can be translated into different batches, depending on the materials chosen to fulfill the oxide requirements. Materials can be changed to "fit" a specific formula until the desired results are reached after testing.

An important fact to remember is that glazes can have exactly the same chemistry, or chemical formula, but with the use of different materials supplying the oxides. This means that the final or melted quality of the same formula can vary. In the United States there is a wide selection of materials, but in some countries the choice is limited. However, the glaze calculation method makes it possible to move anywhere and keep essentially the same glazes.

It would be possible, but not practical, to compound new glazes from chemical formulas all the time. People also prefer the familiarity that results from using the same glazes repeatedly.

Still, we need to understand the method of making up a new glaze formula according to specifications, and how to change an old formula, and then to fit the raw materials to it so that the glaze can in fact be mixed. Working a formula to a batch, or a batch to a formula, requires that you know the molecular weight of the oxides being used. Zinc oxide (ZnO), for instance, contains only zinc and oxygen and has

a molecular weight of 81. However, frits and feldspars, which may form part of a glaze, are more complicated materials with extensive chemical formulas of their own. These can be written in the three columns, RO–R₂O, R₂O₃, and RO₂, like a glaze. Take Kingman feldspar as an example. This is a material found in the ground in Kingman, Arizona, which until recently could be bought from a ceramic supplier. It has a glaze-like formula:

K₂O .75   Al₂O₃ 1.4   SiO₂ 4.5
Na₂O .25

As in glaze formulas, the numbers in the left column total 1. The sum of all the portions of molecules in this feldspar (i.e. its molecular weight) is 578, calculated by multiplying the atomic weights of the various atoms in the molecules by the molecular equivalents of those molecules, and then totaling them.

The chemical formulas and molecular weights of other naturally occurring frits and feldspars used in ceramics are found in the charts on pages 307 and 309–11.

It is not necessary to understand a great deal of chemistry in order to compound glaze formulas or to calculate them into batches. Remember that glaze formulas are always written in three columns — think of fluxes "on the left," viscosity controllers "in the middle," and glass-formers "on the right." Remember too that the formula is a proportional relationship of these oxides, based on their molecular weights. Using these formulas and the information contained in the charts on pages 301–2, 307, and 309–11, you can work out the weights (in grams) of the raw materials in a glaze batch.

CALCULATING FORMULA TO BATCH

You may have a formula that has been worked out from a "parts by weight" batch which needs changing, or perhaps different materials are needed to "fit" it than were involved previously. Or you might just have made up a formula, and need to work it from formula to batch so you can try it out. For whatever reason, you need to be able to translate that glaze formula into a batch, to make it possible to weigh out the new glaze in grams.

Here is a very simple low-fire glaze formula, extremely simple because it has only one oxide in the RO–R₂O column — lead oxide (PbO). Lead is the only oxide that is active enough to carry the fluxing function of the RO column on its own.

PbO 1.0   Al₂O₃ .2   SiO₂ 1.0

How do you make a batch of this formula?

Step 1. Make a chart collecting the oxides given in this formula. Write the oxides across the top of the chart, with room at the left to write the raw materials downward as they are supplied to fulfill these oxide requirements:

	PbO	Al₂O₃	SiO₂

Step 2. Choose raw materials, one at a time, to supply the oxides given in the formula. Start with the RO–R₂O oxides. Lead carbonate is a source of PbO (p. 296). As you have seen in the fusion button tests (p. 151), it melts into a clear yellowish transparent glass at low temperature. It intensifies color, and is thus the preferred choice for nonfunctional objects. It is readily available and a more pure source than red lead, litharge, or galena, unless you happen to be where those materials are local. Lead carbonate has the formula $2PbCO_3 \cdot Pb(OH)_2$, yielding a total of 3 lead oxides (3 PbO).

Next, decide to use clay to supply the alumina and some of the silica. More silica is usually needed in glazes than can be supplied totally by silica-containing materials, such as clay. This will be revealed as the calculation is done.

Step 3. This involves filling in the chart. To know how much each of the materials you have selected for the batch can be used to fit the above formula, you must divide the amount you want in the glaze by the amount you have of each material. You will need to look up the molecular formula of each material on the appropriate charts.

For this formula calculation, divide the amount of lead oxide needed in the glaze (1.0) by the amount in the material (i.e. by the 3 PbOs collected from the lead carbonate formula in Step 2):

$$1.0 \div 3.0 = .33$$

You therefore use .33 equivalents of the material lead carbonate. To see if this fulfills the need for lead oxide, multiply the equivalents of the material by the number of PbOs in the material:

$$.33 \times 3 = .99, \text{ or for all practical purposes } 1.0$$

Write this on the chart to show that the lead oxide has been supplied, and make an X on the chart in the appropriate column to show this is so:

	PbO	Al₂O₃	SiO₂
Needed in glaze:	1.0	.2	1.0
Lead carbonate .33 × 3 PbO	.99		
	X		

Then deal with the two oxides in the clay molecule, alumina and silica. The molecular formula of clay is $Al_2O_3 \cdot 2SiO_2 \cdot 6(OH)_2$. The rule is: divide the amount you need by the amount you have to get the equivalent of raw material. To see how much that equivalent supplies of each oxide in the material, multiply the equivalent by the amount of each oxide in the material.

	PbO	Al₂O₃	SiO₂
Needed in glaze:	1.0	.2	1.0
Lead carbonate .33 × 3 PbO	.99		
Clay .2 × 1 Al₂O₃ .2 × 2 SiO₂	X	.2	−.4
			.6
Silica .6 × 1 SiO₂		X	.6
			X

Once the chart has been worked out, you need only use the molecular equivalents of the raw materials on the left side of the chart. To obtain the batch weight, (or "parts by weight" of the batch), multiply each molecular equivalent by the molecular weight of that material. You could then measure out these batch weights in grams to obtain the correct amounts of each oxide for mixing the dry glaze. However, it is better to convert the batch weights into percentages, which you can use to prepare any quantity of glaze you may want, and which will serve as a useful comparison with other glazes. Round off the answers to the nearest whole percent.

MATERIAL	MOL. EQ.		MOL. WT.		BATCH WT.	% WT.
Lead carbonate	.33	×	775	=	255.75	61
Clay	.6	×	222	=	133.20	32
Silica	.5	×	60	=	30.00	7
					418.95	100

Using the same method, now try working out a more complicated glaze formula:

PbO .30	Al₂O₃ .3	SiO₂ 2.5
K₂O .05	B₂O₃ .3	
Na₂O .15		
CaO .35		
MgO .15		

Step 1. Fit raw materials to this formula. Always start with the material containing the greatest amount of oxides, such as feldspar or frit. For this particular glaze try using the feldspar nepheline syenite, which has the following formula:

Na₂O .75	Al₂O₃ 1.11	SiO₂ 4.63
K₂O .25		molecular weight = 462

In order to find out how much, in molecular equivalents, of the whole raw material (nepheline syenite) is to be used in the above glaze formula, divide the amount you need by the amount you have. In other words, divide the amount you need in the glaze by the amount you have in the feldspar.

In this case, you have .75 Na_2O and you want .15 Na_2O in the glaze:

$$.15 \div .75 = .2$$

Feldspar or any material having more than one oxide must be divided in this way through each component to see which oxide yields the smallest number (amount of oxide). Naturally, only as much of the whole material can be used as will supply the smallest number in the formula — if any more is used, there will be too much of some oxides in the glaze formula.

Na_2O	$.15 \div .75 = .2$	Al_2O_3	$.3 \div 1.11 = .27$
K_2O	$.05 \div .25 = .2$	SiO_2	$2.5 \div 4.63 = .5$

Of these four answers .2 is the smallest, therefore .2 equivalents of nepheline syenite is the largest amount of the feldspar that can be used in this glaze.

Step 2. Make the chart and begin to fill it in, as you did in the previous exercise. The charts in the previous section (pages 296–300) will help you find sources for the various oxides. Molecular formulas for these raw materials are given in the chart on page 301.

Step 3. To see how much of each oxide is satisfied by the material, multiply the molecular equivalent of the nepheline syenite which can be used (i.e. .2) by each of the oxides in the formula of that material. Put the answers in the chart, in the appropriate columns. Subtract those oxides not satisfied by .2 nepheline syenite (i.e. alumina and silica) and bring down the remainders to the next line. Mark an X under those oxides satisfied by the .2 nepheline syenite.

(It helps to bring down every number that is still wanted in the glaze, so that the incomplete chart can be read across on one line, opposite each raw material, as you are doing your calculations.)

Step 4. With the feldspar worked, take the simplest material next, which is lead oxide, and which may be satisfied with lead carbonate. Divide the amount you need (.3) by the amount you have (3 PbO). Multiply this answer (.1) by the number of lead oxides in the raw material (3), and write the answer in the chart (.30).

Step 5. Looking at the remaining oxide requirements, it is natural to think of supplying MgO with dolomite, which also contains CaO. Calculate this by the method used in Steps 3 and 4. When dolomite proves not to satisfy all the CaO needed, Gerstley borate (colemanite) is a good selection for the next material because it contains CaO and B_2O_3, also required by this glaze.

Different material selections could have been made; for instance, whiting for all the CaO, magnesium carbonate for all the MgO, and boric oxide for the B_2O_3. However, magnesium carbonate is a material that often causes crawling and boric oxide is a soluble and therefore unstable material — although these choices would not be wrong, the former decisions are better.

Step 6. The only remaining oxides to be satisfied are Al_2O_3 and SiO_2. Clay and silica, as materials containing these oxides, naturally come to mind; always leave these to the last in suplying any glaze formula. Work out the clay first, because it contains both oxides, and the silica last.

.078 Al_2O_3 is needed and 1 Al_2O_3 is contained in the oxide formula of clay. Divide .078 by 1; the answer is .078. To know how much .078 clay will bring to the glaze in Al_2O_3 and SiO_2, multiply .078 by the formula of clay, or by 1 Al_2O_3 and by 2 SiO_2. This allows .078 Al_2O_3 to be written under what was needed and is now satisfied, and .156 (.078 × 2) to be written under the silica. Subtract that from the silica already there to find that 1.414 is still owed.

		PbO	K_2O	Na_2O	CaO	MgO	Al_2O_3	B_2O_3	SiO_2
Step 2	Needed in glaze:	.30	.05	.15	.35	.15	.30	.30	2.5
Step 3	Nepheline syenite .2 × unity		.05	.15			.30 −.222		2.5 −.93
Step 4	Lead carbonate .1 × 3 PbO	.30	X	X			.078		1.57
	Bring down all numbers of oxides still required in the glaze to see at a glance what is still needed.								
Step 5	Dolomite .15 × 1CaO + 1MgO	X	X	X	.35 −.15	.15 −.15	.078	.30	1.57
	Gerstley borate .1 × 2CaO + 3B_2O_3	X	X	X	.20 −.20	X	.078	.30 −.30	1.57
Step 6	Clay .078 × 1Al_2O_3 + 2SiO_2	X	X	X	X	X	.078 −.078	X	1.57 −.156
	Flint 1.414 × 1SiO_2	X	X	X	X	X	X	X	1.414 −1.414
		X	X	X	X	X	X	X	X

Silica can be provided as SiO_2 (flint). Multiply 1.414 equivalents of SiO_2 by the 1 SiO_2 in the material and you find the requirement satisfied.

Step 7. With the chart filled in and the oxides satisfied, multiply each molecular equivalent of the raw materials on the chart (e.g. .2 nepheline syenite) by the molecular weight of each material to get the batch weight (or "parts by weight" of the batch).

MATERIAL	MOL. EQ.		MOL. WT.	BATCH WT.	% WT.
Nepheline syenite	.2	×	462	92.4	27
Lead	.1	×	775	77.5	23
Dolomite	.13	×	184	27.6	8
Colemanite	.1	×	412	41.2	12
Clay	.1078	×	258	20.0	6
Flint	1.414	×	60	84.8	24
				343.5	100

Step 8. Calculate the batch on the basis of percentage, as shown above, by dividing each batch weight (or part by weight) by the sum total of all the parts. Round off the answers to the nearest whole percent.

Always write glaze batches on the basis of percentage, or 100 parts, to give you a consistent method of comparing one glaze with another. Percentages also help you to keep in mind proportions of materials for various temperatures and effects. This is the beginning of an intuitive knowledge of glaze.

CALCULATING BATCH TO FORMULA

The other way round, working a batch glaze into its oxide formula, is also computed on a chart. You begin by using the parts by weight or batch weight (i.e. the grams called for in the batch) of each material, then dividing this by the molecular weight of the material to get its molecular equivalent.

Start at the top of the chart by collecting all the oxides that are to be found in the materials of the glaze. Begin with $RO-R_2O$ column oxides on the left and end with alumina and silica on the right. Then it is a process of multiplying the molecular equivalents of each material by the oxide formula of the same material, collecting the answers in columns on the chart, and adding each column. The column totals comprise what is called the "empirical" formula of the glaze.

You need to translate the empirical formula to the "unity" basis, as explained on page 302. Do this by dividing each oxide in the column totals by the total of the $RO-R_2O$ oxide group. The whole formula is now put on the basis of the $RO-R_2O$ column. In the final unity formula the $RO-R_2O$ column always adds to 1 or close to it (such as .99 or .98). The universal proportioning of the formula allows you

to discuss glazes on an oxide basis, just as putting anything on the basis of percentage allows you to understand proportions of a given whole. The empirical formula is always taken to the unity formula for this reason.

Here is an example of the method of calculating a batch to a formula:

Cone 04 Matt (Batch)

MATERIAL	PARTS BY WEIGHT
Lead carbonate	387
Whiting	60
Zinc oxide	36
*Kingman feldspar	252
Calcined clay	132
Flint	54

*To do this calculation you will need to know the oxide molecular formula of Kingman feldspar:

Na_2O .245 Al_2O_3 1.065 SiO_2 6.38

K_2O .755 molecular weight = 578

Step 1. Divide each of the parts by weight in the batch by the molecular weight of the material, to get the molecular equivalents of the material.

MATERIAL	PARTS		MOL. WT.		MOL. EQ.
Lead carbonate	387	÷	775	=	.500
Whiting	60	÷	100	=	.600
Zinc oxide	36	÷	81	=	.446
Kingman feldspar	252	÷	578	=	.437
Calcined clay	132	÷	222	=	.595
Flint	54	÷	60	=	.900

Step 2. Collect the oxides contained in the batch on a chart like this:

BATCH	PbO	CaO	ZnO	Na₂O	K₂O	Al₂O₃	SiO₂
Lead carbonate .5 × 3	1.5						
Whiting .6 × 1		.6					
Zinc oxide .446 × 1			.446				
Kingman feldspar .437 × ————				.107	.33	.465	2.785
Calcined clay .595 × ——						.595	1.19
Flint .9 × 1							.9
Totals	1.5	.6	.446	.107	.33	1.060	4.875

$RO-R_2O$ column total = 2.982

Multiply the molecular equivalent of each material by each molecular oxide formula: hence lead carbonate, the formula of which yields 3 PbO, is multiplied by .5:

$$3 \times .5 \text{ is } 1.5.$$

Put each answer in the appropriate column of the chart above. In the case of feldspar and clay, as with any material containing more than one oxide, be sure to multiply the molecular equivalent by each oxide in the material. Add the columns and write the totals at the bottom of the chart.

Step 3. The formula must now be put on a unity basis, to standardize it with other glaze formulas for reasons of comparison. To do this, take the $RO-R_2O$ column total, which is 2.982 in this case. Divide each oxide in the formula by this sum. Add up the $RO-R_2O$ column again — the total should be 1. Divide all other oxides on the chart by the total (2.982), to put the whole formula on the basis of unity.

PbO .503	Al_2O_3 .355	SiO_2 1.632
CaO .201		
ZnO .149		
K_2O .111		
Na_2O .036		
___1.000___		

Having worked through these examples of calculating a glaze — from formula to batch, and from batch to formula — you can apply the same method to any glaze. In addition to the charts on pages 301–2, giving atomic weights of elements and molecular composition and weights of common oxides, you will need to refer to the following charts for the feldspars and frits you may come across in different glaze formulas. Chemical analysis of these compounds in percentages can be found along with other reference information about commercial frits, on pages 309–11.

FELDSPARS

Feldspars are a group of crystalline minerals (making up 60 percent of the earth's crust) that are aluminum silicates with varying amounts of potassium, sodium, calcium, and/or lithium. They have softening points ranging from cone 4 to 9, depending on their composition, and function as fluxes in glaze formulas. Feldspar formulas and molecular weights may vary slightly, depending on where they are mined, so check the analysis of the feldspars you are using periodically with your dealer to be sure you have the correct data for your calculations.

Chemical composition and molecular weights, for use in glaze formula calculations

FELDSPAR	COMPOSITION			MOL. WT.
Plastic vitrox (feldspathic clay)	K_2O .842 MgO .058 Na_2O .055 CaO .045	Al_2O_3 1.693	SiO_2 14.634	1139.4
Minpro	Na_2O .572 K_2O .380 CaO .048	Al_2O_3 1.145	SiO_2 8.00	671
Cornwall stone	K_2O .356 Na_2O .340 CaO .304	Al_2O_3 1.075	SiO_2 8.10	667
Kingman	K_2O .755 Na_2O .245	Al_2O_3 1.065	SiO_2 6.38	578
Buckingham	K_2O .740 Na_2O .260	Al_2O_3 1.026	SiO_2 6.34	571
G–200	K_2O .610 Na_2O .280 CaO .110	Al_2O_3 1.06	SiO_2 6.11	555.6
Nepheline syenite	Na_2O .750 K_2O .250	Al_2O_3 1.11	SiO_2 4.65	462
Lithospar	CaO .461 Li_2O .407 Na_2O .098 K_2O .034	Al_2O_3 .14 Fe_2O_3 .04	SiO_2 1.79	174.8
Gerstley borate	CaO .630 MgO .194 Na_2O .176	Al_2O_3 .025 B_2O_3 1.050	SiO_2 .352	155

FRITS

Frits are commercially prepared combinations of oxides for low-fire glazes. The chart below lists the most commonly used Ferro frits.

Chemical composition and molecular weights, for use in glaze formula calculations

FRIT NO.	FORMULA			MOL. WT.
3403	PbO .874 Na_2O .126	Al_2O_3 .175	SiO_2 2.5	370
3124	Na_2O .256 K_2O .016 CaO .728	Al_2O_3 .279 B_2O_3 .497	SiO_2 2.65	280
3195	Na_2O .311 CaO .689	Al_2O_3 .405 B_2O_3 1.10	SiO_2 2.76	342
3230	Na_2O .60 K_2O .20 ZnO .08 CaO .02 BaO .10	Al_2O_3 none	SiO_2 2.3	225

DEVISING NEW GLAZE FORMULAS

Suppose you need to make up a new glaze, to fulfill the look you want and the temperature and atmosphere you wish to use. Before you can write a proper formula, you need to know the limits of the various oxides you can use to achieve the results you want.

The following glaze limit chart is a useful guide. It gives you a selection of formulas, each with approximate upper and lower limits of oxides, for use within a range of cones. You can adapt these formulas to fit your own specification. The chart begins with a low-fire lead glaze; notice that you can use as little as .7 PbO or as much as 1.0 (the lower the cone you wish to use, the more lead you will need). Remember that the RO–R$_2$O column must always total 1.0; if you use .7 PbO, you will need to supply a further .3 molecular equivalents of one or more other RO–R$_2$O oxides.

The alumina and silica "limit" range is also given. Generally, the lower the cone, the less you should use. For matt finish, use more alumina; for bright or gloss finish, use less alumina and more silica. The same rationalization works in glaze formulation at all temperatures.

After devising an arbitrary formula, calculate one or more batches from various materials that fit this formula, then mix up the batch and test it. If the result is not what you want, go back and adjust your formula. Remember, the "limit" formulas are only guides, not absolutes. You can use different oxides, or more or less than the amounts given here, as long as the RO–R$_2$O column adds up to 1. These figures are averages; experiment with your own formulas.

GLAZE "LIMIT" FORMULAS

TYPE OF GLAZE	CONE RANGE	LIMIT FORMULA					
Raw lead – low temp.	015–07	PbO	.7–1.0	Al$_2$O$_3$	.05–.2	SiO$_2$	1.0–1.6
		CaO	.0–.3				
		KNaO	.0–.2				
Alkaline – leadless	015–07	KnaO	.5–.7	Al$_2$O$_2$	.05–.1	SiO$_2$	1.5–2.5
		CaO	.3–.5	B$_2$O$_3$	.0–1.0		
Raw lead – bright	06–4	PbO	.1–.7	Al$_2$O$_3$	.15–.35	SiO$_2$	1.5–2.5
		CaO	.1–.4	B$_2$O$_3$	.0–.6		
		KNaO	.1–.3				
		ZnO	.0–.2				
		MgO	.0–.15				
Colemanite – leadless	06–4	KNaO	.2–.3	Al$_2$O$_3$	.25–.35	SiO$_2$	2.5–3.5
		CaO	.2–.6	B$_2$O$_3$	.3–.9		
		BaO	.0–.3				
		MgO	.0–.2				
		ZnO	.0–..4				
Raw lead – bright	02	PbO	.5	Al$_2$O$_3$	.25	SiO$_2$	1.75
		CaO	.3				
		KNaO	.2				
Raw lead – matt	02	PbO	.4	Al$_2$O$_3$	.35	SiO$_2$	1.5
		ZnO	.1				
		CaO	.1				
		BaO	.2				
		KNaO	.2				
Fritted whiteware transparent lead borosilicate	1–5	PbO	.2–.3	Al$_2$O$_3$	.25–.35	SiO$_2$	2.5–3.5
		KNaO	.2–.3	B$_2$O$_3$	.3–.7		
		CaO	.35–.5				
		ZnO	.0–.1				
Bristol stoneware	4–8	KNaO	.25–.4	Al$_2$O$_3$	.35–.55	SiO$_2$	2.5–4.0
		CaO	.1–.3				
		MgO	.0–.2				
		ZnO	.15–.4				
Stoneware or porcelain	8–12	KNaO	.2–.4	Al$_2$O$_3$	.3–.5	SiO$_2$	3.0–5.0
		CaO	.4–.7				
		MgO	.0–.3				
		ZnO	.0–.2				

To change from bright to matt:
1   change alumina and silica, raise Al$_2$O$_3$ and lower SiO$_2$;
2   leave Al$_2$O$_3$ and SiO$_2$ the same and substitute .1 ZnO for .1 PbO; substitute .2 BaO for .2 CaO. Zinc has a tendency to soften matt.

DATA AND CONVERSIONS
FELDSPARS, FRITS, AND CLAYS

FELDSPARS – ANALYSIS BY PERCENTAGE

FELDSPAR	K_2O	Na_2O	Li_2O	CaO	MgO	B_2O_3	Al_2O_3	Fe_2O_3	SiO_2	TiO_2
Plastic vitrox (feldspathic clay)	6.92	.30		.22	.20		15.16		77.20	
Minpro	5.32	5.23		.04			17.44		71.97	
Cornwall stone	5.01	3.15		2.55			16.43		72.86	
Kingman	12.28	2.63					18.80		66.29	
Buckingham	12.18	2.80					18.34		66.68	
G–200	10.32	3.12		1.10			19.41		66.05	
Nepheline syenite	5.08	10.06					24.49		60.37	
Lithospar	2.50	4.65	.11	.20			10.89	.05	81.60	
Gerstley borate		5.96		20.33	4.47	42.36	14.68		12.20	
Westspar	5.30	6.20		1.30	1.20		19.90	4.67	60.32	1.11
Custer	10.43	3.00		.30	Trace		17.54	.08	68.65	
K–spar	6.19	4.62		1.98	.05		15.23	.14	71.73	.06
N–spar	.25	7.26		.57	.13		14.33	.23	77.13	.10
Kona F–4	4.80	6.90		1.70	Trace		19.64	.04	66.92	

Feldspar analyses (above) and formulas (p. 307) have been included to show that they look like glaze batches and formulas — they are nature's glazes, so to speak. Similarly, frit analyses and formulas appear like glaze ones, but are manufactured. You can calculate a feldspar or frit from formula to batch, or from batch to formula, just as shown with glazes in the previous section.

FERRO LEAD-BEARING FRITS – ANALYSIS BY PERCENTAGE

FRIT NO.	PbO	MgO/CaO	Na_2O	K_2O	Al_2O_3	B_2O_3	SiO_2	TiO_2	ZrO_2	F
3302	52.6		2.1		4.8		40.5			
3403	69.8		.4	1.3	2.4		28.1			
3417	30.5	4.5	1.5	1.9	3.0	12.6	43.6		2.4	
3419	59.2		6.5			14.5	19.8			
3465	6.6	6.6	14.7			19.3	52.8			
3476	63.2					19.8	17.0			
3482	29.1	3.3	2.7	3.9		6.0	43.1	9.7		2.2
3485	44.4		6.1			13.9	35.6			
3489	67.6	5.6					26.8			
3493	30.4	4.4	1.6	1.8		12.6	46.1			

FERRO LEADLESS FRITS – ANALYSIS BY PERCENTAGE

FRIT NO.	Na₂O	Na₂F₂	K₂O	CaO	ZnO	B₂O₃	Al₂O₃	SiO₂
3124	5.6		6.0	14.5		12.5	10.0	56.8
3134	10.2			20.1		23.2		46.5
3264	21.0					21.9	7.1	50.0
3269	17.7	3.5	10.0		.9	16.7	12.8	48.4
3270	9.3		4.9	8.9		18.7	8.9	50.3
3271	13.0			10.6		21.8		54.6
3278	15.2			6.8		21.8		56.2

PEMCO LEAD-BEARING FRITS – ANALYSIS BY PERCENTAGE AND MOLECULAR FORMULA

FRIT NO.	COEFFICIENT OF EXPANSION*	MOL. WT.		K₂O	Na₂O	CaO	ZnO	PbO	Al₂O₃	B₂O₃	SiO₂	ZrO₂	F
Pb–41	8.6	256.3	% Analysis				5.4	72.2		9.0	13.4		
			Mol. Formula				.17	.83		.33	.57		
Pb–63	6.8	363.9	% Analysis		3.6	4.5		30.5	3.4	12.6	43.0	2.4	
			Mol. Formula		.21	.29		.50	.12	.66	2.60	.07	
Pb–83	10.4	271.1	% Analysis		6.4			59.2		14.4	20.0		
			Mol. Formula		.28			.72		.56	.90		
Pb–349	6.5	312.9	% Analysis	2.7	1.8	10.4		17.1	6.2	8.0	53.8		
			Mol. Formula	.09	.09	.58		.24	.19	.36	2.80		
Pb–716	8.1	247.5	% Analysis			5.6		67.6			26.8		
			Mol. Formula			.25		.75			1.10		
Pb–723	9.0	291.8	% Analysis		1.5			71.2	2.4		24.9		
			Mol. Formula		.07			.93	.07		1.21		
Pb–740	6.7	192.7	% Analysis		1.2		20.0	56.8	2.0		20.0		
			Mol. Formula		.04		.47	.49	.04		.64		
Pb–742	6.5	359.1	% Analysis		3.6	4.5		31.0	3.4	13.0	43.5	1.0	
			Mol. Formula		.21	.29		.50	.12	.66	2.60	.03	
Pb–1038	6.8	297.1	% Analysis	.3	2.7		7.6	43.5	5.0	5.0	35.9		
			Mol. Formula	.01	.13		.28	.58	.14	.21	1.78		
Pb–1307	7.8	240.5	% Analysis		2.2	5.4	8.7	39.9	6.3	9.2	28.3		
			Mol. Formula		.08	.23	.26	.43	.15	.32	1.13		
Pb–1K75	8.3	362.4	% Analysis	1.9	1.8	5.5		28.4	3.8	13.0	40.8	1.2	3.6
			Mol. Formula	.08	.10	.36		.46	.13	.68	2.48	.04	.70

*122–842 °F (50–450 °C) × 10⁻⁶

This chart and the following one show differences in composition as related to expansion.

PEMCO LEADLESS FRITS – ANALYSIS BY PERCENTAGE AND MOLECULAR FORMULA

FRIT NO.	COEFFICIENT OF EXPANSION*	MOL. WT.		K₂O	Na₂O	Li₂O	CaO	CaF₂	MgO	BaO	SrO	ZnO	CdO	Al₂O₃	B₂O₃	SiO₂	ZrO₂	F
P–25	10.0	326.0	% Analysis	5.4	14.7		.5						.7	12.1	16.9	49.7		1.8
			Mol. Formula	.18	.76		.03						.03	.38	.78	2.65		.29
P–54	8.9	190.9	% Analysis		10.4		20.0								23.3	46.3		
			Mol. Formula		.32		.68								.64	1.47		
P–64	7.8	205.3	% Analysis	.4	4.8		6.0	4.0		8.0			16.0	1.0	10.0	39.8	10.0	
			Mol. Formula	.01	.16		.22	.11		.11			.39	.02	.29	3.6	.17	
P–311	7.0	275.4	% Analysis	.7	6.5		14.1							10.0	14.4	54.3		
			Mol. Formula	.02	.29		.69							.27	.57	2.49		
P–609	6.9	254.4	% Analysis	1.1	2.2	1.7	7.1		3.3		8.5			8.0	9.0	59.1		
			Mol. Formula	.03	.09	.14	.32		.21		.21			.20	.33	2.50		
P–626	7.2	374.8	% Analysis		5.6					27.4				5.4	12.4	49.2		
			Mol. Formula		.33					.67				.20	.67	3.07		
P–760	8.9	383.7	% Analysis	8.1	7.3								7.4	4.3	16.3	56.6		
			Mol. Formula	.33	.45								.22	.16	.90	3.62		
P–786	7.2	284.2	% Analysis	3.0	2.0		11.5				8.7			6.8	8.8	59.2		
			Mol. Formula	.09	.09		.58				.24			.19	.36	2.80		
P–830	8.6	271.1	% Analysis		14.9		7.2								21.6	56.3		
			Mol. Formula		.65		.35								.84	2.54		
P–926	8.4	226.2	% Analysis	.3	8.5		17.0							5.0	18.7	50.5		
			Mol. Formula	.01	.31		.68							.11	.61	1.90		
P–930	6.8	299.2	% Analysis		4.3		5.4				17.3			4.1	15.4	52.3	1.2	
			Mol. Formula		.21		.29				.50			.12	.66	2.60	.03	

*122–842°F (50–450°C) × 10⁻⁶

Various companies manufacture frits. The following are numbers of frequently used frits that have similar composition to Ferro's:

FERRO	O'HOMMELL	PEMCO	GLOSTEX	FERRO	O'HOMMELL	PEMCO	GLOSTEX
3134	14	P–54	BF–14	3465	18	P–609	
3264	5		SF–25	3470	11		
3269	25	P–2301	V–3	3482	2		
3271	49			3485			LB–75
3278	K3			3489		P–716	LCS
3403	71	P–723	L–71	3476			LB–88
3417	24	P–63	G–24	FB132D	49		
3419	33	P–83	F–23	3493		P–742	

KENTUCKY-TENNESSEE CLAY CO.

KENTUCKY BALL CLAYS

		OLD MINE NO. 4	KENTUCKY SPECIAL	KENTUCKY NO. 12	K–T IVORY	KENTUCKY NO. 40
PHYSICAL PROPERTIES	Crude Appearance	Medium Gray	Dark Brown to Black	Dark Brown to Black	Brown	Dark Brown
	Particle Size, % < 1μ	64	54	55	52	36
	% Water of Plasticity	41	49	50	36	48
	Dry M.O.R.* — per square inch	650	750	650	560	550
	% Linear Dry Shrinkage	6.0	6.3	6.0	5.0	5.8
	% Total Shrinkage — Cone 5	14	16	14	10	13
	% Total Shrinkage — Cone 12	17	19	18	13	17
	% Absorption — Cone 5	10	14	14	14	15
	% Absorption — Cone 12	1	2	4	5	4
	Fired Color — Cone 12	Light Gray White	Light Cream White	Cream White	Ivory	Cream White
	Pyrometric Cone Equivalent	32	32	32	31	32
CHEMICAL ANALYSIS	SiO_2	51.7%	49.6%	50.5%	58.7%	53.8%
	Al_2O_3	31.0	29.3	28.3	25.2	26.4
	TiO_2	1.6	1.5	1.6	2.4	1.5
	Fe_2O_3	0.8	1.0	0.9	0.6	0.9
	CaO	0.4	0.3	0.5	0.3	0.2
	MgO	0.5	0.2	0.6	0.4	0.3
	K_2O	1.2	1.0	1.1	1.0	1.2
	Na_2O	0.5	0.3	0.3	0.3	0.4
	Loss on Ignition	12.5	16.8	16.7	11.4	15.1
	Outstanding Properties	Medium grain size, strong, clean firing, good color.	Medium grain size, very strong dark clay, excellent plasticity.	Medium grain size, strong dark clay, excellent platicity.	Coarse grained, fast casting, medium strength, very good draining properties.	Coarse grain size, strong dark clay, very good plasticity.

TENNESSEE BALL CLAYS

		JACKSON	TENN. NO. 5	MARTIN NO. 5	TENN. NO. 9	TENN. NO. 10
PHYSICAL PROPERTIES	Crude Appearance	Medium to Dark Gray	Dark to Light Brown	Light Gray	Gray	White to Gray
	Particle Size, % < 1μ	75	53	28	67	68
	% Water of Plasticity	40	37	36	36	35
	Dry M.O.R.* — per square inch	670	560	440	370	360
	% Linear Dry Shrinkage	5.0	4.0	5.0	3.5	3.6
	% Total Shrinkage — Cone 5	12	12	11	10	11
	% Total Shrinkage — Cone 12	16	14	14	15	14
	% Absorption — Cone 5	11	10	11	17	10
	% Absorption — Cone 12	1	2	0.2	3	2
	Fired Color — Cone 12	Gray White	Gray White	Gray White	Light Cream White	Light Cream White
	Pyrometric Cone Equivalent	32½	32	31½	32½–33	32½–33
CHEMICAL ANALYSIS	SiO_2	54.4%	53.6%	58.0%	51.8%	50.2%
	Al_2O_3	30.1	29.6	26.8	30.8	33.2
	TiO_2	1.6	1.5	1.3	2.0	1.5
	Fe_2O_3	0.9	0.7	0.8	0.7	0.8
	CaO	0.4	0.4	0.5	0.6	0.5
	MgO	0.3	0.4	0.4	0.4	0.3
	K_2O	0.3	1.5	1.9	0.8	0.7
	Na_2O	0.1	0.5	0.4	0.3	0.6
	Loss on Ignition	12.2	11.9	10.4	12.4	12.2
	Outstanding Properties	Fine grained, strong, good color, all purpose.	Medium grained excellent casting clay. Long deflocculation range. Excellent drainage.	Coarse grained, very fast casting. Low dope, long deflocculation range. Non-thixotropic, low shrinkage.	Medium strength, fast oxidizing. Excellent extruding and pressing and heat shock properties.	Medium strength, fast oxidizing, excellent extruding and pressing properties.

*Strength Test: Modulus of Rupture Specimens, De-aired, Extruded: 50% Clay, 50% Flint. All clay mine companies will furnish similar data to this chart upon request.

BINDERS USED WITH CLAYS AND GLAZES

CLASSIFICATION	TYPE	HOW TO ADD
Ceramic binders		
	clay	dry or in suspension
	kaolin	dry or in suspension
	bentonite	dry or in suspension
	montmorillonite	in suspension
	hectorite	in suspension
Organic binders		
Flour	corn flour	dry or in solution
	gluten flour	in solution
	tapioca flour	in solution
Starch	potato starch	in solution
	dextrine	in solution
Gum	arabic	in solution
	tragacanth	dry or in solution
	locust bean	in solution
Resin	polyvinyl alcohol	in solution
	phenol formaldehyde	in solution
Wax	paraffin wax	in emulsion
	carbo wax	in solution
Cellulose acetate	methyl cellulose	in solution

The above binders, although more generally used in industry, can aid all clay bodies, engobes, and glazes in workability.

WATER LOSS IN CLAY DRYING (1)

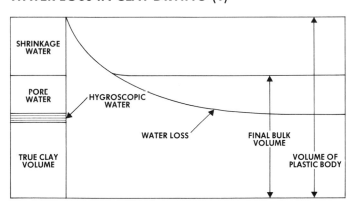

The total height of the box on the left represents the total volume of any plastic body. Reading from top to bottom, in drying, the shrinkage water is lost and the bulk volume is represented by the rest of the box, which is the final bulk volume. After this point has been reached the piece does not undergo any more shrinkage in drying, even though the pore water and hygroscopic water are driven off. The curve represents the total water loss.

Shrinkage water — that part of the free water that is removed during shrinkage.

Pore water — the free water remaining in the mass after shrinkage has ceased.

Hygroscopic water — the water that can be removed only at elevated temperatures. It depends upon the amount of water present in the surroundings.

Chemically combined water — the water that can be driven off only at temperatures above those normally used in drying.

WATER LOSS IN CLAY DRYING (2)

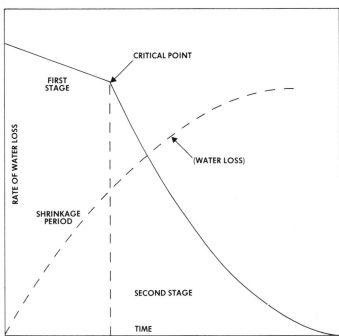

The diagram indicates the initial stage of drying, in which the rate of water loss is controlled only by atmospheric conditions; and the second or final stage, in which the rate of loss is controlled by the characteristics of the body, in addition to the atmospheric conditions. The critical point indicates the maximum limit of surface shrinkage due to drying.

Clay body shrinkage during drying and firing (a major cause of ware cracks) is aided by *even* water evacuation on the shelf and in the kiln. Shrinkage takes place dramatically in the first two stages of firing, critical especially to large works. Different clays have different shrinkage behavior, so test in controlled conditions.

TRIAXIAL DIAGRAM SHOWING AREAS OF COMMERCIAL WARES

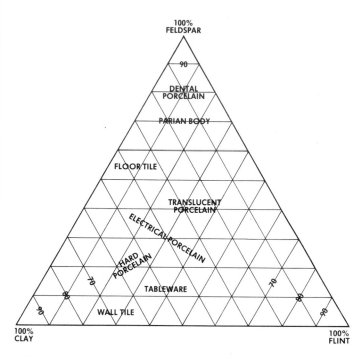

All real porcelains are within the diagram above; low-temperature porcelains require frits, ground glass, or other active flux.

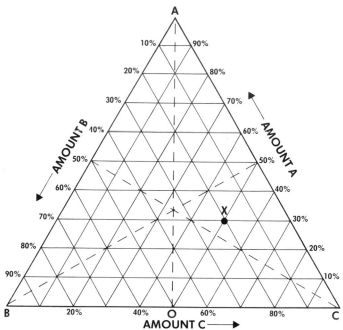

How to read a triaxial diagram Triaxial diagrams are very useful when blending three components to make a mixture. The components, which may be indicated as A, B, and C, are placed at the vertices of the triangle ABC. The light lines within the triangle represent divisions of 10%.

To obtain the composition of any point on the diagram, draw perpendiculars from each vertex to the opposite side. One such line, drawn from vertex A to opposite side BC, is indicated as AO. At the intersection of this line with BC there is zero quantity of A present, indicating that any composition along BC would include only component B and component C. In other words, each of the base lines of the triangle AB, BC and AC represent two-component systems.

Assume the point X, the composition that we are trying to determine. Follow the line AO upward toward A; the point falls on the third line up. Since each line represents 10%, this indicates that there is 30% of A present in the mixture. In the same manner, the amounts of B and C can be determined, all lines parallel to AC indicating successive 10% increments of B and all lines parallel to AB indicating 10% increments of C. The given point lies on the second division along the perpendicular line from B to AC, and on the fifth division from C to AB, meaning that in addition to the 30% of A there is 20% of B and 50% of C in the mixture.

Note that the 10% lines mean decreases in the percentage of any component of the system as you move in a direction away from the vertex of the triangular diagram indicating 100% of that component.

TEMPERATURES AND CONES

TEMPERATURE CONVERSION CHART

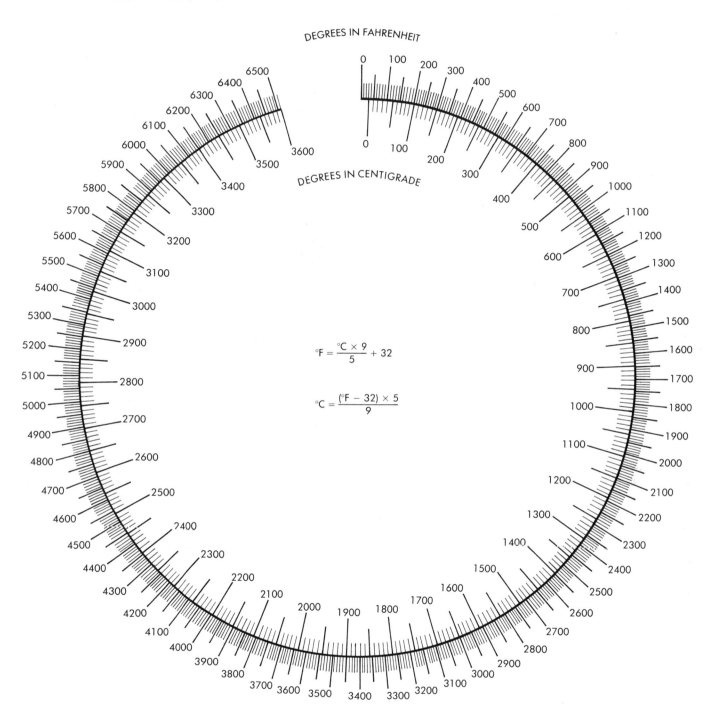

DEGREES IN FAHRENHEIT

DEGREES IN CENTIGRADE

$$°F = \frac{°C \times 9}{5} + 32$$

$$°C = \frac{(°F - 32) \times 5}{9}$$

TYPICAL FIRING TEMPERATURES OF CERAMICS

	TEMP. °C	TEMP. °F
Heavy clay products:		
Common brick – surface clay	871–982	1600–1800
Common brick – shale	982–1093	1800–2000
Face brick – shale	1065–1204	1950–2200
Face brick – fireclay	1148–1260	2100–2300
Fack brick – surface clay	954–1010	1750–1850
Enamel brick	1148–1260	2100–2300
Paving brick (vitrified)	1093–1232	2000–2250
Structural clay tile – surface clay	871–982	1600–1800
Structural clay tile – shale	982–1093	1800–2000
Structural clay tile – fire clay	1065–1148	1950–2100
Drain tile	926–1037	1700–1900
Sewer pipe	1110–1271	2030–2320
Roofing tile	1071–1171	1960–2140
Terracotta	1132–1271	2070–2320
Pottery:		
Ceramic cooking pots	1121–1176	2050–2150
Flowerpots	860–1010	1580–1850
Stoneware (chemical)	1454–1482	2650–2700
Stoneware (once-fired)	1270–1330	2318–2426
Earthenware or semi-vitreous ware – bisque	1250–1290	2282–2354
Earthenware or semi-vitrous ware – glost	1190–1250	2174–2282
Artware – bisque	1010–1204	1850–2200
Artware – glost	982–1315	1800–2400
Pottery decals	704–815	1300–1500
Refractories:		
Firebrick – clay	1260–1398	2300–2550
High alumina	1454–1537	2650–2800
Firebrick – silica	1454–1510	2650–2750
Chrome brick	1454–1648	2650–3000
Magnesite brick	1454–1648	2650–3000
Silicon carbide	1371–1510	2500–2750
Direct bonded basic brick	1648–1760	3000–3200
Whitewares:		
Electrical porcelain	1148–1260	2100–2300
Hotel china – bisque	1204–1260	2200–2300
Sanitary ware – bisque	1204–1315	2200–2400
Hotel china – glost	1037–1232	1900–2250
Sanitary ware – glost	1230–1270	2246–2318
Floor tile	1148–1232	2100–2250
Wall tile – bisque	982–1204	1800–2200
Wall tile – glost	982–1232	1800–2250

	TEMP. °C	TEMP. °F
Porcelain enamels:		
Wet process cast iron enamels	621–760	1150–1400
Dry process cast iron enamels	843–927	1550–1700
Sheet iron ground coat enamels	760–871	1400–1600
Sheet iron cover coat enamels	748–843	1380–1550
A–19 coating	860–882	1580–1620
Solaramic	927–1093	1700–2000
Aluminum	482–593	900–1100
Electronic and newer ceramics:		
Steatites	1260–1348	2300–2460
Aluminas	1537–1760	2800–3200
Titanates	1288–1371	2350–2500
Ferrites	1198–1454	2190–2650
Beryllia	up to 1871	up to 3400
Rare earths	1371–2204	2500–4000
Cermets	1593–1704	2900–3100

FAST FIRING CURVE FOR TILE

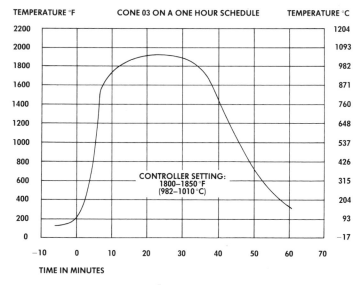

Fast firing is a concept made possible by:

1 constant surveillance and control of the kiln;
2 ability to have even heat treatment;
3 some thermal proof ingredients in the clay body.

The tile curve shown is for a high talc, low clay, white burning composition, maximum temperature 2000 °F (1093 °C), with good thermal shock qualities. The cooling curve is only slightly slower than the firing curve. This one-hour schedule also implies small modules of equal mass; larger pieces of non-talc, high clay body composition will need a slower fire, from three to four hours to 2300 °F (1260 °C).

CHEMICAL AND PHYSICAL CHANGES IN CLAY DURING FIRING

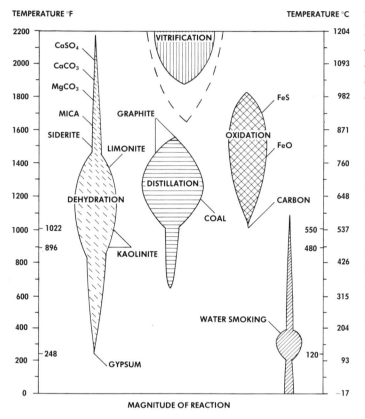

TEMPERATURE °F

TEMPERATURE °C

MAGNITUDE OF REACTION

Massive changes take place during water smoking and dehydration periods of the fire, when physical and chemically combined water leaves the ware. This diagram shows dehydration peaking between 1000 and 1400°F (537 and 760°C), following an initial water smoking peak of 300°F (148°C); ware can still blow during dehydration. Leaving the kiln door or lid open a crack until the stage is finished is advisable, particularly on fast-fire schedules. Oxidation and vitrification stages are not hazardous except where clays with gross impurities are involved.

MELTING POINTS OF SOME COMPOUNDS AND MINERALS

COMPOUND OR MINERAL	TEMP. °F	TEMP. °C
Alumina	3722	2050
Andalusite	3301	1816
Andalusite (commercial)	3011	1655
Arsenous oxide	392	200
Barium carbonate	2480	1360
Barium chloride	1760	960
Barium oxide	842	450
Barium sulfate	2876	1580
Bauxite	3695	2035
Bauxite (commercial)	3272–3668	1800–2020
Borax	red heat	
Calcite	4658	2570
Calcite (commercial)	3803–4505	2095–2485
Calcium carbonate (dissociates)	1517	825
Calcium fluoride	2372	1300
Calcium oxide	4658	2570
Calcium sulfate (gypsum) (dissociates)	1652	900
Chromium oxide	4226	2330
Cobaltic oxide	1661	905
Cobalt nitrate	133	56
Copper oxide (cuprous) (Cu_2O)	2210	1210
Copper oxide (cupric) (CuO)	1947	1064
Corundum	3695	2035
Corundum (commercial)	3362–3686	1850–2030
Cyanite	3301	1816
Cyanite (commercial)	3056	1680
Diaspore	3695	2035
Diaspore (commercial)	3488	1920
Diatomaceous earth	3119	1715
Diatomaceous earth (commercial)	3002	1650
Dolomite	4658–5072	2570–2800
Dolomite (commercial)	3497–4505	1925–2485
Ferric oxide	2818	1548
Ferrous oxide	2586	1419
Fireclay (high grade)	3020–3128	1660–1720
Fireclay (low grade)	2912–3002	1600–1650
Flint	3119	1715
Fluorspar	2372	1300
Forsterite	3470	1910

COMPOUND OR MINERAL	TEMP. °F	TEMP. °C
Ganister	3119	1715
Gibbsite	3695	2035
Gibbsite (commercial)	3200–3686	1760–2030
Halloysite	3227	1775
Kaolin	3164–3245	1740–1785
Kaolinite	3245	1785
Kyanite	3308	1820
Lead oxide (Litharge) (PbO)	1616	880
Lead oxide (Minium) (Pb_3O_4) (dissociates)	932–986	500–530
Lime	4658	2570
Limestone	4658	2570
Magnesite (dissociates)	5072	2800
Magnesite (commercial)	3632–5072	2000–2800
Magnesium carbonate (dissociates)	662	350
Magnesium oxide (approx.)	5117	2825
Magnetite	2800	1538
Manganese dioxide	570	1058
Mullite	3290	1810
Mullite (commercial)	3254	1790
Nickel oxide	752	400
Orthoclase feldspar (dissociates)	2138	1170
Potassium carbonate	1616	880
Potassium chromate	1787	975
Potassium dichromate	748	398
Potassium nitrate	639	337
Potassium oxide	red heat	

COMPOUND OR MINERAL	TEMP. °F	TEMP. °C
Quartz	3119	1715
Rutile (dissociates)	3452	1900
Rutile (commercial)	2966	1630
Silica	3119	1715
Silicon carbide (decomposes)	3992	220
Sillimanite	3301	1816
Sillimanite (commercial)	3290	1810
Sodium carbonate	1567	853
Sodium chloride	1458	792
Sodium nitrate	595	313
Sodium oxide	red heat	
Sodium sulfate	1616	880
Spinel	3875	2135
Spinel (commercial)	3479	1915
Tin oxide	2066	1130
Titanium oxide (dissociates)	3452	1900
Whiting (dissociates)	1517	825
Zircon (dissociates)	4622	2550
Zircon (commercial)	3452–4172	1900–2300
Zirconia	4892	2700
Glass-forming silicates:		
Na_2SiO_3	1992	1089
K_2SiO_3	1789	976
$PbSiO_3$	1418	770
$BaSi_2O_5$	2599	1426
Beta $CaSiO_3$	2804	1540

The action of individual materials is important in the preparation of glasses, glazes, enamels, bodies, colors, and refractories; the interaction among minerals is even more important. Ceramic material combination-melt data is available in ceramic engineering books. The potter knows from experience that silica, a high melter by itself, reacts with whiting as low as 1700 °F (926 °C). Many materials, when united, form new compounds at surprisingly low temperatures; melts are changed for various temperatures by accessing the correct minerals.

Melting is a thermal process whereby a solid is converted to the liquid phase. Factors influencing melts, for glaze, aside from composition, are (a) rate of fire, (b) fineness of particle size; a glaze ground for 20 minutes in a ball mill will melt faster and more smoothly than one with a coarser texture.

The eutectic point (the point at which two refractory materials, when put together, melt surprisingly low) is a fact of certain material combinations; learn through experience or look up a chart. Pre-melted, reground materials such as frits melt more easily and lower the second time, in the glaze mix. This explains why glazes made from the same molecular formula but using different materials can vary in temperature and look.

TEMPERATURE EQUIVALENTS FOR ORTON STANDARD PYROMETRIC CONES (1)

Most of us do not control the rate of heating in a kiln, but it is important to notice the effect on cones of the time factor in firing. The chart below gives the pyrometric cone equivalent, the point at which the cone is at 3 o'clock.

LARGE CONES	TEMP. INCREASE PER HOUR			
CONE NO.	108°F	60°C	270°F	150°C
022	1085°F	585°C	1112°F	600°C
021	1116	602	1137	614
020	1157	625	1175	635
019	1234	668	1261	683
018	1285	696	1323	717
017	1341	727	1377	747
016	1407	764	1458	792
015	1454	790	1479	804
014	1533	834	1540	838
013	1596	869	1566	852
012	1591	866	1623	884
011	1627	886	1641	894
†010	1629	887	1641	894
09	1679	915	1693	923
08	1733	945	1751	955
07	1783	973	1803	984
06	1816	991	1830	999
05	1888	1031	1915	1046
04	1922	1050	1940	1060
03	1987	1086	2014	1101
02	2014	1101	2048	1120
01	2043	1117	2079	1137
1	2077	1136	2109	1154
2	2088	1142	2124	1162
3	2106	1152	2134	1168
4	2134	1168	2167	1186
5	2151	1177	2185	1196
6	2194	1201	2232	1222
7	2219	1215	2264	1240
8	2257	1236	2305	1263
9	2300	1260	2336	1280
10	2345	1285	2381	1305
11	2361	1294	2399	1315
12	2383	1306	2419	1326
13	2410	1321	2455	1346
14	2530	1388	2491	1366
15	2595	1424	2608	1431
16	2651	1455	2683	1473
17	2691	1477	2705	1485
18	2732	1500	2743	1506
19	2768	1520	2782	1528
20	2808	1542	2820	1549
23	2887	1586	2894	1590
26	2892	1589	2921	1605
27	2937	1614	2961	1627
28	2937	1614	2971	1633
29	2955	1624	2993	1645
30	2977	1636	3009	1654
31	3022	1661	3054	1679
31½				
32	3103	1706	3123	1717
32½	3124	1718	3146	1730
33	3150	1732	3166	1741
34	3195	1757	3198	1759
35	3243	1784	3243	1784
36	3268	1798	3265	1796
37	N.D.	N.D.	N.D.	N.D.
38	N.D.	N.D.	N.D.	N.D.
39	N.D.	N.D.	N.D.	N.D.
40	N.D.	N.D.	N.D.	N.D.
41	N.D.	N.D.	N.D.	N.D.
42	N.D.	N.D.	N.D.	N.D.

SMALL CONES	TEMP. INCREASE PER HOUR	
CONE NO.	540°F	300°C
022	1165°F*	630°C*
021	1189	643
020	1231	666
019	1333	723
018	1386	752
017	1443	784
016	1517	825
015	1549	843
014	1596	870*
013	1615	880*
012	1650	900*
011	1680	915*
010	1686	919
09	1751	955
08	1801	983
07	1846	1008
06	1873	1023
05	1944	1062
04	2008	1098
03	2068	1131
02	2098	1148
01	2152	1178
1	2154	1179
2	2154	1179
3	2185	1196
4	2208	1209
5	2230	1221
6	2291	1255
7	2307	1264
8	2372	1300
9	2403	1317
10	2426	1330
11	2437	1336
12	2471	1355

P.C.E. CONES	270°F	150°C
12	2439°F	1337°C
13	2460	1349
14	2548	1398
15	2606	1430
16	2716	1491
17	2754	1512
18	2772	1522
19	2806	1541
20	2847	1564
23	2921	1605
26	2950	1621
27	2984	1640
28	2995	1646
29	3018	1659
30	3029	1665
31	3061	1683
31½	3090	1699
32	3123	1717
32½	3135	1724
33	3169	1743
34	3205	1763
35	3245	1785
36	3279	1804
37	3308	1820
38	3362	1850*
39	3389	1865*
40	3425	1885*
41	3578	1970*
42	3659	2015*

* Temperatures approximate. See note 3.

N.D. Not determined.

† Iron-free (white) are made in numbers 010 to 3. The iron-free cones have the same deformation temperatures as the red equivalents when fired at a rate of 140°F (60°C) per hour in air.

Notes:

1 The temperature equivalents in this table apply only to Orton standard pyrometric cones, when heated at the rates indicated, in an air atmosphere.

2 Temperature equivalents are given in °F and the corresponding °C. The rates of heating shown at the head of each column of temperature equivalents were maintained during the last several degrees of temperature rise.

3 The temperature equivalents were determined at the National Bureau of Standards by H. P. Beerman (see *Journal of the American Ceramic Society*, Vol. 39, 1956), with the exception of those marked (*).

4 The temperature equivalents are not necessarily those at which cones will deform under firing conditions different from those under which the calibrating determinations were made. For more detailed technical data, please write the Orton Foundation.

5 For reproducible results, care should be taken to ensure that the cones are set in a plaque with the bending face at the correct angle of 8° from the vertical, with the cone tips at the correct height above the top of the plaque. (Large cone 2 in [5.08 cm]; small and P.C.E. cones 15–16 in [38.10–40.64 cm].)

TEMPERATURE EQUIVALENTS OF ORTON CONES (2)

The data below differs from the previous chart because of the different degree rises in temperature. Remember that cone temperatures are approximate — it is always best to watch the cones.

CONE NO.	TEMP. INCREASE PER HOUR		CONE NO.	TEMP. INCREASE PER HOUR		CONE NO.	TEMP. INCREASE PER HOUR	
	68°F	20°C		212°F	100°C		1112°F	600°C
022	1085	585	23	2876	1580	39	3389	1865
021	1103	595	26	2903	1595	40	3425	1885
020	1157	625	27	2921	1605	41	3578	1970
019	1166	630	28	2939	1615	42	3659	2015
018	1238	670	29	2984	1640			
017	1328	720	30	3002	1650			
016	1355	735	31	3056	1680			
015	1418	770	32	3092	1700			
014	1463	795	32½	3137	1725			
013	1517	825	33	3173	1745			
012	1544	840	34	3200	1760			
011	1607	875	35	3245	1785			
010	1634	890	36	3290	1810			
09	1706	930	37	3308	1820			
08	1733	945	38	3335	1835			
07	1787	975						
06	1841	1005						
05	1886	1030						
04	1922	1050						
03	1976	1080						
02	2003	1095						
01	2030	1110						
1	2057	1125						
2	2075	1135						
3	2093	1145						
4	2129	1165						
5	2156	1180						
6	2174	1190						
7	2210	1210						
8	2237	1225						
9	2282	1250						
10	2300	1260						
11	2345	1285						
12	2390	1310						
13	2462	1350						
14	2534	1390						
15	2570	1410						
16	2642	1450						
17	2669	1465						
18	2705	1485						
19	2759	1515						
20	2768	1520						

TEMPERATURE EQUIVALENTS OF SEGER CONES

CONE NO.	MELTING POINT		CONE NO.	MELTING POINT		CONE NO.	MELTING POINT	
	°F	°C		°F	°C		°F	°C
021	1202	650	01a	1976	1080	20	2786	1530
020	1238	670	1a	2012	1100	*26	2876	1580
019	1274	690	2a	2048	1120	27	2930	1610
018	1310	710	3a	2084	1140	28	2966	1630
017	1346	730	4a	2120	1160	29	3002	1650
016	1382	750	5a	2156	1180	30	3038	1670
015a	1454	790	6a	2192	1200	31	3074	1690
014a	1499	815	7	2246	1230	32	3110	1710
013a	1535	835	8	2282	1250	33	3146	1730
012a	1590	866	9	2336	1280	34	3182	1750
011a	1616	880	10	2372	1300	35	3218	1770
010a	1652	900	11	2408	1320	36	3254	1790
09a	1688	920	12	2462	1350	37	3317	1825
08a	1724	940	13	2516	1380	38	3362	1850
07a	1760	960	14	2570	1410	39	3416	1880
06a	1796	980	15	2615	1435	40	3488	1920
05a	1832	1000	16	2660	1460	41	3560	1960
04a	1868	1020	17	2696	1480	42	3632	2000
03a	1904	1040	18	2732	1500			
02a	1940	1060	19	2768	1520			

* Numbers 21 to 25 are obsolete

CONVERSION CHARTS

Units of flow

Units		U.S. gallons per minute	Million U.S. gallons per day	Cubic feet per second	Cubic meters per hour	Liters per second
U.S. gallon per minute (U.S. G.P.M.)	=	1	.001440	.00223	.2270	.0631
1 million U.S. gallons per day (M.G.D.)	=	694.5	1	1.547	157.73	43.8
1 cubic foot per second	=	448.8	.646	1	101.9	28.32
1 cubic meter per hour	=	4.403	.00981	1	.2778	
1 liter per second	=	15.85	.0228	.0353	3.60	1
1 miner's inch (M.I.)	I =	11.22	.001618	.0250		
	II =	8.98	.01294	.0200		
	III =	11.69	.01682	.0260		
	IV =	12.58	.01811	.0280		

A miner's inch legally set by British Columbia, 35.7 M.I. = 1 second-foot.
Usual practice in Southern California, 50 M.I. = 1 second-foot = 448.8 G.P.M.

Power, work, and heat

1 ton refrigeration = 200 B.T.U. per min

Latent heat of ice = 144 B.T.U. per lb

1 B.T.U. = 778 ft lbs

1 watt hour = 2655.4 ft lbs = 3.412 B.T.U.

1 kilowatt (1000 watts) = 1.3405 horsepower = 59.6 B.T.U. per min

1 horsepower = .746 kilowatt

1 pound (force) = 32.2 poundals

1 mech. horsepower = 42.4 B.T.U. per min 33,000 ft lbs per min

1 boiler horsepower = 33,479 B.T.U. per hr Evaporation of 34.5 lbs of water per hr from water at 212 °F (100 °C)

Water of plasticity of different kinds of clay

Crude kaolin	36.69–44.78
Washed kaolin	44.48–47.50
White sedimentary kaolin	28.60–56.25
Ball clays	25.00–53.30
Crucible clays	26.84–50.85
Refractory bond clays	32.50–37.90
Glass-pot clays	19.64–36.50
Plastic fire clays	12.90–37.40
Flint fire clays	8.89–19.04
Saggar clays	18.40–28.56
Stoneware clays	19.16–34.80
Face brick clays	14.85–37.50
Sewer pipe clays	11.60–36.20
Paving brick clays	11.80–19.60
Brick clays	13.20–40.70

Hardness scale (Mohs' Scale)

MINERAL	HARDNESS	SCRATCH TEST
Diamond	10	
Corundum	9	
Topaz	8	Chemical porcelain
		Spark plug porcelain
Quartz	7	Insulator porcelain
		Insulator porcelain glaze
		Chemical porcelain glaze
		Stoneware
Orthoclase	6	Spark plug porcelain glaze
		Chemical glassware
		Vitreous enamels
		White earthenware
Apatite	5	Bottle glass
Fluorite	4	
Calcite	3	
Gypsum	2	
Talc	1	

Weights and measures

LINEAR

1 angstrom (Å) = 10^{-8} cm

1 millimicron (mμ) = .001 micron (μ)

1 micron (μ) = .001 millimeter

1 centimeter = 10 millimeters

1 centimeter = .3937 inches

1 meter = 100 centimeters

1 meter = 3.281 feet

1 mile = 1,760 yards

1 mile = 5,280 feet

1 kilometer = .62137 miles

1 rod = 5.333 yards

AREA

1 radian = 57.29578 degrees

1 square centimeter = .155 square inches

1 square meter = 10.764 square feet

1 acre = 43,560 square feet

1 square mile = 640 acres

VOLUME

1 cubic centimeter = .061 cubic inches

1 cubic centimeter = .03384 fluid ounces

1 cubic foot = 1,728 cubic inches

1 cubic yard = 27 cubic feet

1 cubic meter = 35.314 cubic feet

1 U.S. gallon = 3.785 liters

1 liter = 1,000 cubic centimeters

1 liter = 61 cubic inches

1 U.S. gallon = .13395 cubic feet

1 U.S. pint = 28.875 cubic inches

WEIGHT

1 gram = .03528 ounces

1 kilogram = 1,000 grams

1 kilogram = 2.205 pounds

1 ounce = 16 drams

1 pound = 16 ounces

1 pound = 7,000 grains

1 pound = 453.6 grams

1 short ton = 2,000 pounds

1 long ton = 2,240 pounds

1 gram/cc. = .03614 lbs/cu in

1 gram/cc. = 62.43 lbs/cu ft

1 lb/cu ft = .1337 lb/gal

POWER

1 B.T.U. = 778 ft lbs

1 B.T.U. = 2.928×10^{-4} kW.-hrs

1 B.T.U. = 3.927×10^{-4} H.P.-hrs

1 H.P. = 33,000 ft lbs per minute

1 H.P. = 746 Watts

1 H.P. = .746 kW

1 boiler H.P. = 9.8156 kW

1 H.P. hr = 2.547 B.T.U.

1 kW = 737.3 ft lbs per second

1 kW-hr = 3.413 B.T.U.

1 joule = .7376 ft lbs

ARTISTS' TECHNIQUES

This is a sampling of surfaces and treatments from a selection of experienced clayworkers. Trying things others have done is a good way to learn.

When following someone else's batch use the following guidelines. (1) Engobe and glaze batches are listed in percentages or in parts by weight. Either way, batches can be compounded by weighing on scales or by volume proportion. For consistency, always repeat the method previously applied. (2) Most glaze and engobe batches require clay; either china clay (kaolin) or ball clay is usually used. Alternatively, fire clays or surface clays can be used. The choice will make a difference to the look of the glaze. To experiment, vary the type of clay in a glaze batch. (3) Generally, when feldspar is required, use a potash spar such as G–200 or similar. Soda feldspars, such as nepheline syenite, melt more easily than potash spars, and should be chosen for glaze accordingly. (4) Some materials used for low-temperature glazes, such as lusters and fuming salts, may be poisonous if eaten, or may cause a rash on contact. It is wise to use them for decorative rather than utilitarian purposes.

RUDY AUTIO'S ENGOBE DECORATION

Parts by weight

China clay 1

Ball clay ½

Nepheline syenite ½

Feldspar 1

Silica 1

I add colorants to this, such as 8 to 10 percent Zircopax for white, or smaller percentages using copper oxide and cobalt; I also use stains in standard percentages.

I like to use the engobes wet on soft clay, using sgraffito technique to draw through. Then I spray and brush on a light coating of Gerstley borate to seal the engobe, and once-fire to cone 5; or I use a mixture of Pemco frit 239, 10 percent ball clay, and a tablespoon of Epsom salts for each 35.3 oz (1000 g) for suspension. I may refire using commercial low-fire glazes, or fire to a higher temperature using a cone 10 glaze. Or I refire with 95 percent of another low-fire glaze like Frit IV148 with 5 percent ball clay plus gum and colorants or commercial stains for reds, oranges, blues, greens, etc.

ELAINE CARHARTT'S GLUE

I want artists to know about the glue I like, PL 400, produced in the U.S.A. by Chemrex, Inc., Minneapolis, Minnesota. It is generally used in the construction business for putting up siding. After gluing large pieces together I cover the joints with wood putty and they do not show.

JERRY CHAPPELLE'S YELLOW WOOD ASH GLAZE

Hardwood ash 19.0%

G–200 feldspar 28.0%

Whiting 9.5%

Silica 28.0%

Yellow ochre 9.5%

Red iron oxide 2.0%

Rutile 4.0%

Fire to cone 10. Versatile with iron, copper, or cobalt oxides brushed under or over the glaze, or mixed into it in varying amounts.

KRIS COX'S SAGGAR FIRING METHOD

Place the following next to the pieces in the saggar:
   Sawdust. For dark areas; where pot is glazed, glaze will not mature.
   Vermiculite. Used next to or sandwiched amongst sawdust to make an oxidized area.
   Particle board. Often creates dramatic flashes.
   Oxides and carbonates. Copper carbonate, cobalt carbonate for coloration.
   Potassium dichromate. Can produce brilliant flashes, and sometimes green areas, if sprinkled around the piece.
   Here is the batch for a glaze, electric-fired to cone 04.

Lead carbonate 62%

Custer feldspar 20%

Cornwall stone 4%

Barium carbonate 10%

EPK china clay 4%

It must be applied very thick to achieve a "dry lake bed" look. Colorants for this glaze: 6 percent chrome oxide gives a brilliant red, some green, and when potassium dichromate is next to it, a brilliant yellow; 2 percent blue stain — with added materials in the saggar, color will vary from true blue to eggshell blue to a soft yellow. Variation: spray potassium dichromate over any color for intense contrasts.

CHRISTINE FEDERIGHI'S SLAB PROCESS

For construction of large figures I use various hollow cardboard tubes with newly rolled slabs of clay. Then additions and subtractions are made by cutting and pinching. The handling of clay is spontaneous and direct. It is an attitude I'm after. The clay body is mainly ball clay which makes a plastic, sturdy, pliable working material that I fire to cone 04. The surface is painted raw with sigilatta or low-fire engobes or glazes. At times I work back into the fired surface with paint.

KEN FERGUSON'S SHINO GLAZE

I have a strange new "wrinkle" to add to the book: carbon-trap Shino-type glazes can benefit from extra firing, but not to high temperature. If the glaze is on thick enough and is refired in a gas-fired bisque kiln, the gas and impurities from the greenware pots will get into this glaze. The temperature need not exceed cone 04.

Carbon-trap glazes will reflux very low, cone 06, and there are flashes and craze marks that darken and add a rich patina to the glaze. I have been told that Shino potters put wood in the kiln as it cools from red to black heat, firing that way for about one hour. The original carbon-trap glaze is:

F—4 feldspar	43%
Soda ash	10%
Ceramic grade spodumene	38%
EPK china clay	9%

It needs lots of reduction, heavy and mild, from cone 014 onward; never let it completely out of reduction. It can crawl and blister with too much gas pressure and will not heal in subsequent firings. Additions of 56 percent nepheline syenite and 7 percent ball clay to the above batch make it a bit more safe but bland.

MARGARET FORD'S LOW-FIRE UNDERGLAZES, CHINA PAINTS, AND LUSTERS

My colors are commercial underglaze stains and commercial low-fire glazes used straight from the bottle or by mixing them. I often leave the underglazes unglazed. I use several types of china paints, pre-mixed Versa color, and Willoughby's dry pigments. I employ an oil-based medium for both airbrushing and hand painting. The lusters are from Hanovia. I only occasionally use underglaze pencils — I prefer Chem-Clay pencils from Standard Ceramic Supply. I may refire many times.

CHARLES FREEHOF'S LUSTER PROCESS

I use commercial preparations like Hanovia Liquid Bright Gold. I follow the directions but find that cone 022 is too high a temperature for what I want. I fire considerably lower — exactly what I don't know. There is no substitute for just keeping an eye on the work in the kiln. I check the progress of the luster decoration about every 10 to 15 minutes.

MICHAEL FRIMKESS' THROWING TECHNIQUE

With practice I have finally managed to throw with absolutely no water whatsoever, most recently for some ginger jars. I made 60 (I practiced until I was able to retain 30 in a row), lost 30 and got 20 of relatively the same size. I am going to try doing it with a set of teapots now — I won't use a drop of water. It has taken me a long time to learn how to do this.

RON GALLAS' BUILDING PROCESS

The parts are spontaneously cut from thick slabs of leather-hard clay, then dried and bisque fired. This approach frees me from the constraints of traditional form-making. The parts are then glaze fired. Using this stock pile of fired, colored forms, I begin to add and subtract, sometimes cutting with a brick saw to make parts fit. After construction, the joints are then drilled, pinned with steel pins, and glued.

DALE GAYNOR'S UNFIRED ADOBE PROCESS

The best adobe today is stabilized with emulsified asphalt, which hardens the clay and makes it waterproof. Indians have used pinon pitch and the juice of mesquite bean pods, and Africans have used the liquor of the locust bean for the same purpose. Present-day ingredients for hardening adobe and earth include cement, polymers, epoxies, and enzymes, as well as asphalt.

Fortified adobe has a minimum shrinkage and can be built on and added to when dry. It is excessively fragile during the first 24 hours. To aid plasticity, experiment with binders such as straw or any dried plant material available. The use of wire mesh permits thinner walls.

WAYNE HIGBY'S RAKU PROCESS

Clay body for white raku

Pine Lake fire clay 59.0%

OM4 ball clay 17.5%

Talc 17.5%

Crystal silica 6.0%

Clay body for red raku

PBX fire clay 45%

Gold Art 18%

Red Art 23%

Talc 5%

Crystal silica 9%

1–2–3 white glaze
Parts by weight

Silica 1

EPK china clay 2

Gerstley borate 3

Blue-green glaze

1 cup 1–2–3 wet + 1 teaspoon copper carbonate

Green glaze

1 cup 1–2–3 wet + 2 teaspoons copper carbonate

Rocks and cliffs orange-brown glaze

1 part 1–2–3 wet + 1 part iron oxide

Water blue glaze

Frit 3110 74%

Soda ash 11%

Gerstley borate 5%

China clay 5%

Silica 5%

Plus copper carbonate 1%

White engobe

Ball clay 41.7%

Silica 41.7%

Frit 3304 16.6%

I bisque fire at cone 08, glaze fire at approximately cone 08. I apply the glaze with a brush, meanwhile masking areas with a rubber resist material which I remove before firing. The ware is fired only once after the bisque. Refiring doesn't work well for me. When the glaze is shiny it is removed from the kiln with tongs. A variety of effects can be achieved by removing pieces at different degrees of heat or glaze melt. I place the hot pot in a hole in the ground lined with damp straw and then cover it with more damp straw. To make the glaze crackle I remove the piece after it has been in the straw for 30 seconds, expose it to the air very briefly, and re-cover it in the pit for an extended cooling and gentle reducing, sometimes lasting up to half an hour.

RICHARD HIRSCH'S RAKU COLORING

(1) Commercial opaque underglazes are airbrushed first, then translucent underglazes, then the piece is bisqued to cone 06. (2) The raku firing or post-firing process involves the use of metallic salts such as cupric chloride, cupric sulphate, ferric chloride, nickel chloride, or cobalt chloride. They are sprayed on when the vessel is removed from the raku kiln. The piece is hot and the metallic salts fuse to the surface. The process is often repeated to build up a surface and a depth. (3) I smoke-reduce the piece using raw cotton

which flashes, reduces, smokes chemically, and visually alters each piece. (4) To build up even further surfaces and create another dimension, I mix epoxy resins with oil paint or stain. (5) I exclusively use fiber wire kilns because they are light. I recommend the use of fiber 1 in (2.54 cm) thick; at least double the thickness for the kiln wall or heat will be lost. Large kilns can be made with wire and fiber. I would rate the following materials: first Fiberfax (Carborundum); second Insol Blanket (A. P. Green); third Kaowool (Babcock and Wilcox).

DEBORAH HORRELL'S BONE NESTS

The nest forms that I construct are made from slip-cast porcelain bones laid into a thrown and fired bowl-shaped saggar. The bones are then painted with glaze so that the joining areas are glazed together inside the saggar. After the entirety has been fired, the nest form is removed from the bowl, exposing a free-standing nest.

WILLIAM HUNT'S THERMAL-SHOCK-PROOF PERLITE BODIES

Bone dry greenware with approximately 50 percent perlite in the body can be raku fired raw without cracking. Put the pre-warmed, dry, unglazed ware into a red hot kiln at 1500 °F (815 °C) for quick bisque firing. As soon as the pot looks red hot, remove it, cool, then glaze decorate and raku fire again to melt the glaze. Objects can be made and fired in minutes.

Perlite is available in at least two sizes: small particles like grog (up to $1/12$ in or 2 mm), and larger particles (up to $1/5$ in or 5 mm) more the size of vermiculite (expanded mica). Perlite reduces the weight of the finished object by about 20 percent.

Perlite bodies will survive if fired unevenly or with a torch. Here is a batch for a coarse handbuilding body, fired from low to high (cone 9):

Perlite 1 part by volume (13% by weight)

Any stoneware body (dry) 1 part by volume (87% by weight)

The following makes a coarse throwing body for large work, and can be fired up to cone 9:

Perlite 1 part by volume (7% by weight)

Any stoneware body (dry) 2 parts by volume (93% by weight)

DOUGLAS JOHNSON'S "PROPANE PRIMITIVE" TECHNIQUE

For large pots, bring the reduction or carbonizing to the piece. Open the kiln door or lid and cover the fired piece with sawdust, leaves, oil, garbage, grass, or whatever; results are a varied, mottled, black and gray-red finish that has the interest of a "primitive" surface.
(1) Load kiln allowing some spaces for distribution of reduction material. (2) Fire to bisque red heat (1500 °F [815 °C] or so). (3) Immediately fill the kiln or cover the work with the reduction material using a shovel that won't burn. (4) Within minutes, wet down to "freeze" the reduction and cool the kiln. (5) Remove pots and scrub them. (6) Oil, grease, or wax surfaces. Most primitive pots have a rich patina from use, so it seems consistent to approximate that appearance by modern methods.

ELLICE JOHNSTON'S CRYSTALLINE GLAZE

Ferro frit 3110 52.0%

Zinc oxide 24.3%

Silica 23.7%

I always add a few teaspoons of Epsom salts and a teaspoon of gum tragacanth to crystalline glazes and fire to cone 10.

These color additions have worked well: (1) 3% manganese + 2% copper carbonate; (2) $1/4$% cobalt + 2% copper carbonate; (3) 4% titanium dioxide + 3% iron chromate; and (4) 1% black copper oxide + 2% rutile.

For me the best crystals are achieved by taking the kiln to cone 10 rapidly in four hours, dropping rapidly to 2020 °F (1104 °C) and holding for four hours there. I believe that fritting the whole batch produces more dramatic crystals, and I am making a frit furnace.

RANDY JOHNSTON'S OVERGLAZE ENAMELS

These enamels are for painting on already glazed and fired earthenware, stoneware, or porcelain; refire to cone 015 or until they look shiny inside the kiln.

Green

White lead 61.2%

Frit 3134 8.2%

Silica 25.5%

Copper oxide 5.1%

Red

White lead 5.9%

Frit 3134 58.8%

Silica 11.8%

Red iron oxide 23.5%

Yellow

White lead 75.8%

Silica 23.0%

Red iron oxide 1.2%

Plus a pinch of chrome oxide

Blue

White lead 70%

Frit 3185 7%

Silica 22%

Copper oxide 1%

Dark red

White lead 16%

Silica 3%

Red iron oxide 81%

Purple

White lead 46.3%

Frit 3185 46.3%

Silica 5.9%

Manganese dioxide 1.5%

Grind enamels very fine, in a ball mill jar or mortar and pestle. The Japanese grind for many days. Use gum, sugar, and vinegar, or tea, for suspension and bonding to the glazed piece.

JUN KANEKO'S GLAZE AND ENGOBE

For everything I use:

Cone 6 transparent glaze

Soda feldspar 44.6%

Gerstley borate 17.7%

Barium carbonate 18.2%

Whiting 7.3%

China clay 2.4%

Silica 9.8%

Cone 6 white engobe for dry clay

EPK china clay 22.7%

Ball clay 22.7%

Feldspar 18.2%

Borax 4.5%

Frit 3819 13.7%

Silica 18.2%

Plus 15–20% stain for colors

Cone 6 white engobe for wet clay

China clay 40%

Ball clay 20%

Gerstley borate 20%

Silica 20%

Plus 15–20% stain for colors

JENS ART MORRISON'S MULTICOLOR TECHNIQUE

I use experimental found red clays which I dry and crush with a rolling pin. Then I press them into a wet white talc or clay body, roll the slabs, and let them dry. After making shapes from them, I rub more found clay on to the surface of the leather-hard clay, cover it with colored engobes, and build up a multi-colored surface while the clay is still moist. Slurry can also be laid over it.

I use a lace tool and scrape some of the top layer away, exposing the white ground which can be stained or glazed later. A toothbrush is used to round the clay after carving. I use commercial underglazes on the bisque with clear glaze at cone 06, and cone 019 gold. After firing I buff with steel wool and sandpaper and use an electric polisher to weather the surface.

ANDY NASISSE'S FLAMEWARE BODY AND ENGOBES

This is a medium temperature flameware, fired cone 06–02, capable of withstanding great thermal shock and multiple firings. Fired shrinkage at cone 06 is 6 percent.

AP green fire clay 30%

Georgia kaolin, number 6 tile 10%

Ball clay 20%

Pyrophylite 10%

Spodumene 20%

Talc 10%

Plus 5% sand or grog and 1% nylon fiber

Here are two fusable engobes, fired to cone 014, for use on greenware, bisque, or over glazes, with multiple firings.

Parts by weight

Gerstley borate 1½

China clay 1

Silica 1

Plus colorants

Gerstley borate 1

Talc 1

Ball clay 1

China clay 1

Plus colorants

My favorite stains are Mason's Number K3364 turquoise, Number 126 vivid blue, Number 705 lavender, Number 6319 vanadium yellow, Number 150 black, and Number 1221 Saturn orange.

DON SCHAUMBURG'S GLAZE RESIST

I brush bisque tiles with manganese, black iron oxide, and copper carbonate in an oil base and glaze over it in patterns with thick opaque white. As the glaze is firing it pulls away from the oily oxide base, forming puddles and varied textures. The tiles are then reduced in sawdust to give color and luster.

NORMAN SCHULMAN'S PORCELAIN FOR SALT

This once-fire cone 9 porcelain clay body is good in salt or reduction firing. Once-fired in salt it is strong, translucent, and luminous; dried with care it does not crack or warp. It shrinks about 17 percent.

Georgia kaolin, Number 6 tile 35%

Georgia kaolin 8%

Pyrophilite 5%

F—4 feldspar 30%

Flint 22%

Here is an engobe that fires cone 2—10.

Kaolin 10%

Ball clay 20%

Nepheline syenite 20%

Whiting 15%

Silica 20%

Zircopax 15%

I especially like Harshaw's orange Number 475 and yellow G5100; I use Mason's black; Blythe pink M145, sky blue and lilac, 10 to 30 percent.

DAVID SHANER'S FAMOUS SHANER RED

Apply thin to enhance redness; thick is greenish-red. Fire to cone 9 reduction.

Custer feldspar 46%

Whiting 19%

Bone ash 4%

Talc 4%

China clay 22%

Red iron oxide 5%

JOHN AND SUSANNE STEPHENSON'S ENGOBES

We use Mason stains and Harshaw's 475 burnt orange in engobes for low fire, stoneware, and porcelain. All the stains can be used on bisque as washes. Crimsons, alpine rose, and almost all of the chrome tin pinks hold best below cone 9 in oxidation; however, bubble pink, which is a manganese alumina pink, works well in reduction as does the Harshaw orange. We use the stains in an engobe for both raw clay and bisque. We call it cowslip.

Ball clay 19.4%

Kaolin 17.7%

Nepheline syenite 23.4%

Borax 4.3%

Silica 26.7%

Zircopax 8.5%

10 to 15% stain is added to this. The usual amount of metallic oxides can also be used. We substitute fire clay for kaolin in the above batch for a variation on stoneware. It is earthier, toning down some colors, and it fits better. We use a combination of brushing on the engobe, then airbrushing into it. After bisque firing, darker engobe colors may be worked in for another fire.

Mason stains are used to produce the following colors at all temperatures; color is always better on a white body or in a white engobe. Sea green Number 6268 12%; black Number 6600 10%; bubble gum pink Number 6020 10%; Saturn green Number 6121 15%; Victoria green Number 6225 10% pale; teal blue Number 6305 8%; praseodymium yellow 20%; and lavender body stain Number 6319 15%. The slip with black stain in it produces a flat black; a warmer black comes from 1% cobalt, 6% red iron oxide, and 2% copper carbonate in the engobe.

BRUCE VAN VALEN'S ENGOBE FOR BRUSHWORK ON PORCELAIN

This is a white engobe for bone dry porcelain fired cone 8–11.

Tennessee Number 1 ball clay 33.2%

English china clay 23.8%

Custer feldspar 17.0%

Borax 4.7%

Silica 16.6%

Zircopax 4.7%

For painting color on porcelain, metallic oxides give more vibrant color than stains. It is best to put in much greater percentages of color than are usual in engobes.

Oxides added to color engobe

25% iron oxide — Celadon under clear, gold under matt

50% iron oxide — Dark brown with iron flashes under celadon

1–8% cobalt oxide — Blue under anything, purple or lavender under magnesia glazes

1–5% cobalt oxide, 12% black iron oxide, and 6% manganese dioxide — A "gosu" type of blue, like the Chinese blue on white porcelain

3% cobalt oxide, 3% manganese dioxide, and 3% iron oxide — Subtle, but pure blue under clear

25% iron, 5% ilmenite, and 6% rutile — Gold under clear

If you wish to use Sumi-type brushes, paint generally with brown-haired ones, as they are the most resilient, but use white bristles for washes. The new Chinese brushes are as good as or better than the Japanese ones.

LISA WOLKOW'S SCULPTURE BODY

Cone 04 dark earthenware

Calvert china clay 20%

Gold Art clay 30%

Red Art clay 20%

Pine Lake fire clay 20%

Talc 10%

Cone 04 white earthenware

Kentucky ball clay 30%

EPK kaolin 40%

Flint 15%

Kingman or G–200 feldspar 15%

LIST OF ARTISTS

The following clayworkers are mentioned in the book but do not appear in the Portfolio.

Jane Ford Aebersold
Teaching: Bennington College
Studio: Bennington, Vermont

Jane Arnold
Studio: New York City

Jan Axel•
Studio: New York City

Ralph Bacerra
Teaching: Otis-Parsons Art Institute
Studio: Eagle Rock, California

Paul Berube
Teaching: University of Massachusetts
Studio: Amherst, Massachusetts

Sandra Blaine
Teaching: University of Tennessee
Studio: Knoxville, Tennessee

Cynthia Bringle
Studio: Penland, North Carolina

Harriet Brisson
Teaching: Rhode Island College
Studio: Rehoboth, Massachusetts

Regis Brodie
Teaching: Skidmore College
Studio: Saratoga Springs, New York

Joan Campbell
Studio: Sydney, Australia

Elaine Carhartt
Studio: Los Angeles, California

Judy Chicago
Studio: Santa Monica, California

Darryl Clark
Studio: Ashland, Oregon

Joyce Clark
Studio: Saratoga, California

Tom Coleman
Studio: Las Vegas, Nevada

Raul Coronel
Studio: Santa Monica, California

Kris Cox
Studio: Venice, California

Burlon Craig
Studio: Lincoln, North Carolina

Pat and Dave Dabbert
Studio: Michigan City, Indiana

Bill C. Davis
Teaching: California State University, Northridge
Studio: Northridge, California

Dora de Larios
Studio: Culver City, California

Marilyn Dintenfass
Studio: Westchester, New York

David DonTigny
Teaching: Pennsylvania State College
Studio: State College, Pennsylvania

Robert Duca
Studio: Estell Manor, New Jersey

Jack Earl
Studio: Lakeview, Ohio

Margaret Ford
Studio: Seattle, Washington

Mary Frank
Studios: New York City and Woodstock, New York

Charles Freehof
Studio: New York City

Don Frith
Teaching: University of Illinois
Studio: Champaign-Urbana

David Furman
Teaching: Pitzer Graduate School, Claremont Colleges
Studio: Laverne, California

Dale Gaynor
Studio: Mendecino, California

George Geyer
Teaching: University of California, Riverside
Studio: Los Angeles, California

John Glick
Studio: Famington Hills, Michigan

Dorothy Hafner
Studio: New York City

Walter Hall
Teaching: University of Hartford
Studio: Hartford, Connecticut

Ken Hendry
Studio: Fort Collins, Colorado

Jolyon Hofsted
Teaching: Queens College, City University of New York
Studio: Long Island, New York

Deborah Horrell
Studio: Columbus, Ohio

Bruce Howdle
Studio: Mineral Point, Wisconsin

Robert Hudson
Studio: Cotati, California

Clayton James
Studio: Seattle, Washington

Douglas Johnson
Teaching: University of Wisconsin, River Falls
Studio: River Falls, Wisconsin

Randy Johnson
Teaching: University of Wisconsin, River Falls
Studio: River Falls, Wisconsin

Elena Karina
Studio: Washington D.C.

Pat Kenny
Studio: Los Angeles, California

Gene Kleinsmith
Teaching: Victor Valley College
Studio: Apple Valley, California

Grace Knowlton
Studio: Palisades, New York

Peter Kuentzel
Teaching: Miami-Dade Community College
Studio: Miami, Florida

Jay Kvapil
Teaching: California State University, Long Beach
Studio: Long Beach, California

Gunnar Larsen
Studio: Gustavsberg, Sweden

Bruno Lavadiere
Studio: Hadley, New York

James Lawton
Studio: Bluffton, South Carolina

Marilyn Levine
Studio: Oakland, California

Marge Levy
Teaching: University of Michigan
Studio: Ann Arbor, Michigan

Lucy M. Lewis
Studio: Acoma Pueblo, New Mexico

Victoria Littlejohn
Studio: Laguna Beach, California

Patrick Loughran
Studio: New York City

Michael Lucero
Studio: Brooklyn, New York

James Makins
Teaching: Philadelphia College of Art
Studio: New York City

Patriciu Mateescu
Studio: Dayton, New Jersey

Frank Matrenga
Studio: Manhattan Beach, California

Berry Matthews
Studio: State College, Pennsylvania

Harrison McIntosh
Studio: Claremont, California

Nan and James McKinnell
Studio: Fort Collins, Colorado

Tom McMillin
Teaching: California State University, Northridge
Studio: Huntington Beach, California

Ray Meeker
Studio: Pondicherry, South India

Don Miller
Teaching: University of Wisconsin, River Falls
Studio: River Falls, Wisconsin

Judy Moonelis
Studio: New York City

Charles Nalle
Studio: Wilmington, Delaware

Andy Nasisse
Teaching: University of Georgia
Studio: Athens, Georgia

Eric Nelson
Studio: Seattle, Washington

Frederick L. Olsen
Studio: Pinon Crest, California

Judy Onofrio
Studio: Rochester, Minnesota

Rina Peleg
Studio: New York City

Susan Peterson
Teaching: Hunter College, City University of New York
Studio: Carefree, Arizona

Taäg Peterson
Studio: Arlee, Montana

Robert Piepenburg
Teaching: Oakland Community College
Studio: Ann Arbor, Michigan

Todd Piker
Studio: Cornwall Bridge, Connecticut

Rick Pope
Teaching: University of Montana
Studio: Bozeman, Montana

Faith Banks Porter
Studio: Pacific Palisades, California

Elsa Rady
Studio: Venice, California

Don Reitz
Studio: Clarkdale, Arizona

M. C. Richards
   Studio: Uniondale, Pennsylvania
Linda Rosenus
   Teaching: California State University, San
   Jose
   Studio: San Jose, California
Judith Salomon
   Teaching: Cleveland Institute of Art
   Studio: Cleveland, Ohio
Don Schaumburg
   Studio: Tempe, Arizona
Jeff Schlanger
   Studio: New Rochelle, New York
Randall Schmidt
   Teaching: Arizona State University
   Studio: Tempe, Arizona
Norman Schulman
   Studio: Penland, North Carolina
Robert Segall
   Studio: New York City
Nancy Selvin
   Teaching: Laney College
   Studio: Berkeley, California

Tzaro Shimaoka
   Studio: Mashiko, Japan
Peter Shire
   Studio: Los Angeles, California
Deborah Smith
   Studio: Pondicherry, South India
Joe Soldate
   Teaching: California State University, Los
   Angeles
   Studio: Pasadena, California
Robert Sperry
   Studio: Seattle, Washington
Ann Stannard
   Studio: Morgan, Vermont
Jim Stephenson
   Teaching: Pennsylvania State College
   Studio: State College, Pennsylvania
John Stephenson
   Teaching: University of Michigan
   Studio: Ann Arbor, Michigan
Tom Supensky
   Teaching: Towson State University
   Studio: Towson, Maryland

Byron Temple
   Studio: Louisville, Kentucky
Barbara Tipton
   Studio: Calgary, Canada
Lynne Turner
   Studio: Oakland, California
Bruce Van Valen
   Studio: Bethel, Connecticut
Kurt Weiser
   Teaching: Arizona State University
   Studio: Tempe, Arizona
Robert M. Winokur
   Teaching: Tyler School of Art
   Studio: Horsham, Pennsylvania
Elsbeth S. Woody
   Teaching: Baruch College, City University of
   New York
   Studio: New York City
Malcolm Wright
   Studio: Marlboro, Vermont
Yiannes
   Studio: Brooklyn, New York
Arnold Zimmerman
   Studio: Brooklyn, New York

CERAMICS MAGAZINES

AUSTRALIA

Ceramics: Art and Perception
   35 William Street
   Paddington, Sydney, NSW 2021
Crafts Art Magazine
   P.O. Box 363
   Neutral Bay Junction, NSW 2089
Pottery in Australia
   2/68 Alexander Street
   Crow's Nest, NSW 2065

ENGLAND

Ceramic Review
   21 Carnaby Street
   London W1V 1PH

FRANCE

**L'Atelier, Société Nouvelle des Editions
Créativité**
   41 rue Barrault
   75013 Paris
La Céramique Moderne
   22 rue Le Brun
   75013 Paris

GERMANY

Keramik Magazin
   Steinfelder Strasse 10
   W–8770 Lohr am Main
Neue Keramik
   Unter den Eichen 90
   W–1000 Berlin 45

GREECE

Keramiki Techni
   P.O. Box 80653
   185 10 Piraeus

ITALY

Ceramica Italiana Nell'Edilizia
   Via Firenze 276
   48018 Faenza

NETHERLANDS

Foundation COSA
   P.O. Box 2413
   3000 CK Rotterdam
Kerameik
   Kintgenskswn 3
   3512 GX Utrecht

SPAIN

Bulleti Informatiu de Ceramica
   Sant Honorat 7
   Barcelona 08002
Ceramica
   Paseo de la Acacias 9
   Madrid 5

U.S.A.

American Ceramics
   9 East 45 Street
   New York, NY 10017–2403
American Ceramic Society Journal
   757 Brooksedge Plaza Drive
   Westerville, OH 43081–6136
Ceramics Monthly
   P.O. Box 4548, 1609 Northwest
   Boulevard
   Columbus, OH 43212
Studio Potter
   P.O. Box 65
   Goffstown, NH 03045

MUSEUM COLLECTIONS

Museums offer the best research area for historical and sometimes for contemporary ceramics. This unique collation provides information about the world's great ceramic collections. Research shows an amazing extent and quality of examples in museums of many types — art, archeological, ethnological, and historical — and a mass of information in the catalogs and other documentations these institutions produce. Museums make archival holdings that are not on permanent display available by appointment, and slides can be had from most, on request.

This selection is listed alphabetically by country, with special in-depth coverage of the U.S.A. arranged by state. From the 6,000 American museums with ceramic objects, 750 were selected to receive questionnaires and requests for data. Responses were edited from the 500 repositories with the most substantial holdings. Object totals for the American museums are listed in parentheses, as stated by the curators; however, collections change — museums are constantly in the process of accessioning, deaccessioning, and purchasing.

This impressive list of institutions and collections provides a profound study basis for all areas of ceramics.

ALBANIA

Museum of Archaeology and Ethnography
Tirana
Ceramics from Greek and Roman periods.

ALGERIA

Museum of Popular Arts and Traditions
Algiers
African and European pottery.
National Museum of Antiquities
Algiers
Phoenician and Roman pottery; Islamic faience.

ANGOLA

Angola Museum
Museu de Angola
Luanda
African pottery.

ARGENTINA

Isaac Fernandez Blanco Museum of Spanish American Art
Museo Municipal de Arte Hispano-Americano "Isaac Fernandez Blanco"
Buenos Aires
Ceramics from the Colonial period.
José Hernandez Museum of Popular Art
Museo de Motivos Populares Argentinos "José Hernandez"
Buenos Aires
Pre-Colonial pottery.
National Museum of Oriental Art
Museo Nacional de Arte Oriental
Buenos Aires
Ceramics of Far and Near East, especially China, Japan, Persia.

AUSTRALIA

Art Gallery of South Australia
Adelaide
European and Asian, particularly Thai, ceramics.

Art Gallery
Melbourne
Oriental and European ceramics.
Art Gallery of New South Wales
Sydney
Chinese, Japanese, Persian ceramics; 18th c. Victorian English porcelain.

AUSTRIA

Austrian Museum of Applied Art
Österreichisches Museum für angewandte Kunst
Vienna
14th–16th c. Italian, French, German ceramics; 16th c. majolica; Chinese porcelain; 18th c. European ceramics.
Exhibition of the Former Court Collections of Tableware and Silver
Schausammlung der ehemaligen Hoftafel und Silberkammer
Vienna
18th–19th c. porcelain table services from the Imperial household; Vienna and Meissen porcelain.
Museum of the History of Art Collection of Antiquities
Kunsthistorisches Museum
Vienna
Greek 5th–3rd c. B.C.; pottery from Cyprus; Etruscan and Roman pottery.

BELGIUM

Ridder Smidt van Gelder Museum
Kunsthistorische Musea
Antwerp
Chinese and European porcelain; Sèvres and Dresden china.
Chinese Pavilion
Brussels
Collection of porcelain from the Far East.
Provincial Museum of Arts and Crafts
Provinciaal Museum voor Kunstambachten het Sterckshof
Deurne
Pottery of Middle Europe.
Ceramics Museum
Mons
17th–19th c. ceramics.

CAMEROON

Museum of Negro Art
Yaounde
Ceramics of different African regions.

CHINA

Bampo Village Museum
Bampo (east of Xian)
Neolithic site of the Yangshao culture; Stone Age wheel-thrown ceramic funerary urns.
Guangdong Historial Museum
Canton (Guangzhou)
Prehistoric clay from Guangdong province; in-depth Ming.
Ceramics Museum (Tsingtas)
Chingtehchen
Excellent Sung celadons from this region.
Zhejiang Provincial Museum
Hangzhou
Early porcelains from local Han excavations.
Town Museum
Luoyang
Han and T'ang tomb artifacts.
Forbidden City, Palace Museum
Peking (Beijing)
Treasures of rulers covering 5,000 years; important ancient Han clay works; Sung and Ming masterpieces.
Shanghai Museum of Art and History
Shanghai
Especially fine Han, Sui, T'ang; some Sung and Ming; European ceramics since A.D. 1600.
Shaanxi Provincial Museum
Xian
1974 excavation of life-size warriors and horses from the site of Emperor Ch'in Shih Huang Ti (c. 221–206 B.C.)'s gigantic tomb purported to contain 10,000 figures. The figures, each one different, were broken by the next Emperor and are being painstakingly put together now; about 300 are exhibited in the museum and in various other places in China.
Henan Provincial Museum
Zhengzhou
Extraordinary collection of Neolithic clay

wares and the early dynasties: Yang, Shang, Han, T'ang, Chou, and Sung, from this province.

COLOMBIA

Museum of Anthropology
Museo Antropologico
Manizales
Ceramics of the Quimbaya, Colima and Tayrona cultures.

Museum of Pre-Columbian Ceramics
Exposicion Permanente de Ceramica Indigena
Manizales
Pre-Columbian ceramics.

CYPRUS

Cyprus Museum
Nicosia
Pottery from Neolithic and Chalcolithic periods to the Roman age; terracotta figures.

CZECHOSLOVAKIA

Museum of Czech Porcelain
Muzeum Ceskeho Porcelanu
(Umeleckoprumyslove Muzeum, Praha)
Klasterec Nad Ohri
18th–20th c. Czech porcelain.

Museum of Applied Art
Prague
Ancient and contemporary Czech and other European ceramics.

DENMARK

Museum of Decorative Art
Danske Kunstindustrimuseet
Copenhagen
Pottery and porcelain from the Middle Ages to the present day.

National Museum
Nationalmuseet
Copenhagen
Viking ceramics; Oriental and Classical antiquities.

Kolding Museum
Kolding, Jutland
Danish and other European porcelain.

DOMINICAN REPUBLIC

National Museum
Museo Nacional
Santo Domingo
Pre-Columbian ceramics.

EGYPT

Greco-Roman Museum
Alexandria
Coptic, Roman, and Greek pottery and terracotta statuettes.

Coptic Museum
Old Cairo
Pottery of the ancient Mediterranean area to the 12th c.

Egyptian Antiquities Museum
Cairo
Material from pre-dynastic and Pharaonic sites; tomb of Tutenkhamun.

Egyptian National Museum
Cairo
Collections from prehistoric times until 6th c. A.D., Coptic and Islamic periods.

Museum of Egyptian Civilization
Cairo
Egyptian pottery, all ages.

ENGLAND

American Museum in Britain
Bath, Avon
17th–19th c. American craft, including American Indian and Pennsylvania Dutch ceramics.

Holburne of Menstrie Museum
Bath, Avon
18th c. porcelain; 20th c. pottery study center.

Cecil Higgins Art Gallery
Bedford, Bedfordshire
18th–20th c. European porcelain.

City Museum and Art Gallery
Birmingham, West Midlands
14th–20th c. ceramics; ethnographic works of various cultures.

Brighton Museum and Art Gallery
Brighton, East Sussex
Folk art; ethnography; pottery and porcelain, particularly Staffordshire; Art Nouveau and Art Deco.

Corinium Museum
Cirencester, Gloucestershire
Romano–British excavation; mosaics from the site and a mosaic workshop reconstruction.

Colchester and Essex Museum
Colchester, Essex
Archeological material.

Royal Crown Derby Museum
Derby, Derbyshire
History and products of the three Derby porcelain and china factories from 1750.

Gulbenkian Museum of Oriental Art and Archeology
Durham, County Durham
Egyptian, Islamic, Chinese, and Japanese pottery and porcelain; antiquities.

City Art Gallery and Art Museum
Leeds, West Yorkshire
English pottery; Leedsware.

British Museum
London
Fine collections of the world's clay, especially British and medieval European; Oriental from prehistoric times; Greek and Roman.

Percival David Foundation of Chinese Art
London
Extensive collection of Sung, Yuan, Ming, and Ch'ing Dynasty ceramics, many formerly owned by Chinese emperors.

Wallace Collection
London
European 17th and 18th c. ceramics.

William Morris Gallery
London
Works by the famous founder of the Arts and Crafts movement.

Victoria and Albert Museum
London
Comprehensive collection of ceramics of the world; excellent Islamic luster, Chinese T'ang, medieval European, Renaissance, Victorian, and contemporary.

Athenaeum Gallery of Modern Art
Manchester
English pottery, including slipware, stoneware, lead-glazed, and creamware; European and Chinese ceramics.

Nottingham Castle Museum
Nottingham, Nottinghamshire
Medieval ceramics; Wedgwood.

Ashmolean Museum of Art and Archaeology
Oxford, Oxfordshire
European ceramics, Chinese and Japanese porcelain, Islamic pottery.

Verulamium Museum
St. Albans, Hertfordshire
Excavation of Roman site and museum; wonderful early unglazed wheel-thrown pots.

City Museum
Stoke on Trent, Staffordshire
Staffordshire, European, South American, near Eastern, and Oriental ceramics.

Minton Museum
Stoke on Trent, Staffordshire
History of the Minton works.

Sir Henry Doulton Gallery
Stoke on Trent, Staffordshire
Royal Doulton collection and history.

Spode Museum
Stoke on Trent, Staffordshire
Early Spode "bone" and "stone" china.

Wedgwood Museum
Stoke on Trent, Staffordshire
Historical collection of Wedgwood.

Washington Old Hall
Washington, Tyne and Wear
Collection of Delftware at the ancestral home of George Washington.

Bantock House Museum
Wolverhampton, West Midlands
English painted enamels and "japanned" ware; Worcester porcelain, Staffordshire, and Wedgwood jasper.

Dyson Perrins Museum
Worcester, Hereford and Worcester
Worcester porcelain since 1751.
York City Art Gallery
York, North Yorkshire
Modern stoneware.

FINLAND

National Museum of Finland
Suomen Kansallismuseo
Helsinki
Ethnographic collection covering the whole world, especially North Africa, Central Europe and the Balkans, Siberia, Mongolia, Tibet, North and South America.

FRANCE

Grimaldi Museum
Antibes, Alpes-Maritimes
Picasso ceramics; Roman antiquities.
Georges Pompidou Center
Paris
Some historical, mostly contemporary ceramics; claywork of the Impressionists and abstract painters.
Guimet Museum
Paris
Far Eastern ceramics.
Louvre
Paris
Outstanding collection of Middle Eastern, Egyptian, Roman, Greek, Etruscan, Medieval, Oriental.
Museum of Decorative Arts
Paris
Middle Ages to present-day European ceramics.
National Museum of Modern Art
Paris
Contemporary European ceramics.
Picasso Museum
Paris
Exceptional collection of Picasso's ceramics in a remarkable historic building; Diego Giacometti furniture.
Maeght Foundation
Saint-Paul-de-Vence, Alpes-Maritimes
Sculpture and ceramics by Miro, Chagall, Leger, Rouault, and Alberto Giacometti.
Sèvres National Museum of Ceramics
Sèvres, Hauts-de-Seine
History of ceramics from prehistoric times to the present day.

GERMANY

Museum of Far Eastern Art
Staatliche Museen preussischer Kulturbesitz, Museum für ostasiatische Kunst
Berlin
Far Eastern ceramics since the 3rd millennium B.C.

Museum of Islamic Art
Staatliche Museen preussischer Kulturbesitz, Museum für islamische Kunst
Berlin
8th–18th c. Islamic ceramics.
Pergamon Museum: Collection of Greek and Roman Antiquities
Staatliche Museen zu Berlin, Antiken-Sammlung
Berlin
Greek, especially terracottas; Roman pottery.
Pergamon Museum: Far Eastern Collection
Staatliche Museen zu Berlin, ostasiatische Sammlung
Berlin
Late Stone Age to 20th c. Chinese ceramics.
Pergamon Museum: Near Eastern Museum
Staatliche Museen zu Berlin, vorderasiatisches Museum
Berlin
Ceramics of the Near East.
State Art Collections: Porcelain Collection
Staatliche Kunstsammlungen Dresden, Porzellansammlung
Dresden
Chinese pottery of the Han, Wei, T'ang periods; Chinese porcelain of the Sung periods and the 15th–18th c.; Japanese porcelain of the 17th–18th c.; Meissen porcelain of the 18th c.
Museum of Arts and Crafts
Museum des Kunsthandwerks, Grassi-Museum
Leipzig
13th–19th c. German pottery, stoneware; Oriental stoneware, faience; 15th–18th c. Spanish majolica; 17th–18th c. European faience; European and Oriental porcelain.
Municipal and District Museum
Stadt- und Kreismuseum
Meissen
Meissen porcelain.

GREECE

Museum
Aegina
Early Corinthian vases; Attic vases; local pottery; Neolithic to Archaic.
Benaki Museum
Athens
Ancient pottery; Chinese ceramics from Neolithic times to the 19th c.
National Archeological Museum
Athens
Ancient Greek pottery from the Geometric to the Hellenistic period, from nearly all parts of Greece.
Archeological Collection
Hearia
Pottery from the Archaic to the Roman period.
Archeological Museum
Iraklion (Heraklion), Crete

Comprehensive and important collection of pottery from all periods of the Minoan civilization; pottery, statuettes, and figurines of the Geometric, Archaic, Classical, and Hellenistic periods.
Palace of Knossos
Knossos, Crete
Large ceramic jars from Greek excavations.
Archeological Museum of Rhodes
Rhodes
Neolithic, Geometric, Archaic, and Classical pottery, statuettes, and terracottas; 5th c. B.C. vases.

HONG KONG

City Museum and Art Gallery
Hong Kong
Pottery, porcelain, mostly Chinese.
Fung Ping Sham Museum of Chinese Art and Archeology
Hong Kong
Oriental pottery and porcelain.

HUNGARY

Museum of Applied Arts
Iparmuveszeti Muzeum
Budapest
European porcelain, faience, stoneware, pottery.

INDIA

Government Museum and National Art Gallery
Madras
Archeology; early Mohenjo-daro.
Delhi Fort Museum, Archeological Museum
New Delhi
Indian, Tibetan; figures, ancient to 12th c.

INDONESIA

Central Museum
Jakarta
Porcelain of China and South Asia.
Museum Pusat
Jakarta
4,500 pieces, 500 shards; China from Han to Ming; Japan; Indo-China, Thailand from Swankhalok and Sukhothai; Near East (Persia, Arabia); Europe (Germany, Netherlands).

IRAN

Iran Bastan Museum (Iranian National Museum)
Tehran
6,000 years of Iranian ceramics; Chinese ceramics.

ISRAEL

Museum of Ancient Art
Haifa
Greek and Roman sculpture, terracottas.
Ceramics Museum
Museum Haaretz
Tel Aviv
Study collection; contemporary pottery.

ITALY

International Ceramics Museum
Museo Internazionale delle Ceramiche
Faenza
Italian ceramics; modern pottery by Matisse, Picasso, Chagall, Leger, and Lurcat; representative collection of contemporary ceramics of the world.
Archeological Museum
Museo Archeologico
Florence
Ceramics from Cyprus, Crete, Rhodes, Greece; vases and terracottas.
Museum of Ceramics
Museo delle Ceramiche
Forli
Ceramics, especially Italian.
National Ceramics Museum
Museo Duca di Martina alla Floridiana
Naples
China and porcelain, both Italian and foreign.
National Museum of Oriental Art
Museo Nazionale d'Arte Orientale
Rome
Prehistoric ceramics from Iran; 9th–15th c. glazed pottery; Chinese, Japanese, Korean ceramics.
Villa Giulia National Etruscan Museum
Museo Etrusco Nazionale di Villa Giulia
Rome
The best collection of Etruscan ceramics.
Etruscan Museum (Vatican Museums)
Museo Etrusco
Vatican City
Vases of Etruscan and Attic art.

JAPAN

National Museum of Modern Art
Kyoto
Contemporary ceramics of the world.
Kurashiki Mingeikan
Kurashiki-Shi
Folk art, particularly of Japan.
Ohara Art Museum
Kurashiki-Shi
Ceramics and sculptures from Persia and Turkey; retrospective collections of Hamada, Leach, Kawai, and Tomimoto.
Hamada Museum
Mashito, Tochigi-Ken
Hamada retrospective and folk art of all cultures.

Fujita Art Museum
Osaka
Chinese and Japanese ceramics.
Japan Handicraft Museum
Osaka
Ceramics of all cultures.
Municipal Museum
Osaka
Archeological ceramics, especially Shong in the Mamoyama period.
Idemitsu Art Gallery
Tokyo
Pottery from old kiln sites in Japan, China, Korea, Middle and Near East.
Mingeikan Museum of Art
Tokyo
Folk art of all cultures; also includes early work of Leach and Hamada.
Tokyo National Museum
Ueno Park, Tokyo
Outstanding collection of prehistoric Jomom, Yayoi, Sue, Haniwa; pottery and porcelain from the Nara period to the present from China, Korea, Vietnam, Thailand; Middle and Near East; Europe; North and South America.

KENYA

National Museum/Fort Jesus Museum
Mombasa
Chinese porcelain; Islamic earthenware.

KOREA

National Museum
Seoul
Pottery of the old Silla dynasty (5th–6th c. A.D.); Korean pottery and porcelain of the Koryo dynasty (10th–14th c.).

MALAGASY REPUBLIC

Museum of Art and Archeology
University of Madagascar
Isoraka, Tananarive
Pottery from local highlands; aboriginal and later pottery from excavations in China and Arab sites in the northwest and east.

MALAYSIA

Museum of Asian Art
Muzium Seni Asia
Kuala Lumpur
Asiatic, ancient to 19th c.; Southeast Asian and Chinese ceramics; Islamic pottery.
National Museum
Muzium Negara
Kuala Lumpur
Ethnographic ceramics of the Malay culture.

Sarawak Museum
Sarawak
Chinese ceramics of the T'ang/Sung and Ming/Ching Dynasties.

MEXICO

Diego Rivera Museum of Anahuacalli
Mexico City
Pre-Hispanic ceramics collection of Diego Rivera.
National Anthropology Museum
Museo Nacional de Anthropologia
Mexico City
Extraordinary collection of archeological and ethnological ceramics of Mexico and the Americas.
José Luis Bello and Gonzalez Museum
Museo de Arte "José Luis Bello y Gonzalez"
Puebla
Chinese, Japanese, French, and German porcelain.

NETHERLANDS

E. A. Klatte Collection
Collectie E. A. Klatte
Amsterdam
Delft pottery; Chinese porcelain.
National Museum: Department of Far Eastern Art
Rijksmuseum, Afd. Aziatische Kunst
Amsterdam
Chinese and Japanese porcelain.
National Museum: Department of Sculpture and Industrial Art
Rijksmuseum, Afd. Beeldhouwkunst en Kunstnijverheid
Amsterdam
Chinese and Islamic ceramics.
Paul Tetar van Elven Museum
Delft, Zuid
18th–19th c. Chinese and Japanese porcelain; Delft pottery.

NIGERIA

National Museum
Lagos
African art.

PERU

Rafael Larco Herrera Museum
Museo Arqueologico "Rafael Larco Herrera"
Lima
Pottery from Mochira, Nazca, Chimu, Inca periods.

POLAND

Museum of Decorative Arts
Muzeum Rzemiost Artstycznych
Poznan
Oriental and European ceramics.

Wilanow Museum
Muzeum w Wilanowie
Warsaw
Faience; Japanese, Chinese, German porcelain; Polish ceramics.

PORTUGAL

National Museum of Archeology and Ethnology
Museu Nacional de Arqueologia e Etnologia
Lisbon
Portuguese and Hispano-Arabian glazed tiles of the 16th—18th c.

ROMANIA

Art Museum
Muzeul de Arta al R. S. Romania
Bucharest
Oriental and Near Eastern porcelain.

SCOTLAND

Aberdeen University Anthropological Museum
Aberdeen, Grampian
Greek, Roman, ancient Egyptian, and early Chinese ceramics; urns from prehistoric burials in Scotland.

Hunty House Fine Arts Museum
Edinburgh, Lothian
Scottish pottery.

Royal Scottish Museum
Edinburgh, Lothian
Ethnography of the Americas; Oriental ceramics; primitive pots from various cultures.

Art Gallery and Museum
Glasgow, Strathclyde
Broad collection of western European ceramics; Neolithic, Egyptian, Greek, and Cypriot.

SENEGAL

Museum of Black African Art
Ifan Museum
Dakar
African ceramics.

SINGAPORE

Art Museum and Exhibitions Gallery
University of Singapore
Classical Chinese ceramics; Chinese export wares; Islamic pottery; Thai and Annamese ceramics.

SPAIN

Museum of Ceramics
Museo de Ceramica
Barcelona
Spanish ceramics from the Middle Ages onward.

Picasso Museum
Museo Pablo Picasso
Barcelona
Ceramics by Picasso.

National Museum of Decorative Arts
Museo Nacional de Artes Decorativas
Madrid
Spanish and Far Eastern ceramics.

SWEDEN

Gustavsbergs Fabriker Museum
Gustavsberg
Historical and contemporary Scandinavian ceramics; emphasis on Swedish.

Asiatic Museum
Stockholm
The King's extensive collection of Oriental ceramics, primarily Chinese from prehistoric to Sung and Ming.

Museum of Far Eastern Antiquities
Medelhavsmuseet-Grek.-Rom. Avdelningen
Stockholm
Chinese Stone Age ceramics (largest collection outside China), and unusually fine collection of Han to Ming Dynasties.

National Museum
Stockholm
Representative general collection; contemporary Swedish and European artists.

SWITZERLAND

Museum of Greek and Roman Art
Antikenmuseum
Basel
Attic vases, Roman terracottas and vases.

Arianna Museum
Lausanne
International collection of contemporary ceramics, particularly from the U.S.A.

Ceramic Collection
Keramische Sammlung
Zürich
18th c. Swiss porcelain and faience.

Museum of Applied Art Bellerive
Kunstgewerbemuseum und Museum
Zürich
European and non-European ceramics.

Swiss National Museum
Schweizerisches Landesmuseum
Zürich
Many cultures, especially European; Winterthur faience; ceramic stoves.

TAIWAN

National Museum of History
Taipei
Chinese pottery, porcelain.

National Palace Museum and National Central Museum
Taipei
Chinese ceramics from Shang to Ch'ing Dynasties.

THAILAND

Jim Thompson House
Bangkok
Sawankalok pottery (13th—14th c.); Benjarong porcelain.

National Museum
Bangkok
Asian ceramics, particularly good examples of Thai.

TUNISIA

Museum of Islamic Art, National Institute of Archeology and Arts
Musee d'Art Islamique du Dar-Hussein
Tunis
Islamic ceramics.

TURKEY

Archeological Museum of Istanbul
Istanbul Arkeoloji Muzeleri
Istanbul
Amlash, Sumerian, Egyptian, Greek, Roman.

Museum of Turkish and Islamic Art
Turk ve Islam Eserleri Muzesi
Istanbul
Turkish and Islamic ceramics, especially lusterwares.

U.S.A.

Total number of objects in a collection shown in parentheses

ALABAMA

Bellingrath Gardens and Home (785)
Theodore
Dedicated mostly to porcelain: Meissen, Dresden, Sèvres, Old Paris, Wedgwood, Worcester, Copland, Staffordshire,

Queensware, Chelsea, Royal Doulton, Bow, Bennington, Capodimonte, Jacob Petit, Derby, English Parian ware, Boehm.

Birmingham Museum of Art (2,050)
Birmingham
Basically 18th c. European: fine collection of Wedgwood (1,400), English and European porcelain (300); contemporary (100); Oriental collection covering 5,000 years, and representing every culture (250).

Fine Arts Museum of the South at Mobile (160)
Mobile
Wide range chronologically and stylistically; most is contemporary, American folk, and Mayan.

Montgomery Museum of Fine Arts (201)
Montgomery
General collection ranging from Roman lamps to modern sculpture.

ARIZONA

Heard Museum (3,000)
Phoenix
Historic Southwestern pottery to the 20th c.; contemporary northwestern Mexico pottery; collection of New Mexico pottery from the late 1800s.

Museum of Northern Arizona (12,000)
Flagstaff
Archeological: 10,000 whole, cataloged, specimens of Anasazi, Sinagua, Hohokam, and other prehistoric Southwestern groups, A.D. 500 to 1600. Ethnographic: 2,000 cataloged specimens of Hopi, "most complete contemporary collection known to date" (1,200), 75% with maker's name, date, location of manufacture; Navajo (200), Pai groups, Rio Grande Pueblos (400), A.D. 1600 to present.

Phoenix Art Museum (500)
Phoenix
Chinese ceramics; mostly porcelains of the 10th–18th c.; majority are blue and white. European porcelain, mostly 18th c.; contemporary ceramics.

University Art Collections (660)
Arizona State University
Tempe
19th c. crockery; early 20th c. art pottery; contemporary ceramics and ceramic sculpture from 1940s to the present.

ARKANSAS

Collection of University of Arkansas Museum (800)
Fayetteville
Mostly prehistoric North American Indian, 80% from Arkansas, A.D. 1000–1500. Some Southwestern U.S. Mimbres culture, several hundred prehistoric pots of Mexico, Panama, and South America; a few Greek

and Roman; some American Indian ethnographic.

CALIFORNIA

Asian Art Museum of San Francisco (3,500)
Golden Gate Park
San Francisco
The extensive Avery Brundage Collection of Asian art; collections of Chinese blue and white porcelains and Kosometsuke; full representation of the ceramic development and contribution of China, Japan, and Korea from prehistoric to modern times; greater Persian and Southeast Asian early wares.

Bowers Museum (441)
Santa Ana
Toy dishes (200); ceramic forms mainly of English manufacture, partial sets of dishes and single pieces (200). Ethnic collection of 64 complete ladles of North American Anasazi culture. Pre-Columbian Mexican and Mesoamerican bowls, vases, stirrup vessels (60). Crocks and whitewares, 1920–30, manufactured by Bauer or Pacific of Los Angeles.

Craft and Folk Art Museum
Los Angeles
Contemporary American ceramics, including 14 place settings, called "The White House Collection," made by individual craftspersons for the Honorable Rosalind Carter in 1978.

De Saisset Museum (100)
University of Santa Clara
Santa Clara
Mid-19th c. Royal Vienna Beehive plates; 19th c. Meissen from Germany; 18th and 19th c. French Sèvres; ceramics by Picasso.

Fine Arts Museums of San Francisco (700)
California Palace of the Legion of Honor
M. H. de Young Memorial Museum
Decorative Arts Collection
San Francisco
The strengths of the collection are in red-figure Greek pottery; 16th c. majolica and stoneware; 18th c. English and continental porcelain, stoneware, and earthenware.

Galleries of the Claremont Colleges (1,300)
Claremont
Montgomery Art Gallery-Pomona College: Pre-Columbian and Southwestern U.S. (500). Lang Art Gallery-Scripps College: Californian ceramics 1950–70 (700).

Huntington Library and Art Gallery (200)
San Marino
18th c. Sèvres and Chelsea; Wedgwood; a few Chinese pieces. •

J. Paul Getty Museum (600)
Malibu
Ancient ceramics: Greek and Roman; Attic, Apulian, Etruscan, Campanian from 6th c. B.C. to 1st c. A.D. (436); decorative arts: Western European (Baroque, Rococo,

Neoclassical); sets of French Sèvres, German Meissen, and incorporated examples of 17th–18th c. Japanese and Chinese ceramics.

Los Angeles County Museum of Art (thousands)
Los Angeles
Ancient Iranian, 6000 B.C., seals, ceilings, tablets; Amlash vessels; classic Greek pottery; eastern Mediterranean glazed ware; African; Pre-Columbian, especially Peruvian, Central American, and Pre-Classical Mexican; Oriental prehistoric and dynastic; contemporary 20th c.

Los Angeles County Museum of Natural History (1,300)
Los Angeles
Ethnological pottery from Pueblo and other Southwest U.S. cultures within the past 100 years; South America, Asia, Africa, Oceania (800). Historical pottery concentrating on American history with specialization in California and the Southwest (500).

Lowie Museum of Anthropology U.C. (thousands)
Berkeley
Old and New World archeology, primarily Peru and Egypt, plus examples from many small-scale societies in the ethnographic holdings.

Mills College Art Gallery (800)
Oakland
Emphasizes contemporary American ceramics from the 1960s; also includes modern Japanese, Chinese, Pre-Columbian, American Indian.

Norton Simon Museum of Art at Pasadena
Pasadena
Contemporary ceramic pieces include John Mason's 1961 "Black Cross" and firebrick sculpture "Pasadena 1974"; Peter Voulkos' 1958 "Black Divide Butte."

Oakland Art Museum (500)
Oakland
Contemporary Californian artists, with an emphasis on ceramics of the region, 1880 to the present, vessels, objects, sculpture (400). Collection also includes china painting, Arts and Crafts Movement art pottery, early Craftsman era.

Pacific Asia Museum
Pasadena
Good small collection of Oriental ceramics.

Riverside County Art and Culture Center (119)
Edward Dean Museum of Decorative Arts
Cherry Valley
Primarily European decorative porcelains and earthenwares; some Asian pieces.

San Diego Historical Society (several hundred)
San Diego
Pottery by Southern Californian native Americans, from large ollas to small bowls. Restored fragments and whole objects from San Diego Presidio excavations; late 18th,

early 19th c. Chinese, Japanese, English, and Mexican; late 19th, early 20th c. American dishes and household items; American art pottery; ceramics by contemporary local potters.

San Diego Museum of Art (1,200–1,400)
San Diego
About half the pieces are Asian, primarily Chinese from the Chou to Ch'ing Dynasties; some Japanese and Korean ceramics. European and American tablewares, 17th–20th c.; 300 Dutch tiles, 17th–18th c.; significant holdings of Persian, Syrian and Hispano-Moresque pottery 11th–15th c.; San Diego potters, c.1910–50.

San Diego Museum of Man (6,110)
San Diego
Southern Californian Indians; prehistoric and historic Southwest U.S.; pre-Hispanic Mexico and South America, especially Peru; ethnographic Mexico; contemporary Southwest Pueblo Indian potters.

San Francisco Museum of Modern Art (66)
San Francisco
American ceramic figurative sculpture from the first half of the century, mostly terracotta; important contemporary Californian ceramic sculpture.

Santa Barbara Museum of Art (1,000)
Santa Barbara
The majority of pieces are Oriental: Chinese Han to Ch'ing, Japanese, mostly of the last few hundred years; Korean; Pre-Columbian figures; some contemporary American pieces.

Southwest Museum (several thousand)
Los Angeles
Principally Southwest American Indian, historic and prehistoric; also Mexico, Central and South America; excellent library and catalogs.

Stanford University Museum of Art (hundreds)
Stanford
European ceramics from 17th c. to early 20th c. (50); Asian, particularly Japan and China; Southwest Native American pottery.

Triton Museum of Art (260)
Santa Clara
Majolica tin-glazed earthenware, primarily American and English, 19th and 20th c.

U.C.L.A. Museum of Cultural History (5,000)
Los Angeles
Non-Western and folk art; Mexican, Peruvian, and African.

U.C.L.A. Sculpture Garden
Los Angeles
Peter Voulkos' "Gallas Rock."

University of California Art Museum (7)
Berkeley
Contemporary ceramics.

COLORADO

Colorado Springs Fine Arts Center (104)
Colorado Springs

American art pottery, mostly by Van Briggle (45); a sampling of Oriental, ancient Near East, Egypt, Greek and Roman, European, Southeast Asian, contemporary U.S.

Denver Art Museum (3,500–4,500)
Denver
Greek-Roman, Etrurian and Phoenician; terracotta utility vessels, sculpture, decorative arts; Egyptian faience figures. European ceramics: Italian majolica, English porcelain, Deruta majolicas, terracotta sculpture, decorative arts. Asian ceramics: Persia, China, Japan, Southeast Asia, Korea, predominantly Chinese porcelains, sculpture and decorative arts (1,000). Native American Indian and Pre-Columbian: all of the Pueblo Indian pottery arts, historic to 20th c. (1,000); also all of the Pre-Columbian cultures of Mexico and South America. American contemporary ceramics from colonial times to 20th c., including 19th c. salt-glazed and lusterware.

Koshare Indian Museum (2,000)
La Junta
Prehistoric and contemporary Indian pottery (1,000), mostly U.S.A., some Central and South American. Prehistoric collection includes classic Mesa Verde pottery (50), and Casas Grande effigy pottery.

Pioneers Museum (3,174)
Colorado Springs
Van Briggle art pottery, Art Nouveau style, 1901–40s.

Pueblo Metropolitan Museum Associate (300)
Pueblo
American and European historic decorative ceramics, 1870–1925.

Sangre de Cristo Arts and Conference Center (25)
Pueblo
Contemporary work, mostly by local artists.

CONNECTICUT

Bruce Museum (50)
Greenwich
Includes Chinese, Egyptian, American, and European.

Hill-Stead Museum (75)
Farmington
Chinese Han, Sung, Ming, Ch'ing Dynasties; 17th and 18th c. Italian majolica; 18th c. Oriental oxblood porcelains; 19th c. English lusterware.

Peabody Museum of Natural History
Yale University
New Haven
Archeological and ethnological, various cultures.

Wadsworth Atheneum
Hartford
Morgan collection of English and European porcelain.

Webb-Deane-Stevens Museum (800)
Wethersfield
18th c. English Delft; 19th c. English pearl ware, 19th c. American utilitarian stoneware; late 18th to early 19th c. Chinese export porcelain for the American market; mid-19th c. European dinnerwares.

Yale University Art Gallery (200)
New Haven
Pieces made in America, as well as those made in Europe or the Orient for the American market, from the 17th c. to the present. Major styles in this time frame are represented.

DELAWARE

Hagley Museum
Wilmington
18th–19th c. English earthenware and porcelain; Chinese export wares of the 18th and 19th c.

Winterthur Museum (Henry Francis Du Pont) (7,500–10,000)
Winterthur
Chinese export porcelain; English ceramics 1600–1900; emphasis on work of 18th–19th c. Pennsylvania German potters. All pieces are documented as having been made or used in the U.S.A.

DISTRICT OF COLUMBIA

Corcoran Gallery of Art (399)
Washington, D.C.
15th to 18th c. European: French and Italian majolica (120), Delft (45), Palissy (34); figurines of early Greek and Roman origin (200).

Daughters of the American Revolution Museum (1,000)
Washington, D.C.
Decorative objects made or used in America, 1700–1850; ceramics pertaining to Revolution war heroes, and George Washington in particular; includes British and Chinese examples.

Dinock Gallery
George Washington University (75)
Washington, D.C.
Late and post classic Pre-Columbian vessels and figures from the Mayan regions of Mexico, Western Mexico, and Guatemala; some 19th c. decorative arts pieces; a few contemporary works.

Freer Gallery of Art (12,533)
Washington, D.C.
Far East: extensive Chinese and Southeast Asian collection with emphasis on Chinese Han to Ming (6,930); Japan with emphasis on 16th, 17th c. stoneware, Kyoyaki porcelain (885); Korea with emphasis on Koryo celadon (245); Near East including all periods and styles of the Islamic world; Egypt, Iraq, Iran, Syria, Turkey (680); American Pewabic pottery (35).

Hillwood
Washington, D.C.
18th–19th c. Russian; 18th c. French porcelain.

Hirschorn Museum and Sculpture Garden (200)
Smithsonian Institution
Washington, D.C.
European, c. 1730–1960, and American, c. 1935–80, contemporary ceramic sculptures (52); early Greek and Roman, 2000 B.C. Amlash, African, and Haniwa (23); Pre-Columbian, particularly terracotta vessels (124).

Museum of African Art
Washington, D.C.
African collection, all periods.

National Gallery of Art (206)
Washington, D.C.
Chinese porcelain, various dynasties (166); 16th c. Italian majolica (40).

National Museum of American History (16,000)
Smithsonian Institution, Division of Ceramics and Glass
Washington, D.C.
Western ceramics dating from the 16th c. through the present day, with emphasis on ceramic forms and types made and used in America, and on continental porcelain; Chinese porcelain made for the Western market.

National Museum of Natural History (179,000)
Department of Anthropology
Smithsonian Institution
Washington, D.C.
Ethnological collection: 19,000, classified according to culture; Asian, African, Oceanian, Native American. Archeological collection: 160,000 (mostly shards), classified according to locality; America's prehistoric cultures; scattered materials from the rest of the world, particularly the Mediterranean.

Renwick Gallery (55)
National Museum of American Art
Smithsonian Institution
Washington, D.C.
Contemporary U.S.A. ceramics with an emphasis on American clay artists' porcelain of recent vintage.

Society of the Cincinnati (500)
Washington, D.C.
Oriental porcelain: Chinese Han to Chi'en Lung, and 17th–18th c. Japanese Imari; Limoges, Wedgwood, and other dinner services.

White House (thousands)
Washington, D.C.
Several thousand pieces of late 18th, 19th, and 20th c. Presidential porcelain dinner services; 465 pieces of sculpture and decorative arts; Chinese export porcelain, French, English, American 19th c. vessels and sculpture.

FLORIDA

Cummer Gallery of Art (844)
Jacksonville
The "most complete collection of Meissen porcelain tableware dated between 1710 and 1750 to be found in the U.S.A.," Wark collection (720); Chinese porcelains: T'ang, Sung, Ming, Ch'ing, especially K'ang Hsi, Yung Cheng, Ch'ien Lung (101); a few Japanese, Pre-Columbian and black figure Greek.

Florida State Museum
University of Florida
Gainesville
Several million archeological pottery shards, including aboriginal from the Ceramic Archaic Period, c. 2000 B.C., to c. 1500–1700; European earthenwares; Caribbean works and a collection from the Weeden Islands; some on exhibit, majority in archives for research.

Florida State University Art Gallery (900)
Tallahassee
Outstanding Pre-Columbian, emphasis on Nazca, Chancay, Lambayeque, Chimu, Mochu.

Henry Morrison Flager Museum (1,000 +)
Palm Beach
19th c. to 1930: French, English, Italian, German, Chinese, mostly porcelain dinner services: Napoleon III dinner services, Marie Antoinette plates, Louis Philippe dinner service, Capodimonte dinner and dessert service; provincial painted earthenware vases and jardinières.

Jacksonville Art Museum (750)
Jacksonville
Chinese pottery and porcelain dating from the Early Neolithic period to the Ch'ing; a small number of Pre-Columbian Central and South American; small number of contemporary U.S.

Jacksonville Museum of Arts and Sciences (250)
Jacksonville
Pre-Columbian, mostly Mayan, Late Classic, and Costa Rican-Huetar; contemporary Southwest Indian Pueblo; contemporary Mexican folk pottery.

Lightner Museum (several thousand)
St. Augustine
Late 19th c. Royal Doulton, Leeds, Minton, Wedgwood, Royal Worcester. Porcelain 18th–20th c.: Chinese Rose Medallion, Royal Vienna, Dresden, Meissen, Russian porcelain urns, Korean "vase of 1,000 monkeys," American Rookwood.

Loch Haven Art Center (300)
Orlando
Pre-Columbian 2000 B.C. to A.D. 1500, 58 significant cultural styles of sculptured vessels, effigies, religious, and utilitarian objects.

Lowe Art Museum (1,500)
Coral Gables
Pre-Columbian; Chinese and Japanese,

particularly Ch'ing Dynasty; American Indian Pueblo and others; European, German, French, Dutch.

Morikama Museum of Japanese Culture (10)
Delray Beach
Japanese folkware, tea ceremony ware, and contemporary stoneware displayed in a traditional Japanese-style building.

Museum of Fine Arts (167)
St. Petersburg
Varied collection of European and American porcelains, 18th, 19th and 20th c. figures, plates, serving accessories. Oriental porcelain and pottery from 1200 B.C. to 19th c., including K'ang Hsi region, Ch'ing Dynasty. South American pottery and earthenware, A.D. 400–600.

Tampa Museum (147)
Tampa
All Pre-Columbian regions from Peru to Mexico and from three major areas of Pre-Columbian civilization: Central Andes, Mesoamerica, Intermediare; emphasis on Columbia, Peru, Guatemala, and Panama.

University of Florida Gallery (122)
Gainesville
Pre-Columbian, outstanding Peruvian; contemporary U.S.A. from Florida.

University of South Florida Gallery (211)
Tampa
Pre-Columbian (150); modern clay sculptures.

GEORGIA

American Camellia Society (140)
Fort Valley
Edward Marshall Boehm porcelain sculptures, especially of camellias.

Columbus Museum of Arts and Sciences (200)
Columbus
Ancient Greek, European Doughty, and Boehm Bird collections; North and South American Indian; West Georgia and East Alabama Indian.

High Museum of Art (500)
Atlanta
Emphasis on 17th to early 19th c. English; 19th and early 20th c. southern pottery; contemporary U.S.A.

HAWAII

Bishop Museum
Honolulu
Fine group of archeological potsherds, general prehistoric, pre-contact Pacific areas; Lapita pottery.

Contemporary Arts Center of Hawaii (62)
Honolulu
Contemporary ceramics by artists who were born in, or have some connection with, Hawaii.

Friends of Iolani Palace (500)
Honolulu
*Table china, generally factory-made
Victorian from Europe or the Orient,
created for Hawaiian kings and queens,
1840s to early 1890s.*

Honolulu Academy of Arts (1,530)
Honolulu
*Classic Mediterranean cultures, including
Greek vases (60); Islamic works, the
majority from Persia, and a few rare Syro-
Egyptian Fostat types (100); traditional
European, English, and American wars
(250); Pre-Columbian, North American
Indian and African ceramics (70);
Southwest Asian including Ban Chien wares
from Thailand (50); Chinese prehistoric to
Ch'ing and export wares, Japanese from
Jomon wares onward, including tea
ceremony objects, Nabeshima ware, pots
by folk-revival artists, such as Hamada and
Kawai, and Korean, including Koryo
celadons (1,000).*

IDAHO

Boise Gallery of Art (15)
Boise
Contemporary work by Idaho potters.

ILLINOIS

Art Institute of Chicago (thousands)
Chicago
*Major areas, periods, and types in classical
ceramics: Greek vases and terracotta
statues; African, Oceanian, American,
European, Near and Far Eastern; some
contemporary work from Europe and the
U.S.A.*

Chicago Historical Society (500)
Chicago
*American, German, other European, 19th
to early 20th c.; collection of Chicago-
made ceramics.*

**Cultural Arts and University Museums
(300)**
Southern Illinois University at Edwardsville
Edwardsville
*Silla kingdoms to the Koryo and Yi
Dynasties from the Stroup Korean Pottery
Collection (225); Pre-Columbian Mexico,
Southern Illinois University Master of Fine
Arts ceramists.*

David and Alfred Smart Gallery (600)
University of Chicago
Chicago
*Ceramics from all periods, antiquity to the
present, West and Far East; impressive
collection of classical Mediterranean
cultures.*

Field Museum of Natural History (50,000)
Chicago
*Archeological and ethnological early 19th
to 20th c. with outstanding ceramics of
Southwestern U.S. Indians, Peru, Iraq-*

*Sumerian, China from Shang to Han,
Melanesia and New Guinea; strong
collection from Mexico and Amazon areas;
Pompeian and Etruscan, Pharaonic Egypt
and Roman, Madagascar, Malaysia,
Indonesia, and the Philippines; Melvina
Hoffman's famous bronze (from the clay
sculpture) of Maria Martinez, the potter of
San Ildefonso Pueblo.*

Freeport Art Museum (172)
Freeport
*Turn of the century art pottery, mostly
European; Southwestern American Indian
c. 1880–1920; 19th c. European
decorative; Oriental; Turkish tiles.*

**Krannert Art Museum
University of Illinois (600)**
Champaign
*16th–20th c. European; 19th–20th c.
American, emphasis in 20th c.; 7th–20th c.
Chinese; 9th–8th c. B.C. Greek; Pre-
Columbian c. 900 B.C.–A.D. 1470.*

Lakeview Museum of Arts and Sciences (60)
Peoria
*Mostly 19th c. Illinois-made jugs and urns;
18th–19th c. European and American
decorative ceramics; 19th c. Oriental.*

Maurice Spertus Museum of Judaica (100)
Chicago
*Archeological pottery, primarily modern
ceremonial pieces.*

**Museum of Anthropology
Northern Illinois University (200
ethnographic pieces, several thousand
archeological shards)**
Dekalb
*Southwest Indian, prehistoric, late
prehistoric, and contemporary; recent
pottery from New Guinea, Indonesia, and
the island of Kythnos, Greece.*

Oriental Institute (thousands)
University of Chicago
Chicago
*Every ceramic period from every
civilization in the ancient Near East,
including Egypt, Mesopotamia, Palestine,
Turkey, Iran, Nubia. Covering c. 7000 B.C.
to Islamic periods.*

Peoria Historical Society (1,050)
Peoria
*Decorative art works, primarily dinner
services, 1840–90 (900); French and
German porcelain; English stoneware;
Peoria pottery.*

University Museum, Southern Illinois (75)
University at Carbondale
Carbondale
*19th c. American jugs, crocks, and jars;
19th c. Kirkpatrick pottery works of Anna,
Illinois; pieces from 1930 to the present.*

INDIANA

**Evansville Museum of Arts and Science
(1,189)**
Evansville
Wide span of chronology and provenance;

*anthropological collection of American
Indian (236), Mexican, Central and South
American, Near Eastern (286);
contemporary U.S.A. (275) and other
countries, primarily Europe (273).*

Fort Wayne Museum of Art (20)
Fort Wayne
Small, diverse collection.

Indiana University Art Museum (300)
Bloomington
*Includes ancient, African, Asian, European,
and contemporary ceramics.*

Indianapolis Museum of Art (2,000)
Indianapolis
*Eastern: Chinese, Japanese, Korean, and
Southeast Asian; Western: 18th c.
porcelain, English and German figures from
Chelsea, Bow, Derby, Worcester, Meissen,
Nymphenburg. American Indian, Asia
Minor, Assyrian, Austrian, Babylonian,
Cypriot, Danish, Dutch, Egyptian, French,
Greek, Irish, Italian, Mexican, Persian,
Peruvian, Pre-Columbian, Roman, Spanish,
Syrian; contemporary U.S.A.*

**Tippecanoe County Historical Society
(1,000)**
Lafayette
*General collection, some on display, many
in storage.*

**Valparaiso University Art Galleries and
Collections (25)**
Valparaiso
*Palestinian pottery pieces 3100–2300
B.C.; Chinese vases, c. A.D. 1700.*

IOWA

**Brunnier Gallery, Iowa State University
(500)**
Ames
*Works from European porcelain factories,
18th and 19th c., with good representation
of the late Baroque and Neoclassical styles;
emphasis on work from the Meissen
factory, 1720–1800, and the Worcester
factory of the 18th c.; Chinese from Hao to
Ming Dynasties.*

Central Iowa Art Association (122)
Marshalltown
*Study collection including a diversity of
contemporary and historical work from a
broad variety of geographical sources.*

Putnam Museum (several thousand)
Davenport
*Prehistoric, rare Hopewell and Mississippi
culture American pottery; Nazca, Chimu,
Aztec, Pre-Columbian; 18th Dynasty
(1530–1410 B.C.) Egyptian; Greek pottery
600–500 B.C.*

KANSAS

Birger Sandzen Memorial Gallery (37)
Lindsborg
*Contemporary works with a loan collection
of figures by Rosemary L. Bashar.*

Edwin A. Ulrich Museum of Art (285)
Wichita State University
Wichita
Southwest American Indian prehistoric and contemporary pottery; contemporary U.S.A. sculptures; large Joan Miró ceramic mural on the museum façade.

Spencer Museum of Art (2,000)
University of Kansas
Lawrence
General collection; extensive 19th c. ceramics from the U.S.A. and Great Britain; also ceramics from France, Germany, Japan, Korea, and China.

Thomas County Museum (2,000)
Colby
European: Meissen, Capodimonte, Royal Vienna, Sèvres.

Topeka Public Library and Gallery (350)
Topeka
Majority from the turn of the century, Art Nouveau American and European; contemporary U.S.A. mostly from Kansas.

Wichita Art Association (200)
Wichita
Good collection representative of U.S.A. contemporary ceramics; purchase awards of the National Ceramics and Decorative Art Exhibitions from 1946 to 1972.

Wichita Art Museum
Wichita
Large collection of Doughty and Boehm birds; Pre-Columbian ceramics; smaller collections of 19th c. Meissen and American lusterware; 18th c. faience. A few works by Henry Varnum Poor and Maria Martinez.

KENTUCKY

Berea College Museums
Berea
Good collection of Southern folk ceramics.

Kentucky Museum (550)
Bowling Green
Local ceramics with a history of use and/or manufacture in the area; commercial and "country" household items, including miniatures from the late Victorian era, and Tropicana ware.

Library of the Louisville Presbyterian Theological Seminary (175–300)
Louisville
Pottery pieces from the Bible lands dating from 3000 B.C. to A.D. 70 with an emphasis on Palestine.

University of Kentucky Art Museum (107)
Lexington
10th–11th c. Iranian, Mazandaran, Sani; 12th–13th c. Kashan or Sultanabad; 14th–15th c. Syrian; Japanese 19th c. Royal Satsuma, 17th–18th c. Oribe, Edo period; Western Mexican, Nayarit, Colima, Calima, Chimila, Tairona, Ecuadorian, Quillacinga; English, French, German; 19th c. Chinese Ch'en, Ming, Ch'ing.

LOUISIANA

Anglo-American Art Museum (100)
Louisiana State University
Baton Rouge
British, American, Chinese export; 18th c. to 1930 German and French pieces; early to mid-19th c. Sophie Newcomb pottery.

Longue Vue Center for Decorative Arts (2,000)
New Orleans
British with emphasis on U.K. creamware and pearlware, 18th–20th c.; Chinese export wares.

Louisiana Arts and Science Center (75)
Baton Rouge
Northwest American Indian; contemporary pottery by Cynthia Bringle.

Louisiana State Museum (500–600)
New Orleans
Ceramics made or used in Louisiana, early 18th c. to 1940; Louisiana prehistoric pottery A.D. 1200–1500; art pottery produced at the Newcomb College Pottery 1895–1940; English and French ceramics 1810–60; study collection and related archives.

Middle American Research Institute (2,000)
Tulane University
New Orleans
Anthropological collection of Latin America, mostly pre-Hispanic, late Classic, A.D. 500–1000; vessels from Honduras; modern ethnographic pieces from Latin America; North American archeological ceramics.

New Orleans Museum of Art
Tulane University
New Orleans
Newcomb-style pottery produced at Newcomb College during and after the turn of the century; Japanese pottery from the Edo period.

Newcomb College
Tulane University
New Orleans
Newcomb pottery, 1900s.

R. W. Norton Art Gallery (400)
Shreveport
Large collection of 18th and 19th c. Wedgwood; contemporary porcelain.

MAINE

Bowdoin College Museum of Art (550)
Brunswick
Ancient, Greek, Oriental, English, miscellaneous.

William A. Farnsworth Library and Art Museum (250)
Rockland
English, mostly Wedgwood, 1800–1900s; English lusterware and portrait pitchers, 1700 to early 1800s; American, mostly Dedham 1896–1943; Central American pottery, mostly undated Indian.

MARYLAND

Baltimore Museum of Art (3,000)
Baltimore
Chinese porcelain from Han to Ch'ing Dynasties; 18th–19th c. Chinese export porcelain; 19th c. English Staffordshire earthenware; 18th–19th c. Wedgwood earthenware, Worcester, and Caughley porcelain; 18th–19th c. French porcelain; Pre-Columbian Peruvian; contemporary Southwest American Indian works from the U.S.A., England, Italy, and Sweden.

United States Naval Academy (300)
Annapolis
A few pieces from the ancient world; emphasis on 19th and 20th c. U.S.A., Europe, and the Far East. Functional service pieces, commemorative urns, and vases used or owned by famous naval officers aboard U.S. naval ships, or to commemorate naval officers, ships, or events.

MASSACHUSETTS

American Antiquarian Society (325)
Worcester
A collection of Staffordshire pottery with American subjects.

Berkshire Museum
Pittsfield
Near Eastern, Egyptian, Greek, Chinese.

Busch-Reisinger Museum
Harvard University (125)
Cambridge
Work of artists from Central and Northern Europe: Danish, Swedish, Swiss, Austrian, Dutch, German, 16th–20th c.; strongest holdings in German porcelain, Meissen, Nymphenburg, Dresden, 18th c.

Essex Institute (5,500)
Salem
Representative collection of ceramics used or made in Essex County, Massachusetts; strong in English and Chinese export; American, especially New England, 1650–1900.

Fogg Art Museum
Harvard University
Cambridge
Greek vases, black-figured, red-figured, and earlier examples of geometric and Corinthian; Chinese ceramics: large collection of Ming and Ch'ing enamelled porcelain, glazed stonewares, Sung and Yuan Dynasties; Wedgwood.

Historic Deerfield (2,500)
Deerfield
English ceramics and Chinese export porcelain from 17th c. to 1850; some American, Dutch and French pieces, early to mid-19th c.

Museum of the American China Trade (3,500)
Milton
Chinese export porcelains for European

and American markets of the late 18th to late 19th c., some domestic Chinese ceramics and related Asian ceramics. Emphasis: the influence of Chinese export on Western ceramic designs and forms. American-owned pieces include those used by Washington, Jefferson, and Paul Revere.

Museum of Fine Arts (extensive)
Boston
Asiatic collection: 8,000 Japanese pieces, 2,000 Chinese; European decorative arts: terracotta sculpture, figural porcelain and soft-paste, Chinese export porcelain, European provincial; classical and Egyptian pottery; early American pottery and porcelain; major contemporary works.

Old Sturbridge Village (1,450)
Sturbridge
New England-made redware (350) and stoneware (100); English and Chinese imported wares, c.1750–1850, limited to those found in rural, non-coastal New England (1,000).

Peabody Museum of Archeology and Ethnology (thousands)
Harvard University
Cambridge
Pottery from North America: prehistoric and historic, particularly the Mississippi Valley and the Southwest; Central America: primarily Maya, Costa Rica, Panama; Mexican ethnological pieces; South America, primarily Peru; African pottery.

Ropes Memorial, Essex Institute (800)
Salem
Chinese export and English export porcelains used by members of the Ropes family 1720–1907.

Smith College Museum of Art (400)
Northampton
Chinese and Japanese ceramics, for study purposes only.

Society for the Preservation of New England Antiquities (1,000)
Boston
Displayed in 35 museum houses, and a study collection maintained in storage areas, available on written request; English, American, and Chinese export 17th to early 20th c., mostly late 18th to late 19th c.; concentrates on pieces with New England origins or history. Utilitarian and household objects, particularly complete sets to visually recreate New England lifestyles; all types of wares: strengths in New England redware and stoneware, Federal period Chinese export porcelain, English transfer-printed wares, lusterware, mochaware, Parian ware.

Sterling and Francine Clark Art Institute (419)
Williamstown
European porcelains: Sèvres, Meissen, Vienna, Hochst, tablewares, and figures, 18th–19th c.

Wellesley College Museum (170)
Wellesley

Chinese, Greek, Italian, Japanese, Korean, other.

Worcester Art Museum
Worcester
General collection, including Pre-Columbian and 18th c. North American.

MICHIGAN

Albion College (500)
Department of Visual Arts
Albion
General collection of American ceramics, including significant Pewabic group; U.S.A. art pottery and contemporary; Japanese folk pottery.

Cranbrook Academy of Art Museum (250)
Bloomfield Hills
20th c. American ceramics (171); 20th c. European; ancient Egyptian; Greek; Near Eastern; Pre-Columbian; Chinese and Japanese.

Detroit Institute of Arts (2,000)
Detroit
European, emphasis on English wares; Eastern/Oriental, emphasis on Chinese and Japanese ceramics; North and South American; ancient Greek; 19th and 20th c. U.S.A.; Pewabic pottery.

Ella Sharp Museum (300)
Jackson
Victorian period household and decorative art ceramics, late 1800s to early 1900s: Haviland and Minton ironstone, Parian, Bennington, Staffordshire, Van Briggle, Rookwood, Meissen, Satsuma, Capodimonte, Limoges, Noritake, Royal Bayreau.

Flint Institute of Arts (975)
Dewaters Art Center
Flint
Primarily Oriental, pre-20th c.; European and American, 19th and early 20th; contemporary U.S.A.

Greenfield Village and Henry Ford Museum
Edison Institute
Dearborn
Ceramics made in continental U.S.A. from the 17th c. to 1950. English and European ceramics used in the U.S.A. soon after their date of manufacture.

Kalamazoo Institute of Arts (65)
Kalamazoo
General collection with an emphasis on contemporary American ceramics.

Michigan Historical Museum (3,000)
Lansing
18th and 19th c. English Chelsea, Bow, Worcester, New Hall, Leeds creamware, Longport, Doulton, Staffordshire, Wedgwood, Clews, Minton, Davenport, Stevenson, Alcock, mochaware, Staffordshire spatter, luster-glazed earthenware; 19th c. American decorated redware, stoneware, brown Rockingham-

type ware, Pennsylvania and New England slipware, stoneware, salt-glazed pottery, Parian ware; lotus ware; continental ceramics; 18th c. Meissen, Royal Vienna, 19th and 20th c. Capodimonte, Sèvres, Limoges.

Michigan State University (125)
Kresge Art Center Gallery
East Lansing
Prehistoric, Egyptian, Cycladic, Greek, Roman, Pre-Columbian, Oriental (mostly Chinese, some Japanese and Haniwa); contemporary.

University of Michigan Kelsey Museum of Ancient and Medieval Archeology (6,300)
Ann Arbor
Excavated material from Egypt and Iraq, late Roman and Parthian; Greece and Iran, broad chronological range; Cypriot; Italian.

University of Michigan Museum of Anthropology (3,000)
Ann Arbor
Prehistoric and ethnographic pottery from North America, South America, Africa, Asia; emphasis on China, Eastern and Southwestern U.S.A.

University of Michigan Museum of Art (200)
Ann Arbor
2000 B.C. to contemporary; emphasis on Near Eastern and Far Eastern; special collection of contemporary Japanese ceramics; American Pewabic pottery.

MINNESOTA

Benedicta Arts Center (175)
College of Saint Benedict
St. Joseph
Asian ceramics, predominantly Japanese 17th–19th c., including China, Korea, Thailand (100), and New Guinea (20). Remainder are contemporary Asian wares, and historic to modern wares from Europe and U.S.A.

Minneapolis Institute of Arts (1,800)
Minneapolis
Far East: Chinese Neolithic through 18th c. Ch'ing, including porcelain, 600–19th c. (178) and pottery 1523 B.C.–19th c. (147); 17th–20th c. Japanese (23), Korean (34): Silla, Koryo, Ti periods; 16th c. Thai; Near Eastern (147); North and South American native Indian (211); ancient (14); American and European porcelain and pottery, primarily 1750–1850 (937); English lusterware and French faience "thought to be among the largest and best in the world," Meissen tablewares, German stoneware, 16th c. Italian majolica, Chinese export porcelain, Dutch tin-glazed earthenwares; contemporary U.S.A.

University Gallery
University of Minnesota (300)
Minneapolis
Contemporary stoneware by American and

English potters; 18th and 19th c. porcelain: English, German, Chinese, Italian; 12th–15th c. Chinese, Korean; 9th and 10th c. Persian.

Walker Art Center (16)
Minneapolis
United States 20th c. contemporary.

MISSISSIPPI

Cobb Institute of Archeology
Mississippi State University
Mississippi State
Archeological collection, prehistoric America: North American Indian, largely from Mississippi; Meso- and South American. Historic collection: Near Eastern, Israel, and Jordan; Greek and Roman periods; current folk ceramics from North America and non-American sources.

University Museums
University of Mississippi
Ancient Greek and Roman pottery; South American clay tablets; Egyptian.

MISSOURI

Museum of Art and Archeology (1,000)
University of Missouri
Columbia
Ancient Greek, Roman, Cypriot, Iranian; Islamic; Pre-Columbian; Chinese and Japanese; 19th c. European.

Nelson Gallery-Atkins Museum (4,700)
Kansas City
English pottery, 14th–19th c. (1,100); Chinese pottery and porcelain 2000 B.C. to 19th c. (2,000); Japanese ceramics 16th–19th c. (350); Persian 9th–13th c. (150); contemporary.

Principia College (100)
St. Louis
American Indian, Chinese pottery and decorative arts.

Saint Louis Art Museum (6,265)
St. Louis
Most major styles and periods: Chinese (650), Japanese (30), Korean (30), Southeast Asian (30); ancient Egyptian, Greek, Roman and Islamic (175); English and American (500–600); Southwest prehistoric to modern (250); Pre-Columbian (4,500); extensive collection of well-known contemporary ceramic artists.

Springfield Art Museum (400)
Springfield
19th c. American factory productions; European ceramics; some Pre-Columbian pieces.

University of Missouri Museum of Anthropology (1,000)
Columbia
One of only two collections in the U.S.A. from Eastern Guatemala, emphasizing ceramics made in the last 50 years for local use rather than the tourist trade.

MONTANA

Rockaday Center for the Arts (5)
Kalispell
Contemporary U.S.A.

NEBRASKA

Nebraska Wesleyan University (10)
Lincoln
Contemporary from Nebraska.

Stuhr Museum of the Prairie Frontier (62)
Grand Island
Southwest American Indian; some early American pottery.

University of Nebraska Art Galleries (130)
Lincoln
Mostly 20th c. U.S.

NEW HAMPSHIRE

Colony House Museum (1,000)
Keene
Hampshire pottery, Keene, New Hampshire, 1871–1923; English Staffordshire.

NEW JERSEY

Art Museum of Princeton University (2,300)
Princeton
Ancient Mediterranean (700); post-Classical continental Europe (300); British (200); Pre-Columbian (100); Islamic (125); Far Eastern, including Chinese export (850); contemporary (25).

Campbell Museum (300)
Camden
Soup tureens, primarily 18th c., European porcelain and earthenware; Oriental examples; contemporary U.S.A.

New Jersey State Museum (5,000)
Trenton
Represents the history of the ceramic industry in New Jersey, 18th c. to the present.

Newark Museum (4,159)
Newark
Ancient (625); European porcelain (306); English porcelain (129); U.S.A. porcelain (110); European pottery (296); English pottery (595); U.S. pottery: New Jersey ceramics and art pottery (395), ethnological South American, Mexican, and Indian pottery (540); Oriental and Near Eastern pottery and porcelain (1,163).

NEW MEXICO

Institute of American Indian Research
Santa Fe
One of the most extensive of all study collections of native American ceramics.

Laboratory of Anthropology (7,422 plus potsherds)
Santa Fe
Potsherd collection from 8,000 archeological sites, including 4,500 restorable potsherds. The Anthropology Bureau maintains a reference collection of 300 named prehistoric and historic pottery types. Prehistoric pottery includes Anasazi culture from Mesa Verde, San Juan, Acoma, Kayenta, Rio Grande regions (4,550); Mexico, Central and South America. Historic pottery dates from 1882: Pueblo pottery from Keres, Tewa, Tiwa, Towa, Zuni, Hopi, Tortugas (2,582); non-Pueblo, Meso and South American (2,782). Contemporary Indian pottery includes work from Maria Martinez and family, Tafoya family, Nampeyo family, Marie Chino, Lucy Lewis, Santana Melchor, etc.; good reference library.

Museum of International Folk Art (15,000)
Santa Fe
International figurative and utilitarian folk art with emphasis on Latin America, Mexico, Guatemala, Spain, Italy, 18th–20th c.; houses the renowned world folk collections of Alexander Girard.

Museum of New Mexico (250)
Santa Fe
Tableware 1820–1930, majority of work from Northern Europe and eastern coast of the U.S.A.

Museum of San Ildefonso
San Ildefonso Pueblo
Historical and contemporary pottery of the region and the pueblo; educational displays.

Roswell Museum and Art Center (90)
Roswell
Prehistoric and historic Pueblo pottery; contemporary U.S.A. ceramics.

University of New Mexico
Maxwell Museum of Anthropology (5,000)
Albuquerque
Archeological pieces of Southwestern native America with examples of every pueblo from 1880 to present; fine Mimbres collection.

NEW YORK

Albany Institute of History and Art (900)
Albany
18th and early 19th c. Chinese export porcelain; late 17th and 18th c. Dutch and English Delft; first half of the 19th c. American Patriotic Staffordshire.

Albright Knox Art Gallery (60)
Buffalo
Contemporary ceramic sculpture.

American Craft Museum
New York
Contemporary U.S.A. ceramics; collection is in storage; special arrangements can be made for viewing.

American Museum of Natural History (hundreds of thousands)
New York
Broad geographical, cultural, and chronological range, including Pre-Columbian, African Asiatic, American Indian; one of the great museums.

Asia Society (126)
New York
Asian ceramics: strongest in Indian and Southeast Asian sculpture and Chinese Sung, Ming, Ch'ing Dynasties; Japanese Edo-period ceramics; also fine examples of Korean, Koryo period.

Dewitt Historical Society of Tomkins County (100)
Ithaca
Local history collection, 1790–1900, primarily lusterware and locally made stoneware.

Everson Museum of Art (1,200)
Syracuse
Emphasis and commitment is to ceramics; world collections from all periods and styles: chiefly U.S.A. ceramics from 1896 to present; extensive English porcelains; European and Oriental, ancient to modern; in depth Chinese from Han to Ch'ing. Over 200 contemporary U.S.A. ceramic exhibition purchase awards from the Everson Annual, 1936 to 1972.

Frick Collection (324)
New York
Oriental porcelains, 17th and 18th c.; French Saint-Porchair porcelains of the 16th c.; French Sèvres; Vincennes porcelains of the ancien régime.

Guggenheim Museum
New York
Joan Miró "Portal," and other contemporary ceramics.

Herbert F. Johnson Museum of Art
Cornell University
Ithaca
Contemporary U.S.A. ceramics.

Hinckley Foundation (20–30)
Ithaca
American 19th c. salt-glazed stoneware and earthenware; miscellaneous late 18th and 19th c. ceramics.

Hispanic Society of America (1,550)
New York
Prehistoric to modern pottery focusing on the Iberian peninsula: Aeneolithic pre-Roman, Roman, Oriental, Visigothic, Arabic, and Hispano-Moresque lusterware emphasis, also Spanish, Portuguese, Mexican pottery and modern Spanish tiles.

Historic Cherry Hill (2,500)
Albany
Chinese export porcelain: Mandarin, Rose Medallion, Nanking, Canton; French hard-paste porcelain, late 18th–20th c.; English earthenware; American Rookwood.

Home Sweet Home Museum (1,500)
Long Island
English wares made 1790–1850, including a large collection of lusterware, Adams "Kyber" pattern (300), Blue Staffordshire (100).

Hyde Collection (75)
Glen Falls
Decorative art ceramics from many periods.

Madison County Historical Society (150)
Oneida
Household pieces, 1820–1920, with emphasis on objects made or used in Madison County.

Metropolitan Museum of Art (many thousands)
New York
One of the great collections of the world covering all cultures and all periods: ancient Near East emphasizing Persian (879); primitive; Egyptian; Islamic; Minoan; Greek and Roman. Far East: Chinese, 3000 B.C. to early 20th c., numerically greatest in wares of the Ch'ing Dynasty (5,000); Japanese, 3000 B.C.–1979, strongest in Edo period (1,000); Korean, 5th–19th c. celadon wares (500). European sculpture and decorative arts emphasizing English, French, and German porcelain (9,000); Medieval (230). American decorative arts; 20th c. works. Extensive study archive collections available by appointment.

Munson-Williams-Proctor Institute (250)
Utica
European, American, and Oriental ceramics, mostly 19th to early 20th c.; English: Copeland, Ferrybridge, Staffordshire, Minton, mochaware, Delftware, luster, Liverpool, Wedgwood; 19th c. French and German; American: Tucker, Art Nouveau, American Pottery Co., Dedham, Marblehead, Old Moravian, Rookwood, redware, New York State stoneware; Chinese and Japanese porcelains.

Museum at Stony Brook (50)
Stony Brook
American and English, 19th c.

Museum of American Folk Art (135)
New York
General folk ceramics (18) and chalkware (117).

Museum of the American Indian (1 million)
Heye Foundation
New York
Large and fine collection of archeological and ethnographic Pre-Columbian North and South American Indian pottery, prehistoric to present; library and archives; moving soon to Washington, D.C.'s Smithsonian Institution.

Museum of the City of New York (1,000)
New York
Wares manufactured in New York City or purchased and used by New Yorkers, predominantly 19th c. ceramics; collection of transfer-printed Staffordshire with New York City scenes.

The Museum of Modern Art
New York
"Good Design" prototypes; Miró and Noguchi ceramic sculptures.

New York Historical Society (hundreds)
New York
New York redware and salt glaze, 18th–19th c.; Dutch and English wares, 18th–19th c.

New York State College of Ceramics
Alfred University
Alfred
19th and 20th c. ceramics, mostly by artists; some industrial.

New York State Historical Association (400)
Cooperstown
New York State clay products and wares used in the state, emphasizing salt-glazed stoneware, 19th c.

New York State Museum (500)
Albany
19th c. stoneware and Staffordshire.

Parrish Art Museum (88)
Southampton
Porcelain birds (59) and blossom sprays (6) by Doughty; Chinese terracotta statues and Blanc de Chine figures from Han Dynasty to 19th c. (23).

Rensselaer County Historical Society (3,000)
Troy
19th c. decorative and domestic pottery and china.

Skidmore College Art Association (200)
Saratoga Springs
Teaching collection of Dutch and British Delft; Pre-Columbian; 18th and 19th c. Chinese and Japanese; 19th c. French Sèvres; contemporary Southwest Indian.

Syracuse University Art Collections (600)
Syracuse
Ceramics (200): Old Silla, United Silla, Koryo period, Yi Dynasty; contemporary folk ceramics from Africa, India, Japan; contemporary American art pottery.

University Art Gallery (388)
State University of New York
Binghampton
Wedgwood (269); 19th c. Chinese (61); Pre-Columbian (33); Egyptian pre-Dynastic and 18th Dynasty (21); Greek (2).

Vanderbilt Museum (42)
Centerport
Chinese and other Oriental pieces, especially porcelain jars; terracotta and buff clay Roman and Greek oil jars; tile tables, tiled courtyards, ornamental wall decorations.

Whitney Museum of American Art (25)
New York
Ceramic sculpture of well-known U.S.A. artists, 20th c.

NORTH CAROLINA

Ackland Art Museum (24)
University of North Carolina
Chapel Hill
North Carolina folk pottery; contemporary ceramic sculpture.

Arts and Science Museum (40)
Statesville
Pre-Columbian pots and other objects in clay; southern folk pottery; contemporary work by North Carolina potters.

Asheville Art Museum (25–30)
Asheville
Collection of Southern folk pottery, especially by Walter Stephens; Oriental 19th c.; contemporary U.S.A.

Duke University Museum of Art (3,150)
Durham
Pre-Columbian (3,000); Classical: Mycenaean, geometric, Orientalizing, and Archaic periods (100); Chinese porcelains primarily from the Ch'ing and Ming Dynasties.

High Point Historical Society Museum (40)
High Point
North Carolina production pottery from late 19th to early 20th c.; local folk pottery.

Mint Museum (3,340)
Charlotte
Comprehensive collection of early Chinese dynastic wares, Japanese, Korean, Middle Eastern, French, German, Italian, Dutch, Spanish, English pottery and porcelain (particularly Wedgwood) (2,500); American art pottery; Pre-Columbian (800); contemporary, primarily southeastern U.S.A.

Mint Museum of History (1,500)
Charlotte
Pottery made in America during the last 200 years, especially from the larger ceramic centers, emphasizing North Carolina folk pottery.

Museum of Early Southern Decorative Arts (250)
Winston-Salem
English types found in the South prior to 1821; Southern-made wares through 1860.

North Carolina Museum of Art
Raleigh
Pre-Columbian pottery; Western and non-Western decorative arts; ancient pottery; some contemporary regional pieces.

Seagrove Potters Museum
Seagrove
Southern folk pottery; installation includes photographic documentation and explanations of process.

Tryon Palace Restoration Complex (300)
New Bern
English ceramics and Chinese ceramics made for the export market, 18th and 19th c.

OHIO

Allen Memorial Art Museum
Oberlin College (550)
Oberlin
Oriental: Korean, Japanese, Chinese; ancient: Cypriot, Greek, Egyptian, Etruscan, Roman, Mycenaean. Before 1800: English, Dutch, German, French, Italian; after 1800:

European, English, French, American, especially Rookwood.

Butler Institute of American Art
Youngstown
Contemporary Ohio ceramics.

Canton Art Institute (67)
Canton
Clewell art pottery, metal-clad vases; contemporary ceramics.

Cincinnati Art Museum (2,500)
Cincinnati
16th c. to present, Western countries; area of emphasis U.S.A., especially Rookwood; English 18th and 19th c. and French 18th c. wares, some German and Italian.

Cincinnati Museum of Natural History (300)
Cincinnati
Fired and non-fired pottery of local prehistoric material, Western American Indian material, some Mesoamerican, some ancient Egyptian. Not generally available to the public, but to scholars by appointment.

Cleveland Museum of Art (2,000)
Cleveland
Ancient Egyptian and Greek, Italian majolica, English and French porcelain, Pre-Columbian, North American Indian, Korean, Chinese, Japanese, contemporary American.

College of Wooster Gallery (150)
Wooster
Mesopotamian clay tablets (28); Native American pots (6); Peruvian (2); classical Cypriot, Roman and Hellenistic (75); 17th–19th c. Chinese porcelain (25); Amlash/Ardabil ancient Persian (16); contemporary (15).

Dayton Art Institute (500)
Dayton
Pre-classic period pottery of Mexico and the Neolithic period of China, to 20th c. American works; emphasis on Asia, Pre-Columbian, and Islamic ceramics.

Denison University Galleries (200)
Granville
Eastern and Western collection; Chinese (100), Burmese (23), Cuna Indian (25), American Indian (20).

East Liverpool Museum of Ceramics (4,000)
Columbus
Extensive representation of pottery wares produced by East Liverpool potteries, 1840–1920.

Massillon Museum (385)
Massillon
American Indian, luster, majolica, Massillon, Mexican, Oriental, redware, Rockingham, Rookwood, Roseville, stoneware, tile, Weller, whiteware, yellowware, contemporary Ohio artists.

Miami University Art Museum (several hundred)
Oxford
Greek and Roman; Islamic; ancient Near East; Egyptian; Pre-Columbian; American

Indian; 18th and 19th c. European and American.

Taft Museum (200)
Cincinnati
Chinese porcelain: K'ang Hsi and Ch'ien Lung periods of Ch'ing Dynasty (200 pieces); Italian majolica, first half of 16th c.

Toledo Museum of Art (1,900)
Toledo
Extensive world collection extending from Egyptian pre-Dynastic vessels of 4th millennium B.C. to 20th c. American. Emphasis upon Greek vases (350), 16th–18th c. French, American, and European (850); Far Eastern: Chinese and Japanese (650); Islamic (50).

Zanesville Art Center (5,000)
Zanesville
Egyptian from 4000 B.C.; contemporary American, emphasis on Zanesville area pottery; Southeast Asian and Chinese pottery.

OKLAHOMA

Philbrook Art Center (1,600)
Tulsa
American Indian: various tribes and styles (1,000); Oriental; Chinese, Japanese; Indo-Chinese, broad time range (450); antiquities: primarily Greek and Roman; American and European miscellaneous decorative artwares; contemporary U.S.A.

Thomas Gilcrease Institute of American History and Art (7,949)
Tulsa
Pre-Columbian, prehistoric, historic and contemporary North American Indian; most to be viewed by appointment.

University of Oklahoma at Norman Museum of Art (200)
Norman
Primarily Oriental, 6th to 19th c. China, Japan, Korea; some Pre-Columbian, African, American Indian; contemporary U.S.A.

OREGON

Horner Museum
Oregon State University (150–200)
Corvallis
Oriental porcelain, cloisonné, etc.; ethnographic jars or jugs from 1880s to 1920s.

Portland Art Museum (710)
Portland
Classical; Pre-Columbian; American; European; Near East and North African; Chinese; Japanese; Chinese export porcelain.

University of Oregon Museum of Art (426)
Eugene
Chinese: Han Dynasty to early 20th c., including T'ang tomb sculpture (over half of collection); Japanese: Edo period (one quarter of collection); American; European; Korean; Mongolian; Persian; Tibetan;

Mexican, Gandharan pieces, ranging from Pre-Columbian to contemporary; contemporary U.S.A.

PENNSYLVANIA

Allegheny College Art Gallery (25)
Meadville
Japanese, some Chinese and Korean; contemporary British.

Buten Museum of Wedgwood (10,000)
Merion
Ceramics produced by Josiah Wedgwood and his successors in England.

Carnegie Institute Museum of Art (1,000)
Pittsburgh
Ancient to contemporary, majority are European. Also Renaissance; Baroque Bozetti; 18th c. terracotta; transfer-printed English wares; some majolica; 18th c. faience.

Chester County Historical Society (2,000)
West Chester
18th, 19th, some 20th c. ceramics from Chester county homes and collectors; including Tucker porcelain made in Philadelphia (1825–38).

Frick Art Museum (23)
Pittsburgh
Chinese porcelains of the Ch'ien Lung and K'ang Hsi periods.

Landis Valley Farm Museum
Lancaster
Pennsylvania Dutch, Moravian, and other local domestic wares.

Naomi Wood Collection at Woodford Mansion (250)
Philadelphia
Early American household goods of redware and slipware; Leedsware; Oriental export and English Delft, primarily 18th c.

Packwood House Museum (3,000–4,000)
Lewisburg
Local ware, 1790 onward. Pennsylvania redware and stoneware; some Chinese porcelain; English earthenware 1820–90.

Pennsylvania State University Museum of Art (260)
State College
Peruvian Pre-Columbian, 700 B.C.–A.D. 1500; Oriental: Chinese, Eastern Chou to Ch'ing Dynasties, Korean, early Silla to mid Koryo periods, Japanese 19th–20th c.; ancient Greek and Roman: Minoan c. 1200 B.C. to early Christian c. A.D. 300; European and U.S.A. 20th c.

Philadelphia Museum of Art (500)
Philadelphia
Excellent collections; Chinese, prehistoric through Ch'ing Dynasty with exceptional T'ang pieces (3,000), 6th–20th c. Japanese (350); 5th–9th c. Korean (50); Tucker porcelain; Pennsylvania German ceramics, primarily pre-1850 (200); late 13th–16th c. Thai (100); 12th–18th c. Near Eastern, primarily Turkish and Persian (65); Griffin, Smith and Hill, Phoenixville majolica (55);

20th c. U.S.A. Large collection of European decorative art.

Renfrew Museum and Park (670)
Waynesboro
19th c. American pottery and folk sculpture, Bell pottery (130); English Chinese export (Canton: 250); English Stafford-shire spatterware (130); English sprig and berry (60); miscellaneous English (100).

University Museum
University of Pennsylvania (thousands)
Philadelphia
Archeological and historical pottery, spanning the history of ceramic production from ancient to modern; extensive objects of the Mediterranean, Near Eastern, South and East Asian, Egyptian, Syro-Palestinian; American, Oceanic, and African.

Valley Forge Historical Society (1,100)
Valley Forge
Early pottery: Staffordshire and kindred types, Leeds, Liverpool, Gaudy Dutch, Rockingham, "historic blue" (1,000); Chinese export.

Westmoreland County Museum of Art (50)
Greensburg
Victorian U.S.A.; increasing 20th c. collection.

RHODE ISLAND

Haffenreffen Museum of Anthropology (2,500)
Brown University
Bristol
Historic and prehistoric New World emphasis, examples from most regions of North and South America; also European, African, Asian, and Pacific.

Rhode Island School of Design Museum of Art
Providence
Includes 18th c. European porcelain.

SOUTH CAROLINA

Charleston Museum (1,000)
Charleston
18th and 19th c., emphasis on South Carolina "Edgefield" potters.

Columbia Museum of Art and Science (200)
Columbia
Chinese export; Meissen; 20th c. commercial manufactured wares, and good collection of contemporary clay.

Gibbes Art Gallery (20)
Charleston
Mostly Chinese import and export ware.

SOUTH DAKOTA

Culture Research Center, Blue Cloud Abbey (200)
Marvin
Southwest American Indian: Maria pottery

(25), and Pueblo pottery; Guatemalan and Peruvian pottery, including Inca, 500 B.C.

TENNESSEE

Houston Antique Museum (thousands)
Chattanooga
Extensive 19th c. European, American, and Oriental ceramics and glass, and one of the largest collections of lusterware in the world.

TEXAS

Bayou Bend Collection (1,700)
Museum of Fine Arts
Houston
Wares exported to or produced in America from 17th c. to mid-19th c.; strong in 17th and 18th c. Delft ware; 18th c. American salt-glazed stonewares and agatewares; works from W. E. Tucker's American China Manufactory (1826–38).

Dallas Museum of Fine Arts (661)
Dallas
Pre-Columbian, primarily Peruvian (215); Chinese export porcelain (66); English china (60); contemporary ceramics and sculpture (69); classical, Near East and Egypt, Orient, Africa, North American Indian.

El Paso Museum of Art (1,000)
El Paso
Prehistoric Indian; El Paso phase pottery (black and brown); Mimbres; Casas Grandes (utilitarian and Ramos ware); 19th and 20th c. American Indian; Baroque and Rococo European, including Meissen.

Forth Worth Art Museum (37)
Fort Worth
Japanese; Greek–Roman; Peruvian; Pre-Columbian; small contemporary collection.

Harrison County Historical Museum (800)
Marshall
History of Harrison county, 400 B.C. to 1980; Caddo Indian.

International Museum of Cultures (100)
Dallas
Contemporary Quichua, Ecuador, and Shipibo, Peru.

Japanese Art Museum (3,000)
Corpus Christi
Special rare collection of Hakata "dolls" of Japan, 20th c., depicting historical and folk figures.

Kimbell Art Museum (44)
Fort Worth
Chinese; Japanese; Korean; Pre-Columbian; prehistoric to 19th c.

Marion Koogler McNay Art Institute (20)
San Antonio
Southwestern Indian; contemporary works of Henry Varnum Poor, C. L. Turner.

Museum of Fine Arts, Houston (350)
Houston
European: French and English 18th c.,

primarily Worcester; extensive North American Indian; Pre-Columbian earthenwares; some Chinese.

UTAH

Brigham Young University Art Gallery (100)
Provo
Contemporary works by Utah artists; some Chinese ceramics.

VERMONT

Bennington Museum (5,000)
Bennington
Bennington pottery: includes stoneware, Rockingham, Flint enamel, graniteware, Scroddledware, red and yellow wares, Parian porcelain, colored porcelains, and other variations made in Bennington 1793–1890s; ceramics made in other parts of Vermont and New England; small collection of European and Chinese export porcelain.

Robert Hull Fleming Museum (200)
University of Vermont
Burlington
Majority are of 19th c. American; Southwest Native American; Chinese; Japanese; contemporary, mostly Vermont artists.

Shelburne Museum (1,800)
Shelburne
General collection of primarily late 18th and 19th c. pieces, including transfer-printed ware, mocha, Oriental export, spongeware, Rockingham combware, among others, emphasizing ceramic types found in 17th, 18th, and 19th c. America.

VIRGINIA

Association for the Preservation of Virginia Antiquities (1,000)
Richmond
Mainly English and American household decorative arts used in furnishing the association's 13 historic site museums, 17th–19th c.

Chrysler Museum (900)
Norfolk
Oriental, late Neolithic to 20th c., contemporary; also emphasis on English and American art pottery.

Colonial Williamsburg Foundation (4,000)
Williamsburg
English, late 17th to early 18th c.; some Chinese export porcelain; American pottery and German stonewares.

Mount Vernon Ladies' Association of the Union
Mt. Vernon
Early American domestic wares in George Washington's kitchen.

Oatlands (5)
Leesburg

Maria Martinez pots from the 1920s.

Roanoke Museum of Fine Arts (300)
Roanoke
Classical Greek and Roman; 19th c. Japanese; English and continental; contemporary American.

University of Virginia Art Museum (650)
Charlottesville
Pre-Columbian: West Mexican, Vera Cruz, Mayan; Chinese: early pottery, K'ang Hsi; European: late 18th to early 19th c. English and continental porcelain; ancient Mediterranean: South Italian, Cypriot.

Virginia Museum of Fine Arts (2,300)
Richmond
Collection covers the spectrum of ceramic styles, periods, nationalities: American, Chinese, French, German, Korean, Japanese, Persian, Greek, Roman, Egyptian, Mexican, Peruvian; emphasizes Greek pottery: mainland, Minoan, Mycenaean; also South Italian; contemporary U.S.A.

WASHINGTON

Evergreen Galleries
Evergreen State College
Olympia
West Coast functional and sculptural ceramics.

Henry Art Gallery (241)
Seattle
Contemporary ceramics, primarily Northwest artists (109); Japanese pottery (132).

Seattle Museum of Art
Seattle
Oriental collection; Pre-Columbian; contemporary U.S.A. and others.

WASHINGTON, D.C.

See District of Columbia

WEST VIRGINIA

Mansion Museum, Oglebay Institute (750)
Wheeling
English and local American pottery industry products from the late 19th c.

WISCONSIN

Elvehjem Museum of Art (600)
Madison
Ancient Greek emphasis; South Italian; Oriental: 18th and 19th c. European; Chinese export porcelain.

John Michael Kohler Center (100)
Sheboygan
Functional ware from Europe and the U.S.A., late 19th to early 20th c.; works by contemporary American artists created in the Center's Arts/Industry program.

John Nelson Bergstrom Art Center and

Mahler Glass Museum (168)
Neenah
A.D. 1000–1500: Pre-Columbian Esmeraldas culture pottery, Ecuador; 18th–20th c. tableware: Viennese and English Royal Worcester Doughty figurines.

Johnson Wax Collection, Johnson Cultural Center
Racine
Contemporary American ceramics, special collection.

Kohler Co. (70)
Kohler
Works by contemporary U.S.A. artists, most of which were made at the sanitary-ware factory in the Artists-in-Industry program.

Leigh Yawkey Woodson Art Museum (200)
Wausau
Porcelain bird figures designed by Doughty and crafted at Royal Worcester Porcelain Factory (100); Worcester porcelain dinnerwares (30); other 1880–1950 ceramics (70).

Milwaukee Public Museum (5,000)
Milwaukee
Worldwide archeological and ethnological, emphasizing Pre-Columbian from Mexico, Central and South America (3,000); American Southwest.

Paine Art Center and Arboretum (370)
Oshkosh
Chinese; English; American.

State Historical Society of Wisconsin (3,740)
Madison
Mostly English 19th c.; continental porcelain; U.S.A. pottery, emphasizing Wisconsin wares.

Theodore Lyman Wright Art Center, Beloit College (180)
Beloit
General collection of ancient Egyptian, Greek and Capuan terracotta lamps and tomb figures; Chinese, Japanese, and Korean porcelain wares; good collection of Korean celadons.

U.S.S.R.

National Ceramic Museum
Kuskovo
European and Russian ceramics.

Hermitage Museum
Leningrad
Ancient, Near and Far East, Russian ceramics.

Museum of Porcelain
Leningrad
18th–20th c. European and Russian porcelain.

WALES

Aberystwyth Arts Centre, University College of Wales
Aberystwyth, Dyfed
British studio pottery.

GLOSSARY

ABSORPTION
(1) Method of measuring density; also a factor in the use of plaster molds and **bats**. (2) The taking up of water in the pores of a fired clay piece, the percentage of which indicates hardness and determines the definition of earthenware, stoneware, or porcelain.

ALBANY SLIP
A natural common **surface clay** which becomes a shiny brown or black glaze from cone 4 upwards.

ALUMINA
Alumina oxide, Al_2O_3, is the viscosity controller in glaze, and the binder that holds glaze on another surface; it is also important as a component of the clay molecule.

ANAGAMA
Tube-like single chamber hill kiln; predecessor **noborigama**, a multi-chamber hill kiln of Oriental style.

ANECDOTAL
Verbal description (of a firing).

ASH
The residue ash made by burning tree, plant, or vegetable material; can be used alone or with other materials for glaze at stoneware temperatures; it is traditional in the Orient where wood has been a common fuel; volcanic ash can also be used.

BALL CLAY
Highly plastic clay which fires off-white; workable, fine-grained, sedimentary clay used in white earthenware, china, and porcelain bodies, engobes, and glazes; found in the U.S.A. in Kentucky and Tennessee.

BALL MILL
Motorized cylinder used for mixing glaze, grinding found materials, and crushing **calcined** mixtures; can be a roller machine with jars (for smaller quantities).

BAMBOO KILN
Climbing kiln, a kind of tube kiln for wood firing.

BASALT WARE
Black unglazed stoneware, first developed by Wedgwood in England.

BAT
Any slab used as a base for throwing or handbuilding clay; also applies to a trough used to dry **slurry** clay to the plastic state; usually made of plaster, pressboard, plywood, or bisqued clay.

BATCH
A mixture of materials or ingredients calculated by parts or weight.

BELLEEK
A thin, highly translucent, frit-containing porcelain body which is fired to nil absorption at low temperature, covered with a soft glaze. The name comes from a town in Ireland where the unusual china is still manufactured.

BISQUE, BISCUIT
Unglazed but fired ware, usually accomplished in a low temperature firing prior to the glaze fire; also applies to unglazed ware fired high, as in porcelain bisque.

BLISTERING
Bubbles formed in the glaze during the firing due to liberation of gases or impurities, caused by firing that is too fast or immature, or caused deliberately by putting into the glaze a material such as trisodium phosphate, which will promote decorative bloats or blisters.

BLOATING
Occurs in clay bodies when they are overfired, contain air, or have added bloat ingredients.

BLOCK AND CASE
To make a mold of a mold, i.e. case the block.

BLUNGER
A mixer with revolving paddles for liquid mixes; can be used to make casting slip, to re-mix scrap clay, and to mix glaze.

BODY
A combination of natural clays and non-plastics, especially formulated to have certain workability and firing characteristics.

BONE ASH
The mineral calcium phosphate, or ash from bones; found in Europe and the Orient and used in clay bodies; used as a glaze flux in the U.S.A.

BONE CHINA
Porcelain of high translucency made with bone ash, produced mainly in England and Japan; highly prized but not technically superior to feldspathic porcelain bodies made in the U.S.A.

BTU
British Thermal Unit. Unit of heat by which fuels are rated; amount of heat needed to raise one pound (U.S. pint, 16 fl oz) of water one degree Fahrenheit; all carbonaceous fuels including dung and other organics can be listed according to efficiency, by BTU value.

BURNISHING
Polishing with a smooth stone or tool on leather-hard clay or slip to make a surface sheen, bonfired or low-fired (the surface will not stay shiny at temperatures above 2000°F [1093°C]); the traditional process used in North and South American Indian pottery.

CALCINING
Firing in red heat to remove physical and chemical moisture; treatment for surface clays and other high-shrink materials such as zinc oxide, colemanite, and trap rock, to prepare them for use in glazes.

CALIPERS
Two-pronged device for measuring inside and outside diameters.

CANDELING
Leaving a kiln on very low heat for a long time without changing the input — an expensive and inefficient practice.

CARBON CORE
A condition resulting from using reduction atmosphere too much, too long, or too soon during firing of stoneware bodies containing iron; results in brittle or broken ware.

CASTING
Process of forming shapes by pouring **deflocculated** liquid clay slip into plaster molds for duplication or mass production.

CELADON GLAZE
French name for a sea-green glaze with a small percentage ($\frac{1}{2}$ to 2 percent) of iron as the colorant, fired in reduced atmosphere; innumerable variations of green, gray-green, blue-green and gray; a stoneware or porcelain glaze first used by Oriental potters.

CELSIUS (°C)
Measurement of temperature used in many countries.

CENTERING
Pushing a mass of clay on center with the centrifugal motion of a potter's wheel.

CERAMICS
Art and science of forming objects from earth materials containing or combined with silica, produced with the aid of heat treatment at 1300°F (704°C) or more.

CHINA
(1) A porcelain clay body, with up to 1 percent absorption, usually translucent; industry fires high to vitrification and glazes low; studio potters usually fire clay and glazes together to high temperatures by the traditional Oriental method, or make low-fire porcelain by the European method. (2) **Whiteware**, vitreous and hard, sometimes translucent. (3) A general term used in the trade when discussing any kind of tableware.

CHINA CLAY
Primary or secondary **kaolin**, refractory, not very plastic, white-burning, rare in the world, found in the U.S.A. in a few southeastern states; used in the blending of all **whiteware** and porcelain bodies.

CHUCK
A cylindrical form used to put pots in or over, used upside-down for foot trimming on a potter's wheel.

CLAY
Theoretically $Al_2O_3 \cdot 2SiO_2 \cdot 6H_2O$; fine-grained earth materials formed by the decomposition of igneous rock; when combined with water, clay is plastic enough to be shaped; when dry, it is strong; and when subjected to red heat or above, it will become progressively more dense and rock-like.

CLAY BODY
See **BODY**.

CLAY SLIP
See **SLIP**.

CODDLE
Wall built around a model to contain the plaster in forming a mold, made of materials such as clay, wood, linoleum, or cardboard.

COILING, COIL-BUILDING
Age-old method of constructing hollow forms by rolling and attaching ropes of soft clay.

CONES
Pyrometric cones, Orton or Seger brand, are 2 in (5 cm) pyramids made of clay and glaze constituents that soften and bend at specific temperatures. Cones are placed in the kiln during firing as a guide, and to indicate the final heat; they are classified by numbers coded to their softening point.

CONSTRUCTS
(accent on first syllable) (1) Constructions in clay made by various plastic methods, wheel or hand thrown. (2) Broken, cut, glued, taped, or otherwise held combinations made from bisqued or glazed pieces.

CORDIERITE
A magnesium aluminium silicate with low expansion characteristics, used for kiln furniture.

CORE
The interior of a piece, or a frame or stuffing on or over which work can be supported; combustible core materials can burn out in the kiln; rigid cores should be removed before the clay shrinks.

CRACKLE
Decorative and intentional fissures netting the surface of a glaze due to a variation in expansion and contraction of the glaze and the clay body.

CRAWLING
Glaze that has separated into mounds on the clay surface during firing, generally caused by fluffy or high-shrink materials in the raw glaze; sometimes called alligator glaze.

CRAZING
A faulty and unintentional cracking of the glaze due to a variation in body and glaze expansion and contraction. **Crackle** is the term used when these fissures are desired for decoration.

CROSS-DRAFT KILN
Kiln with burners across from each other so that the atmosphere circulates in a criss-cross pattern and then up and down before exiting via a flue.

CRYSTALLINE GLAZES
Large crystals grown on the glaze surface during firing and cooling, primarily induced by high zinc oxide and low alumina content in the glaze.

CUPRIC, CUPROUS
Pertaining to copper: cupric compounds contain CuO; cuprous compounds contain Cu_2O.

DAMPER
Adjustable shutter to control draft at the kiln flue.

DE-AIRING
Process of removing air from plastic clay mixtures either by hand **wedging** or by mechanical means in a vacuum chamber.

DECAL
Ceramic pigments photo-screened or pattern-screened on to flexible decal paper for transfer to bisque or over glaze; can be bought or made. Same as transfer.

DEFLOCCULANT
Electrolyte or catalyst that causes clay and water mix to become liquid faster with a minimum addition of water; examples are sodium silicate, soda ash, Calgon, tannic acid, and Darvon.

DEFLOCCULATE
To function as an electrolyte in a clay casting slip mixture; to cause clay and water mix to become liquid faster with a minimum addition of water.

DELFT WARE
Buff-colored earthenware covered with a white tin-enamel glaze and decorated with cobalt blue overglaze painting on the unfired glaze. First made in Holland and later in England in the 1600s, and still made today.

DELLA ROBBIA
Richly modeled ceramic reliefs, tin-enameled with **majolica** overglaze pinks, yellows, blues, and greens, produced at Florence in the 15th century by the della Robbia family.

DEVITRIFY
To overfire, or fire in such a way that a clay or other surface is spoilt.

DIPPING
The application of an **engobe** or glaze by immersing areas of the piece quickly and allowing the excess liquid to drain off.

DOWNDRAFT KILN
Kiln with fire entering at the side or base, where heat is forced around, up, and down through the ware, and finally exits via a flue at the back of the chamber.

DRESSING
Soaping or greasing a wood or plaster form before casting a mold.

DRY FOOT
No glaze on the footrim; usual for stoneware and porcelain because the clay body is fired to density.

DUNTING
The explosion-like cracking or breaking of pots from sudden changes of temperature on cooling, or from wrong clay body composition.

EARTHENWARE
All ware with a permeable or porous body after firing; by definition earthenware has 10 to 15 percent absorption.

ELASTICITY
When referring to clay, its ability to be maneuvered without breaking.

ENAMELS
(1) As applied to pottery: low-temperature glazes, usually applied over other glazes. (2) As applied to metals: transparent or opaque glaze that melts lower than the copper, silver, or gold on which enamel is used as the decorative finish; usually fired about 1300 °F (704 °C).

ENGOBE
A liquid clay slip colored with metallic earth oxides or glaze stains applied to wet or leather-hard ware for decoration; also natural clays of different colors applied on raw ware for decoration. Engobe can be covered by glaze or used alone.

EUTECTIC POINT
The point at which two or more materials together melt lower than either one separately.

EXTRUSION
Forcing plastic clay through an **auger** or form, mechanically or by hand, to change its shape.

FAHRENHEIT (°F)
Measurement of temperature used in the U.S.A.

FAIENCE
A general word covering low-fire colored clay bodies, such as Egyptian paste. Often a misused term, it is more particularly a French name for the tin-enameled earthenware made in the Italian town of Faenza during its period of Hispano-Moresque influence.

FELDSPAR
Mineral found in granite which melts around 2300 °F (1260 °C), used as a **flux** in clay bodies and glazes. When feldspar rock loses its alkaline content through decomposition, it becomes **kaolin** and is thus the origin of clay.

FERRIC, FERROUS
Pertaining to iron: ferric compounds contain tervalent iron; ferrous compounds contain bivalent iron.

FILTER PRESS
A machine for removing enough water from a clay slip to make plastic clay; used in industry as the best means of achieving homogeneity and plasticity in a clay body.

FIREBOX
The chamber of certain kilns into which the fuel is fed and in which the initial combustion takes place.

FIRE CLAY
Secondary clay that withstands high temperature and has varying amounts of free silica in addition to the clay molecule; prevalent throughout the world.

FIRE CLAY CEMENT
(1) Mixture of dry fire clay and sodium silicate, for mending kiln cracks or laying brick. (2) Commercial mix for building kilns, made from refractory cement, **grog**, and clay; the same as mortar.

FIRING
(1) Heating in a kiln to the required temperature for clay or glaze, at least to red heat, 1300 °F (704 °C); most enamel-on-copper melts from 1300 to 1600 °F (704 to 871 °C); most clay and glaze matures between 2000 and 2300 °F (1093 and 1260 °C). (2) Bonfiring in a pit or on the ground.

FIRING CURVE
The track made by joining points on a graph, showing the relationship between change in temperature and firing time.

FIT
Good or bad adjustment of a fired glaze to a clay body or metal.

FLAMBE GLAZE
Reduced copper glaze giving variegated effects of red and blue; originally developed by Chinese potters in the Sung Dynasty.

FLANGE
The tiny shelf on which a lid sits, or the extension on the lid that fits into a vessel.

FLATWARE
Dishes, plates, saucers, and low bowls are called flatware in the pottery industry to distinguish them from hollow ware.

FLINT
Quartz, silica, sand, and flint are terms applying to minerals used in clay bodies and glazes containing nearly 100 percent silica oxide; the minerals are similar but not identical.

FLOCCULATE
To thicken a clay suspension by the addition of an acid, such as acetic acid.

FLUE
(1) The passageway for flames in kilns — essentially the combustion space; the flue is the area around the stacking space. (2) The place of escape for the products of combustion from the chamber.

FLUX
A material or mixture having a low melting point or lowering the melting point of other materials. One of the three main components of glaze; also used to increase density in clay bodies; examples include lead, borax, lime, **feldspar**, and **frit**.

FOOT
Base or bottom of a piece.

FRIT
Mixture that is melted, cooled quickly by quenching the molten mass in cold water, and ground to a fine powder. Fritting renders soluble glaze ingredients, such as soda ash, insoluble, and poisonous materials, such as lead, non-poisonous. Made commercially or in the studio.

GANG MOLD
One mold of many separate objects.

GLAZE
Glassy melted coating developed by chemicals and heat on a clay or metal surface; technically, an impervious silicate coating formed by the fusion of inorganic materials. Glaze has a similar oxide composition to glass, but also includes a binder. Glaze provides decoration and color, prevents penetration of liquids or acids, and yields a matt or glossy, easily cleaned, functional surface.

GLAZE STAINS
Fabricated ceramic colorants from metallic oxides mixed in combination with other elements to widen the glaze decorating palette, manufactured to be stable at various temperatures; sold by code number, color, and company.

GRAVITY-FEED KILN
Kiln where the ware moves very fast through the firing and cooling cycle; used for industrial **talc** body floor and wall tiles.

GREENWARE
Finished leather-hard or bone-dry clay pieces not yet fired; raw ware.

GROG
Crushed or ground-up fired clay, purchased commercially or made by the potter; used to reduce shrinkage, yield texure, give fired clay more resistance to temperature change, help in even drying and firing, and help large pieces to stand up during construction. More than 30 percent grog addition may cause too much porosity and reduce fired strength.

GUM ARABIC
A natural tree gum used as a drying and adhering agent when applying overglaze enamels or when reglazing a piece which has previously been glaze-fired. A synthetic gum such as CMC or metho-cellulose can be used instead; it has the advantage of being water soluble and will not ferment.

HANIWA
Japanese ceramics of the first few centuries of the Christian era, characterized by simple warrior and horse images.

HARD-PASTE PORCELAIN
Sometimes called true porcelain; a body composed of **kaolin**, filler, and **flux** that when fired to density is white, **vitreous**, and translucent where thin. Hard-paste porcelain fires the clay body and glaze together to the top temperature; soft-paste porcelain is bisqued high and glazed low, as in the dinnerware industry today.

HOLLOW CASTING
Pouring liquid clay slip into a hollow plaster mold to create a shell of specific shape.

HOLLOW WARE
A trade term for hollow dinnerware forms.

IMPERMEABILITY
In ceramics this term refers to the property which results when clay forms have been rendered non-porous by vitrification, i.e., which have achieved maximum density without melting in a kiln.

INTAGLIO
Depressed surface decoration, the reverse of bas-relief.

JIGGER AND JOLLY
A jigger is an adjustable arm that holds a profile-tool or template for one side of a shape pressed against clay on a plaster mold; the mold revolves on a jolly or power-driven spindle. Many commercial wares are made by this process, either on hand-jigger machines or with total automation.

JOMON
Blackened, coiled, textured, sometimes cord-marked Japanese ware thought to date from 10,000 to 200 B.C.

KAKI GLAZE
Traditional glaze from the village of Mashiko, Japan, created by grinding local rock; according to Shoji Hamada it was named for the color that a persimmon is on October 24.

KAOLIN
Anglicized form of the Chinese word for **china clay**. Pure kaolin is rare; it is a perfectly white-burning, high-firing natural clay that can be either primary or secondary in terms of geological formation; it is the essential component of porcelain bodies and an ingredient in many glazes.

KICKWHEEL
A potter's machine for working clay with a centrifugal motion propelled by kicking.

KILN
Furnace for firing clay, slumping glass, or melting enamels; studio kilns can achieve temperatures up to 2500 °F (1371 °C), depending on their construction materials; they can be fueled carbonaceously, organically, or electrically.

KILN FURNITURE
Refractory slabs, posts, and setters for supporting ware in the kiln; handmade or purchased.

KILN WASH
Half clay, half silica, mixed with water to coat kiln shelves.

KOREAN KILN
Climbing kiln, a type of hill kiln for wood firing.

LEAD
The most active glaze **flux** at low temperatures; found in red lead, litharge, and lead carbonate; poisonous in the raw, unfritted state; the flux in crystal glass mixtures.

LEATHER-HARD
Cheese-hard stage which clay reaches before being bone-dry; stiff enough to support itself, but can still be altered.

LIMESTONE
Impure calcium carbonate, whiting, $CaCO_3$, chalk; a much-used high-temperature glaze ingredient and an auxiliary body **flux** in porcelains.

LOOSE-BRICK KILN
Kiln constructed without mortar.

LUSTER
A brilliant iridescent metallic film on glaze, formed from certain metallic salts in reduction; the technique was developed by the potters of Persia and Valencia during the Middle Ages.

LUTING
A cross-hatch and moistening method of putting together coils, slabs, or other clay forms in the wet or leather-hard stage; the same as **scoring**.

MAJOLICA
The decorative application of coloring oxides and stains over an unfired glaze that fuses into the base glaze during firing, leaving fuzzy edges. The term comes from the island of Majorca. The della Robbia workshop was famous for Majolica during the 15th century. Also the term for a kind of white color, and historically for certain white undecorated earthenwares.

MAJOLICA GLAZE
An opaque glaze with a glossy surface, usually white, generally opacified by tin oxide; a base for colored stain overglaze decoration; traditionally thought of as Italian and Spanish, also used at Delft, Holland, and in Persia.

MAQUETTE
See **model**.

MASTER MOLD
The plaster shape from which repeated copies of a mold can be made.

MATT
Dull, non-reflecting surface; in the case of glaze, due to deliberate composition or to immature firing.

MATURING
Reaching the temperature in a kiln which develops desired properties in the ware; or the stage that materials, bodies, or glazes need to reach in order to be durable. Potters talk about mature glazes, mature bodies, referring to the look and feel of density. Most clays and glazes have a long maturing range, at any point of which they could be deemed mature.

MICA
A sheet-like mineral found in small flakes in some natural clays; the material that shimmers in many low-fire pots of primitive cultures.

MICRON
$1/1000$ of a millimeter, equals 0.0000394 of an inch; a measurement used for defining glaze thickness.

MILLEFIORE
Similar to *neriage*; a traditional technique in glass and clay where several, or many, slabs of color are combined in patterns, drawings, or shapes and cut through in cross-section to make many similar ones.

MIMBRES
A group of Indians in Southwestern U.S.A. who made a unique contribution to clay art from about A.D. 900 to 1200.

MISHIMA
Carved decoration in leather-hard clay, covered with **engobe** and ribbed off when drier, leaving engobe inlaid in the carving.

MODEL
An initial form in clay, plasticine, plaster, or a found object, from which a mold will be made for reproduction; maquette.

MOLD
Usually a plaster form, single or multi-pieced, which will be used to reproduce any number of accurate copies of the original model in clay or plaster.

MORTAR
See **fire clay cement**.

MOSAIC
A pictorial composition made of many small shapes, usually ceramic, glass, or stone.

MUFFLE
A wall or barrier within a kiln to keep the direct action of flame from the ceramic ware.

MULLITE
The aluminium silicate crystal created during firing to vitrification that gives strength to stoneware and porcelain as opposed to earthenware; can be formed as low as 1832 °F (1000 °C) but is not insured until 2100 °F (1148 °C).

NEUTRAL ATMOSPHERE
An atmosphere in a kiln that is neither completely oxidizing nor completely reducing.

NOBORIGAMA
Climbing kiln, the basic tube kiln, with chambers which can be fired individually.

NOTCH
A key used to register two halves of a plaster mold.

OFF-THE-HUMP
Method of throwing many small forms consecutively from one large mound of clay.

ONCE-FIRING
Glazing leather-hard or dry ware and firing to maturing temperature (this skips the first bisquing); frequently used in commercial production; often the method in salt and wood firing.

OPALESCENT GLAZE
Glaze with a milky moonstone or translucent quality.

OPEN FIRING
Firing in which the flames play through the exposed wares, either in an updraft periodic open-fire kiln with no **muffle** wall or in the open with no kiln.

OVERGLAZE ENAMEL PAINTING
Painting fluxed ceramic colors over glazed ware and fusing them on to the fired glaze in a separate low-temperature firing; developed centuries ago in China and Japan; similar to but not the same as commercial china paint technique.

OXIDATION, OXIDIZING FIRE
Opposite of a reducing fire; the firing of a kiln where combustion of the fuel is complete; the atmosphere contains sufficient oxygen to allow all elements in the clay and glaze to receive the molecules of oxygen needed for their oxidized colors.

PALISSY WARE
French **faience** with tin enamel glaze decorated in bright colors, developed during the 16th century.

PARIAN WARE
Unglazed porcelain, looking like marble, used primarily in the manufacture of Victorian statuettes and doll heads; translucent, highly fluxed.

PATINA
Surface effect, in the case of ceramics, normally an unusual surface developed during firing.

PEACHBLOOM GLAZE
A copper reduction glaze famous in Sung Dynasty China, yellow-pink and red with green specks.

PEEPHOLE

A view or observation hole in the wall or door of a kiln; should be large enough to see into the kiln easily during the fire; also used for pulling draw-trials and tests during firing.

PESTLE AND MORTAR

Device for grinding substances by hand.

PHOTO-EMULSION

In the context of ceramics, the process of developing a photograph directly on to a ceramic piece.

PINCHING

Moving and shaping clay, usually with the fingers.

PIT FIRING

Firing to accomplish ceramic hardening in a hole in the ground or a cave.

PLASTER

The mineral gypsum, with the chemical composition of calcium sulfate, used for clay reproduction and as a work surface.

PLASTICITY

Workability; clay is the only material having real plasticity, meaning the ability to form into any shape, and to get progressively harder in the same shape on being fired to 1300 °F (704 °C) and above. Other materials such as **talc** can be said to have clay-like plasticity.

PORCELAIN

Mechanically strong, hard, frequently translucent, fired clay body with zero absorption; pieces are bisqued at low-fire and glazed high, or bisqued high and glazed low. Porcelain is dense and **vitreous**, the strongest of all clay bodies unless very thin.

POTTER'S WHEEL

A horizontal disk revolving on a vertical shaft, propelled by a treadle, a motor, by kicking, or other means. Ancient potters' wheels were sticks in the ground with a wood or stone slab on top, or one rock rotating on another. The flywheel can today revolve by various pedal devices from a motor or pulley, by gear reduction, or simply by kicking; there are hand, kick, and electric wheels. **Throwing** is done on a potter's wheel.

POTTERY

A losely-used term; often means earthenware or just any clay piece that has been fired.

PRESSING

Forming plastic clay in a plaster mold or other form, by laying it against the mold face.

PRIMARY CLAYS

Clays found today on the spot where they were geologically formed; only **kaolins** (**china clays**) are such; they are whiter-burning, more refractory, and less plastic than secondary kaolins.

PROFILE LINE

Outside or inside line of a shape; the line formed when a shape bisects space.

PUG MILL

A horizontal machine with blades used to bring clay into a workable plastic state and to extrude it in a given shape; provides no de-airing unless the clay goes through a vacuum chamber.

PYROMETER

A calibrating instrument on the outside of a kiln, used with a **thermocouple** inside the kiln to measure temperature during firing. Pyrometers are used to indicate temperature and heat rise at all times during the fire; **cones** are used to culminate the firing, and are the real indication of heat absorption.

PYROMETRIC CONES

See **cones**.

RAKU

A firing or a type of ware; porous groggy ware, with or without a glaze, put into and pulled out of a hot fire, sometimes smudged with smoke after firing; developed in Japan during the 1600s; now a widely used "happening" technique.

RAW GLAZE

(1) Unfired glaze. (2) Glaze containing no **frit**.

REDUCING AGENT

(1) Material put into a body or glaze that yields carbon monoxide on firing, or robs it of oxygen molecules; an example is fine-ground silicon carbide. (2) A material that will reduce the kiln atmosphere, such as asphalt, oil-soaked rags, grass, wood, or mothballs; particularly useful for luster firing.

REDUCTION, REDUCING FIRE

Opposite of an oxidizing fire; the firing of a kiln with an atmosphere of reduced oxygen, where combustion of the fuel used in firing is incomplete. This often affects fired color: copper in reduction is ox-blood red, in oxidation green; iron in reduction is celadon, in oxidation amber yellow or brown.

REFRACTORY

Resistant to melting or fusion; a ware or material that does not fuse under 2500 °F (1371 °C); a substance that raises the melting point of another material. Refractory materials are the basis of high-temperature ceramics.

RESIST

(1) Wax, varnish, latex, or other substance applied in pattern on a surface to cover an area while the background is treated with another material or color. (2) Cerumel A, a water-soluble synthetic wax used for resist decoration with engobes and glaze.

RIB

A tool used in throwing a pot to shape or straighten it; made of rubber, wood, gourd, or metal.

RO, R₂O₃, RO₂

The symbols that make up the three columns of a glaze formula: RO, any element that combines with one oxygen atom; R_2O_3, those elements with three oxygen atoms per two of the original substance; RO_2, those elements requiring two atoms of oxygen per molecule.

ROOKWOOD

An important early American art pottery and china factory in Ohio; closed in 1940.

RUTILE

Impure titanium dioxide, used as a matting agent in glazes or as a tan-orange colorant.

SAGGAR

(1) Refractory container or fire-clay box in which pottery is stacked during firing for protection from direct flame; can be used routinely in wood-burning kilns. (2) A container for holding fuming materials such as metal oxides, chemical salts, and organic substances, that will act on the ware in the saggar during the fire.

SALT FIRING

Traditionally, rock salt is thrown into the fire at the maturing temperature of the clay until an orange-peel textured clear glaze appears; contemporarily, any sodium put into a kiln at any temperature, or during a post-firing after a work has already been fired once; salt is deleterious to kiln bricks.

SAWDUST FIRING

Firing with sawdust to blacken the ware.

SCORING

A cross-hatch and moistening method of putting together coils, slabs, or other clay forms in the wet or leather-hard stage; the same as **luting**.

SECONDARY CLAYS

Clays that have been removed from the spot of original formation by physical or chemical forces after decomposition; all clays except primary **kaolins**.

SGRAFFITO

To scratch through one surface to another; the decoration of leather-hard clay by scratching through a layer of colored **engobe** to the surface below, or decorative scratching through an unfired glaze.

SHARDS

Fragments of pottery; the state in which many ancient clayworks are found, from which they are restored; remains of civilizations used by archeologists and other scientists to study human culture.

SHIVERING

Cracking off of the glaze due to compression during cooling, or over-finishing of the clay pot (especially at the edges), or **carbon core** caused by too much reduction.

SHRINKAGE
Contraction of clays or bodies in drying and firing, caused by the loss of physical and chemical water and the achieving of molecular density.

SIGILLATA
See **terra sigillata**.

SILICA
Oxide of silicon, SiO_2; found abundantly in nature as quartz, sand, and flint; the essential oxide in ceramics.

SILICA INVERSION
The change in the silica molecule as it expands from alpha to beta quartz at 500 °F (260 °C) and 1000 °F (537 °C) in the firing and cooling cycle; cracking can be caused by firing or cooling certain clay bodies too quickly at these temperatures.

SILICATE OF SODA
A solution of sodium silicate used as a **deflocculant** in clay casting slips. The pottery industry uses N brand with 36.7 percent solid, a ratio of soda to silica of 1 to 3.3, and a specific gravity of 1.395.

SINTERING
The process by which frits are manufactured: materials are heated together in a crucible inside a furnace until fused and molten, then poured into cold water, shattered, and reground for use.

SIZE
A soap coating applied in several layers to prevent plaster from sticking to plaster; used, for example, on the plaster model for a plaster mold; can be liquid green or special pottery soap; any oil or vaseline serves the purpose but non-specialist sizes will obscure detail.

SKOVE KILN
Kiln built of the brick products that are to be fired and taken down after firing so the bricks can be used.

SLAB
Flat piece of clay from which shapes can be fabricated.

SLAKING
Breaking down clay or other ceramic materials in water.

SLIP
A suspension of ceramic materials in water; generally refers to casting slip for molds; can mean a liquid clay **engobe** for decorating or a glaze slip.

SLIP GLAZE
The glaze that results from firing a clay past its maturing temperature until it melts; usually low-firing common **surface clays** taken to high temperature.

SLURRY
Thick suspension of one or more ceramic materials in water.

SOAPING
Applying liquid soap in a prescribed fashion to a piece of plaster to prevent it from sticking to plaster that is cast against it.

SOLAR KILN
Kiln capturing the sun's rays on a clay surface through the use of mirrors; a very limited area can be fired by very extensive use of reflectors.

SOLID CASTING
Casting liquid clay into the void created by two or more pieces of a mold; the thickness of the shape can vary.

SPECIFIC GRAVITY
Density of a liquid slip compared with that of water, to indicate viscosity; water has a specific gravity of one; casting slip generally has a specific gravity of 1.7.

SPIRAL WEDGING
Kneading clay with a pivoting motion to remove air pockets and make the texture homogeneous.

SPLIT BAMBOO KILN
Climbing kiln, a kind of tube kiln for wood firing.

STAIN
Watercolor wash on bisque with metallic coloring oxides or commercial glaze stains; also a term referring to glaze stain.

STEATITE
A form of **talc** used instead of clay by the ancient Egyptians for carving shapes to which glazes were applied.

STILTS
Spurs, pins, and other refractory clay pieces manufactured for use in supporting ware during firing.

STONEWARE
Hard, dense, and durable ware generally fired to 2150 °F (1176 °C) or above; a body with 0 to 5 percent absorption, regardless of firing temperature.

SURFACE CLAY
Common surface clay is one of the geological types of clay; it can be on the surface of the ground, but does not have to be; it is low-firing and generally colored.

SUSPENSION AGENT
Substance sometimes needed to hold glaze particles in a liquid suspension: Epsom salts, bentonite, CMC gum, and magnesium carbonate should be experimented with in small (1 percent) amounts; sodium hydroxide is the suspension agent used in sigillata.

TALC
Hydrated magnesium silicate; a glaze ingredient but also used in **whiteware** bodies in place of clay; has clay-like properties but lacks real plasticity. Talc bodies were developed in ancient Egypt and then revived in the early 1900s on the West Coast for commercial low-temperature bodies; fast-firing, has low thermal shock, fires very white.

TENMOKU
Japanese name for a type of glaze used especially by the Chinese during the Sung Dynasty; glaze with metallic circular markings whose rich black appearance at stoneware and porcelain temperatures is caused by an overabundance of iron oxide (10 to 15 percent) in a feldspathic glaze fired in reduction and cooled fast; also known as oilspot glaze.

TERRACOTTA
Used to describe iron or rust-red colors; an art historian's term for low-fired, unglazed, generally red-colored ware; a term for pottery or clay.

TERRA SIGILLATA
Low-fired claywork with a sheen resulting from burnishing; an extraordinarily fine-ground clay suspension in water that shines when applied as a coating and fired at low temperature (the molecular structure changes at high fire, destroying the sheen); the surface on Attic Greek wares.

THERMOCOUPLE
Wiring device placed inside the kiln to register heat and transfer it to a temperature gauge (**pyrometer**) outside the kiln.

THROW-AND-COIL
An age-old process of creating ceramic shapes using both wheel-throwing and coil-throwing additions.

THROWING
The process of forming pieces on a revolving potter's wheel from solid lumps of clay into hollow forms.

TIN ENAMEL
An opaque glaze containing tin oxide, usually on earthenware; developed historically in Persia, middle Europe, Spain, and Italy; fired in oxidation to low or medium temperature.

TIN OXIDE
A low temperature opacifier giving brilliant whites and sometimes lustrous sheen; used in the manufacture of pink stains, in combination with lead and chrome.

TOOTH
Texture or quality of coarseness in a clay body; necessary in clay to make it lift and support weight in handbuilding; results from the addition of fine grog, sand, or any slightly coarse particles; some clays have natural tooth.

TORQUE
In the context of potters' wheels, the continuous rotation of the machine against the force of the thrower's motions.

TRAILING
A method of decorating with engobe or glaze squeezed out of a bulb from a small orifice or poured from a narrow lip.

TRANSFER
See **decal**.

TRANSLUCENCY
Ability to transmit scattered light, not quite transparent.

TRANSPARENT
Clear, like window glass; can be colored or colorless; clay texture or decoration easily shows through a transparent glaze.

TRIM SHELF
Ledge in a plaster mold which allows in extra slip and enables the trimming of an even edge.

TROMPE L'OEIL
"Deceptive" portrayal of an object; making something unreal look as real as possible.

TURNING
(1) Trimming a piece in leather-hard condition on a wheel. (2) Term used for **throwing** in some cultures and in the southern United States.

UNDERCUT
An angle in a model for a mold that impairs the removal of the model and necessitates another piece to the mold.

UNDERGLAZE or U.G.
(1) Ceramic pigments blended of metallic oxides and other ingredients and ground to various degrees of fineness; manufactured pigments are designated underglaze stains, overglaze stains, and body stains, according to usage. (2) A name used by commercial manufacturers for a glaze product that stays put and does not melt.

UPDRAFT KILN
Kiln in which the fire is underneath or at the low end of the tube or chamber; heat moves up through the ware and out of a flue at the top.

USHABTI
Small figures made of Egyptian paste, used as funerary items in ancient times.

VISCOSITY
Property of flow; a highly viscous glaze is "stiff," does not flow much during the fire, and generally results in a matt surface; a glaze of low viscosity is fluid, vacillates during the melt, is usually glossy, and can cause other glazes or decoration to become fluid.

VITREOUS
Glass-like, hard, dense.

WAX
Melted paraffin wax (which is not water soluble) mixed with kerosene or benzine for ease of application, used on clay, bisque, or between glazes for resist techniques; also commercially produced water-soluble waxes such as Ceremul A.

WEDGING
Kneading a mass of clay to expel air and make the mass homogeneous; plastic clay should be wedged before use or if it is to be re-used or stored.

WHITEWARE
All ware with a white or ivory color after firing; made from **kaolin** and ball clays plus **flux** and filler, and can be fired at any temperature; can be a **talc**-type body fired at low temperature.

ZIRCOPAX
Trade name for a zirconium opacifier used to make glaze white at temperatures above cone 5, and in reduction atmospheres; Ultrox, Opax, and Superpax are alternatives.

ANNOTATED BIBLIOGRAPHY

This list — one of the most extensive of its kind — starts with general books on ceramics and is then followed by a section on ceramic history, compiled alphabetically according to location. Old books are included because of their continuing interest or unique subjects. College, university, museum and other libraries are the sources for these texts, and also for a wealth of exhibition catalogs of individual and group shows. Finally, there is a brief technical section; however, most technical ceramic engineering and materials science books have not been cited; they are available in the engineering libraries of the world.

Major comprehensive ceramic book collections can be found at the New York State College of Ceramics, Alfred University, New York; the American Ceramic Society Headquarters, Columbus, Ohio; and the National Art Library at the Victoria and Albert Museum, London.

GENERAL BOOKS ON CERAMICS

Axel, Jan, and McCready, Karen. *Porcelain Traditions and New Visions.* New York: Watson-Guptill, 1981. A survey of contemporary ceramists working in porcelain; traces the development of porcelain from its inception to the present day; illustrated.

Barber, Edwin A. *Lead Glazed Pottery.* New York: Doubleday, Page & Co., 1907. Historical sketches, review of processes, characteristics and examples of glazed, sgraffito- and slip-decorated wares; still a valuable document of 19th-century discoveries in lead-glazed pottery.

Berenshon, Paulus. *Finding One's Way with Clay: Pinched Pottery and the Color of Clay.* New York: Simon & Schuster, 1972. The pinch method of making pots; discussion of movement and rhythm in clay, from the author's view as a potter/dancer; colored clay body information; sensitive photographs.

Binns, C. F. *The Potter's Craft.* New York: Van Nostrand, 1947. First published in 1910 by the father of studio ceramics in this country, first Dean of the College of Ceramics, Alfred, New York, the man who said, "The path to strength and beauty leads through fire"; still an excellent basic clay and glaze text.

Birks, Tony. *The Art of the Modern Potter.* New York: Van Nostrand Reinhold, 1976; reissue, Radnor, Pennsylvania: Chilton, 1989. A selection of contemporary British sculptural potters with a brief introduction to each; photographs from private collections.

——. *Hans Coper.* New York: Icon Editions, Harper & Row, 1983. For the first time the entire range of this unusually creative and influential potter's work is presented; a selection of drawings is included.

——. *Lucy Rie.* Radnor, Pennsylvania: Chilton, 1989. A lovely book about the life and work of this well-known potter.

Bohrod, Aaron. *A Pottery Sketchbook.* Madison: University of Wisconsin, 1959. Fifties-style drawings by a well-known Midwestern painter on pots; some explanation of techniques.

Buckley, Cheryl. *Potters and Paintresses; Women Designers 1870–1955.* London: Women's Press, 1990. English women potters' work during the 19th and 20th centuries.

Campbell, James Edward. *A Guide to Information Sources of Pottery and Ceramics.* Detroit: Gale Research, 1978. A reference bibliography of books on ceramics according to area of the world and country. Brief lists of collections, organizations, and periodicals.

Cardew, Michael. *Pioneer Pottery.* New York: St. Martin's Press, 1976; reissue, Oxford, New York: Oxford University Press, 1989. A wealth of technical information about clays and glazes, with some discussion of this British craftsman's many years of potting and teaching in Africa.

Charleston, Robert L. *World Ceramics.* New York: McGraw-Hill, 1968. A comprehensive history of pottery and porcelain from early antiquity to 1966; emphasis on Europe, Near East, and Far East; color illustrations and more than 1,000 black and white photographs.

Chicago, Judy. *The Dinner Party.* New York: Doubleday, 1979. This well-known painter's story of what she learned about clay fabrication and decoration for her epic work.

Clark, Garth. *Ceramic Art: Comment and Review 1884–1977.* New York: Dutton, 1978. An overview of the literature and a discussion of individuals involved in claywork during this century.

——. *Michael Cardew.* Tokyo: Kodansha International, 1976. The story of a potter and a scholar, graduate of Oxford University, pupil of Bernard Leach, teacher in Africa for 25 years, maker of redware and stoneware at Wenford Bridge, philosopher in spite of himself.

——. *The Mad Potter of Biloxi, George E. Ohr.* New York: Abbeville Press, 1989. Biography and interpretation of this early 20th-century potter who is now famous.

Colbeck, John. *Pottery Technique of Throwing.* New York: Watson-Guptill, 1969; reissue, 1988. Traditional wheel techniques fully illustrated in black and white.

Cooper, Emmanuel. *A History of World Pottery.* 2nd rev. ed., New York: Larousse, 1981; 3rd ed., Radnor, Pennsylvania: Chilton, 1988. Compact survey of the history of pottery covering major types and groups, from Mesopotamian civilization to contemporary times.

Cordoza, Sidney. *The Art of Rosanjin.* Tokyo, New York: Kodansha International, 1987. Photographs and biography of this unusual clay artist by his foremost collector.

Counts, Charles. *Pottery Workshop.* New York: Macmillan Publishing, 1973, 1978. A manual for beginning potters about all the basics.

——. *Common Clay.* Anderson, South Carolina: Droke House/Hallux, 1971. An odyssey of, and tribute to, traditional Southern Appalachian potters and their work.

Coyne, John, ed. *The Penland School of Crafts Book of Pottery.* New York: Bobbs-Merrill, 1975. Potters who have taught at Penland discuss and illustrate their favorite techniques.

Ford, Betty. *Ceramic Sculpture.* New York: Reinhold, 1964. Illustrated guide to making hollow-built clay sculptures, especially animals, on a relatively large scale; information about textures and colored clays.

Forsyth, Gordon. *20th Century Ceramics.* London: The Studio Limited, 1936. Survey of 20th-century international ceramics, craftspersons, materials, and processes, and the state of the industry from the British point of view, with photographs.

Fournier, Robert. *An Illustrated Dictionary of Practical Pottery.* 2nd rev. ed., New York: Van Nostrand Reinhold, 1981. Extensive, practical dictionary including definitions, charts, analyses, formulas, materials, and equipment, techniques, and processes.

Gilot, Françoise. *Life with Picasso.* New York: McGraw-Hill, 1965. Contains a wonderful chapter on Picasso's ten-year experimentation with claywork at the Ramie's Madoura pottery in Vallauris, France; the forms, the colors, the wood firing, and the village.

Hofsted, Jolyon. *Ceramics.* New York: Golden Press, 1967. A basic paperback for beginners; illustrated.

Honey, William B. *The Art of the Potter.* New York: Whittlesey House, 1950. A non-technical description of techniques and a discussion of pottery esthetics; written for the collector.

Jouffray, Alain, and Teixidor, Joan. *Miró Sculpture.* New York: Leon Amiel, 1974. Miró's sculpture, 1930–72, much of it in clay; full-page black and white photographs and color plates; excellent discussion of his collaboration with ceramist Joseph Llorens Artigas, begun in 1944.

Kemp, Dorothy. *Slip Ware: How to Make It.* Rev. ed., London: Faber & Faber, 1962. Presents a rationale and program for a course in making slipware; details of materials needed, techniques, and processes; black and white photographs.

Kenny, John B. *Complete Book of Pottery Making.* Radnor, Pennsylvania: Chilton, 1976. First written in 1949; most useful for its chapter on molds.

Lakofsky, Charles. *Pottery.* Dubuque, Iowa: William C. Brown, 1968. A short work about the basics by a long-time teacher and potter.

Lane, Peter. *Studio Porcelain: Contemporary Design and Techniques.* Radnor, Pennsylvania: Chilton, 1980. A comprehensive book on modern porcelain representing 117 potters from England, Europe, Canada, and the U.S.A.

Larney, Judith. *Restoring Ceramics.* New York: Watson-Guptill, 1979. Techniques of pottery repair.

Leach, Bernard. *A Potter's Book.* New York, London: Transatlantic Arts, Faber & Faber, 1946; 18th ed., 1965. The classic book on studio pottery; excellent first chapter "towards a standard"; description of materials and techniques used by this famous British potter; the story of his pottery and its development; some history of his Oriental training.

——. *A Potter's Challenge.* New York: Dutton, 1975. A discussion of the esthetics of pottery as Bernard Leach saw them; photographs.

——. *A Potter's Work.* London, Tokyo, New York: Adams & Maclay, Kodansha International, 1967. Introduction and biographical notes by J. P. Hodin; Bernard Leach selected sketches and pots of his own, covering 55 years, 1911–66, with notes about all the plates.

Marshall, Richard, and Foley, Suzanne. *Ceramic Sculpture, Six Artists.* Seattle: University of Washington Press, 1981. Analyses of the work of Arneson, Gilhooly, Mason, Price, Shaw, and Voulkos, from the Whitney Museum exhibition, with color illustrations and full-page black and white photographs.

Matson, Frederick. *Ceramics and Man.* Chicago: Aldine Publishing, 1965. Very interesting archeological and ethnological research of prehistoric and historic ceramics, particularly unglazed pottery; philosophy of societal pot-making; technical descriptions.

Nelson, Glenn C. *Ceramics, A Potter's Handbook.* 5th ed., New York: Holt, Reinhart, & Winston, 1984. An introduction to ceramics and the basics of clay techniques; profusely illustrated.

Nigrosh, Leon. *Low Fire.* Wooster, Massachusetts: Davis Publications, 1980. Low-temperature firing methods and decorating techniques; includes adobe, raku, discussions of kilns, Egyptian paste, majolica, and photo-clay; black and white and color photographs.

Nordness, Lee. *Jack Earl.* Chicago: Perimeter Press, 1985. Many photographs; discussion of the unusual sculpture and method of working of this clay artist.

Paak, Carl E. *The Decorative Touch: How to Decorate, Glaze, and Fire Your Pots.* Englewood Cliffs, New Jersey: Prentice-Hall, 1981. Just what the title says.

Piccolpassi, Cipriano. *The Three Books of the Potter's Art.* London: Victoria and Albert Museum, 1934. Historically important early work on ceramics, translated from a 15th-century treatise.

Poor, Henry Varnum. *A Book of Pottery: From Mud to Immortality.* Englewood Cliffs, New Jersey: Prentice-Hall, 1958. This American painter, who was also a good and fanciful potter, informally discusses beginning clay techniques as well as his philosophical and artistic concerns; photographs, Poor's drawings, clay formulas, and studio layout.

Ramie, Georges. *Picasso's Ceramics.* New York: Viking, 1976. Hundreds of photographs, many in color, of the ceramics of Picasso; wonderful visual and technical information.

Rhodes, Daniel. *Stoneware and Porcelain.* Radnor, Pennsylvania: Chilton, 1956; rev. ed., 1975. A philosophical, technical, and esthetic treatise on high-fired ware by the late American potter and Professor Emeritus of the New York State College of Ceramics at Alfred University.

——. *Tamba Pottery.* Tokyo, New York: Kodansha International, Harper & Row, 1970. Traces the past 600 years of pottery making in this traditional region of Japan; describes techniques and tools used; based on the work of a particular family in Tamba.

Richards, Mary Caroline. *Centering.* Middletown, Connecticut: Wesleyan University Press, 1969, distributed by Columbia University Press. A poetic relating of the centering of clay on the potter's wheel to the centering of one's self, by a respected clay artist and philosopher.

Sanders, Herbert H. *How to Make Pottery.* New York: Watson-Guptill, 1974. A remake of the 1950s Sunset series book on ceramics.

Savage, George. *Pottery Through the Ages.* London: Cassell, 1963. Defines over 3,000 terms relating to wares, materials, processes, styles, patterns, and shapes, from antiquity to the present day. Introductory list of the principal European factories and their marks; excellent for collectors.

Savage, George, and Newman, Harold. *An Illustrated Dictionary of Ceramics.* New York: Van Nostrand Reinhold, 1974. Over 3,000 entries with brief descriptions relating to wares, materials, processes, styles, and patterns from all historical periods; lists principal European factories and marks.

Schafer, Thomas. *Pottery Decoration.* New York: Watson Guptill, 1980. Historical and contemporary decorative techniques; how-to; black and white and color photographs.

Slivka, Rose. *Peter Voulkos.* New York: New York Graphic Society, 1978. Lively discussion and serious consideration of one of the foremost clayworkers of this century; full page color and black and white photographs.

Speight, Charlotte. *Hands in Clay.* Sherman Oaks, California: Alfred Publishing, 1979; 2nd ed., Mountain View, California: Mayfield Publishing, 1989. Part one, ceramic history; part two, clay working techniques.

Walters, H. B. *Catalogue of the Terracottas in the Department of Greek and Roman Antiquities.* London: British Museum, 1903. A full discussion of the ancient methods of working in terracotta; various uses of things made from surface clays, the circumstances in which the ancient figures were found, and their history; very useful information.

Weiss, Gustav. *The Book of Porcelain.* New York, Washington, D.C.: Praeger Publishers, 1971. Extensive history of Far Eastern and European porcelain from its origins; some photographs.

Weiss, Peg, and others. *Adelaide Alsop Robineau, the Glory of Porcelain.* Syracuse, New York: Syracuse University Press, 1981. The life and extraordinary work in porcelain of this late 19th and early 20th-century grande dame; lists her glaze batches and experiments; illustrates the extensive Everson Collection.

Wildenhain, Marguerite. *The Invisible Core; A Potter's Life and Thoughts.* Palo Alto, California: Pacific Books, 1973, 1986. An autobiography of Wildenhain's early years, Bauhaus student days, immigration to the U.S.A., and her establishment of the Pond Farm Pottery in California; black and white photographs.

——. *Pottery, Form, and Expression.* New York: American Craftsmen's Council: 1959; Palo Alto, California: Pacific Books, 1986. One of the best descriptions of a personal attitude toward clay.

Wong, Jade Snow. *Fifth Chinese Daughter.* 1950; rev. ed., Seattle: University of Washington Press, 1989. The autobiography of a woman ceramist who overcame family odds for education and success.

Wood, Beatrice. *I Shock Myself.* San Francisco: Chronicle Books; reissued, 1988. The autobiography of one of America's most interesting contemporary potters.

Woody, Elsbeth. *Handbuilding Ceramic Forms.* New York: Farrar, Strauss, & Giroux, 1978. Description of materials and techniques of handbuilt ceramics and how these are used by artists; batches for clay bodies and glazes; photographs.

Wykes-Joyce, Max. *7,000 Years of Pottery and Porcelain.* London: P. Owen, 1958. A history of pottery and porcelain, ancient to modern, describing the people who made and make them, and the people who used and use them; many black and white photographs.

Yanagi, Soetsu. *The Unknown Craftsman: A Japanese Insight into Beauty.* Adapted by Bernard Leach. Tokyo, New York: Kodansha International, 1972; reissued, 1986. A selection of writings by the late Soetsu Yanagi on the Buddhist meaning of beauty; adapted with the help of translator Mihoko Okamura; foreword by Shoji Hamada. In the 1920s to 1950s, in international lectures and articles, Yanagi articulated the contemporary Japanese folk craft movement called *mingei*, exemplified in the ideas and work of his potter friends and colleagues, Hamada, Leach, and Kawai.

CERAMIC HISTORY

GENERAL

Barber, E. A. *Salt Glazed Stoneware, Germany, Flanders, England, and the United States.* New York: Doubleday, Page & Co., 1907. Interesting old book discussing traditional methods of salt glazing at high temperature.

Cox, Warren E. *The Book of Pottery and Porcelain.* New York: L. Lee Shepard, 1944; 2 vols., New York: Crown, 1953, 1970. A reissue of this classic survey of world ceramics; emphasis on Europe, China, and the United States, dating from ancient times to the contemporary period; 3,000 illustrations in two volumes; includes American Indian pottery, and pottery and porcelain marks.

AFRICA

Clark, C., and Wagner, L. *Potters of Southern Africa.* New York: Hacker, 1974. A study of 14 contemporary potters from pottery workshops; black and white photographs.

Fagg, William, and Picton, John. *The Potter's Art in Africa.* London: British Museum, 1970. An exhibition catalog; brief text and many photographs of ceramic works and village scenes; includes the tools used; lists all pieces from the exhibition according to area and country.

ANCIENT

Poulik, Joseph. *Prehistoric Art.* Translated by R. Finlayson Samsour. London: Spring Books, 1956. A general treatment of prehistoric art in Czechoslovakia, with many fine examples of pottery from Neolithic times to the Roman age.

Rafael, Max. *Prehistoric Pottery and Civilization in Egypt.* Washington, D.C.: Pantheon Books, Bollingen Foundation, 1947. The three early Egyptian cultures and their pottery styles; illustrated with drawings.

Stiles, Helen. *Pottery of the Ancients.* New York: E. P. Dutton, 1938. Ceramic and mosaic survey of ancient Mediterranean and Mesopotamian cultures and the Orient, to the 18th century; also touches briefly on Indian and Turkish pottery.

ASSYRIA

Andrae, Walter. *Coloured Ceramics from Ashur and Earlier Ancient Assyrian Wall-Paintings.* London: K. P. Paul, Trench, Trubner, 1925. Short introduction to what makes Assyrian ceramics unique in ceramic history. Beautiful hand-drawn and colored plates of decorative motifs, earthenware, walls, and slabs.

BELGIUM

Helbig, Jean. *Le Céramique Bruxelloise du Bon Vieux Temps.* Brussels: Editions du Cercle d'art, 1946. Ceramics of Brussels, primarily from the 18th century; bibliography and photographs; text in French.

BULGARIA

Bakurdjiev, Georgi. *Bulgarian Ceramics.* Sofia: Bulgarski Hudozknik, 1955. Bulgarian pottery from ancient to modern times.

BYZANTINE

Rice, David Talbot. *Byzantine Glazed Pottery.* Oxford: Clarendon Press, 1930. Entire Byzantine period covered; bibliography.

CHINA

Beurdeley, Cecile and Michel. *A Connoisseur's Guide to Chinese Ceramics.* New York: Harper & Row, 1974. A general review of the history of Chinese ceramics, prehistoric to 20th century; photographs, drawings, maps, and chronology; glossary of technical terms and extensive bibliography.

Eumorfopoulos, Georges. *The Georges Eumorfopoulos Collection: Catalogue of the Chinese, Korean and Persian Pottery and Porcelain.* London: E. Benn, 1925–28. The great classic limited edition; fine photographs of famous works, large format; worth searching for a library that owns this six-volume series.

Gompertz, Godfrey. *Chinese Celadon Wares.* London: Faber & Faber, 1958; 2nd rev. ed., London: Faber & Faber, 1980. A well-illustrated history of Chinese celadon stonewares and porcelains which incorporates both European and Oriental scholarship on the subject.

Hobson, R. L. *Handbook of Pottery and Porcelain of the Far East.* London: Oxford University Press, 1948. A survey of the British Museum collections from China, Korea, Japan, from ancient times to the 19th century, by one of the foremost experts in the field.

——. *Chinese Pottery and Porcelain.* 2 vols., reprint, New York: Dover, 1976. Volume I discusses broad classifications of wares from three early dynasties; volume II surveys Ming and Ch'ing porcelain.

——. *The Art of the Chinese Potter, from the Han Dynasty to the End of the Ming.* New York: Alfred Knopf, 1923. One of the best books in this area, with 192 examples of some of the finest Chinese pottery, plus the history of Chinese pottery from the Han to the Ming Dynasty; large color photographs.

Honey, William B. *The Ceramic Art of China and Other Countries of the Far East.* London: Faber & Faber, 1945. Survey of Chinese potters throughout history with an emphasis on the wares; brief coverage of Indo-China, Korea, and Japan. Half of the book is devoted to black and white and color plates.

——. *The Ceramic Art of China.* London: Faber & Faber, 1954. More specific than his other books about the ceramic art of China; a survey of the art of Chinese potters from earliest times to the present day; list of Chinese dynasties and reigns; many photographs.

Lan, P'u. *The Potteries of China. Translated by Geoffrey R. Sayer.* London: Routledge & Kegan Paul, 1951. Translation of T'ao-Lu, a main source of knowledge about Chinese ceramics from native sources; appendices.

Medley, Margaret. *The Chinese Potter.* New York: Charles Scribner & Sons, 1976. Based on the technique of manufacture and the conditions under which the wares were produced. Also a general history of earthenware, stoneware, and porcelain through the evolution of techniques; excellent diagrams and photographs.

——. *Yuan Porcelain and Stoneware.* London: Pittman, 1974. The first book devoted entirely to a scholarly discussion of pottery of the Yuan (Mongol) period of Chinese history, especially focusing on the 14th and 15th centuries. Detailed description of styles and types; black and white and color plates.

CRETE

Levi, Doro. *Early Hellenic Pottery of Crete.* Princeton, New Jersey: Princeton University Press, 1945. The origins of Greek art and ceramics based on the author's archeological excavations in Crete.

DENMARK

Flor, Kai. *Jais Nielsen Keramik.* Copenhagen: A. Jensen, 1938. Introduction to and reproductions of works of the early 20th-century Danish ceramist Jais Nielsen; translated into English and French.

ENGLAND

Bemrose, Geoffrey. *Nineteenth Century English Pottery and Porcelain.* London: Faber & Faber, 1952. A discriminating view of the pottery and porcelain movements in 19th-century England.

Blacker, J. F. *The ABC of English Salt-Glaze Stoneware, from Dwight to Doulton.* London: S. Paul & Co., 1922. English salt-glaze stoneware, mainly from the 18th century; colorfully written, illustrated in black and white, containing interesting information for today's potter about traditional salt glaze.

Cooper, Ronald G. *English Slipware Dishes 1650–1850.* London: Alec Tiranti, 1968. Good photographs of these wonderful pots.

Honey, William B. *English Pottery and Porcelain.* London: A. & C. Black, 1969. A concise history of English pottery from medieval times to the 19th century; many illustrations.

Lewis, Griselda. *A Collector's History of English Pottery.* New York: Viking Press, 1970. Historical chronology from the Stone Age to the present day, presented through photographs, with an introduction.

Wingfield Digby, George F. *The Work of the Modern Potter in England.* London: Murray, 1952. English art potters from the early 1920s to the early 1950s; black and white photographs.

EUROPE

Haggar, Reginald George. *The Concise Encyclopedia of Continental Pottery and Porcelain.* New York: Hawthorne Books, 1960. A comprehensive summary of European porcelain from its beginnings; selections of impressed and incised marks; color and black and white photographs; bibliography of foreign-language books in this field.

Honey, William B. *European Ceramic Art from the End of the Middle Ages to about 1815.* 2 vols., London: Faber & Faber, 1963. Comprehensive dictionary of all the words and names likely to be met in the study of European ceramic art; begins with late medieval and covers every European pottery or porcelain of importance up to 1815; color and black and white illustrations.

Stiles, Helen. *Pottery of the Europeans.* New York: E.P. Dutton, 1940. Broad survey of European pottery; emphasis on social and historical significance; illustrations.

FRANCE

Honey, William B. *French Porcelains of the Eighteenth Century.* London: Faber & Faber, 1950. Study of 18th-century French porcelain, mainly soft-paste; list of marks; color and black and white photographs.

Lane, Arthur. *French Faience.* London: Faber & Faber, 1963. Survey of white tin-glazed pottery or "faience," descriptions and history from medieval times until the 18th century in France; many illustrations.

GERMANY

Honey, William B. *German Porcelain.* London: Faber & Faber, 1954. Study of German porcelain from the 18th century; color and black and white photographs.

Rontgen, Robert E. *The Book of Meissen.* Exton, Pennsylvania: Schiffer, 1984. Excellent book on the ceramics of this important factory.

GREECE

Arias, Paolo Enrico. *A History of 1,000 Years of Greek Vase Painting.* Translated, revised by B. Shelton. New York: Harry N. Abrams, 1962. A view of the development of Greek vase painting through 100 full-page plates, descriptive catalog, and commentary.

Beasley, John Davidson. *Attic Red-Figure Vase Painters.* 2nd ed., 3 vols., Oxford: Clarendon Press, 1963; rev. ed., Berkeley: University of California Press, 1986. Historical directory: volume I covers earliest pot painters to early classical painters; volume II covers early classical to 4th-century painters; volume III is a list of indices.

Boardman, John. *Athenian Black-Figure Vases.* London, New York, Toronto: Oxford University Press, 1974. 383 black and white photographs and the history of each style, from 700 to 500 B.C.

Cook, R. M. *Greek Painted Pottery.* 2nd ed., New York: Harper & Row, 1972. Comprehensive study from a stylistic and chronological viewpoint; chapters on preservation and handling of vases; glossary of important terms.

Higgins, R. A. *Greek Terracottas.* New York: Barnes & Noble, 1967. History of terracottas from 7000 B.C. to A.D. 100, according to region and period; introduction to materials and methods; black and white and color photographs; extensive bibliography of this field.

Lacy, A. D. *Greek Pottery of the Bronze Age.* New York: Barnes & Noble, 1967. Neolithic to Late Cycladic historical survey; pencil drawings, photographs, and watercolors of patterns and vessels.

Lane, Arthur, *Greek Pottery.* 3rd ed., London: Faber & Faber, 1971. Survey of Greek pottery from the beginning, interestingly written; color and black and white photographs.

ISLAMIC

Atil, Esin. *Ceramics from the World of Islam.* Washington, D.C.: Freer Gallery of Art, 1973. Exhibition catalog filled with black and white and color photographs, showing both inside and side views of the work with full descriptions.

Fukai, Shinji. *Ceramics of Ancient Persia.* New York: Weatherill, Tankosha, 1981. Dynastic origins and development of Persian ceramics; color photographs with commentaries.

Lane, Arthur. *Early Islamic Pottery: Mesopotamia, Egypt and Persia.* London: Faber & Faber, 1958.

——. *Later Islamic Pottery: Persia, Syria, Egypt, Turkey.* 2nd ed., London: Faber & Faber, 1971. The development of Islamic pottery after the 13th century; maps, color and black and white photographs.

Rackham, Bernard. *Islamic Pottery and Italian Majolica.* London: Faber & Faber, 1959. Study of glazing techniques of Islamic and Italian overglaze painting; color and black and white photographs.

Wilson, Oliver. *Persian Lusterware.* London, Boston: Faber & Faber, 1985. Color plates and discussion of all Islamic lusterware.

ITALY

Lane, Arthur. *Italian Porcelain.* London: Faber & Faber, 1954. History of the development of Italian porcelain as opposed to the more familiar earthenware; list of marks; color and black and white photographs.

Liverani, Giuseppe. *Five centuries of Italian majolica.* New York: McGraw-Hill, 1960. Full-page color plates complement the text dealing with various aspects of the subject: origins, characteristics, styles, influences, to the 17th century.

——. *Museo Internazionale delle Ceramiche.* Faenza, Italy: published in association with Itinerari dei Musei e Monumenti d'Italia, Rome, 1950, 1956, 1963. Illustrated catalog with a selection of works from the only international ceramic museum in the world; foreword in Italian, French, English, and German. Photographs and their informational listings cover a selection of worldwide ceramics from the 7th century B.C. to 1952.

Vaughn, Agnes Carr. *Those Mysterious Etruscans.* New York: Doubleday, 1964. Supposed story of the people who lived 2,500 years ago, left no written language, and were expert artists in clay objects and sarcophagi.

JAPAN

Adachi, Barbara. *The Living Treasures of Japan.* Tokyo, New York: Kodansha International, 1973. Wonderfully illustrated and interestingly written book about the artist-craftsmen selected and subsidized by the Japanese government as the most honored persons in their fields.

Cort, Louise Allison. *Shigaraki Potter's Valley.* Tokyo, New York: Kodansha International, 1984. The best reference work on this famous village and its wares.

Fujioca, Ryoichi. *Shino and Oribe Ceramics.* Tokyo: Kodansha International, 1976. A well-illustrated description of the techniques and forms of these famous folk wares.

Jenyns, Roger. *Japanese Porcelain.* London: Faber & Faber, 1965. A history of Japanese porcelain with small but numerous black and white photographs, 17th to 20th century.

Kidder, Edward J. *Prehistoric Japanese Arts: Jomon pottery.* Tokyo, Palo Alto, California: Kodansha International, 1968, 1971. The best reference for Jomon pots; large-folio book presenting a representative survey of the Jomon culture; many wonderful photographs and maps labeling pottery sites.

Leach, Bernard. *A Potter in Japan 1952–1954.* London: Faber & Faber, 1960. Leach's return to Japan in 1952, for the first time since his ceramic study in the early 1900s; the story of his travels and of his marriage to the American potter Janet Darnell.

——. *Hamada, Potter.* Tokyo: Kodansha International, 1975; reissued, 1990. Recollections of Shoji Hamada, the famous Japanese potter, with translations of articles by Hamada and a section from his sketchbook; color retrospective plates of his work.

——. *Beyond East and West.* New York: Watson-Guptill, 1978; reissued, Boston: Faber & Faber, 1985. Bernard Leach's last book; the philosophy of his life and work.

Mikami, Tsugio. *The Art of Japanese Ceramics.* New York: Weatherill/Heibonsha, 1972. Overview of origins and development of the ceramic culture in Japan; prehistoric low-fired pottery, early stoneware and porcelain development, and ancient kilns; filled with photographs.

Munsterberg, Hugo. *Folk Arts of Japan.* Tokyo: Charles E. Tuttle, 1959. The best reference book in this field; map of folk pottery locations, descriptions of work and techniques, photographs; preface by Yanagi.

Peterson, Susan. *Shoji Hamada: A Potter's Way and Work.* Tokyo, New York: Kodansha International, Harper & Row, 1974. The philosophy and work of Shoji Hamada, a leading potter of Japan and the National Treasure of folk pottery; his way of work and life, descriptions of the throwing, decorating, and wood-firing processes; information about the organic natural material glazes.

Sanders, Herbert H. *The World of Japanese Ceramics.* Tokyo, New York: Kodansha International, Harper & Row, 1968; reissue, 1990. Techniques, processes and glazes used by contemporary and folk potters of Japan, extracted through personal interviews; photographs of ceramic work, process steps, tools, and kilns.

KOREA

Griffing, Robert P. *The Art of the Korean Potter.* New York: Asia Society, 1968. History of Silla, Koryo, and Yi pottery, with handsome black and white and color photographs, commemorating a 1968 exhibition.

Honey, William B. *Korean Pottery.* London: Faber & Faber, 1955. Historical survey; many photographs.

Kim, Chewon and Won-Yong-Kim. *Treasures of Korean Art: 2,000 Years of Ceramics, Sculptures, and Jeweled Arts.* New York: Harry N. Abrams, 1966. Profusely illustrated survey of Korean ceramics, sculpture, gold, bronze, and lacquer from prehistoric times; chronology, bibliography.

MEXICO

Cervantes, Enrique. *Loza Blanca y Azulejo de Puebla.* Mexico: 1939. History of tile making in Puebla, Mexico; list of artists; list of factories; extensive color and black and white photographs; text in Spanish.

Whitaker, Irwin and Emily. *A Potter's Mexico.* Albuquerque: University of New Mexico Press, 1978. Contemporary Mexican pottery; firing techniques, clays, pottery centers, and artists; color and black and white photographs.

NATIVE AMERICA

Blair, Mary Ellen and Laurence. *Margaret Tafoya, a Tewa Potter's Heritage and Legacy.* West Chester, Pennsylvania: Schiffer Publications, 1986. Story and photographs of the famous head of a dynasty at Santa Clara Pueblo, New Mexico.

Brody, J. J.; Scott, Katherine J.; and LaBlanc, Steven. *Mimbres Pottery, Ancient Art of the American Southwest.* New York: Hudson Hill Press, 1983. One of the best selections of photographs of this material; includes Mimbres history from Indian oral culture.

Chapman, Kenneth M. *The Pottery of the San Ildefonso Pueblo.* 1925; 2nd ed., Albuquerque: University of New Mexico Press, 1970. Written when Maria and Julian Martinez were becoming world-famous for their black pottery; illustrates the pot making and bonfiring process, with decorative patterns and antecedents,and stories about the pueblo.

Dillingham, Rick. *Seven Families in Pueblo Pottery.* Albuquerque: University of New Mexico Press, 1975. Small, helpful book of genealogy with photographs.

Guthe, Carl Eugen. *Pueblo Pottery Making.* 1925; reprint, New York: AMS Press, 1980. A classic; wonderful description and step-by-step diagrams of the making of pots at San Ildefonso Pueblo, New Mexico, in the early 1900s.

Harlow, Francis H. and Frank, Larry. *Historic Pueblo Indian Pottery.* Santa Fe, New Mexico: Museum of New Mexico Press, 1967, 2nd ed., West Chester, Pennsylvania, Schiffer Publications, 1990. Analysis of Southwestern pottery from 1600 to 1880; many photographs.

Marriott, Alice. *Maria, the Potter of San Ildefonso.* Norman, Oklahoma: University of Oklahoma Press, 1952. The life story, up to 1943, of the famous Pueblo Indian potter, mostly concerned with cultural and ethnographic information; black and white drawings by La Farge.

Peterson, Susan. *Maria Martinez, Five Generations of Potters.* Washington, D.C.: Smithsonian Institution Press, 1978; available from U.S. Government. Chronological photographs and descriptions of pots from 1900 to the present, from Maria to her great-great-grandchildren; catalog of an exhibition at the Renwyck Gallery, 1978.

——. *The Living Tradition of Maria Martinez.* Tokyo, New York: Kodansha International, Harper & Row, 1977; rev. ed., 1989. The definitive book on this famous American Indian potter from San Ildefonso Pueblo and her potting family of five generations; specific intformation on techniques, particularly of making the black pottery; 88 pages of color, 66 pages of black and white photographs.

——. *Lucy M. Lewis, American Indian Potter*. Tokyo, New York: Kodansha International, 1984. Lucy Lewis, her family and pots, selected historical Acoma pots, a glimpse of Acoma Pueblo and its life, and documentation of the traditional pottery techniques, presented in 225 color and 127 black and white photographs.

NETHERLANDS

Fourest, H. P. *Delftware: Faience Production at Delft*. New York: Rizzoli, 1980. Pottery made at Delft during the 17th and 18th centuries; extensive photographs.

ORIENTAL

Koyama, Fuji and Pope, John A. *Oriental Ceramics: The World's Great Collections*. 12 vols., Tokyo, New York: Kodansha, Charles E. Tuttle, 1976. An unprecedented series of large volumes documenting great Oriental collections in the world's museums. Each volume has full-page plates of a selection of work; museums covered include the national museums of Japan and Korea, the British and Iranian Museums, the Metropolitan and the Freer.

Koyama, Fujio and Figgess, John. *Two Thousand Years of Oriental Ceramics*. New York: Harry N. Abrams, 1961. Black and white photographs and full-page color illustrations presenting a survey of the development of Oriental ceramics, based on pre-World War II information.

ROMAN

Charleston, R. J. *Roman Pottery*. New York: Pittman, 1955. Pottery of the Roman Empire selected for its esthetic value; many plates.

SOUTH AMERICA

Bushness, Geoffrey. *Ancient American Pottery*. New York: Pittman, 1955. A brief historical development, by country, of the pottery from the ancient civilizations of Central and South America, contrasted with that of the Southwestern United States.

Litto, Gertrude. *South American Folk Pottery*. New York: Watson-Guptill, 1976. Extensive coverage of contemporary South American pottery; filled with black and white photographs of techniques, processes, kilns, market places, and wares.

SOUTHEAST ASIA

Brown, Roxanna. *The Ceramics of South-East Asia, Their Dating, and Identification*. Kuala Lumpur: Oxford University Press, 1977, 2nd ed., 1988. Text and drawings of patterns and shapes, presenting new information about the ceramics and pottery of Vietnam, Cambodia, Thailand, and Laos; black and white and color photographs.

SPAIN

Frothingham, Alice Wilson. *Lusterware of Spain*. New York: Hispanic Society of America, 1951. The regional histories of the manufacture of luster — a special kind of luminous glaze — and its development in Spain, from source material of early Spanish literature; black and white photographs of regional wares.

Vaca, Gonzales P. Diodoro. *Historia de la Ceramica de Talavera de la Reina y Algunos Datos Sobre le de Puente del Arzobispo*. Madrid: Editoria Nacional, 1943. Treats the historical development of ceramics and tiles in the town of Talavera, Spain; black and white photographs; text in Spanish.

THAILAND

Spinks, Charles Nelson. *The Ceramic Wares of Siam*. Bangkok: Siam Society, 1978. History of kiln sites and excavations, with emphasis on Sarwankhalok, Sukhothai, celadons, and painted wares; a comprehensive history to the present.

TURKEY

Oz, Tahsin. *Turkish Ceramics*. Ankara: Turkey Press, Broadcasting and Tourist Department, 1954. Historical discussion of the development of Turkish tiles and ceramics and the buildings from which they came; includes a section on Turkish pottery, its characteristic shapes, motifs, and decorations; color reproductions of the motifs and wall tiles.

U.S.A.

Clark, Garth. *American Ceramics 1876 to Present*. New York: Abbeville Press, 1987. 20th-century potters, pottery, and sculpture; extensive biographies; good color photographs.

Donhauser, Paul S. *History of American Ceramics*. Dubuque, Iowa: Kendall/Hunt Publishing Co., 1978. Overview of the growth and development of studio pottery in the United States; black and white photographs.

Harrington La Mar. *Ceramics in the Pacific Northwest*. Seattle: University of Washington Press, 1979. Historical survey of the 20th-century ceramic development of this region, and of contemporary living potters; many photographs.

Levin, Elaine. *The History of American Ceramics*. New York: Harry N. Abrams, 1988. Ceramics 1607 to present, from pipkins to contemporary; lavishly illustrated.

Quimbi, Ian M. G., ed. *Ceramics in America*. Charlottesville: University Press of Virginia for Winterthur Museum, 1973. A study of ceramics from a cultural viewpoint and as social history. The 14 papers that comprise this conference report contrast and compare early American culture as influenced by a primarily European ceramic tradition.

Spargo, John. *Early American Pottery and China*. New York: Century Co., 1926. Classic handbook for collectors of Early American china and pottery, giving details of collectable items; well illustrated.

Stiles, Helen. *Pottery in the United States*. New York: E. P. Dutton, 1941. One of the few survey books on ceramics in the U.S.A., from the landing of the pilgrims to about 1935; includes some early studio potters.

Watkins, Laura. *Early New England Potters and Their Wares*. 2nd rev. ed., Cambridge, Massachusetts: Harvard University Press, 1968. The best book on this subject by an important scholar in the field; a comprehensive study, especially of redware, with a checklist of early New England potters; good photographs.

Zug, Charles. *Turners and Burners, the Folk Potters of North Carolina*. Chapel Hill: University of North Carolina Press, 1986. The fascinating story of the traditional potters.

TECHNICAL BOOKS

Andrews, A. L. *Ceramic tests and Calculations*. Rev. ed., New York, London: J. Wiley, Chapman & Hall, 1967. Self-testing problems in glaze calculation; very specific explanations of glaze chemistry and behavior; excellent preparation for technical glaze compounding.

Bourry, Emile. *Treatise on Ceramic Industries*. London: Scott, Greenwood & Co; U.S.A. D. Van Nostrand, 1901. Still one of the great definitive works on all types of clay bodies, fabrication techniques, glazing, and firing of everything imaginable, by the man who invented the Bourry-box kiln.

Brodie, Regis. *The Energy-Efficient Potter*. New York: Watson-Guptill, 1982. Firing pottery and energy conservation.

Brody, Harvey. *The Book of Low-Fire Ceramics*. New York: Holt, Reinhart, & Winston, 1980. The craft of pottery with emphasis on low-fire techniques.

Chappell, James. *The Potter's Complete Book of Clay and Glazes*. New York: Watson-Guptill, 1977. Cross referenced book covering a wide range of glazes with 1,500 clay body and glaze formulas which include mixing, application, and firing instructions.

Colson, Frank A. *Kiln Building with Space-Age Materials*. New York: Van Nostrand Reinhold, 1975. How to build kilns with all of the new lightweight insulating materials: castable fiber and block; burner and door information.

Conrad, John W. *Ceramic Formulas: The Complete Compendium*. New York: Macmillan, 1973; rev. ed., 1980. Glaze batches of all kinds, all temperatures. Caution: nothing works the same in anyone else's kiln.

Cooper, Emmanuel and Royle, Derek. *Glazes for the Studio Potter*. London: B. T. Batsford, 1987. Glaze materials, formulating glazes, scientific structure and formulas, firing, special effects, development of techniques, charts, and tables.

Frazer, Henry. *Glazes for the Craft Potter*. New York: Watson-Guptill, 1974. A British book on glaze composition and molecular glaze calculation, based on British materials.

Frith, Donald. *Moldmaking for Ceramics*. Radnor, Pennsylvania: Chilton, 1985. All you ever wanted to know about mold making.

Graebnier, Joseph. *Chinese Stoneware Glazes*. New York: Watson-Guptill, 1975. Technical information on historical Chinese glazes, particularly of the Sung Dynasty; formulas, batches; color photographs.

Hamer, Frank and Janet. *Clays*. New York: Pittman/ Watson-Guptill, 1977. A small book on the origins and chemical and physical properties of clay; clay body formulation and preparation.

——. *A Potter's Dictionary of Materials and Techniques*. New York: Watson-Guptill, 1975; rev. ed., 1986. Comprehensive coverage of sources and character of materials, clays, and glaze construction.

Hetherington, A. L. *Chinese Ceramic Glazes*. South Pasadena, California: P. D. and Ione Perkins, 1948. A classic; excellent technical discussion of celadons, copper reds, and tenmokus, based on chemical analyses of Chinese pot shards; surface effects from the Han to the Manchu Dynasties; 2,000 years of glaze.

Lawrence, W. G. *Ceramic Science for the Potter*. Philadelphia: Chilton, 1972; rev. ed., 1982. Scientific information for those without a scientific background; a clear explanation of clays and glazes, by the Dean Emeritus of the College of Ceramics at Alfred University.

Newcomb, Rexford, Jr. *Ceramic Whitewares*. New York: Pittman, 1947. Much-used technical textbook covering white clay body and glaze chemistry, preparation, and firing.

Norton, F. H. *Ceramics for the Artist Potter*. Cambridge, Massachusetts: Addison-Wesley Publishing, 1956. How-to-do-it study of ceramic work by the Dean Emeritus of ceramic engineering at Massachusetts Institute of Technology.

——. *Elements of Ceramics*. Cambridge, Massachusetts: Addison-Wesley Publishing, 1952. A basic ceramic engineering textbook, including glass.

Olsen, Frederick. *The Kiln Book*. Radnor, Pennsylvania: Chilton, 1982. Originally written for another publisher 15 years ago, now reissued; good general information about all types of kilns and burners, especially wood-firing data.

Parks, Dennis. *A Potter's Guide to Raw Glazing and Oil Firing*. New York: Scribner's, 1980. All aspects of the single firing process, discussion of oil fuel, and the author's testimonial to rural living combined with claywork.

Parmelee, C. W. (edited posthumously). *Ceramic Glazes*. Chicago: Industrial Publications, 1948; rev. and expanded ed., Boston: Cahners, 1973. Excellent reference and technical resource, the classic glaze text.

Piepenburg, Robert. *Raku Pottery*. New York: Macmillan, 1972. Ceramic skills and techniques utilized in the making of raku; black and white and color photographs.

Reigger, Hal. *Raku: Art and Technique*. New York: Van Nostrand Reinhold, 1970. A well-illustrated, interesting book by a potter who has spent much of his life dealing with found materials and firing in the natural environment.

Rhodes, Daniel. *Clay and Glazes for the Potter*. New York: Greenberg, 1957; rev. ed. Radnor, Pennsylvania: Chilton, 1973. Technical as well as general information about clays, clay bodies, and glazes.

——. *Kilns*. Radnor, Pennsylvania: Chilton, 1968, 1982. Historic development of kilns: design, construction, and operation; tables, photographs, and three-dimensional drawings for kiln construction.

Rosenberg, Carol. *Slip Casting*. Basset, California: Keramos Books, 1979. Technical manual of materials, tools, molds, casting procedures, problems, and solutions to producing multiple forms; easy to follow.

Ruscoe, William. *Glazes for the Potter*. London: Academy, 1974; New York: St. Martin's Press, 1974, 1977. From the author's experiences, this book teaches the making and mixing of glazes through minimal calculations and formulas; glossary.

Sanders, Herbert. *Glazes for Special Effects*. New York: Watson-Guptill, 1974. Especially about crystalline glazes, by the man who has worked with them longest in our time; color and black and white photographs. Remember, it is impossible to duplicate anyone else's effects without identical conditions.

Searle, A. B. *The Clayworker's Handbook*. 5th rev. ed., London: C. Griffin, 1949. The classic extensive manual, geared toward the commercial manufacture of articles from clay and allied materials, but interesting for artists; graphs, black and white photographs.

——. *The Glazer's Book*. 2nd rev. and enlarged ed., London: Technical Press, 1948. One of the first books written particularly about glaze.

Troy, Jack. *Salt-Glazed Ceramics*. New York: Watson-Guptill, 1977. Compendium on salt glazing with historical background; artists at work, technical methods, and processes; many photographs.

Wilson, Hewitt. *Ceramics: Clay Technology*. New York: McGraw-Hill Book Co., 1927. A handbook summarizing the elements of clay technology and ceramic engineering; still the definitive book on clay.

ACKNOWLEDGEMENTS

John Calmann & King Ltd and the author wish to thank the institutions and individuals who have kindly provided photographic material for use in this book, and especially the Garth Clark, Charles Cowles, Allan Frumkin, Nancy Hoffman, and Max Protetch galleries. Where museums are given in the captions they are not duplicated below.

Vanessa Adams took all the fabrication photographs of Susan Peterson in chapter 2, the glaze sequence photographs in chapter 3, the clay and glaze tests in chapter 4, and a number of the historical photographs in chapter 6. Unless otherwise credited, the majority of the rest of the photographs were taken by Susan Peterson.

1   Vanessa Adams
2   Jon Barber
12–13   Virginia Garner
14   (Coper) Ceramic Review
16   Jack L. Peterson
16–17   Margot Granitsas
18   D. James Dee
19   Ken Whitbeck
22   Vanessa Adams
29   Anthony Cuñha
30   Mary Randlett
36   (DonTigny) Pennsylvania State University Photographic Services, UDIS
39   (Levine) D. James Dee
43   (Duckworth) Jim Hedrich, Hedrich-Blessing
        (Howdle) Paul Dagys
44   Bengt H. Malmqvist
45   (Selvin) Charles Frizzell
        (Horrell) Steven Young
47   ("Red-X") Los Angeles County Museum of Art
50   (Voulkos) Rose Slivka
        (Coleman) John Nance
58   (Sperry) Ed Marquand
        (Kenny) Bob Lopez
        (Hafner) S. Baker Vail
59   (McIntosh) Gail Reynolds Natzler
74   (Loughran) James Kiernan
        (Kleinsmith) D. and C. H. Bickham
75   (Turner) Colin C. McRae
83   (Piker) Glynne Robinson Betts and Donald Pahl Heiny
96   (Stephenson) Pennsylvania State University Photographic Services, UDIS
        (Mateescu) Slocomb/ Borsari
101   Willard Gallery
108   S. Baker Vail
109   (Levy) Gary Sinick

113   Palm Springs Desert Museum (Schenck & Schenck Photography)
119   (Glick, finished plate) Bob Vigiletti
122   (Wright) Siegel Studio
137   Douglas M. Parker
138   Douglas M. Parker
145   Museum of Fine Arts, Boston
161   Rick Paulson
165   Smithsonian Institution, Washington, D.C.
181   Bill Scott
186   Ed Marquand
187   Colleen Chartier
192   (Nepal) Jack L. Peterson
197   (Nelson) Mary Randlett
201   (James) Mary Randlett
218–19 British Museum
6.2   © James Mellaart
6.7   Hirmer Fotoarchiv
6.11   Hirmer Fotoarchiv
6.14   Hirmer Fotoarchiv
6.22   Werner Forman Archive
6.29   The Ancient Art and Architecture Collection
6.30   Werner Forman Archive
6.41   © Photo R.M.N.
6.46   The Bridgeman Art Library
233   (Picasso) © Photo R.M.N.
233   (Rouault) Musée National d'Art Moderne, Centre Georges Pompidou
6.56   Mexicolore
235   (Geyer/McMillin) Libby Jennings
238   (Kwali) Rosenthal Art Slides
244–5   Bemis Foundation
246   (Adair) Doug Welsh
        (Andreson) Gail Reynolds Natzler
        (Arneson) M. Lee Fatherree

247   (Autio) Bruce S. Rose
248   (Baldwin) Robert Noonan
250   (Boyden) Jim Piper
        (Brady) Michele Maier
251   (Caruso) M. Ruta
252   (Chappelle) Ken Krakow
        (Christensen) Ole Buenget
253   (Cichocka) Czesław Chwiszczuk
254   (Costanzo) Schopplein Studio
        (Counts) Ellen Carey Goldman
255   (Cushing) Steve Myers
        (Davis) J. Anthony
257   (Dillingham) Herbert Lotz Photography
        (Duckworth) Jim Hedrich, Hedrich-Blessing
258   (Farrell) Lakeside Studio, Michigan
259   (Ferguson) E. G. Schempf
262   (John Gill) Steve Myers
264   (Hepburn) Bemis Project, Omaha
        (Higby) Steve Myers
266   (Karnes) Ralph Gabriner
267   (Klam) Udo Hesse
        (Koblitz) Susan Einstein
268   (Kopylkov) L. Heyfits
        (Kristiansen) Ole Haupt
        (Krystyniak) A. Krystyniak
269   (Langsch) Lausanne Museum
        (Larson) Per-Anders, Nacka Foto
270   (David Leach) Ceramic Review
        (Janet Leach) Peter Kinnear Photography
        (Leedy) Gary Sutton
271   (Mackenzie) Jerry Mattiason
272   (Manthey) B. Kuhnert
        (Mariscal) Jim Woodson
273   (Meyers) W. Montgomery

274   (Mintzberg) Al Kilbertus
275   (Juanita Jiminez Mizuno) Douglas M. Parker
        (Möhwald) Klaus-Eberhard Göltz
276   (Morrison) Bob Nishihira
        (Nagle) Roger Gass
279   (Parry) Brian Oglesbee
281   (Raman) Peder Björkegren
282   (Rice) Dean Nagle
        (Rothman) Laughmiller
283   (Savoie) Paul-Emile Rioux
284   (Saxe) John White
        (Imre Schrammel) Imre Schrammel
        (Severijns) Peter Bors
285   (Slee) Zul Mukhida
287   (Troy) Rick Sara
289   (Welsh) Richard Sargent
290   (Williams) Bill Finney
        (Winokur) Eric Mitchell
291   (Wood) John White
        (Woodman) John White
        (Yanagihara) Takash Hatakeyama
315   Encyclopedia of Chemical Technology
317   (Typical firing temperatures) J. T. Robson, Consultant
317   (Fast firing curve) R. T. Vanderbilt Co., Inc.
320   The Edward Orton Jr. Ceramic Foundation
321   (Orton cones 2) The Edward Orton Jr. Ceramic Foundation
322   (Units of flow) Joshua Hendy Iron Works, Pomona Pump Co. Div.
322   (Water of plasticity) Ries: Clays — Occurrence, Properties, and Uses, John Wiley & Son, Inc.
322   (Hardness scale) Louis Navias: J. Am. Ceram. Soc., 2, 69 (1929)

INDEX

WITHDRAWN